"Creative and methodical, clear and matu[...] *the Trinity* ably demonstrates the existence of Trinitarian thought throughout the New Testament as it systematically examines the six orders used by the New Testament in its seventy-five occurrences discussing the Father, Son, and Spirit. This important volume is exegetically driven, historically aware, theologically nuanced, pastorally helpful, and worthy of attention."

—Christopher W. Morgan, California Baptist University

"This is a rich book that gleans many important theological and practical insights from a topic that almost no one has given much thought to: the different sequences by which the members of the Trinity are referred to in the New Testament. In addition to the widely known Father-Son-Spirit sequence, Professor Durst explores the meaning and significance of five other sequences found in the New Testament, yielding many fascinating new insights. He also shows many practical ways in which attention to these different orders can transform people's prayer lives and their understanding of God. This book will amply repay careful study."

—David M. Howard Jr., Bethel Seminary

"After mature and focused deliberation upon God as Trinity, Rick Durst offers his greatest gift yet to the church. While he is grounded in biblical exegesis, aware of history's movements, and engaged with contemporary systematics, Durst never fails to remind us that there are practical, liturgical, and prayerful dimensions to the Trinity. For this magnificent and helpful rehearsal of the variety of Trinitarian manifestations in Scripture, we are thankful!"

—Malcolm B. Yarnell III, Southwestern Seminary

"Rick Durst opens up the underlying Trinitarian patterns of the New Testament texts and shows us their practical consequences. This is a book that will teach us again the varied ways in which we can delight in the richness of God's life and the many ways in which our lives can reflect God's life."

—Steve Holmes, University of St. Andrews

REORDERING THE

TRINITY

SIX MOVEMENTS OF GOD IN THE NEW TESTAMENT

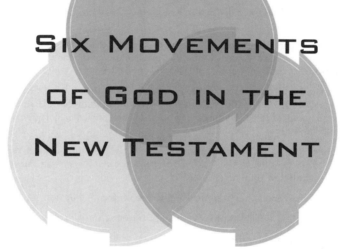

RODRICK K. DURST

Kregel
Academic

Reordering the Trinity: Six Movements of God in the New Testament
© 2015 Rodrick K. Durst

Published by Kregel Publications, a division of Kregel, Inc., 2450 Oak Industrial Dr. NE, Grand Rapids, MI 49505-6020.

Unless otherwise noted, all Scripture quotations are taken from the Holman Christian Standard Bible®, Copyright © 1999, 2000, 2002, 2003, 2009 by Holman Publishers. Used by permission, Holman Christian Standard Bible®, Holman CSB®, and HCSB® are federally registered trademarks of Holman Bible Publishers.

Scripture quotations marked NIV are taken from the Holy Bible, New International Version®, NIV®. Copyright © 1973, 1978, 1984 by Biblica. Used by permission of Zondervan. All rights reserved worldwide. (www.zondervan.com)

Scripture references marked KJV are from the King James Version. Public domain.

The Greek font GraecaU is available from www.linguistsoftware.com/lgku.htm, +1-425-775-1130.

Library of Congress Cataloging-in-Publication Data

Durst, Rodrick K., 1954-
  Reordering the Trinity: six movements of God in the New Testament / Rodrick K. Durst.
    pages cm
  Includes bibliographical references and index.
  1. Trinity—Biblical teaching. I. Title.
  BT112.D87 2016
  231'.044—dc23
                                                          2015020518
ISBN 978-0-8254-4378-7

Printed in the United States of America

15 16 17 18 19 / 5 4 3 2 1

To Kristi,
faithful and encouraging partner,
and to my students.

Contents

Acknowledgments / 9
List of Charts and Tables / 11
Introducing the "Trinitarian Matrix" / 13

PART 1: Considering Four Key Questions

Chapter 1:   The Status Question: The Search for Trinitarian Significance in Contemporary Theology / 29
Chapter 2:   The Data Question: The Trinitarian Matrix in the New Testament / 63
Chapter 3:   The Antecedent Question: Triadic Presence in the Hebrew Scriptures / 83
Chapter 4:   The Historical Question: The Karma of Dogma—The Trinity in Tradition / 123

PART 2: The Contextual Question and the Trinitarian Matrix

Chapter 5:   The Sending Triad: Father-Son-Spirit as the Missional Order / 159
Chapter 6:   The Saving Triad: Son-Spirit-Father as the Regenerative Order / 183
Chapter 7:   The Indwelling Triad: Son-Father-Spirit as the Christological Witness Order / 199
Chapter 8:   The Standing Triad: Spirit-Father-Son as the Sanctifying Order / 221

Chapter 9:   The Shaping Triad: Father-Spirit-Son as the Spiritual
              Formation Order / 241
Chapter 10:   The Uniting Triad: Spirit-Son-Father as the Ecclesial
              Order / 265

PART 3: Everyday Applications and Further Resources

Chapter 11:   The Application Question: Becoming a Functional Trini-
              tarian for Everyday Worship, Life, and Ministry / 287

APPENDIXES

Appendix A: New Testament Census of Triadic Occurrences / 307
Appendix B: Glossary of Trinitarian Terms / 319
Appendix C: Spiritual Formation Exercise #1: Trinitarian
              Prayers / 325
Appendix D: Spiritual Formation Exercise #2: Forty-two Days of
              Trinitarian Devotion / 327
Appendix E: Explaining the Trinity to Children and to Adolescents / 331

BIBLIOGRAPHY AND INDEXES

Bibliography / 339
Scripture Index / 363
Author and Topic Index / 365

Acknowledgments

It takes a village to write a book. I have many people to acknowledge and thank. Brad Sargent provided superb editorial work and developed the book indexes, and Dr. Rex Shaver provided critical assistance for journal research matters. I also want to thank the Golden Gate Baptist Seminary president and trustees for the sabbatical leave to do much of the research and some of the writing. I also want to acknowledge that it was Dr. Fred Mabie at Kregel Publications who encouraged me to submit the proposal that led to this book. When I first proposed this book, I was asked if I liked to engage in controversy. I replied that if the biblical truth is controversial, then yes, I engage in controversy. The real truth of the matter is that I simply wanted to investigate whether this biblical theological lacuna is authentically significant or merely a chimera.

I also want to thank my faculty colleagues, especially Rick Melick, John Shouse, Earl Waggoner, and Dwight Honeycutt, for their interest and dialogue about the book, especially in its earliest stages. David Howard heard me read parts of this book in plenary sessions of the graduate seminar weeks at Golden Gate Seminary, and he was the one who encouraged me to design a grading system to evaluate the intentionality of each of the Trinitarian instances that I had identified. Harry Hahne encouraged me not to exclude some of the triadic references even though they might not register as "A" or even "B" instances. The students in my Christian theology courses have been subjected to the early stages of this research and have always returned encouragement and challenges to get it published. I want to acknowledge the helpfulness of my colleague, Don Miller, who often asked, "Did you get your pages written today?" and suggested that he would buy and might read the book. Finally, I want to thank my wife and my father-in-law who were absolutely reliable sources of encouragement and prayer in this process.

One of my mentors in ministry, Dr. James Coffee, of Community Baptist Church in Santa Rosa, California, urged me early in my preaching and teaching to "keep the main thing as the main thing." Surely the great truth of the Triune God is a "main thing" in the distinctively Christian way of thinking and living. To that end this book is dedicated.

The Second Sunday of Advent
Rodrick Durst
San Rafael, California 2014

List of Charts and Tables

Chart 2.1 New Testament Triadic Pattern Frequencies / 70
(also appears in Chapter 11)

Chart 2.2 Triadic Occurrences in Major New Testament Areas / 72

Table 2.3 Triadic Orders Comparison Chart / 81

Table 5.1 The Missional Order References: Father, Son, Spirit / 160

Table 6.1 New Testament Occurrences of the Son-Spirit-Father Triad / 184

Table 7.1 New Testament Occurrences of the Son-Father-Spirit Triad / 200

Table 8.1 New Testament Occurrences of the Spirit-Father-Son Triad / 225

Table 9.1 New Testament Occurrences of the Father-Spirit-Son Triad / 242

Table 10.1 New Testament Occurrences of the Spirit-Son-Father Triad / 266

Appendix Chart 1 New Testament Census of Triadic Occurrences / 309

Appendix Chart 1A Trinitarian References in the Gospels / 313

Appendix Chart 1B Trinitarian References in the Book of Acts / 314

Appendix Chart 1C Trinitarian References in the Pauline Epistles / 314

Appendix Chart 1D Trinitarian References in Hebrews Through Revelation / 316

Appendix Chart 1E Summary and Totals for Triadic Locations and Gradations / 317

Introducing the "Trinitarian Matrix"

The Father is incomprehensible, the Son is incomprehensible, and the whole thing is incomprehensible. Something put in by theologians to make it more difficult.
　　　　　　　　　　　　—Dorothy Sayers, *Creed or Chaos* (1949)[1]

The nudge to write this book came during a Thursday night systematic theology course in 1997. My students reflected the multi-ethnicity of Christianity globally. To affirm those ethnic origins and to reflect the divine love for diversity, I intentionally exposed them to a number of theologians writing outside the traditional North Atlantic perspective, among them Jung Young Lee's 1996 *The Trinity in Asian Perspective*.[2]

While Lee abandons the biblical text too early to pursue his cultural analysis, he does make two contributions to contemporary Trinitarian thinking.[3] First, he challenges readers to take seriously the diversity of the triadic orders in the New Testament. Lee's work encourages thoughtful reflection on the potentially unique meaning of each of the Trinitarian orders. His work does serve to call for a plainer reading of the triadic occurrences found in the New Testament, which is the subject of this book.

1. Dorothy Sayers, *Creed or Chaos* (New York: Harcourt and Brace, 1949), 22.
2. Jung Young Lee, *The Trinity in Asian Perspective* (Nashville: Abingdon Press, 1996).
3. Veli-Matti Kärkkäinen, *The Trinity: Global Perspectives* (Louisville: Westminster John Knox Press, 2007) 316–335. In this recent work, the author also critically selected Lee's work as making a contribution to understanding the Trinity from an Asian perspective.

Second, Lee carefully weighs the cultural impact respectively of the Father-Son-Spirit order, which he calls the Patriarchal order; the Son-Father-Spirit order, which he calls Filial; and the Spirit-Father-Son order, which is deemed the Matriarchal order.[4] Lee suggests that Asian culture expects the older male of the home to be introduced first and then the firstborn son. So, the economic order of Father-Son-Spirit works well in the Asian context. He also affirms the Son-Father-Spirit order as culturally understandable because sometimes the Asian son takes over the leadership and support of the household when the father becomes aged. However, says Lee, the Asian mind would reject any introduction of the wife/mother before the father or son. If the Spirit represents the matriarchal in the triadic order, according to Lee, Asian minds would accept neither an order of Spirit-Son-Father nor Spirit-Father-Son. In light of this proposed rejection, Lee then moves his exploration from triadic orders in the text to a full blown evaluation of the Trinity in the context of the *yin/yang* worldview characteristic of Asian culture.

Despite his premature departure from the biblical sources and insights, Lee lays some groundwork for examining the warp and woof of the biblical triadic orders in the New Testament. It was this groundwork that suggested a classroom prayer experiment in Trinitarian theology, which I will describe shortly.

TRINITARIAN "DISORDER" IN 2 CORINTHIANS 13:13

The Trinitarian mystery snags our attention in at least three ways. Here is how I see them, from the most general advancing about our interaction with Scripture down to the most specific about the Trinity.

First, Bible-loving folk usually affirm the plain sense of the Scriptures. Since the Reformation, Protestants have upheld the doctrine of the perspicuity of the biblical revelation. This doctrine affirms that the Bible is understandable by any literate person, subject to the illumination of the Spirit of Christ. It argues that Scripture is not so hard to understand because it is complex, but rather Scripture is hard because it is demanding in terms of application.

Second, the interpretative problem is often that we see in Scripture what we expect to see—not what the text actually says. To quote Chesterton, "The sharpest pleasure of a traveler is in finding the things he did not expect, . . . I mean

---

4. Lee, *The Trinity in Asian Perspective,* 161–162.

the things that are at once so strange and so obvious that they must have been noticed, yet somehow they have not been noted."[5]

Third, with reference to the Trinity, the prevailing expectation is to see the Trinity in the order of Father, Son, and Holy Spirit. In the justly revered Great Commission of Matthew 28:19–20, Jesus mandated baptism of those being discipled in the name of God as Father, Son, and Spirit. This particular Trinitarian order occurs nineteen times in the New Testament, but it is not the only ordering (see Appendix A). Thus, given perspicuity of Scripture, shouldn't we assume that all ordering versions were intentional and have some significance? However, the prominence of the Father-Son-Spirit ordering has become an ingrained assumption that may blind us to any other order. Are we willing to do the work demanded to consider whether that is so, and how it may have affected our faith and practice?

For instance, what is a New Testament reader to think when coming upon the "disorderly" Trinitarian benediction in 2 Corinthians 13:13? There the apostle Paul closes his letter to the Corinthian believers with an unexpected Trinitarian order: "The grace of the Lord Jesus Christ, and the love of God, and the fellowship of the Holy Spirit be with all of you." The triadic order here is Son-Father-Spirit.

Or what about Ephesians 4:6, where Paul speaks of one Spirit, one Son, and one God and Father? This triadic order of Spirit-Son-Father is the exact opposite of the traditional Father-Son-Spirit order.

If these two instances were among the few exceptions, then they might demonstrate the proverbial rule of the expected triadic order of Father-Son-Spirit. That would be neat if it were true, but the biblical evidence points otherwise. There are more than seventy Scriptural references to the three persons of the Godhead, but often in orders different from the baptismal order of Matthew 28. Mathematically, any three entities can be arranged in six different orders. Guess what? The New Testament presents God as three, in all six possible orders, with intriguing regularity! Does this have significance? If so, what might it be? And if so, so what—what differences should that make in our everyday lives as disciples? My own exploration of this part of the Trinitarian mystery may have waited indefinitely, except for what happened in a 1997 Trinitarian prayer exercise.

---

5. Gilbert Keith Chesterton, *The Things I Saw in America* (New York: Dodd, Mead and Company, 1923), 79.

UNEXPECTED BREAKTHROUGH IN TRINITARIAN PRAYER

I shared my preliminary observations on the Trinitarian references with my theology students, in a draft form of the New Testament Census of Triadic Occurrences (Appendix A). My presentation to the students argued that if the New Testament authors wrote prayers and benedictions naming the three persons of the Trinity in six different orders, why couldn't we pray to God in those names in the order that made the most sense to us that night? I proposed a prayer experiment, based on the demonstration that there is ample warrant in the New Testament to call upon the Triune God in any of the six possible triadic orders:

- Father, Son, Holy Spirit
- Father, Holy Spirit, Son
- Son, Father, Holy Spirit
- Son, Holy Spirit, Father
- Holy Spirit, Son, Father
- Holy Spirit, Father, Son

I asked students if they would be willing to pray in class that evening to God in any of the triadic orders that made the most sense to them. Privately, I hoped that they would experiment with a Triune order new to their prayer life. I gave them five minutes to pray silently, and then we held a debriefing session. Many students expressed awkwardness at praying formally in the name of the Triune God in an order other than that of the Matthew 28 baptismal formula: Father-Son-Spirit. Other students expressed how refreshing it was to pray biblically, but in a new order. Some had never directly addressed the Holy Spirit previously and expressed a thrilling freedom as they did so.

Then a female student shared her experience. Having come from a home in which she experienced her father as stern and abusive, she shared that she had always found it difficult to pray to God as Father. But for the first time that evening, she was able to talk to God by the name of Father as she employed the Son-Spirit-Father order as used in Ephesians 2:17–19. Praying to God in this order was a spiritual breakthrough for her.

As I have used this Trinitarian prayer exercise with large groups of students and at church retreats, I continue to hear reports of these kinds of significant breakthroughs for those who follow Jesus. My conclusion then, as now, is that there is much more to intentionally applying the diverse triadic orders than is usually experienced in the life of the churches. This mystery of the triadic orders calls for careful investigation. Such is the purpose of this present work.

NEGLECT OF THE ECONOMIC TRINITY

Despite the recent upsurge in publications on the doctrine of the Trinity, few if any of those studies have turned systematically to the New Testament. The focus has been discussion of the theological issues inherent in the internal intra-relations among the Three as One, the so-called immanent Trinity. Reflection on the external economic Trinity has taken a backseat to searching for refined understanding of the immanent Trinity. Theologians may have conceded, perhaps unconsciously, to the Enlightenment assumption of evolutionary historical development of the doctrine of the Trinity. This Enlightenment view asserts that the Trinity is the result of dogmatic development over the centuries after the apostles.[6] Here are the usual arguments:

- Nothing of the Trinity can be found in the Old Testament.

- The bi-unity of the Father and Son is explicit in the New Testament, but the Trinity is implicit at best.

- The word *Trinity* is not found in the New Testament and was actually coined centuries after the Gospels were written.

- The doctrine of the Trinity is explicitly defined only in the post-apostolic period at Nicaea in 325 CE.

Increasingly, however, contemporary Trinitarian theologians have questioned these assertions by much more closely examining the internal New Testament witness to the God who is Three and One. Arthur Wainwright's 1952 *Trinity in the New Testament*; Boris Bobrinskoy's 1999 *The Mystery of the Trinity*; and, most recently, Allan Coppedge's 2007 *The God Who Is Triune* identify and

---

6. For a recent and articulate presentation of this view, see Marian Hillar, *From Logos to Trinity: The Evolution of Religious Beliefs from Pythagoras to Tertullian* (New York: Cambridge University Press, 2012).

reflect on the multiple triadic witnesses to the Triune God within the New Testament.[7] In this book, I intend to move the discussion from *multiple* to a *multitude* of New Testament textual witnesses to the Trinity. Further, this multitude of divine triadic instances occurs so often and in such a spectrum of orders—but each apparently in specific contexts—that it may well constitute a *matrix* of Trinitarian consciousness.

Trinity is often how the New Testament authors inadvertently think and view reality. This work will explore where these "inadvertent" Trinitarian instances occur and how consistent these occurrences are in their contexts and usage. In other words, do specific triadic orders such as Son-Spirit-Father occur in a consistent context so as to suggest that each triadic order defines or refines that context? For instance, certainly the context of Matthew 28:19–20 is missional and the order invoked is Father-Son-Spirit, but are the other eighteen contexts in which this particular triadic order occurs also missional? We will explore each triadic order in a specific chapter to sound out the relationship (if any) between order and context, and to distill out the application of that order within both our lives as disciples and our life together as the church.

WORSHIP: TRIUNE LIVING, MOVING, AND BEING

There remains one other practical motivation for making a thorough effort to explore the Trinitarian matrix found in the New Testament: worship. God deserves to be worshipped and served as He has revealed Himself. Latin Christianity asserts *lex orandi, lex credendi*: "the rule of prayer is the rule of belief" (and *practice* should be added). Churches live, move, and have their being in and through the Triune Being that is God.

With more than seventy instances, the diverse triadic formulae are so common in the New Testament as to become a default consciousness of its authors. The various instances of the six orders of the three persons of the Triune God construct a Trinitarian matrix for the New Testament. What value in worship and mission might apprehension of each of these divine triads in their biblical context have for the high expectations of the church in the world? What rich contributions toward the significance of the Trinity for faith and practice do they make? To find that out for ourselves, we must first embrace the apparent biblical

---

7. Allan Coppedge, *The God Who Is Triune: Revisioning the Christian Doctrine of God* (Downers Grove, IL: IVP Academic, 2007).

"disorder" of the New Testament references to the Trinity (i.e., orderings that go against our typically ingrained expectation of Father-Son-Spirit). Here are the core questions that this book will answer on implications and ramifications of the triadic references in the New Testament.

KEY QUESTIONS ON THE TRINITARIAN MATRIX

Chapter 1: The status question. Chapter 1 reviews the state of the doctrine of the Trinity. It gives particular attention to what many are calling a "renaissance of the doctrine of the Trinity." Many of these new works aim at a contemporary expression of the significance of the doctrine for everyday life and ministry. However, most of these efforts work from the immanent Trinity, which is somewhat of a mystery in terms of what little Scripture reveals, and is therefore more speculative since no one has access to the inner life of God. My research works from the biblical instances of the six movements outward of the economic (external) Trinity in mission and redemption. I offer this book as a fresh approach to apprehend significance of the Trinity in worship and life.

Chapter 2: The data question. Just how many New Testament occurrences of diverse Trinitarian orders are there? Where are they to be found in the New Testament? Are occurrences widely distributed, or are they clustered in only a few of the twenty-seven books therein? Are some of the orders more frequent than others, or are all the orders fairly evenly represented? We will search for answers to these textual data questions in chapter 2: The Trinitarian Matrix in the New Testament. It presents the data in support of the assertion of a matrix of Trinitarian awareness in the New Testament. If the data on the six triadic orders of the Trinity is not compelling, then the remainder of the book may not be worth writing, much less reading. However, if the data is compelling and valid—which I believe to be the case—then four more questions arise (antecedent, historical, contextual, and application), and I offer one or more chapters addressing each of them.

Chapter 3: The antecedent question. If triadic references are so abundant in the New Testament as to give evidence of an apostolic Trinitarian mindset, how did the apostles and writers of the New Testament learn to think this way? The simple answer, of course, is that they learned it from Jesus. However, what did Jesus have to work with as He taught His followers to pray, think, and live Trinitarian? How much space is there in the first century Palestinian Jewish mind for diversity within the unity that is the Shema, "Hear, O Israel, the Lord your God is One"? (Deut. 6:4). To use the phrase of Richard Niebuhr, can a radical monotheism of differentiation within the profound unity of God be found within what he also described as the "rigid monotheism" taught by the Pharisees and others?[8] Chapter 3: Triadic Presence in the Hebrew Scriptures gives the backstory of the presence and abundance of Trinitarian references in the New Testament. This chapter expands that wider backstory of plurality in the Godhead as uncovered in the first Testament and in the intertestamental works.

Chapter 4: The historical question. The current Trinitarian scholars is not the first biblical theologians to attempt identification and assessment of the multitude of triadic references in the New Testament. Origen in the third century and Calvin in the sixteenth both sought to produce commentaries on each of the books of the Bible.[9] In the fourth century, Hilary of Poitiers interpreted Scripture often to defend Trinitarian faith against the challenges of Sabellian unitarianism and Arian subordinationism. How have the diverse triadic orders been accounted for in these and other significant moments of the Christian faith? How have theologians ancient and contemporary addressed this issue of Trinitarian orders in their biblical and theological writings? What might be the consequences of ignoring the diverse orders of the Trinitarian procession, despite the biblical evidence for diverse usage? Did this actually occur in history, or was the invocation of the diverse triadic orders merely as inadvertent as is the usage of the orders in the New Testament, at least at first blush? Would ardor for one triadic order induce inflexibility in the worship and mission of the church? Did this actually happen in history? Where and when? These questions will be answered in chapter 4: The Karma of Dogma. Here we examine the history and ramifications of the dogmatic tradition at Nicaea. The key turning points in the development of the doctrine will be identified and enhanced by reference to how church leaders have used the triadic texts throughout the history of the church.

Chapters 5 through 10: The contextual question. Is there any contextual consistency regarding where specific triadic orders are found—for instance, in the eighteen contexts where the Son-Father-Spirit is found? Regeneration as an entrance into new life in the kingdom is a recurring theme through the New Testament. When addressing this subject, do the biblical

---

8. Richard Niebuhr, *Radical Monotheism and Western Culture* (Louisville: Westminster John Knox Press, 1960).
9. Calvin wished to omit only the book of Revelation from his project.

authors use a specific triadic order in such contexts? Are specific Trinitarian orders found in similar contexts so as to constitute a pattern of meaning for that specific triadic order? Answers to these questions will be developed in chapters 5 through 10, where each instance of the six triadic orders is catalogued and explored in its biblical context. There is one chapter per triadic order, and in each, I propose related conclusions and applications for our worship, life, and ministry.

- Chapter 5: The Sending Triad: Father-Son-Spirit as the Missional Order

- Chapter 6: The Saving Triad: Son-Spirit-Father as the Regenerative Order

- Chapter 7: The Indwelling Triad: Son-Father-Spirit as the Christological Witness Order

- Chapter 8: The Standing Triad: Spirit-Father-Son as the Sanctifying Order

- Chapter 9: The Shaping Triad: Father-Spirit-Son as the Spiritual Formation Order

- Chapter 10: The Uniting Triad: Spirit-Son-Father as the Ecclesial Order

Chapter 11: The contemporary question. What might be the applications of affirming and engaging the biblical usage of the diverse orders of the Trinitarian procession into the life of the church and into its interaction with the world? Can these positive consequences be seen already in the life of the church? How might the diversity of the triadic orders expressed in the New Testament speak in the current Trinitarian conversations around the social trinity, the Trinity and Islam, and the re-emergence of natural theology and its inevitable return to Trinitarian arguments from creation and humanity? In this concluding chapter, on "Becoming a Functional Trinitarian," I address these questions and recapitulate the findings of the research into a comprehensive view of Trinitarian living and serving for the church in the world. This will integrate with other Trinitarian theologies past and present to offer the contours of a Trinitarian ecclesiology that is grounded in the biblical text.

My Theological Method

The theological method I used in this study could have taken one of three paths. One was Paul Tillich's well-known and sometimes criticized method of correlation, which advocates beginning with an existential question that emerges out of contemporary anxieties and then correlating that question with biblical answers.[10] So Tillich words the anxious question of forgiveness and relationship to the holy God with the response of faith that even though we are unacceptable, we can accept God's acceptance of us in Christ. So, in the case of correlation for the doctrine of the Trinity, what would be the existential question which precipitates development of the biblical and systematic content of the doctrine? How can we have peace within ourselves and union with others without surrendering our autonomy? Or why is loneliness so abundant and so destructive? Both questions lend themselves to discussion of the image of God in humanity. However, as the major means to develop the doctrine, correlation is simply too narrow and would likely lead to missing all the benefit a more systematic approach would develop. Plus, these existential questions can lend themselves to guide the development of the sermons to be supplied at the end of each of the major chapters. These sermons are intended to express the value and application of the doctrine to worship, life, ministry, and the mission of the church.

A second possible path would be to follow the apologetic approach of Lewis and Demarest in *Integrative Theology*.[11] These writers designed their work to move from discussion of current theological controversies to a biblical resolution. Certainly numerous threats to the orthodox presentation of the Trinity have been mounted in our day. The rigid monotheism of Islam pressures against open conversation about the Triune God. The practical monism of most Christians and some megachurch pastors makes discussion of the Trinity seem less necessary and relevant. Tampering with the Trinity to solve the debate between egalitarian and complementarian positions on the roles of women in the church is another issue. Numerous questions could be posed.

---

10. Paul Tillich, *Systematic Theology*, vol. 1 (Chicago: University of Chicago Press, 1951), 1–8; see also Millard Erickson's critique of the method of correlation in his *Christian Theology* (Grand Rapids: Baker Academic, 1983, 1998, 2013), 60.
11. Gordon R. Lewis and Bruce A. Demarest, *Integrative Theology* (Grand Rapids: Zondervan, 1987, 1990, 1994; 2014).

The third method of research, which I use here, follows a traditional systematic rubric not unlike that commended in the evangelical systematic text *Christian Theology* by Millard Erickson.[12]

1. Develop a biblical theology of divine processional movements by reviewing their order in context.
2. Develop historical theology of these processional movements by researching the exegetical and theological materials available from the church fathers to the present.
3. State the conclusions derived from the foregoing research and name the various processions for their effect upon pastoral theology and mission.

YES, BUT WILL IT PREACH? TOOLS FOR MOVING FROM THEOLOGY TO PRAXOLOGY

Sermon starters. As mentioned earlier, one practical application feature of the book is to conclude most chapters with a related "sermon starter." After all, if it is in the Triune God that we live and move and have our being, we ought to be apt to preach and pray in the triune name and way. Therefore, the book includes eight sermons on the doctrine of the Trinity. At the end of each chapter you will find discussion questions to stimulate further reflection and conversation.

Appendixes, Indexes, Bibliography. The appendixes contain the full data chart of the Scripture research for this book. Also included in the appendixes is a glossary of technical Trinitarian concepts, a primer for sharing the Trinity with children and teenagers, and two exercises in Trinitarian spiritual formation. There are also indexes on Scripture and author/topic and an extensive reference bibliography.

HOW TO USE THIS BOOK

For Pastors, Preachers, and Worship Leaders

Pastors are hard pressed to say something memorable each week. The pressure increases when they plan specific doctrinal material. Most pastors have only one sermon on the Trinity in their files.

This book has eight sermons, and ten more sermon themes can be found in chapter 11. If you are an expository preacher working through full books of

---

12. Erickson, *Christian Theology*.

the Bible, use the Scripture index or "New Testament Census of Triadic Occurrences" in Appendix A to see which texts carry Trinitarian truths to be presented.

Worship leaders can find six fresh approaches to worship infused with biblical insight in chapters 5 through 10. If the congregation is facing a season of service, perhaps even suffering service, consider using chapter 6's insights into God standing for believers and enabling believers to stand for Christ no matter what comes. This Spirit-Father-Son movement in song, prayer, video, and Scripture selection captures and recreates the experience of Stephen under pressure in Acts 7.

For Personal Growth

By all means read chapter 2: The Trinitarian Matrix in the New Testament. You may find yourself seeing the texts with freshly opened eyes to what was always there but not visible previously. With that grasp of the thesis that the Trinity was a default consciousness of the writers of the New Testament, browse chapter 3: The Antecedent Question: Triadic Presence in the Hebrew Scriptures, to learn how God had revealed Himself since the beginning as a differentiated Oneness.

Chapters 1 and 4 cover some historical and contemporary theological developments related to the doctrine of the Trinity. You may enjoy these, or you may want to skip them until later. Either way, you are ready for the Trinitarian Prayers (see Appendix C). Most people who have taken this exercise emerge with memorable results. If you really want to stretch yourself, set aside about fifteen minutes every day for forty-two days to practice Trinitarian meditation (see Appendix D). This may do more than anything else to make you a functional Trinitarian.

As a Textbook

The doctrine of the Trinity is core to the curriculum in all schools where Christian ministerial leaders train. Chapters in this book end with discussion questions to aid in reflection upon issues of biblical interpretation, theological and spiritual conception of the triune God, and worship and preaching design. You can use this book in courses related to historical and systematic theology, spiritual formation, and worship and preaching in particular. Each chapter on a specific Trinitarian order considers specific approaches to worship which are reflective of that order. Each of these chapters also provides an example of how to approach that triadic order in a sermon. Finally, the appendixes contain two specific exercises appropriate for courses or retreats focusing on spiritual formation and growth. Both exercises have been field-tested, with memorable results for those who have experienced them.

Best Pages

I subscribe to the theory that good books have a few great pages. Great books have everyone else's great pages on that subject. In my mind, the best pages in this book are the New Testament Census of Triadic Occurrences in the New Testament found in Appendix A. It presents the heart of the research on which this book rests.

The Trinitarian Prayer exercise described in the Introduction and detailed in the Appendix has demonstrated the application power of being functionally Trinitarian in every class session in which I have used it.

Finally, read the headers in chapter 11, as they outline the demands and benefits of living as a functional Trinitarian.

DISCUSSION QUESTIONS

- Having read the introduction of this book, what did you see that you are most looking forward to reading in later chapters?

- Did you look ahead at the "best pages" in the book identified above? What did you think when you glanced at those pages?

- How could there have been more than seventy references in the New Testament to the three persons in the Trinity for two thousand years, and yet this is the first time a book has identified them and explained what they might mean? Would it be more fair to say that theologians from the beginning have noticed triadic presence and patterns in the New Testament, but this is the first time someone has systematically searched for all the pieces of the puzzle?

PART 1:

Considering Four Key Questions

The Status Question: The Search for Trinitarian Significance in Contemporary Theology

That mathematical history. That mind-bending oddity. That strange, even embarrassing idea. Yes, deep within the Christian psyche today seems to be the notion that the Trinity is an awkward and odd irrelevance, an unsightly wart on our knowledge of the true God.

—Michael Reeves[1]

Today the doctrine of the Trinity is being remembered (James White said it is forgotten), rethought (Robert Woźniak and Giuliu Maspero declared it is disputed), and reconstructed (Fred Sanders said it changes everything).[2] The mystery of the Triune God is simply that no words and no human minds can fully apprehend Him. The fundamental mystery of the Christian faith, then, involves recitation of the Hebrew Shema, "Hear, O Israel, the Lord your God is One"—*in the manner in which* Jesus of Nazareth revealed that Oneness as

---

1. Michael Reeves, "Three Is the Loveliest Number," *Christianity Today,* December 2012, 43.
2. James White, *The Forgotten Trinity* (Minneapolis: Bethany House Publishers, 1998); Robert J. Woźniak and Giulio Maspero, *Rethinking Trinitarian Theology* (New York: T & T Clark International, 2012); Fred Sanders, *The Deep Things of God: How the Trinity Changes Everything* (Wheaton, IL: Crossway, 2010).

Father, Son, and Spirit. Human minds are stretched by the mystery of how three may be one and one may be three. Yet there is the command to love God with all our heart, with all our soul, and with all our mind (Matt. 22:37), so failure to attempt to express truth about the Godhead can hardly be faithfulness.

For centuries, systematic theologians have mined the concept of the immanent Trinity as the inner relations between and among the Three in order to explain God's Oneness. The formative truths from reflection on the Trinity have often been fitted with precise technical terms such as *perichoretic* or *hypostatic*. These ancient constructs have added to the mystery and the perceived impracticality and inaccessibility of the doctrine to laity.[3] Yet the doctrine of the Trinity has rightly persisted as a test of orthodox Christian faith for two millennia. You may be surprised to learn that the conservative and influential Evangelical Theological Society has only two doctrinal tests in its required membership statement, one of which is affirmation of the Trinity. Worship of and obedience to the Triune God is not optional for Christians and the church.

In this chapter, I review the fall and rise again of the doctrine of the Trinity in modern theology. I then summarize four ways that recent Trinitarian studies have sought to frame the significance of the doctrine for practical life and ministry: dogmatic, polemical, ecumenical, and practical. Finally, I seek to make the case that a biblical investigation into the way the New Testament invokes the Godhead reveals six practices of the church to be done in the name and power of the Trinity. These practices are what give us the framework for becoming what I call "functional Trinitarians."

MODERN THEOLOGY AND THE FALL
AND RISE OF TRINITARIANISM

Strikes against the Trinity

Mystery can be frustrating, especially to critics of practical reason. Since Kant in the eighteenth century, Christians have been told that this Trinitarian mystery has no practical value, no matter how truthful it may be. We live in the age and imagination of pragmatism where everything distills down to "What works is what I affirm as true." So pastors and priests increasingly neglect this so-called impractical doctrine in their preaching. They trust Trinitarian veneration primarily to the baptismal pronouncement, "I baptize you in the name of

---

3. A glossary of Trinitarian-related theological terms is provided in Appendix B.

the Father and the Son and the Holy Spirit," and perhaps to the benediction at the end of the worship service.

In the nineteenth century, liberal Protestant thinkers including F. C. Bauer and Adolf Harnack told and sold Protestants in particular the dogma that the Trinity is a third-century ecclesiastical development, a doctrinal evolution that is post-New Testament and post–early church. Lay Christians have submitted to the resulting pastoral neglect by reasoning that, after all, the word "Trinity" is not even found in the New Testament. So, from the pew, the best argument for assertion and retention of the doctrine has been the argument of tradition for tradition's sake—or even the fideistic argument: "Jesus said it, so that settles it."

Michael Reeves recently lamented in *Christianity Today*, "That mathematical history. That mind-bending oddity. That strange, even embarrassing idea. Yes, deep within the Christian psyche today seems to be the notion that the Trinity is an awkward and odd irrelevance, an unsightly wart on our knowledge of the true God."[4] However, the late modern and early postmodern mind is not stirred by such paradoxical and impractical logic, so now a surge of new Trinitarian works has been published in the past quarter of a century to reestablish the grounds for and the significance of the doctrine. Most of these authors have built their cases from reflection on the *immanent* Trinity, which is understood as the inner relation between the three modes of God's being: Father, Son, and Spirit.[5] Others have focused on reference to historical theology and tradition. Few have focused on the scriptural invocations of the *economic* Trinity, which economy refers to the external, redemptive movement of the Father sending the Son and Spirit. What have these authors come up with?

From Showcase to Embarrassment

As recently as 2000, John Feinberg made the following confession about the state of the doctrine of the Trinity in his monumental work, *No One Like Him*, "Though this is Christianity's unique doctrine (and in that sense it should be a 'showcase' for Christianity's distinctiveness), many see it as an embarrassment, a case of 'creative mathematics' intended to assert something, though exactly what is

---

4. Michael Reeves, "Three Is the Loveliest Number," 43.
5. Karl Barth most famously introduced moving away from a Trinitarian theology of three persons as the modern understanding of personality and into a "modes of divine subsistence thinking." Of course, criticism has been leveled at Barth for moving this theology toward modalism, the concept of one God carrying out three tasks. See Ted Peters, *God as Trinity: Relationality and Temporality in the Divine Life* (Louisville: Westminster John Knox Press, 1993), 105.

uncertain."[6] How far the esteem for the doctrine has fallen since the fifth century preacher of Gallic France, Caesarius of Arles, declared, *"Fides omnium christianorum in Trinitate consistorum"* ("The faith of all Christians rests on the Trinity").[7]

This theological embarrassment has persisted for 150 years, especially from 1800 to about 1950. It started in 1798, when Enlightenment philosopher Immanuel Kant offered the assertion that "the doctrine of the Trinity, taken literally, has no practical relevance at all. . . . Whether we are to worship three or ten persons in the Deity makes no difference."[8] The pragmatic assumption, presumably, is that if a doctrine has no discernible practical relevance, then there is little lost in its benign neglect. However, my intention is to demonstrate biblically the degree to which the Trinity is a showcase doctrine and how that showcase practically works to the glory of God and the benefit of the church.

To the Attic

Exactly how did the centerpiece of the doctrinal parlor end up relegated to dusty storage in our theological attic? First, the so-called father of modern theology, Friedrich Schleiermacher, took his cue from Kant and shifted the doctrine of the Trinity out of its central place in the Christian mansion and into the appendix of his 1821 theology, *The Christian Faith*. An appendix is of course the literary equivalent of an attic or basement.[9] To be sure, baptisms in Schleiermacher's church in Berlin continued to invoke the name of the Father, Son, and Holy Spirit—no matter the perceived relevance or irrelevance of the doctrine. Worshippers still sang the "blessed Trinity" stanza of "Holy, Holy, Holy," and his retooled pietistic evangelism turned many to the faith.[10] Despite this drift in modern theology with the rising tide of liberal Protestantism, conservative Evangelicals and Catholics continued to teach and preach on the Trinity, though probably more stridently than before in the face of less assurance about the practicality of the doctrine.

---

6. John Feinberg, *No One Like Him: The Doctrine of God*, in the Foundations of Evangelical Theology Series (Wheaton, IL: Crossway Books, 2001), 437.
7. Ibid., viii.
8. Immanuel Kant, "The Conflict of the Faculties," in *Religion and Rational Theology*, trans. and ed. Allen W. Wood and George di Giovanni (Cambridge: Cambridge University Press, 1996), 264.
9. Friedrich Schleiermacher, *The Christian Faith*, H.R. Mackintosh and J.S. Stewart, eds. (New York: T & T Clark, 1999; originally 1821).
10. The lyrics for "Holy, Holy, Holy" were composed by the Bishop of Kolcata, Reginald Heber (1783–1826).

In 1981, Jürgen Moltmann's *The Trinity and the Kingdom* became available in English. In it, Moltmann identifies and analyses two primary causes for the eclipse of Trinitarian thinking and development since the Enlightenment.[11] First, there had been a theological shift away from objective metaphysical orthodoxy and to subjective values. This meant that the scholastic achievements in Trinitarian formulations of immanent Trinity failed to create feelings of utter dependence on the Triune God among the cultured despisers in Frederick Schleiermacher's Berlin congregation. Moltmann rejects the result of Schleiermacher's reworking *The Christian Faith*, that the declaration and celebration of the immanent Trinity gave way to a "practical monotheism." In other words, it appears easier to invoke emotional response to God if God is much more one than three. Threeness takes hard thinking to combine it with Oneness, so thinking took a theological back pew to feeling.

This practical Monarchianism surfaced significantly at the beginning and the end of the twentieth century in US Protestant churches. Historians of the American church identify the 1906 Azusa Street Revival in Los Angeles as the beginning of the Pentecostal expression of Christianity. That movement very nearly fell off the orthodox track to become a monorailed, monarchial, Jesus-only movement. The anti-Trinitarian expression was splintered off so that the main movement could proceed on three rails, with the Holy Spirit being the power rail in the center, of course. Also, by the end of the century, some iconic megachurch leaders have been challenged as neglecting the Trinity in favor of a Jesus-only theology.

Pragmatism is the second cause for decline of Trinitarianism that Moltmann analyzes. As I noted earlier, Kant abruptly asserts that there is no practical value in the doctrine of the Trinity. In the technological age where it is assumed that if it works it must be true, the aged doctrine of the Trinity is deemed too old to be put to use in the executive models of the modern church. There the mantra of emotion is no substitute for activity, and activity is no substitute for productivity. This has several deep historical causes:

- The monocular overfocus of historical tradition on the baptismal order of Father-Son-Spirit.

- The 1,500-year dismantling of the priesthood of believers so that even the missional meaning of the Father-Son-Spirit order was withheld with the cup from the laity.

---

11. Jürgen Moltmann, *The Trinity and the Kingdom* (San Francisco: Harper & Row, 1981).

- The somewhat anti-Semitic habit of asserting the Septuagint Greek translation over the preserved original in the Masoretic Hebrew text, so that the roots of the diversity within the divine Oneness were obscured at best and denied or ignored at worst.

- The postmodern predisposition to distrust authority, metanarratives, and dogmatic institutions, of which the Trinity could be the poster child.

The resulting decline of fresh thinking and theology about the divine Three meant that pastors fretted over what to preach on the annual Trinity Sunday sermon. They trusted that orthodoxy was somewhat satisfied by regular reference to the Trinity during baptisms and benedictions.

The Two Karls and the Trinitarian Reformation

The diminishing state of the doctrine in the West began to reverse in the twentieth century when the two Karls—the Reformed Karl Barth (1886–1968) and the Jesuit Karl Rahner (1904–1984)—fetched the doctrine from the intellectual attic and restored it to the theological parlor.[12] Here are milestones in this Trinitarian Reformation in the twentieth century:

- 1932—Karl Barth publishes the first volume of the fourteen-volume *Church Dogmatics*, with the Trinity as its subject.

- 1943—Oxford theologian Leonard Hodgson issues *The Doctrine of the Trinity*, which lays out the historical development of the doctrine from the New Testament to Calvin with reference to philosophy.

- 1944—The Eastern Orthodox theologian Vladimir Lossky publishes *The Mystical Theology of the Eastern Church*, which unfolds the Trinity as three uncreated existences (*hypostases*) in one uncreated essence (*ousia*).

- 1948—Scottish theologian Donald Baillie publishes his influential *God Was in Christ* and spends a chapter, "Two Trends in Trinitarian

---

12. I am following the astute historical-theological analysis commended by Lesslie Newbigin and his colleague, Harold Turner, in the latter's seminar presented to the Anglican Diocese of Auckland, 29th February 2000, "Theology 1900–1950 in Relation to Society," at http://www.gospel-culture.org.uk/harold_turner.htm (accessed May 14, 2012).

Thought," fusing the near modalism of Barth's approach with the near tri-theism of the social trinity in Hodgson.

- 1962—Methodist professor Arthur Wainwright seeks to reseat the Trinitarian reformation squarely on its biblical references in his *The Trinity and the New Testament.*

- 1967—Karl Rahner's *The Trinity* issues his famous Rule on the inseparability of the economic and immanent Trinitarian formulations, which reflects Barth's influence.

- I would add Hans Urs von Balthasar, the greatest Catholic theologian of the twentieth century, writing in interchange with Barth, when he took the Trinity and the Incarnation as the two fundamental dogmas of Christianity.

That helps give the big picture of the turn in trajectory for the doctrine of the Trinity. Now, here are a few close-up snapshots from the two Karls.

On the Protestant side, Trinity is the centerpiece in Barth's fourteen-volume *Church Dogmatics*. It is the subject of volume 1 (1932 in the German, 1936 in English) and the theological underpinning for all that follows. Barth restores the centrality of the doctrine arguing, "The doctrine of the Trinity is what basically distinguishes the Christian doctrine of God as Christian, and therefore what already distinguishes the Christian concept of revelation as Christian, in contrast to all other possible doctrines of God and concepts of revelation."[13] About Barth's impact on contemporary Trinitarian theology, American Lutheran Robert Jenson concluded, "It can be fairly said that the chief ecumenical enterprise of current theology is the rediscovery and development of the doctrine of the Trinity. It can also be said that Barth initiated the enterprise."[14]

On the Catholic side, Karl Rahner critiqued what he saw as the traditional captivity of the doctrine of the Trinity to medieval Scholastic categories. These ten neo-Aristotelian categories and metaphysical cognates kept theological focus on the intra-Trinitarian relations of the immanent Trinity.[15] Medieval scholastics

---

13. Karl Barth, *Church Dogmatics,* 1/1, 301.
14. Robert Jenson, "Karl Barth," in *The Modern Theologian: An Introduction to Modern Theology Since 1918,* 3rd ed., edited by David F. Ford (New York: Blackwell, 2005), 27.
15. Among the ten Aristotelian philosophical categories are: 1. Substance or essence; 2. Quantity,

endeavored philosophically to refine the abstract, invisible distinctions and relations between the Father, Son, and Spirit to the neglect of exploration of the more concrete, visible economic mission toward creation and humanity. Rahner saw this medieval preoccupation as detaching practical application of the doctrine to Catholic lives. He then proposed the often invoked but recently critiqued "Rahner's Rule," that the economic Trinity is the immanent Trinity and the immanent Trinity is the economic Trinity.[16]

Rahner's assertion brought Trinitarian discussion back down to earth. Discussions of the immanent interrelations of the Three could no longer be detached from the significance of the redemptive mission of the Three earthward. The economic mission of creation and redemption was of course normatively experienced in the incarnation, crucifixion, and resurrection of the incarnate Son. So faithful discussions of the inner relations of the Father, Son, and Spirit must be done in continuity with that mission of the Triune Godhead.

The call for restoration of the centrality and distinctiveness of the doctrine sparked up again with the 1980 British Council of Churches study entitled *The Forgotten Trinity*. More recently, the Evangelical apologist James White published his own version of *The Forgotten Trinity* in 1998, and then Baptist theologian Stanley Grenz published his *Rediscovering the Trinity* in 2004.[17] Today, the doctrine of the Trinity is a fresh field of study and publication, with multiple monographs on the doctrine being published annually in the past decade. The Trinity is a hot topic for doctrinal discussion and practical application. How have those debates and engagements configured themselves? I would suggest that four distinct approaches have been emerging, as we will see in the next section.

THE NEW QUEST FOR TRINITARIAN SIGNIFICANCE

The surge in Trinitarian interest has at least two causes. First, postmodernity has ended the modernist sanctions against supernatural considerations.

3. Quality; 4. Relation; 5. Place or Position in the environment; 6. Time, etc.; see Aristotle, "Categories," in Jonathan Barnes, ed., *The Complete Works of Aristotle*, J.L. Ackrill, trans. (Princeton, NJ: Princeton University Press, 1995), 3–24.

16. Karl Rahner, *The Trinity*, trans. Joseph Donceel (Turnbridge Wells: Burn and Oates, 1970), 22.

17. *The Forgotten Trinity: The Report of the B.C.C. Study Committee on the Trinitarian Doctrine Today* (The British Council of Churches, Inter-Church House, 1989), vol. 2; Stanley J. Grenz, *Rediscovering the Triune God: The Trinity in Contemporary Theology* (Minneapolis: Fortress Press, 2004); and James R. White, *The Forgotten Trinity: Recovering the Heart of the Christian Faith* (Minneapolis: Bethany House Publishers, 1998).

Spirituality is back in vogue. Second, however, this postmodern spirituality is expected to have a green meaning—a practical, sustainable application.

Against this public place background, contemporary Trinitarian theologians are therefore in search of the *contemporary significance* of the doctrine. Their search has been so productive that at least two new studies on the Trinity have been published every year in the last decade.

Published Overviews

With so many new works and authors in the field, buying an introduction has become exceedingly helpful to navigate the theological developments in Trinitarian thinking. Thankfully, several recent books have taken on the important task of interpreting the state of Trinitarian thinking. The earlier Trinitarian "program guides" were published in 1995 and 1998—respectively by John Thompson and the Catholic scholar Anne Hunt.[18] More recently, Nazarene theologian Roderick Leupp, Wesleyan Methodist scholar Jason Vickers, and Fuller Seminary ecumenicist Velli-Marti Kärkkäinen have each published useful overviews of the increasingly rapid growth of Trinitarian studies.[19]

A number of edited collections from the Catholic and Orthodox perspectives of works on the Trinity have appeared from 2012 through 2014 to accelerate this Trinitarian resurgence and to invite others into the conversation.[20]

On the more evangelical side, Oliver Crisp and Fred Sanders edited and published papers from the Los Angeles Theology Conference 2014, entitled *Advancing Trinitarian Theology: Explorations in Constructive Dogmatics*. Also that year, *Two Views on the Doctrine of the Trinity*, edited by Jason Sexton, presented Catholic and evangelical views of the classic Nicene formulation of the Trinity and a Catholic and an evangelical take on the relational view of the Trinity.[21]

---

18. John Thompson, *Modern Trinitarian Perspectives*, (New York: Oxford University Press, 1994); Anne Hunt, *What Are They Saying about the Trinity?*, (Mahwah, NJ: Paulist Press, 1998).

19. T. Roderick Leupp, *The Renewal of Trinitarian Theology: Themes, Patterns & Explorations* (Downers Grove, IL: IVP Academic, 2008); Jason E Vickers, *Invocation and Ascent: The Making and Remaking of Trinitarian Theology* (Grand Rapids: Eerdmans, 2008); and Velli-Matti Kärkkäinen, *The Trinity: Global Perspectives* (Louisville: Westminster John Knox Press, 2007) and see his earlier work, *The Trinity and Religious Pluralism* (Hants: Ashgate Publishing Limited, 2004).

20. Khaled Anatolios, ed., *The Holy Trinity in the Life of the Church* (Grand Rapids: Baker Academic, 2014); Giulio Maspero and Robert Wozniak, eds., *Rethinking Trinitarian Theology: Disputed Questions and Contemporary Issues in Trinitarian Theology*, (New York: T & T Clark, 2012); Christophe Chalamet and Marc Vial, eds., *Recent Developments in Trinitarian Theology: An International Symposium* (Minneapolis: Fortress Press, 2014).

21. While the classical view of the Trinity defines the Triune God in terms of substance and persons,

So far, the search for Trinitarian significance has operated along four approaches: the dogmatic, the polemical, the ecumenical, and the practical. We will look into each of these now.

The Dogmatic Approach

Christianity has ever benefited as orthodox theologians have risen in their times to make a dogmatic defense for the hope of God in Christ. Such dogmatic defenses, however, have been at times more pugnacious than gentle. In *The Forgotten Trinity*, evangelical apologist James White carefully reasoned his defense of the historic doctrine "as the heart of the faith," against any and all ancient and present challenges.[22] The implication of Allan Coppedge's 2007 *The God Who Is Triune* is that to be significant in the twenty-first century, the Trinity must be put in the Reformed way of thinking and that such "revisioning" will align better with the divine ends.[23] Recently deceased Baptist theologian Stanley Grenz had also called for a rediscovering of the Trinity, although he meant that in less of a traditionally dogmatic form and more of a post-foundational social Trinity approach.[24]

The Polemical Approach

Polemics is about defending the faith. It is a necessary, ongoing aspect of doctrinal development because theological heresy may be refuted and anathematized but is never fully eradicated. For instance, the subordinationist thesis that the Son was created by the Father and that there can only be one undifferentiated being in the Godhead continues to break out as an endemic heretical virus. The oft-heard anti-Trinitarian arguments of the Watchtower Society are among the stronger carriers of this theological disease.

The defenders of the traditionally interpreted Qur'an also have intimidated some evangelicals into playing down defense of this showcase doctrine at the street level. Evangelical missionaries to the Muslim world often have personal encounters where mention of the Trinity discourages further conversation with otherwise engaging acquaintances.

---

the relational view defines the Trinity as relations. See Paul S. Fiddes, "Relational Trinity: Radical Perspective," in *Two Views on the Doctrine of the Trinity* (Grand Rapids: Zondervan, 2014), 159.

22. James R. White, *The Forgotten Trinity: Recovering the Heart of the Christian Faith* (Minneapolis: Bethany House Publishers, 1998).
23. Allan Coppedge, *The God Who Is Triune: Revisioning the Christian Doctrine of God* (Downers Grove, IL: IVP Academic, 2007).
24. Stanley J. Grenz, *Rediscovering the Triune God: The Trinity in Contemporary Theology* (Minneapolis: Fortress Press, 2004).

Also, some megachurch pastors—and no doubt many more small church pastors—find that preaching, teaching, and practicing the Triune God takes more thought and discipline than just teaching and preaching Jesus. So their doctrine is an operational monotheism of the Son.

Keen-eyed observers have even quipped that the Episcopalians have the Father, the Baptists have the Son, and the Pentecostals have the Spirit. The choice of hymns and prayer references to God reveal that we are usually Trinity-lite in worship.

The Trinity is trouble. It is a liturgical litmus test of whether or not biblical revelation is the norm for faith and practice. It tests whether a congregation submits more to the textual pressure of the scriptural witness to the Triune God, or to the pressure of public place logic so-called (How can three be one?), or to the pressure of intimidation by cult and non-Christian religious sources (monotheism must mean an undifferentiated One without any inner plurality).

The Protestant historical theologian, Claude Welch, published his *In This Name* in 1952. Rather than a practical or pastoral application of the Trinity, for Welch the Trinity has largely a polemical role in defense of Christian monotheism in a polytheistic world. His study of contemporary Trinitarian doctrine defined the nineteenth-century state of the doctrine as "reduction to a doctrine of the second rank."[25] Thanks to the relegation of the Trinity to a postscript position in Schleiermacher's *Christian Faith* at the beginning of the nineteenth century and those Welch calls a deep suspicion of metaphysical doctrines, over-attachment to the transcendent categories of the immanent Trinity meant that the doctrine held for Protestant liberal thinkers little aid for ethical value judgments in an age committed to finding "what Jesus would do."[26] Welch's assessment of the state of the doctrine among Roman Catholics and what Welch calls evangelical fundamentalists is the value.[27]

At best, then, for these kinds of what Welch calls authoritarian Christianity, the doctrine of the Trinity finds a use as a "defensive" doctrine. Here Welch rather critically picks up on the assertion of Emil Brunner that the Trinity does not arise from the *kerygmatic* gospel proclamation of the church, but rather as a theological defensive doctrine [*Schutzlehre*] for the center of biblical and ecclesiastical faith.[28] So the

---

25. Claude Welch, *In This Name: The Doctrine of the Trinity in Contemporary Theology* (New York: Charles Scribner's Sons, 1952), 3.
26. Ibid., 19, 51.
27. Ibid., 93–94.
28. Ibid., 66. See Emil Brunner, *The Christian Doctrine of God* (Philadelphia: Westminster Press, 1950), 205–240.

doctrine defends the whole of Christian theology against the mere monotheisms of Judaism and Islam and against the polytheisms abounding around the globe.

The Ecumenical Approach

Bridges can be barriers. Western and Eastern Christian denominations find a theological commonality in the Trinitarian formula affirmed at Nicaea in 325 CE, three Persons in one God. So Christianity existed, broadly speaking, in one house, one *economos*. However, over the course of the next millennium, the churches in the West came to use and then dogmatize an additional phrase regarding the Spirit being sent by the Father *and the* Son, *filioque* in the Latin. In 1054, there occurred a Great Schism for reasons theological, ecclesiological, political, and cultural.[29] That Trinitarian ecumenical bridge was closed, with mutual anathemas exchanged between the papacy in the West and the patriarchy in the East. However, significant work is underway to rebuild the house and bridge. Since at least 1979, the Roman Catholic Church has fostered ecumenical dialog with the Orthodox Church.

In October 2003, the North American Orthodox-Catholic Theological Consultation issued a statement entitled, "The Filioque: A Church Dividing Issue?" Among the recommendations were the acknowledgment about limited ability "to make definitive assertions about the inner life of God" and that declaration be made that the condemnation made at the 1274 Council at Lyon of those "who presume to deny that the Holy Spirit proceeds eternally from the Father and the Son" no longer applies.[30]

If four pillars are critical to hold the roof of this ecumenical house up, then certainly theology and ecclesiology represent two such pillars. The theological question is one of understanding and defining the relationship of the Spirit to the Godhead. A number of influential Western theologians have weighed into this discussion in favor of restoring an earlier version of the Creed, perhaps even with a compromise of "from the Father *through the Son.*" Kärkkäinen supports this reversion in his 2007 *The Trinity: Global Perspectives,* as did Yale historical theologian Jaroslav Pelikan, who converted from being an ordained Lutheran pastor to an Orthodox layman in 1998. Of this event, Pelikan liked to say that

---

29. A. Edward Siecienski, *The Filioque: History of a Doctrinal Controversy* (New York: Oxford University Press, 2010).
30. The North American Orthodox-Catholic Theological Consultation, "The Filioque: A Church Dividing Issue?" http://www.assemblyofbishops.org/ministries/dialogue/orthodox-catholic/2003filioque (accessed January 17, 2015).

he had not so much converted to Orthodoxy as "returned to it, peeling back the layers of my own belief to reveal the Orthodoxy that was always there."[31]

For Kärkkäinen, global perspectives on the Trinity rightly involve more than study of its capacity to reunite the churches of the west and east. Kärkkäinen is ecumenical, but he is not pluralistic—he seeks to find common ground for formal union between traditions of the Christian faith, but he seeks no such ground for non-Christian traditions. That distinction is crucial, especially in postmodern cultural climates of relativism and pluralism: Is the Trinity distinctively Christian, or not?

Kärkkäinen does examine the current impact of pluralism on Trinitarian understanding by evaluating the pluralistic Trinitarianism of Raimundo Panikar.[32] Kärkkäinen notes Vanhoozer's 1997 assertion that Panikar is the rare exception, a pluralist who does invoke the Trinity and "believes it to be at the heart of all religions."[33] So, the contemporary conversation around religious pluralism has called into question whether or not the doctrine of the Trinity is distinctive to the Christian faith.

The Catholic theologian Gavin D'Costa describes his intention to honor "the universal salvific will of God" and the particularity of Christ for salvation.[34] According to D'Costa, the Spirit of God is at work in all places and religions that all might be saved, but Christ alone is that means. D'Costa defines Christ's uniqueness as "*totus Deus,* but never *totum Dei;* wholly God but never the whole of God."[35] In other words, the universal work of God in Christ is not universalism in the thought of D'Costa.

Once we have surfaced and examined the full New Testament data on triadic references, we will use those conclusions to address this issue of the so-called "re-

---

31. Timothy George, "Delighted by Doctrine," *Christian History and Biography*, vol. 91 (Summer 2006), 43–45.

32. Veli-Matti Kärkkäinen, *The Trinity: Global Perspectives* (Louisville: Westminster John Knox, 2007), 336–345; cf. Raimundo Panikar, *The Intrareligious Dialogue* (New York: Paulist Press, 1978) and Panikar, *The Trinity and the Religious Experience of Man: Icon-Person-Mystery* (Maryknoll, NY: Orbis, 1973).

33. Ibid., n.1, 336; see also Kevin Vanhoozer, ed., *The Trinity in a Pluralistic Age* (Grand Rapids: Eerdmans, 1997), 58–64.

34. Gavin D'Costa, *The Myth of Christian Uniqueness: Toward a Pluralistic Theology of Religions* (Marynoll, NY: Orbis, 1987), 149; see Loe-Joo Tan, "Gavin D'Costa's Trinitarian Theology of Religion: An Assessment," *New Blackfriars*, vol. 95, Issue 1055, (Jan. 2014), 88–104; and P. Plata, "The Appeal to the Trinity in Contemporary Theology of Interreligious Dialog," PhD Thesis, Katholieke Universiteit, Leuven, Belgium, 2007.

35. D'Costa, *The Myth of Christian Uniqueness*. This is also similar to "Christ defines but does not confine God."

consideration of Christian uniqueness."[36] If there are evidences of the Triune Creator in humanity as made in His image, then may we not look for vestiges of the Trinity within the structure of human existence? Augustine made this argument in his *On the Trinity* in the fifth century CE. There he famously suggested evidence of the Trinity in the threefold aspect of human intellectual life: memory, active recollection as understanding, and action as will and love. The Psalmist asserts that "The heavens declare the glory of God, and the sky proclaims the work of His hands" (Ps. 19:1). *Would not such divine glory be a triune glory?* reasons Augustine. And if indigenous and world religions are reflections of the general revelation in creation, could we not expect to find vestiges or impressions of the Trinity within those traditions, though perhaps in a refracted if not distorted form?[37]

This logic is what guides Panikar.[38] "His invisible attributes, that is, His eternal power and divine nature, have been clearly seen since the creation of the world, being understood through what He has made." Therefore, Panikar critically evaluates the Trinitarian exploration of Hindu theology, looking for vestiges of the Trinity embedded.[39]

Kärkkäinen also reviewed the intercultural approach of Jung Young Lee's *yin/yang* Asian interpretation of the Trinitarian procession. It was Lee's work that sparked the prayer experiment in my graduate theology course described previously.

The Practical Approach

While recovery of the traditional values and truths of the doctrine is inspiring and helpful, modernist and postmodernist publics are not likely to have much patience with tradition-for-tradition's-sake arguments. If the mantra of modernity has been "Question authority!" then those of the postmodern worldview will be asking, "Why have we always done it this way?" or "How did the church speak of God before the Council at Nicaea?" If the mantra of postmodernists is "Question questions!" then their desire may be to hope in mystical experience by invoking the words of Nicene Trinitarian confession without significant interpretation or understanding. However, preferring the

---

36. Gavin D'Costa, *Christian Uniqueness Reconsidered* (Maryknoll, NY: Orbis Books, 1990); see also *The Myth of Christian Uniqueness.*

37. Augustine, *On the Trinity*, Bk. 9, Ch. 3; Phillip Schaff, ed., (Grand Rapids: Eerdmans, 1887/1999), 127.

38. See Bruce Demarest, *General Revelation: Historical Views and Contemporary Issues* (Grand Rapids: Zondervan, 1982).

39. Karl Barth, *Church Dogmatics,* I:I, 8.3–9.2. Barth's critique of the value of vestiges of the Trinity in nature and humanity will be addressed in a later chapter.

experiential to the rational fails to enable much of a gentle defense for the hope that is the Triune God to whom Jesus wrought witness. On this score, two practical issues arise where alternative Trinitarian emphases clash: gender relationships and social activism.

Gender Relations. Proponents of both the egalitarian and the complementarian views of the roles of men and women seek to trump each other with reference to their interpretation of the intra-Trinitarian roles immanent within the One God. Egalitarian theologians from vastly differing traditions offer the same solution. They call it the "social Trinity." The social Trinity is a theological movement to express the equality of intra-relationships among the members of the Trinity. Egalitarian authors propose applications of those Triune relationships as an emancipation charter for humanity and a mandate for egalitarian relationships between men and women. Following the lead of German Reformed theologian Jürgen Moltmann, feminist Catholic theologian Catherine LaCugna, the Australian Anglican Kevin Giles, and the Baptist Stanley Grenz all explore the so-called social Trinity as a way likely to capture contemporary attention.[40]

But complementarians likewise use Trinitarian arguments for their point of view. The dialogue has become heated over the last decade especially, both at the academic and populist levels. For instance, Kevin Giles argues repeatedly in print to show that egalitarian essence and relations within the Trinity are determinative that men and women too have equality of essence and functions in family and church. Making the opposite case, Wayne Grudem and Bruce Ware argue for an eternal role of submission by the Son to the Father, from which they deduce calls for permanent submission of women to men in home and church. [41] The "Evangelical Dean of Theology" Millard Erickson has called both views "tampering with the Trinity," and others have identified these discussions as being "entangled in the Trinity."[42] The Trinitarian Matrix approach

---

40. Kevin Giles, *The Trinity and Subordinationism: The Doctrine of God and the Contemporary Gender Debate* (Downers Grove, IL: InterVarsity Press, 2002); Stanley J. Grenz, *The Social God and the Relational Self: A Trinitarian Theology of the Imago Dei* (Louisville: Westminster John Knox Press, 2001) and *Rediscovering the Triune God: The Trinity in Contemporary Theology* (Minneapolis: Fortress Press, 2004). Catherine Mowry LaCugna, *God for Us: The Trinity and Christian Life* (New York: HarperSanFrancisco, 1993)

41. Bruce A. Ware, *Father, Son, and Holy Spirit: Relationships, Roles and Relevance* (Wheaton, IL: Crossway Books, 2005).

42. Millard Erickson, *Who's Tampering with the Trinity* (Grand Rapids: Kregel, 2009); Randal Rauser, "Rahner's Rule: An Emperor without Clothes?" *International Journal of Theology* vol. 7, no. 1 (January 2005). Note that Erickson identifies his use of "tampering" as a

introduces some fresh biblical insights into this discussion and thereby suggests some possible resolutions.

Social Activism. Meanwhile, British Baptist theologian Paul Fiddes and Croatian theologian Miroslav Volf have developed ethically fruitful interpretations of the social Trinity as their contribution to defining the significance of this doctrine. Fiddes focuses on participation as moving toward a practical and pastoral theology of the Trinity. Volf identifies the Trinity as "Our Social Program." He then combines his full-blown Trinitarian work with an ecclesiology, since humanity in Christ is intended to be corporately in that image. The contention of both works is that oneness, diversity, and economic solidarity in the Triune God must have its reflection in both church and society as corporate *imago dei*, images of God.[43] Less deep in dogmatic analysis, Asbury theologian Stephen Seamands applies Trinitarian theology to pastoral leadership in his award-winning 2005 *Ministry in the Image of God*.[44]

These applied Trinitarian theologies are all somewhat dependent upon or reflective of the studies of Brazilian liberation theologian Leonardo Boff in *Trinity and Society* and feminist Catholic theologian Catherine LaCugna in *God for Us*. LaCugna critiques what she sees as a historical drift into a speculative theology of the immanent Trinity and away from the earlier patristic emphasis on the economic Trinity. She identified this speculative drift as commencing with the Council of Nicaea in 325 CE and climaxing in the West with Aquinas in the thirteenth century. In light of the priority of the redemptive mission of the economic Trinity, Boff and LaCugna worked independently to develop a Trinitarian framework for a relational view of society and personhood. The respective studies in this book on each of the six triadic orders will support LaCugna's contention that the economic view of the Trinity is the source of Trinitarian ethics.

---

reflection of that phrase in the work of Ware himself. See also Fred Sanders, "Entangled in the Trinity: Economic and Immanent Trinity in Recent Theology," in *Dialog: A Journal of Theology,* 40:3 (Fall 2001), 175–182; and *The Image of the Immanent Trinity: Rahner's Rule and the Theological Interpretation of Scripture* (New York: Peter Lang, 2005).

43. Paul S. Fiddes, *Participating in God: A Pastoral Doctrine of the Trinity* (Louisville, KY: Westminster John Knox Press, 2000); Miroslav Volf. "The Trinity Is Our Social Program: The Doctrine of the Trinity and the Shape of Social Engagement," *Modern Theology* 14 (1998): 403–23; and *After Our Likeness: The Church as the Image of the Trinity* (Grand Rapids: Eerdmans, 1998).

44. Stephen Seamands, *Ministry in the Image of God: The Trinitarian Shape of Christian Service* (Downers Grove, IL: InterVarsity Press, 2005)

FROM EMBARRASSMENT BACK TO SHOWCASE: ASSESSING THE STATE OF TRINITARIAN THOUGHT

The vitality of any Christian doctrine is proportional to the number of significant works being produced relative to that doctrine. If this assertion is correct, the Christian doctrine of the Trinity is in good health indeed. Multiple major studies on the Trinity have been published annually since Leonard Boff's 1988 *The Trinity and Society*, which is not to over- or under-emphasize the significance of that work, but merely to establish a rather arbitrary academic marker for a quarter century of serious Trinitarian research and reflection. The "hot buttons" in current Trinitarian research have to do with four concerns:

1. **Forms of Hierarchy.** The incarnational sonship versus eternal generation versus eternal subordination of the Son (see Fred Sanders).

2. **Time and Roles.** "Entanglements" between the immanent and economic Trinity, namely the eternal subordination of the Son and Spirit to the Father versus a functional subordination in time (see Giles, Sanders, and Ware).

3. **Implications for Gender Relations.** The promise of the eternal immanent relation of the Three and/or the economic (incarnational?) relation of the Three for resolving the egalitarian/complementarian debate about biblical manhood and womanhood (see Giles, Ware, and LaCugna).

4. **Robust Relevance.** Less-than-compelling ways of expressing the triune reality of God apart from dogmatic formulations which appear disconnected with lived lives (see Rahner and Sanders).

Despite intense conversations among adherents of Trinitarianism, attacks continue from outside and inside detractors. The Trinity has been marginalized by both the secular worldview of modernity and the disaffection of postmodernity with metanarratives, of which the Trinity is the most meta! Of course Karl Barth both writes against Schleiermacher for relegating the doctrine to the back of his opus *Christian Faith* and then serves as a theological straw man against whom postmoderns can react for Barth's stark advocacy of absolutes and metanarratives. In the realm of the sacred, historical-critical assumptions about the doctrine have also served to obfuscate the significance of the Trinity. The biblical witness to Trinitarian thought patterns and doctrine has been neglected under the assumption that the doctrine is a developmental doctrine largely forged by the church to defend against wrong-headed polytheism or henotheism creeping into the church. C. Kavin Rowe asserts, "The historical-critical approach is correct in a crucial and far-reaching aspect: the doctrine of the Trinity is later than the biblical texts and to suggest that the biblical writers were consciously thinking in later creedal terms is in fact a major anachronistic mistake."[45] Who really wants to be anachronistic?

Trinitarian marginalization has been accelerated by the resurgence of popular or operational "unitarianism" of the kind defended in Buzzard's and Hunting's 1998 *The Doctrine of the Trinity: Christianity's Self-Inflicted Wound* and Buzzard's 2007 *Jesus Was Not a Trinitarian*, and by the resurgence of the philosophical analysis of the Threeness and Oneness in Placher's 2007 *The Triune God: An Essay in Postliberal Theology*.[46] How often the tongue-in-cheek adage is all too true: "The Episcopalians have the Father, the Baptists have the Son, and the Pentecostals have the Spirit!"

Incidentally, the postmodern antidote to contemporary forms of theological unitarianism is presented in the clearly tri-personal and nearly tritheistic Trinitarian narrative in the bestselling work by William Young, *The Shack*.[47] Here, three personal manifestations of the Trinity only manifest in each other's company. Young conceives the Father as a black woman, not unlike the oracle in *The Matrix*; the Son as a Middle Eastern, rough-hewn carpenter; and the Spirit as an Asian woman named Sarayu. *The Shack* is a raw, story-based attempt to retell the significance of the doctrine of the Triune God in a way that might make sense to postmoderns and pagans who have little trouble with tritheism.

The prevailing bifurcation of Trinitarian thinking along the lines of Karl Rahner's immanent and economic Trinity inadvertently sustains this marginalization of the Trinity. Since Rahner, the most creative thinking in the northern hemisphere—Catholic, Orthodox, or Protestant—has centered on

---

45. C. Kavin Rowe, "Biblical Pressure and Trinitarian Hermeneutics," *Pro Ecclesia*, 11, no. 3: 297.
46. Anthony F. Buzzard and Charles F. Hunting, *The Doctrine of the Trinity: Christianity's Self-Inflicted Wound* (McDonough, GA: Restoration Fellowship, 1998), which focuses on New Testament Christology over Old Testament monotheism; and Buzzard's newer, *Jesus Was Not a Trinitarian* (McDonough, GA: Restoration Fellowship, 2007), which tries to make a case that the creed of Jesus was the Hebrew Shema; and William C. Placher, *The Triune God: An Essay in Postliberal Theology* (Louisville: Westminster John Knox Press, 2007).
47. William Young, *The Shack* (Nashville: FaithWords, 2008).

the inner relations of the divine triad. In the 1998 *These Three Are One,* David Cunningham summarizes and even advances this discussion as a revision of the five Thomistic subsistent relations of the Godhead: 1) paternity as the Father initiating; 2) filiation as the Son being eternally generated; 3) spiration as the eternal issuance of the Spirit from the Father; and 4) procession as the emergence of God as Father, Son, Spirit relative to creation, redemption, and restoration.

I commend Cunningham for his advocacy against the individualization of the immanent triad. He writes that when "we think of them [i.e., Father, Son, and Holy Spirit] as separate entities, as distinct centers of consciousness—in short, as isolated individuals," then "one of the most important claims of Trinitarian theology—that the Three are most fundamentally *relations*—is lost from our view" (emphasis in the original).[48] I also applaud Cunningham for his biblical faithfulness to a monotheism that abjures Western overindividualism into a near-operational tritheism. However, he does fall victim to the lure of transcendental/metaphysical Rahnerism. Limiting the discussion of relations to the immanent Trinity fails to recognize that the fundamental theological attribute of God as immanent refers to the mission of God toward His creation in creating, judging, and redeeming.

Rahner's great student and critic, Johann Baptist Metz, discerned that this metaphysical captivity of the Trinity failed to be effectively potent in a holocaust-ridden world. Rather than the focus on the good news of the Triune God transcendent and metaphysical, Metz called for a "political theology" based on the "dangerous memory of Jesus." He meant, as does John Howard Yoder in *The Politics of Jesus,* that the good news of the active mission of the Three in One is seen in the economics and politics of the diverse processional intercessions in the world and in the church.[49] Justo Gonzalez echoes this call away from the Western Trinitarian captivity to the transcendent metaphysical plane and toward external involvement. He affirms the declaration of Tanzanian Catholic Bishop Christopher Mwoleka, that the Trinity is not about God giving "riddles for speculation but examples for imitation . . . it invites

---

48. David S. Cunningham, *These Three Are One* (Oxford: Blackwell Publishers, 1998), 64. Cunningham credits Robert Jenson for underscoring this claim as the "metaphysically revolutionary power of the gospel" breaking out in western theology. See Robert Jenson, *The Triune Identity* (Philadelphia: Fortress Press, 1982), 123.
49. Johann Baptist Metz, *A Passion for God: The Mystical-Political Dimension of Christianity*, J. Matthew Ashley, trans. (New York: Paulist Press, 1998), 150; John Howard Yoder, *The Politics of Jesus* (Grand Rapids: Eerdmans, 1994), 162.

everyone, in a down to earth practical way to imitate the life of the Trinity which is a life of sharing."[50]

Such Trinitarian rigor is easily affirmed in view of the reality that the doctrine of the Trinity is distinctly Christian. So this doctrine makes the Christian message distinct amongst an increasingly competitive market of worldviews.[51] Any marginalization of this doctrine must result in a trivialization of its value in the church too.

Many of the current Trinitarian monographs make serious attempts to defend the relevance of the Trinity for everyday Christian living and ministry. For instance, just prior to his death, Stanley Grenz sought to interpret Christian anthropology as the *imago dei*, based upon the current theological presentation of the so-called "Social Trinity."[52] Paul Fiddes also invokes this perspective in his encouraging pastoral theology of participation in the triune *perichoresis*.[53] This latter discussion of the relevance of the doctrine of the Trinity for Christian worship, ecclesiology, living, and ministry holds my present interest.

My specific interest lies in how the New Testament presentations of the Triune processional movements are relevant for Christian ministry and practice. In his evaluation of the pressure of the biblical texts with Trinitarian intentions, Kavin Rowe describes what he calls the "Trinitarian language" as God's own testimony about Himself and that the abundant instances of such testimony create significant "textual pressure" in support of Triune thinking.[54] He sounds the call in harmony with Brevard Childs for additional exegetical and biblical study. What comes next is a history of that evolving biblical theology of the Trinity in the New Testament.

THE RENEWAL OF BIBLICAL TRINITARIAN THINKING: 1950 TO THE PRESENT

When I first proposed this book, the publisher immediately asked if I liked controversy. I think what he meant was, How could an obscure West Coast seminary professor discover something significant all through the New Testament

---

50. Justo Gonzalez, *Mañana: Theology through Hispanic Eyes* (Nashville: Abingdon Press, 1990), 111–112.
51. As well noted in Kärkkäinen's *The Trinity: Global Perspectives*, Panikkar has identified operating Trinitarian constructs within the Hindu worldview, which Panikkar calls the "cosmotheandric mystery" of the Trinity. See Kärkkäinen, 336
52. Stanley J. Grenz, *The Social God and the Relational Self: A Trinitarian Theology of the Imago Dei* (Louisville: Westminster John Knox Press, 2001).
53. Fiddes, *Participating in God*, 47–48, 71–78.
54. Rowe, "Biblical Pressure and Trinitarian Hermeneutics," 299.

that two thousand years of well-known scholars did not discover. My answer is that many New Testament scholars have been working on the pieces of the puzzle of Trinitarian instances in the New Testament. I have built on their work but also think I may have found in the "Trinitarian Matrix" the missing corner piece that lets us complete the framework for this overarching picture of who the Triune God is. Stay with me, and see if you agree.

1950: Kelly's "Obstinate Triadic Obtrusions"

In 1950, famed patristic scholar J. N. D. Kelly began his now classic *Early Christian Creeds* with an investigation into what may have constituted a proto-*Apostolic Creed*. His primary observations in that research drew attention to what he calls "the triadic pattern" in the following way:

> The Trinitarianism of the New Testament is rarely explicit; but the frequency with which the triadic schema recurs . . . suggests that this pattern was implicit in Christian theology from the start. If these gaps are filled in, however, we are entitled to assume with some confidence that what we have before us, at any rate in rough outline, is the doctrinal deposit, or the pattern of sound words, which was expounded in the doctrinal church in the apostolic Church since its inauguration and which constituted its distinctive message.[55]

Kelly here concludes that the frequent recurrence of triadic patterns in the New Testament materials is part of the content of the deposit of faith. Despite what he deems as "frequent," Kelly goes on to assert that "Explicit Trinitarian confessions are few and far between; where they do occur, little can be built upon them."[56] He identifies 2 Corinthians 13:14 and Matthew 28:19–20 as two explicit instances, which he says have so preoccupied the Trinitarian discussion that other less obvious Trinitarian confessions are overlooked though they are "in reality no less significant."[57] Among such Trinitarian confessions, Kelly quotes 1 Corinthians 6:11; 1 Corinthians 12:4; 2 Corinthians 1:21; 1 Thessalonians 5:18; Galatians 3:11–14; 1 Peter 1:2, and Hebrews 10:29. In

---

55. J. N. D. Kelly, *Early Christian Creeds*, 3rd ed. (London: Longman Group Limited, 1950), 12–13.
56. Ibid., 22.
57. Ibid.

a footnote, he also adds twenty-three additional Trinitarian lineaments which he suggests "might be quoted."[58] He draws three conclusions about these triadic confessions, two of which I would affirm and one of which I find worthy of critique. First, Kelly is searching for the kind of set words that might be used in creeds for catechetical or liturgical purposes, thus he notes that there is no "fixity" in the wordings of these triadic instances. Second, fixity notwithstanding, he identifies an obstinate obtrusion of these triads to such a degree as to constitute "the Trinitarian ground-plan. . . . The impression inevitably conveyed is that the threefold manifestation of the Godhead was embedded deeply in Christian thinking from the start."[59] Finally, Kelly finds these obstinately frequent obtrusions of triadic patterns into the New Testament material to be all the more striking "because more often than not there is nothing in the context to necessitate it."[60]

Obtrusion has the negative connotation of having an unwanted and/or uninvited opinion thrust upon oneself. Kelly finds these frequent triadic occurrences to be obtrusions because he does not discern how the contexts in which they are embedded require such Trinitarian references. I note that all of the triadic instances quoted by Kelly, with the exception of the 2 Corinthians 13:14 benediction, follow the baptismal or economic order of Father-Son-Holy Spirit. Though he footnotes additional instances which do not follow that order, he does not examine or compare the contexts of those alternate triadic orders to discern any contextual clues that necessitate a different triad formulation. Such an examination is a current lacuna in the extensive material available on the Trinity. Kelly observes that "though as yet uncanonized, the New Testament was already exerting a powerful influence; it is commonplace that the outlines of a dyadic and a triadic pattern are clearly visible on its pages."[61]

Taken all together, this means Kelly recognizes the Trinitarian matrix embedded in the New Testament, but he does not understand its significance. The ideas implicit in these early catechetical and liturgical formulae, as in the New Testament writers' use of the same dyadic and triadic patterns, represents a pre-reflective, pre-theological phase of Christian belief. This in no way minimizes their interest and importance. It is out of the raw material thus provided

---

58. Ibid., 22–23.
59. Ibid., 23.
60. Ibid.
61. J. N. D. Kelly, *Early Christian Doctrines*, rev. ed. (San Francisco: Harper and Row, 1978), 88.

by the preaching, worshipping church that theologians had to construct the more sophisticated accounts of the Christian doctrine of the God. Kelly's contribution to the assessment of the abundant occurrences of theological triads in the New Testament is primarily the frank declaration that those triads are inarguably present and that their presence constitutes part of the pre-dogmatic deposit of the faith and witness to the God as One and Three.

1962: Wainwright Defines Trinitarian Patterns

In *The Trinity in the New Testament,* Arthur W. Wainwright defines the Trinitarian pattern as "a strong body of evidence which shows the writers of the New Testament were influenced in thought and expression by the triad 'Father, Son, and Spirit.'"[62] He goes on describe a triadic consciousness of the writers when he asserts, "In none of these passages however are there any clear doctrinal implications about the relationship between the Father, Son, and Spirit."[63] Wainwright asserts further that when the New Testament authors used a triad, they were drawing from something already recognized in the community of faith. He writes,

> John's concern with the problem as threefold would be caused partly by his own experience of the Spirit and partly by the growing tendency in the early Christians to link Father, Son and Spirit together. He is not inventing a triad. He was explaining an association which was already recognized in the Christian community.[64]

The book ends with Wainwright's remarkable conclusion: "One thing is certain. The problem of the Trinity was being raised and answered in the New Testament."[65] So, with Wainwright's addition, scholars are now on the alert to recognize triadic references to the Trinity in the New Testament as a consciousness of the early Christian community.

1980: Kaiser's Experiential Apprehension of the Trinity

In 1980 came the book *One God in Trinity,* edited by Peter Toon and James Spiceland. In the article entitled, "Discernment of Trinity," Christopher Kaiser

---

62. Arthur Wainwright, *The Trinity in the New Testament* (London: SPCK, 1962), 237–247.
63. Ibid., 246.
64. Ibid., 265.
65. Ibid., 266.

builds a case from the prayer life of Jesus for "a suitable empirical basis for the apostolic discernment of the triunity."[66] Kaiser presents seven elements in summation of his case. In the last of these elements, he introduces an important consideration for understanding the triadic processions in the New Testament. He asserts that "Presence of the Spirit [is] discerned to be continual, immediate and intimately related to the apprehension of God as 'Father' and Jesus as 'Son' (Rom. 8:15, Gal. 4:6); implies three, and only three, 'coinhering,' divine persons, one God."[67] Citing these two samples, Kaiser insists that the triadic patterns imply threeness and only threeness within the Godhead. Thus, by their frequency and unvarying presentation of threefoldedness, the triadic patterns both *limit* the internal community to three and underscore the reality of the distinctiveness within the Godhead as *no less than* three.

What else did Kaiser contribute to the ongoing flow of this conversation? His significant word choice of "apprehension" is accurate, since both texts cited speak beyond mere mental assent of a theological truth to an experiential engagement with those truths. Kaiser could have gone on to suggest that the triadic patterns are the way that the church apprehended the God of Jesus Christ in worship, discipleship, and mission.

1986: Boff's Pre-dogmatic New Testament Trinitarian Thinking

In 1986, Leonardo Boff published *Trinity and Society* in his native Portuguese. While noting reliance on some of the work of Arthur Wainwright, Boff characterizes the triadic formulae in the New Testament as "indications of understanding that Jesus Christ, the Father, and the Spirit are equally God," though there "is still no *doctrine* of the Trinity."[68] He examines four triads closely: Matthew 28:19; 2 Corinthians 13:13; 2 Thessalonians 2:13–14; and 1 Corinthians 12:4–6. From there, Boff goes on to list twelve triadic formulae within the epistles of Paul and four additional triads in Hebrews, Revelation, Jude, and 1 Peter.

Boff concludes that these triads express the presence of a faith in the Trinity and thought in Trinitarian form, rather than expressing a clear doctrinal formulation. He notes the significance of these triadic formulae with the acknowledgment that "the mystery of the Trinity will always be obscure in any

---

66. Christopher B. Kaiser, "The Discernment of the Triunity," in *One God in Trinity*, ed. Peter Toon and James Spiceland (Westchester, IL: Cornerstone Books, 1980), 36–37.
67. Ibid.
68. Leonard Boff, *Trinity and Society*, trans. Paul Burns (Maryknoll, NY: Orbis Books, 1988), 34 (italics in the original); see 244 for the reference to Wainwright.

form of expression. But Christian thought must always work on these first suggestions of the awesome mystery of the Father, Son and Holy Spirit. The New Testament passages constitute the supreme revelation of the Mystery."[69] Boff is here challenging theologians and believers to investigate the Triune Mystery in its revelatory form, New Testament triadic instances.

1996: Lee, Torrance, Toon, and Boborinsky

In 1996, four major works on the Trinity were published. Each gave attention to the significance of the triadic patterns in the New Testament for the understanding of the doctrine of the Trinity.

Asian Cultural Correlates for Trinitarian Understanding. Jung Young Lee offers a cultural analysis of the NT triadic patterns in *The Trinity in Asian Perspective*. He states that his work was not intended to supplement or supplant the traditional idea of the Trinity, but rather to complement it.[70] Lee uses the Asian concept of *yin/yang* as a metaphor for understanding the incarnational God/man and to lead into an Asian cultural interpretation of various Trinitarian orders. In his introduction, Lee proposes:

> [S]ix different patterns of intertrinitarian relationships: the Father-the Spirit-the Son (the so-called Asian Trinity), the Father-the Son-the Spirit (the patriarchal or Confucian order), the Spirit-the Father-the Son (Taoist or matriarchal order), the Son-the Spirit-the Father (contextual approach, a reversal of the traditional hierarchical approach), the Son-the Father-the Spirit (new generation approach), and the Spirit-the Son-the Father (Shamanic approach).[71]

Here Lee identifies all six possible combinations of the Trinitarian variables of Father, Son, and Spirit. He also assigns each resulting order a name according to his Asian cultural lens of *yin/yang*. Later in his book, he addresses the significance and acceptability of each triadic order for his cultural context.

Since his concern is to bring Asian cultural analysis to these possible Trinitarian orders, it is perhaps unfair to bring too much attention to the fact

---

69. Ibid., 40.
70. Jung Young Lee, *The Trinity in Asian Perspective* (Nashville: Abingdon Press, 1996), 12.
71. Ibid., 19.

that Lee does not make specific connection to the occurrences of each of the possible orders. However, he does give attention and assessment to the cultural impact and/or acceptance of each order by that culture in the second half of the book. For example, Lee understands the Father-Son-Spirit order to be normative for the Asian sense of age and authority. He understands an order of Son-Father-Spirit also to be acceptable in the Asian culture only when a father is of such age that the son must now take leadership of the household. Lee does not find a Spirit-Father-Son order to be culturally acceptable, if the Spirit is understood to represent the maternal aspect of the divine Godhead.[72]

Lee does not correlate his reflection on the Trinitarian orders with those orders as presented respectively in the New Testament. In a relatively recent analysis of *The Trinity in Asian Perspective*, Veli-Matti Kärkkäinen asserts, "Biblical materials do not play a central role in his [Lee's] theological construction, yet occasionally he backs up his discussion with biblical materials."[73] Lee describes the diverse Trinitarian orders as "all the possible, mathematical combinations of the three persons," but asserts that "traditionally, there was only one way of ordering the divine members of the Trinity: the Father, the Son, the Spirit."[74] In his chapter entitled "The Orders of the Divine Trinity," none of his four biblical citations are to any of the instances of such an order itself. Lee misses the opportunity to fulfill his cultural analysis by failing to fully engage the abundant biblical materials on the triadic orders. Use of such biblical references to triadic orders would have enriched his presentation without "Westernizing it." I do confess that it was Lee's serious reflection on the meaning of each of the triadic orders in the Asian cultural context that challenged me to organize an equally serious reflection of those orders within their biblical contexts. We need such a schema to activate wider missional and discipleship contextualizing for any and all cultures.

I was also challenged by Lee's interpreting the various possible orders by naming each of those orders.[75] He names The Father-Son-Spirit triad "patriarchal." The Spirit-Father-Son order is "matriarchal" and the Son-Father-Spirit order is "filiarchal."[76] As you will see in my research that follows, Lee's work

---

72. Ibid., 152ff.
73. Veli-Matti Kärkkäinen, *The Trinity: Global Perspectives*, 330. Here Kärkkäinen does note in this regard the review of Julie Green, "*Trinity in Asian Perspective*, by J. Y. Lee," *Scottish Journal of Evangelical Theology* 17 (Spring 1999): 67.
74. Lee, *The Trinity in Asian Perspective*, 176.
75. Kärkkäinen also highlights this creative contribution of Lee by listing and briefly describing the naming rationale of Lee relative to each of the six proposed orders, *The Trinity*, 327–328.
76. Ibid., 152–171.

challenged me also to name the biblical processional orders. I depart from Lee's cultural approach and base my naming on the contexts in which the triads occur in Scripture and upon their theological relevance for the church and its mission.

Explicit Witnesses to Implicit Doctrines. Also in 1996, **Thomas Torrance** of the University of Edinburgh published *The Christian Doctrine of God: One Being Three Persons*. This work is a sequel to his 1988 *The Trinitarian Faith*, but here Torrance makes a real contribution to Trinitarian theology. Contrary to the predisposition in the public place to see Trinitarian thought to be post-Apostolic and Conciliar, Torrance demonstrates that the origins of the doctrine of the Trinity are to be found implicitly throughout the New Testament and not as a later derivation from other doctrines. He refers to the Trinitarian triads as *formulae* or *movements*, and he identifies about thirty-eight triads in his footnotes.[77] About these formulae, Torrance writes,

> This Trinitarian revelation of God is deeply imprinted in the Scriptures of the New Testament implicitly informing their witness, so it is hardly surprising that it crops up on the surface here and there in the more explicit form of *triadic formulae*. . . . There are not a few passages in which the Father, Son and Holy Spirit are somewhat loosely associated with one another but without evidence of there being any deliberate coordination of the three divine Persons into a three-fold pattern.[78]

If I am reading Torrance correctly, he is asserting that at least some of the *implicit* doctrine of the Trinity inherent in the New Testament witness exists in the numerous *explicit* Trinitarian triads. He also is asserting that, despite this abundant explicit triadic witness, there is little or no evidence in support of coordinated and meaningful patterns in those triads. Yet in the next chapter, Torrance reconstructs a triadic pattern and attaches significant meaning to that pattern. He writes:

> At the same time the doctrine of the Trinity had the effect of grounding the doctrine of the incarnation in the very cen-

---

77. Thomas F. Torrance, *The Christian Doctrine of God: One Being Three Persons* (Edinburgh: T & T Clark, Ltd., 1996), n.169–171 on pages 70–71.
78. Ibid., 70.

tre of faith in God in such a way as to establish the triune movement of God's self-revelation, from the Father *through* the Son *in* the Spirit, and correspondingly in the Trinitarian movement of faith and devotion in the Church, *in* the Spirit *through* the Son *to* the Father. It is thus that Trinitarian thinking enters into the fabric of all Christian worship and knowledge of the one God, and the doctrine of the Trinity is recognized to constitute the fundamental grammar of Christian dogmatic theology.[79]

Torrance here asserts that the baptismal recitation of the economic triadic pattern, Father-Son-Holy Spirit, receives a faith and devotional response from the church in the triadic formula of Spirit-Son-Father. He previously reviewed this latter order as it was found in what he rightly calls "the influential text" in 1 Corinthians 12:4–6, Galatians 4:4–6, and Ephesians 4:4–6. Torrance does not connect the dots between these three texts and discern the consistency in their respective contexts, namely ecclesiology. However, he does assert that these triadic patterns "do more than prepare the way" for an explicit doctrine of the Trinity by giving "expression to the three-fold structure of God's astonishing revelation of himself. . . . This in the *kerygma* [preaching] and *didache* [teaching] of the Gospel as handed on in the apostolic deposit of Faith, the Father, Son and Holy Spirit, are intimately linked together in the essential devotion and worship of the Church in Christ."

Torrance's evaluation of the abundant triadic pattern witness is twofold. First, he sees that abundant triadic instances are an explicit witness of the implicit doctrine of the Trinity within the New Testament. Secondly, he suggests that the variety in the orders of the triadic patterns means that "already in the apostolic mind there was lodged an implicit belief in the equality of the three divine Persons."[80]

How Binitarianism Integrates with Trinitarianism. Also in 1996, **Peter Toon** published *Our Triune God: A Biblical Portrayal of the Trinity.* Toon believes that the earliest Christian confessions may have been binitarian—Father and Son—but then contends that underlying those confessions was a basic Trinitar-

---

79. Ibid., 82 (emphasis in the original).
80. Ibid., 71

ian consciousness.[81] He argues that, in light of the impact of the Spirit of God on the church at Pentecost, "an explicit binitarianism and an implicit Trinitarianism can therefore be seen to belong to the same Faith." [82]

If there are seventy-plus triadic instances referencing the threefoldedness of God, wouldn't that also constitute explicit Trinitarianism?

Triad Movements Normative in Earliest Christian Communities. In 1996, the Russian Orthodox theologian **Boris Bobrinskoy** wrote *The Mystery of the Trinity: Trinitarian Experience and Vision in the Biblical and Patristic Tradition.*[83] He identifies and interprets multiple Trinitarian schemes in "the New Testament [that allow] us to discern in it several 'movements' of Trinitarian revelation that complement one another, and all seem to have their inevitability."[84] He interprets the Father-Spirit-Christ scheme as "messianic." Here is how he explains this interpretation: "In this schema, the Father is the origin, the Spirit is the mediator who descends and rests on the Son, who permits His incarnation and sends Him. Christ appears then as the One in whom the fullness of the Divinity rests."[85]

Bobrinskoy calls these schemata *taxis,* "orders." He identifies the Son-Father-Spirit order of 2 Corinthians 13:14 as the "Christological *kerygma* . . . [t]he very core of the Christian message . . . it is within the mystery of Christ that we have access to the Father ("the one who has seen Me has seen the Father") and that we receive the fullness of the Holy Spirit."[86]

He goes on to examine what he calls the classic or "filioquist" schema, which "consists of the classical sequence: Father, Christ, and Holy Spirit. In this schema, the Father and the glorified Lord send the Holy Spirit. This is the sequence Father-creation, Christ-redemption, and the Holy Spirit-sanctification in the church."[87]

Bobrinskoy concludes this section on "the mystery of the Trinity in the New Testament" by identifying the Son-Spirit-Father order found in Hebrews 9:14; Ephesians 5:2; Romans 8:11, and especially 2 Corinthians 13:14 as legitimate

81. Peter Toon, *Our Triune God: A Biblical Portrayal of the Trinity* (Wheaton, IL: Bridgepoint, 1996), 117.
82. Ibid., 125.
83. Boris Bobrinskoy, *The Mystery of the Trinity: Trinitarian Experience and Vision in the Biblical and Patristic Tradition* (Crestwood, NY: St. Vladimir's Press, 1996).
84. Ibid., 65–66.
85. Ibid.
86. Ibid., 68.
87. Ibid.

reflections of "the Trinitarian awareness of the early communities."[88] He interprets this schema as "the mystery of the salvation worked out by Jesus Christ, the sanctification of the Holy Spirit, the filial adoption by the Father. It is the Holy Trinity in the work—or the economy—of salvation is professed, prayed to and taught in the New Testament. The redemption accomplished by Christ is therefore offered to the Father, in obedience to His will, in the transparency of the Holy Spirit."[89] Bobriskoy treats and interprets these triads as normative for the Trinitarian awareness of the New Testament community. He almost asks rhetorically, How else would you invoke the mystery of the Trinity?

2001: Feinberg and Differences in Significances of Triadic Orders

John Feinberg's monumental work, *No One Like Him,* discusses the significance of the triadic occurrences under the subheading, "Various NT phenomena suggest equality of the three."[90] I would affirm the logic of Feinberg's assertion: "If the three were inherently unequal, then we might expect a consistent order in listing them whenever they are mentioned together. This might even seem like a formulaic prioritizing of the three. However, the NT refers to the three together in a variety of orders."[91] He goes on to list four different occurrences (Matthew 28:19–20 [F-S-Sp]; 1 Corinthians 12:4–6 and Ephesians 4:4–6 [Sp-S-F]; 2 Corinthians 13:14 [S-F-Sp]; and 1 Peter 1:2 [F-Sp-S]).

Feinberg is carefully using the presence of these diverse orders within the New Testament—*not* to prove the ontological equality of the three persons within the One God, but rather to argue that if there were an ontological hierarchy within the Trinity, then "any ontological point to be made to that effect is totally undercut because the NT writers seem to associate the three as equals and refer to them in no particular order."[92] Feinberg's point is well taken as far as it goes. But his point does not render due account for the large number of uses of each of the six possible triadic orders used in Scripture.

2004: Letham "Reforms" the Trinity

In *The Holy Trinity: In Scripture, History, Theology and Worship*, Robert Letham

---

88. Ibid., 136.
89. Ibid., 137
90. John S. Feinberg, *No One Like Him: The Doctrine of God* (Wheaton, IL: Crossway, 2001), 467.
91. Ibid., 468.
92. Ibid.

publishes the most thoroughgoing analysis to date of the New Testament triadic patterns. His intention is to produce a contemporary Reformed study of the doctrine of the Trinity. He discusses the triadic patterns in the context of his discourse on explicit binitarianism and implicit Trinitarianism. What is not clear is why Letham deems the former to be explicit and the latter to be implicit. He acknowledges his indebtedness to the works of Wainwright and Toon, discussed above. Letham then goes on to identify thirty triadic patterns and to categorize those triads according to processional patterns such as Father-Son-Spirit; its reversal Spirit-Son-Father (Eph. 2:18; 4:4–6; 1 Cor. 12:4–6); as Son-Father-Spirit (2 Cor. 13:14); and as Father-Spirit-Son (Rev. 1:4–5).[93] Letham sees the latter verse as mirroring the messianic passage in Isaiah 42:1. He concludes that there is "no settled pattern in the NT. . . . The expression of the Trinity is rooted in personal salvation and Christian experience, not abstract speculation."[94] Is he then suggesting that post-Apostolic Trinitarian doctrinal discussions might be less experiential and more abstract?

Letham's work includes an excursus exegeting the Trinitarian framework embedded in the epistle to the Ephesians, entitled, "Ternary Patterns in Ephesians."[95] Letham strikingly identifies the Father-Son-Spirit order as characteristic of the "plan of salvation" and its reverse Spirit-Son-Father as the "experience" of that salvation.[96] These analyses represent some of the first attempts to articulate the meanings inherent in or characteristic of a specific triadic procession.

Letham also observes how Paul refers "to the triadic pattern in a natural, unforced, and unself-conscious way."[97] This manner of triadic recitation means for Letham that it expresses a deeply held conviction not requiring extensive explanation because "it was recognized widely, if not universally, among his readership."[98] Here Letham provides a key insight for understanding the frequency and ease of recitation of triadic patterns throughout the New Testament, namely that the references to God in diverse triadic patterns represent the mindset of New Testament authors. They wrote this way because it was the way they learned to think of God from Jesus.

---

93. Robert Letham, *The Holy Trinity: In Scripture, History, Theology and Worship* (Phillipsburg, NJ: P & R Publishing, 2004), 68.
94. Ibid.
95. Ibid., 73.
96. Ibid., 81.
97. Ibid., 75.
98. Ibid., 85.

HOW THESE STUDIES EXPAND OUR
BIBLICAL TRINITARIAN CONSCIOUSNESS

The New Testament presents more than seventy references to the Triune God acting economically or praised doxologically in varied processions of the three persons. The best known is in the baptismal formula, Matthew 28:19–20. There the order is "baptizing them in the name of the Father, and of the Son, and of the Holy Spirit." If this order of Father-Son-Spirit were normative, uniquely authoritative, and represented a sequence of essence from greatest to least, then we should expect to find little or no deviation from that order in the New Testament documents. However, that is not the case; there is no inherent hierarchy evident here. In contrast to this perceived normative order, the gospel witnesses to the baptism of Jesus Himself reflect instead a processional order of Jesus, the descent of the Holy Spirit as a dove, and that followed by the epiphany of the Father's voice, "You are My beloved Son" (Luke 3:21–22). Jude presents still another processional order in verses 20–21: Pray in the Holy Spirit; keep in the love of God; and wait for the Lord Jesus Christ. So this processional order is Son-Spirit-Father. The Corinthian benediction of 2 Corinthians 13:14 introduces another variation from the baptismal order: "the grace of the Lord Jesus Christ . . . the love of God . . . and the fellowship of the Holy Spirit," or S-F-Sp.

Added to the seventy-plus "Trinitarian processional" references in the New Testament, twenty more diverse binitarian processional references are also worthy of note. Sometimes the Father precedes the Son, and at other times it is the reverse. Sometimes the reference is to the relationship between the Father and the Spirit, and sometimes between the Son and the Spirit, with either person leading or following the other in that discussion. The point of the diversity of triadic occurrences must be the indivisibility of the Three; they are indeed One, yet with distinct and variegated movements together.

Fiddes, Lee, and others have made good attempts to establish the relevance and significance of the doctrine of the Trinity for and in the churches. I advocate a different reference point, however. Fiddes and others appear to want to show how a right Trinitarian perspective can make Christian living more effective and worshipful. That is indisputable, but has the feel of a "last ditch" effort to keep a cherished tradition from going extinct. The assertion I want to make in this book is that whenever and wherever Christian life and ministry have been God-glorifying, or personally satisfying or ethically prophetic or socially effective, it is precisely because a Trinitarian processional value has been consciously or unconsciously applied. Far from extinction, the Trinity flourishes everywhere and in every way as the agent of causation in which we live, minister, and have our being.

The much-needed new Trinitarian studies reviewed in this chapter make reference to the economic Trinity, but almost exclusively do so as the economic order of Father, Son, and Holy Spirit. I offer here a systematic New Testament study of the Trinity, and will contend that while the word *trinitas* was not coined until the third century after Christ, Trinitarian thinking was the default consciousness out of which the New Testament authors wrote, worshipped, and ministered. My study shows that, instead of the expected two or three textual witnesses to the Trinity, the New Testament has more than seventy such references. We will explore these and see how to conclude that the Trinity, who is worshipped in the awareness of God's Oneness and Threeness, is not and never has been biblically captive to a normative processional order of Father, Son, and Spirit. The Scriptures regularly "disorder"—or, more accurately, "reorder"—the procession of the Three in One in six different ways, and for six distinct outcomes.

DISCUSSION QUESTIONS—CHAPTER 1

- Having read this chapter on the current state of the doctrine of the Trinity, why do you think there is such a renewed interest in all things Trinitarian? Why are so many books on the Trinity now being written, published, bought, and read?

- Which theologians discussed in this chapter would you like to find out more about and read more deeply? Explain why.

- How might this study on the super-abundant triadic references to the Trinity in the New Testament be received by the scholars currently talking and publishing on the doctrine of the Trinity? Do you think it will help their research, or challenge it? Explain.

CHAPTER 2

The Data Question:
The Trinitarian Matrix in the New Testament

The sharpest pleasure of a traveler
is in finding the things he did not expect
—Gilbert Keith Chesterton (1874–1936)[1]

Over fifty denominations anticipated the release of the Revised Standard Version (RSV) of the Bible in 1952. The RSV was expected to send the long-venerated King James Version into respectful retirement from liturgical use. However, difficulties and disputes with translator choices emerged early and stayed late. The RSV translation omitted the following phrase from 1 John 5:7–8, "bear record in heaven, the Father, the Word, and the Holy Ghost: and these three are one. And there are three that bear witness in earth. . . . "

Cherished misinformation is not easily abandoned. These words had supplied a key explicit reference to the Trinity for 450 years of the 1611 King James Version. Some readers believed that the RSV had taken the Trinity right out of the Bible and backpedaled from support of the doctrine of the God, who is One and Three.

---

1. Gilbert Keith Chesterton, *The Things I Saw in America* (New York: Dodd, Mead and Company, 1923), p. 79.

Muslim and Watchtower critics of orthodox Christianity agreed. To this day, Muslim scholars point out that "this cornerstone of the Christian faith [the Trinity] has been scrapped from the RSV by these thirty-two Christian scholars of the highest eminence backed by fifty cooperating Christian denominations, once again all according to the 'most ancient manuscripts.'"[2]

However, as footnoted in the RSV and in many more recent English translations, only ninth-century or later manuscripts of the Latin *Vulgate* and no Greek manuscript before the fourteenth century contain this creed-like phrase. Equally significant was the absence of 1 John 5:7–8 from the fourth-century Arian controversy, which gave rise to the Trinitarian formula at Nicaea in 325 CE. The phrase "these three are one" would have been choice armament for Athanasius against those who wanted in the name of monotheism to subordinate the Son to the status of a creation of the Father, *if that view had existed in the fourth century*. In this instance, the RSV translators displayed dispassionate honesty about manuscript evidence. That Trinitarian phraseology simply was not to be found in any manuscripts before the ninth century, so the passage was omitted from the Revised Standard Version.

About the same time, the Lutheran ecumenicist Oscar Cullman's influential 1949 *The Early Christian Confessions* was published. It increased momentum away from the pursuit of evidence for the Trinity within the New Testament. Cullman provided a detailed argument in favor of the Trinitarian creed being seen as a post-Apostolic development necessitated as converts moved from Judaism to Hellenism. He reasoned that the monotheism of the Father with its baptism in the name of Jesus (Acts 2:38) evolved historically toward baptism in the name of the Three (Matthew 28:19).[3] The word "Trinity" is of course not found in the Bible. Its invention awaited birth from the third-century apologetic mind of Tertullian.[4]

However, scholarly defenders of New Testament-fostered Trinitarianism were not hard to find. Oxford patristic professor J. N. D. Kelly's *Early Christian Creeds* came out one year after Cullman's work. Kelly searched for consistent wording indicative of Trinitarian creedal formation within the New Testament. He did not find it. What he found instead was something unexpected and nearly ubiquitous. Kelly found a web of triadic references, a Trinitarian matrix in the New Testament.

---

2. Later Unitarians V: Emlyn and Lindsey, http://www.answering-islam.org/Responses/Badawi/Radio/RA200K31.htm (accessed April 15, 2012); see also http://www.blessedquietness.com/journal/resource/1john5–7.htm (accessed April 15, 2012).
3. Oscar Cullman, *The Earliest Christian Confessions* (London: Lutterworth Press, 1949), 27–30
4. Chapter 4 will report that Tertullian's coining the word *trinitas* [trinity] is actually translating Athenagoras' slightly earlier coinage of *trias* as the name for the revealed phenomena of the God who is One and Three.

While the Trinitarianism of the New Testament is admittedly not explicitly in creedal form, he asserted that "the frequency with which the triadic schema recurs . . . suggests that this pattern was implicit in Christian theology from the start."[5] Sometimes the writers acknowledged God as Father, Son, and Holy Spirit and other times the order was Spirit, Son, and Father. From these multiple instances of the divine triadic references, Kelly concluded the following:

> In all of them there is no fixity so far as the wording is concerned, and none of them constitutes a creed in any ordinary sense of the term. Nevertheless, the Trinitarian ground plan obtrudes itself obstinately throughout, and its presence is all the more striking because more often than not there is nothing in the context to warrant it. The impression inevitably conveyed is that the conception of the threefold manifestation of the Godhead was embedded deeply in Christian thinking from the start, and provided a ready-to-hand mould in which the ideas of the apostolic writers took shape. If Trinitarian creeds are rare, the Trinitarian pattern which was to shape all later creeds was already part and parcel of the Christian tradition of doctrine.[6]

What Kelly notes here is the textual pressure toward Trinitarian worship and creedal development supplied by the commonplace "outlines of a dyadic [Father and Son, or Word and Spirit] and triadic pattern clearly visible in its [Scripture's] pages."[7] While agreeing about the "attractive plausibility" of Cullman's scheme of the evolution of the Trinitarian creedal formulae, Kelly found that the New Testament texts themselves indicated otherwise.

The pages of the New Testament make it abundantly plain, as we have had occasion to observe, that the binitarian and Trinitarian schemas were much more deeply impressed on the minds of primitive Christianity than Cullman and scholars of his outlook have been prepared to admit. The juxtaposition of the Father and the Lord Jesus Christ as parallel realities and the collocation of the Father, Son, and Holy Spirit had become categories of Christian thinking long before the New Testament documents were written down.[8]

---

5. J. N. D. Kelly, *Early Christian Creeds*, 3rd ed. (London: Longman Group Limited, 1972), 23.
6. Ibid., 12.
7. Ibid., 88.
8. Ibid., 25–26.

Simply said, the earliest Christians were Trinitarian because that is how they learned to think before, from, and within the New Testament. The Triune God loved them because the Bible told them so.

About the same time, the Methodist chaplain and biblical scholar Arthur Wainwright published *The Trinity in the New Testament*. In his reflection on the internal New Testament witness to Trinitarian thinking, Wainwright concluded, "One thing is certain. The problem of the Trinity was being raised and answered in the New Testament."[9] More than fifty years later, in the 2007 *The God Who Is Triune*, Allan Coppedge affirmed Wainwright's conclusion and observed that the Trinitarian data in the New Testament is of sufficient quantity to demand a fresh approach to its analysis. [10]

This present chapter intends to move from the discussion of *multiple* witnesses by Kelly, Wainwright, and Coppedge to discussion of a *multitude* of New Testament witnesses to the Trinity. My research shows that the quantity of divine triadic instances is so profound and in such a diversity of orders that it constitutes a qualitative *matrix* of Trinitarian consciousness. Trinity is how the New Testament authors inadvertently thought and viewed reality. In this chapter, we will explore these questions:

- Just how many instances of triadic references to the Trinity are there in the New Testament?

- Are those instances largely found in only a few books in the New Testament, or are they spread throughout it?

- Are those triadic instances predominantly in the form of the Matthew 28:19 baptismal order (Father, Son, and Holy Spirit), or are all possible orders of the threefold name found and used proportionately?

- Is there any consistency and correlation between the context in which a specific triadic order is found and why it is used? For instance, is the triadic order of Spirit, Son and Father found in specific contexts, or is it

---

9. Wainwright, *The Trinity in the New Testament*, 266; Thiselton approves this assertion, except for the use of the word *problem*. He suggests "question" in its place (Anthony C. Thiselton, *The Hermeneutics of Doctrine* [Grand Rapids: Eerdmans, 2007], 460).

10. Allan Coppedge, *The God Who Is Triune: Revisioning the Christian Doctrine of God* (Downers Grove, IL: IVP Academic, 2007), 25.

used inadvertently with little discernible meaning between context and triadic order (which was the contention of Kelly)?[11] In chapters 5–10, this question will be explored relative to each of the triadic orders and the contexts in which they are embedded.

As shown in the above review and the overview in chapter 1 of theological development, the issues of exact quantity and orderings have not been consistently addressed yet. Probably these other authors had different questions and historical situations to launch their inquiries. But I would contend that we need a complete census of triadic instances—and a careful notation of their orderings—if we are to discern the most robustly biblical responses to these questions. You will find my full "census chart" of New Testament triadic references in Appendix A. I believe analysis of this data yields critical insights into how the pervasively Trinitarian thinking functioned in the New Testament and early church.

A "DIVINE GENOME" PROJECT

With the beginning of the twenty-first century, humanity became able to know and influence itself genetically. Genes can now be diced, spliced, injected, and induced. By 2005, the globally shared Human Genome Project had mapped the double-helix code first cracked by Watson and Crick in 1953.[12] The senior project administrator, Francis Collins, even published his story of coming to Christian faith in the evocatively titled *The Language of God.*[13] Because the gene sequences are known, genes can be cloned and introduced with amazing healing potentials promised—amidst immense ethical concerns being raised. Such stem-cell and gene-sequencing research has introduced a whole new industry to the stock market, the biotech industry.

Despite the downsides of genetic engineering, the Genome Project offers a great "governing metaphor" for thinking about New Testament Trinitarianism. What exactly is the matrix of triadic sequencing embedded in the biblical materials? How does Trinitarian "spiritual coding" affect the development of life for disciples? What maladies happen when our spiritual DNA has genes that are missing or corrupted?

---

11. Ibid.
12. Alan Lightman, *The Discoveries: Great Breakthroughs in 20th Century Science* (New York: Vintage Books, 2005), 356–371.
13. Francis Collins, *The Language of God* (New York: Free Press, 2006).

As shown in the Inroduction, this "divine genome" project of connecting the Trinity with the New Testament and the church has been underway for some time by Christian scholars, but no one has taken it to completion in the sense of identifying and classifying all the triadic sequences and their implications. That has been my task in this book, along with helping us consider the faith interpretation and practical applications thereof.

CENSUS DISTRIBUTION OF THE SIX TRIADIC ORDERS

Mathematically, any three entities may be grouped into six distinct orders. With three values—Father, Son, and Spirit—six processional orders are potential. The three persons of the Triune God could therefore potentially be grouped in the following orders.

- Father-Son-Spirit
- Father-Spirit-Son
- Son-Father-Spirit
- Son-Spirit-Father
- Spirit-Son-Father
- Spirit-Father-Son

Careful reading of the New Testament for triadic order results in more than seventy instances of Trinitarian references, among which all six orders are found in abundance. To be precise, I have identified seventy-five triadic order passages. These instances can be classified according to the order of the persons named in the Trinity. For instance, the greeting in 1 Peter 1:2 reads "according to the foreknowledge of *God the Father* and set apart by the *Spirit* for obedience and for sprinkling with the blood of *Jesus Christ*. May grace and peace be multiplied to you" (emphasis added). So, the triadic order expressed is Father, Spirit, and Son, for which I will sometimes use the abbreviated form of F-Sp-S.

Another example is found in Acts 10:38 which reads, "how God anointed Jesus of Nazareth with the Holy Spirit and with power." But in the Greek, the text has the order Jesus, God, and Holy Spirit (S-F-Sp).

Using this method, the seventy-five triadic instances found can be organized into six categories of orders, with all six used in surprisingly balanced percentages overall. They do split into two tiers, three triadic orderings that are relatively more frequent, and three that are less. Chart 2.1 shows the following:

- Father-Son-Spirit (F-S-Sp)—the historically predominant order—is used eighteen times, or in twenty-four percent of the instances.

- Son-Spirit-Father (S-Sp-F) is used fifteen times, or in twenty percent of the instances.

- Son-Father-Spirit (S-F-Sp) occurs fourteen times, or in nineteen percent of the occurrences.

So, the top tier of three triadic orders represents sixty-three percent of the Trinitarian witness. Using this method of analysis, the baptismal order F-S-Sp is not nearly as dominant as history and tradition suppose it to be. We tend to assume and act as if F-S-Sp is almost 100 percent of the data, but if the New Testament actually represents first-century Christian practice, they used much more flexibility then than we do now in expressing and addressing God by naming His three modes of being.

What about the second tier of the other three triadic orderings? The remaining thirty-seven percent of the triadic occurrences divide out relatively evenly among them:

- Father-Spirit-Son (F-Sp-S) appears eleven times, for fifteen percent of the total.

- Spirit-Father-Son (Sp-F-S) is used nine times, or twelve percent of the total usage.

- Spirit-Son-Father (Sp-S-F)—the converse image of the baptismal order—is used eight times, for ten percent.

So what questions can we start asking and what conclusions can we start drawing, just from this accumulation of Trinitarian census data? The New Testament displays greater diversity in the expression of the Triune orders than is seen in the contemporary church, at least in its expressions in worship, prayer, and the ordinances. Was this profusion of diverse triadic orders because the formal apostolic creedal order was yet to be settled? Or was this diversity of Trinitarian expression something divine and theological? Are these occurrences inadvertent in their abundant and obstinate recurrence, or are they intentional? Can that intentionality be demonstrated by exegetical and contextual investigation? I do wish to draw one line in the sand about the presence of a multitude of triadic references in the New Testament. Let's suppose that scholars were able to refute ten to twenty-five of those instances. That still means that the New Testament authors thoughtfully articulated their Trinitarian consciousness and worldview in a six fold manner in so many instances that Trinitarian matrix formulation must be incorporated into our theology, liturgy, and life.

In subsequent chapters, I will explore these more specific questions—triadic order by triadic order and instance by instance—before offering any conclusions on them.

Chart 2.1: New Testament Triadic Pattern Frequencies (based on seventy-five instances)

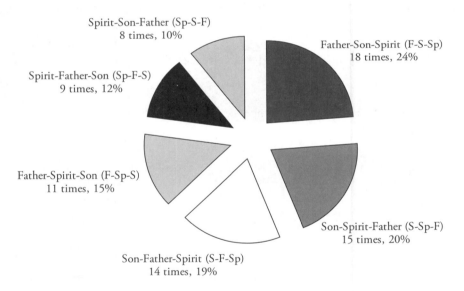

Spirit-Son-Father (Sp-S-F)
8 times, 10%

Father-Son-Spirit (F-S-Sp)
18 times, 24%

Spirit-Father-Son (Sp-F-S)
9 times, 12%

Father-Spirit-Son (F-Sp-S)
11 times, 15%

Son-Spirit-Father (S-Sp-F)
15 times, 20%

Son-Father-Spirit (S-F-Sp)
14 times, 19%

NEW TESTAMENT DISTRIBUTION OF TRIADIC INSTANCES

The New Testament was written by a minimum of nine authors over a minimum of forty or so years. How active were these authors in employing the diverse triadic orders? Are some sections of the New Testament less fertile places to find some of the diverse triadic orders? Which books make the most references to the Triune Godhead and which have no Trinitarian references at all? A summary of the data harvested to answer these questions is posted in Chart 2.2 below. (For the full census of triadic occurrences, see Appendix A. That "master chart" details exactly where Trinitarian references are found, and which triadic ordering I have placed them in.) The data supports a number of conclusions. Here is an overview of key findings.

- The vast majority of New Testament books have one or more instances of triadic references. Of the seventy-five triadic orders identified, here is the frequency in which they are found, by major area of the New Testament:

  - Twenty-eight instances (thirty-seven percent) are found in the epistles of Paul.
  - Nineteen instances (twenty-six percent) are located in the Gospels.
  - Fifteen instances (twenty percent) are located in Hebrews, the general Epistles, and Revelation.
  - Thirteen instances (seventeen percent) occur in Acts.

- Of the twenty-seven books in the New Testament, nineteen of them (seventy percent) have triadic references to the Trinity in one of the six possible orders, and eight of them (thirty percent) have no references.

- Acts has the most occurrences at thirteen, and John and Romans are tied for second highest frequency at ten instances each.

- Five books—Mark, Colossians, 1 Thessalonians, 2 Thessalonians, and Jude—each have one triadic instance.

- Eight books (thirty percent) have no triadic references—four of them Pauline epistles (Philippians, 1 Timothy, 2 Timothy, and Philemon) and four of them general epistles (James, 2 Peter, 2 John, and 3 John).

- When you consider the entire authorship of the New Testament, the one single author who has no triadic references is James. All other authors include the Trinity somewhere in their book(s).

These numbers look substantial, but are they really? Another way to consider the weightiness of the evidence is by an analysis of page content. Of the

680 pages comprising the New Testament, the books *lacking* triadic occurrences represent a mere thirty-eight of those pages; the books *including* Trinitarian references represent 642 pages. So, does that seem like the Trinity is an assumed way of thinking on the part of New Testament authors, or an add-on doctrine gradually developed in the post-Apostolic era? With Trinitarian references in seventy percent of the New Testament books, such a profound and generous distribution of triadic references demonstrates that the Trinitarian way of praying, communing, thinking, and teaching was a part of Christianity from its start.

One might suspect that Trinitarian references might abound in the theologically didactic works of Paul more than in the largely narrative genre employed in the Gospels and Acts. However, these triadic references are found fairly equally in the narrative materials (Gospels plus Acts, forty-two percent of the instances) and the didactic materials (Pauline epistles and other writings, fifty-eight percent). Surely this suggests that early Trinitarian Christianity was both theory and practice, orthodoxy and orthopraxy. Trinity was what the early Christians prayed, preached, and practiced. The witness of the New Testament canon bears this conclusion.

Chart 2.2: Triadic Occurrences in Major New Testament Areas

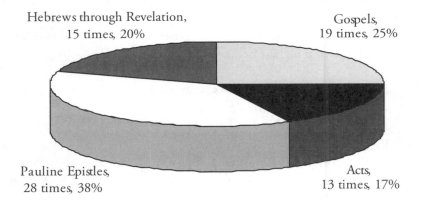

Hebrews through Revelation, 15 times, 20%

Gospels, 19 times, 25%

Pauline Epistles, 28 times, 38%

Acts, 13 times, 17%

These questions are far more than mere academic minutia. Life reflects thought. Jesus asserted that humanity is designed for solidarity between thought and life. "As a person thinks in his heart so is he." Integrity means that our dogmatic theology and our practical theologies influence each other. To invoke the pagan text used by Paul in Athens, if we do "live and move and exist" in God, then doesn't it follow that whenever and wherever the church has moved in procession with God, confirmation and effectiveness would be the result? What were the results if and when the church constricted how it shaped its life to limited movements of the Triune processions? Wouldn't people perceive the church to be rather rigid and narrow if it reduced the generous diversity of the six triadic orders for prayer and worship to one, even if the intention in so doing was to preserve unity and purity? No twenty-first-century pragmatic evaluation should be imposed on these issues. It is the thesis of this book that as the church is made in the image of God and His Son by the leadership of the Spirit, so the Triune God is glorified and enjoyed in proportion to the expression of the diverse Triune orders by the body of Christ. That follows from the common assumption that God should be worshipped and served as He has revealed Himself.

MAKING SENSE OF THE TRIADIC CENSUS, AND "GRADING" THE INSTANCES

G. K. Chesterton suggested that the traveler sees what he sees. The tourist sees what he has come to see." If we are theological *tourists* of the New Testament, we will perceive only the expected Trinitarian order of Father, Son, and Holy Spirit—despite what is actually there. This is not to minimize that particular ordering. After all, this creedal framework was the order pronounced at Christian baptism, in keeping with Matthew 28:19–20. Some unexpected triadic "disorder" from the apostolic authors is acceptable. The benediction at the end of 2 Corinthians is tolerated as an exception that proves the doctrinal rule of order. Clearly in that passage, the writer pronounces a triadic blessing in the order Son, Father, and Spirit: "The grace of the Lord Jesus Christ, and the love of God, and the fellowship of the Holy Spirit be with all of you" (2 Corinthians 13:14).

However, if the eyes of Chesterton's *traveler* are put on to see what has always been waiting for us in the text, then such "disorders" become much more common, varied, and perhaps even a new doctrinal rule. **Research indicates that there are seventy-five Trinitarian references in the New Testament.** Just eighteen instances (twenty-four percent) do follow the expected order of Father, Son, and Spirit. The remaining fifty-seven instances (seventy-six percent) exist in five other diverse orders.

As we will see, some instances are easily identifiable as triadic and Trinitarian by virtue of their brevity and simplicity. Others occurrences are longer and more complex, but still are clearly Trinitarian in their intentionality. I have identified all triadic instances; analyzed their triadic ordering (sometimes the Greek original differs from the English translation); and graded them into one of the following three classifications from A through C, based on their verse configurations.[14]

Grade A. A grade of "A" means that **the usage is brief and usually contained within one verse, with no or very few intervening words.** Certainly the baptismal triadic order in Matthew 28:19 sets a standard for brevity and intentionality. The 2 Corinthians 13:14 benediction mentioned earlier also fits this parameter of brevity in one verse, "The grace of the Lord Jesus Christ, and the love of God, and the fellowship of the Holy Spirit be with all of you." The order expressed here is Son-Father-Spirit. Another Grade A example is the greeting in 1 Peter 1:2, "according to the foreknowledge of God the Father and set apart by the Spirit for obedience and for sprinkling with the blood of Jesus Christ." Here, the triadic order of Father-Spirit-Son occurs in nine words within one verse and in the Greek text. Of the seventy-five triadic usages identified, forty-four instances (fifty-nine percent) were graded "A" due to their brevity and clarity.

Grade B. A grade of "B" means the triadic **usage is found usually with intervening words over two or three verses**. Of the seventy-five triadic usages identified, eighteen instances (twenty-four percent) received a grade of "B."

Acts 2:32–33 reads, "God has resurrected this Jesus. We are all witnesses of this. Therefore, since He has been exalted to the right hand of God and has received from the Father the promised Holy Spirit, He has poured out what you both see and hear." In the Greek text, the order is Son-Father-Spirit or more precisely Son-Father-Son-Father-Spirit. This occurrence falls over two verses and uses nineteen words. Here the Trinitarian usage is inadvertent since the point in Peter's address is to explain the coming of the Spirit at the post-crucifixion/resurrection celebration of Pentecost.

A second example of a "B" triadic instance is found in Ephesians 4:4–6: "There is one body and one Spirit—just as you were called to one hope at your calling—one Lord, one faith, one baptism, one God and Father of

---

14. The data charts, with usage grading for all seventy-five identified triads, can be found in Appendix A.

all." Here the oneness of the church is to be found in the Oneness of God expressed in the triad Spirit-Son-Father. The few intervening words do not obscure the Trinitarian intention, but do move it down in classification to a "B" instance.

Grade C. A grade of "C" means a triadic **usage occurs over two to five verses with intervening words**. Of the seventy-five triadic usages identified, twelve instances (sixteen percent) received a grade of "C."

For example, Acts 11:15–17 reads: "the Holy Spirit came down on them, just as on us at the beginning. Then I remembered the word of the Lord, how He said, 'John baptized with water, but you will be baptized with the Holy Spirit.' Therefore, if God gave them the same gift that He also gave to us when we believed on the Lord Jesus Christ." Here the order might be identified as Spirit-Son-Spirit-Father-Son—or more succinctly, Spirit-Son-Father. While the referents are clearly Trinitarian, the intervening words make the order somewhat disputable for the purposes of this study.

The apostle Paul's discussion of the redeemed life in Romans 8:1–3 is another example of a "C" grade usage. Occurring over three verses and thirty-three words, the passage reads: "Therefore, no condemnation now exists for those in Christ Jesus, because the Spirit's law of life in Christ Jesus has set you free from the law of sin and of death. What the law could not do since it was limited by the flesh, God did." The text exhibits a triadic order of Son-Spirit-Son-Father but has a number of intervening words.

Identifying and grading triadic orders is not an exact science by any means. Other scholars might give specific triads different grades than the ratings I assigned here. However, even if there is a 10 percent change in the grading schema of the census, the undeniable conclusion is that the Trinitarian way of thinking is so common, pervasive, and persistent that it constitutes a default theological consciousness to which the writers defer regularly and at times refer intentionally. Based on the internal evidence in the text of the New Testament, the Trinitarian way of thinking about God was no afterthought developed in the post-Apostolic period, but rather a forethought and centerpiece of first-century Christian prayer and presentation.

Grade NA. I have one unusual occurrence that I have given an NA "not applicable" grading. That is Luke 11:13, and I will explain that when we get there in chapter 7 on Son-Father-Spirit triadic incidents.

Trinitarian Rigidity and Flexibility

This research indicates that the New Testament writers practiced a generous flexibility and an insightful intentionality in application of the diverse triadic orders to Christian life and service. But that analysis still leaves many questions to investigate:

- If the New Testament writers applied diverse triadic order, then isn't that a reflection of the earliest Christian communities?

- How long did that diversity of applying all the possible triadic orders persist in Christian history?

- How did it get constricted to mostly the baptismal ordering, and when?

- How do differences in triadic orders potentially relate to doctrinal divisions among various streams in Christianity?

Theology develops in conflict and community. So as the early Christians encountered theological crises from within (as in the case of Arias) and without (as in the case of Julian the Apostate), there is some expectation that the church might focus on defending the orthodoxy of the Triune God using the most known order, Father-Son-Spirit. Because practice makes permanent, this practice of the baptismal order used by Jesus might have become the permanent and sole order normally used by the church. We will look at this issue in chapter 4, "The Karma of Dogma." Meanwhile, it raises more questions to stimulate our search for interpretations, implications, and applications:

- Was this preference for the baptismal Father-Son-Spirit order a healthy or an unhealthy development?

- Certainly, the defeat of subordinationism and unitarianism by orthodox Trinitarianism was a valued outcome. However, what doxological and missiological footprint would an overemphasis liturgically of the Father-Son-Spirit procession have left in church history?

- Could the Great Schism of the church in 1054 CE reflect conflict between a Western insistence on one Trinitarian order, versus an Eastern insistence on maintaining the New Testament balance of processional orders?

- If there is a significant connection between Trinitarian processional balance and theological health, then it still bears asking: What was or is the effect of neglecting use of the remaining five triadic orders in the ways that the New Testament applies them?

- How might the resonance or dissonance between New Testament processional balance and church practice of the full six triadic orders have affected the life and mission of the church in its history?

- Might this imbalance not be the theological equivalent of asking someone to eliminate one or more of the five basic food groups from his or her diet?

- Another question worthy of attention is, Can church ethical and missional practices reflect diverse processional orders, even when the liturgical practices fail to express those orders? If worship is the engine of ethics and evangelism, how might fuller application of the diverse Trinitarian orders in worship enable more effective Christian community and service?

We will explore such questions as we study each of the triadic orders in chapters 5–10.

MAKING THE TRINITARIAN DATA SING

Research for the sake of research does not have much value. The data must be made to sing! However, before that part of this Trinitarian study begins, it is valuable to state the research gains thus far.

Presuming the Usual Order and What We Lose. Most practicing Christians are reasonably comfortable with the received order of Father, Son, and Spirit for their worship, prayer and other churchly functions. This baptismal order is easily demonstrable biblically, is the movement almost exclusively used when sermons are heard on the Trinity, and on the surface appears to govern how prayers are to be prayed: to the Father in the name of the Son in guidance and passion of the Spirit.

However, when applying only the Father-Son-Spirit order to church life and ministry, the church closes its eyes and ears to seventy-six percent of the New

Testament witness to the Triune God—differences from the assumed ordering in three out of every four passages. How does this constriction seem to affect our witness in the world? In seeking biblical grounds to mount an apologetic and polemical defense for their hope in the Trinity, some Christians become defensive at best and embarrassed at worst about the doctrine. Only twenty-four percent of the available biblical witness to the Trinity is being brought into the conversation. Christians can be too willing to concede that the Trinity is a post-New Testament doctrine; noting the other seventy-six percent of passages could change that.

Exploring the Other Orders and What We Gain. This research brings forward more clearly that Trinitarian thinking is richly embedded into the fabric of the New Testament. It suggests that Trinitarian thinking was the default consciousness of the writers so that they creatively and repeatedly included all possible triadic orders of the Three in One in their gospels and epistles. Confidence and competence increases with the size of accumulated witness. The identification of seventy-five textual witnesses to the Trinitarian way of God's being also ought to encourage and empower Christians to live and witness in that name.

So the song that these seventy-five triadic references sing in unison is, "Holy, holy, holy; merciful and mighty! God in three Persons, blessed Trinity!"[15] That song is good, but the data permits more. The biblical references can be organized into six part harmony, with each of the orders supplying its voice for the whole.

How Can We Make It "Sing"? The data set begs to be analyzed, instance by instance, to determine whether or not, or to what degree, there is something common to the contexts in which specific triadic orders are found. In later chapters, we will do just that—analyzing each of the triadic orders in its respective New Testament context. I will marshal evidence toward considering the commonality of contexts relative to specific triads. Do specific triads, for instance Spirit-Son-Father, normally occur in specific contexts, say in discourse on ecclesiology or on salvation? I offer the following six proposals as possibilities—or even probabilities—of each triadic order and its significance, based on the theme of contexts in which it occurs. I will attempt to show those patterns of connection with context, using exegesis and exposition of the passages wherein the triads have been found.

Here is a preliminary overview of the research and analysis of each of the triads in the Trinitarian matrix of the New Testament. Consider it a quick, curbside chorus on the Holy Trinity in six-part harmony.

---

15.   Reginald Heber (1783–1826), "Holy, Holy, Holy!"

PREVIEWING THE SIX TRIADIC ORDERS
AND THEIR THEMATIC SIGNIFICANCE

The Missional Triad: Sentness (F-S-Sp)

Father-Son-Spirit occurs eighteen times and represents a missional triadic order of sending, sent, and sentness. In the redemptive mission of God, the Father sends the Son and the Son asks the Father to send the promised Spirit at the conclusion of the Son's earthly mission. The baptisms of Jesus and the various versions of the "Great Commission" exhibit this order: Matthew 12:18; 28:19–20; John 1:33; 20:21–22; 5:31–32; 10:38; Romans 1:1–4; 1 Corinthians 2:4–5; 1 Thessalonians 1:2–5.

The Father-Son-Spirit triad works like an apostolic procession which empowers and tests orthodoxy and orthopraxy as *sentness*. This triadic order seems to be primary to the mission of God in Christ in His church.

The Christological Triad: Service (S-F-Sp)

Son-Father-Spirit order occurs fourteen times and represents the christological order. The Pauline benediction in 2 Corinthians 13:14 famously invokes this order. John 14:16; Acts 2:32–33; Ephesians 2:22; Hebrews 2:3–4 and 10:12–16 are other prime occurrences.

The Son-Father-Spirit order may be above all else the christological procession, which moves the Church as the body of Christ to maintain service despite difficult times. Temporally, humiliation precedes exaltation, the cross comes before the crown. Sacrificial *service* looks to be the primary meaning of this triadic order.

The Ecclesial Triad: Oneness/Giftedness Unity/Diversity) (Sp-S-F)

Spirit-Son-Father is the least represented triadic order, with only seven occurrences. A preliminary investigation suggests that this is likely the ecclesial triadic order. As the exact counterpoint to the Father-Son-Spirit triad, instances are found in 1 Corinthians 12:4–6 (different gifts, but the same Spirit . . . different ministries, but the same Lord . . . different activities, but the same God . . ."); Ephesians 4:4–5 (one Spirit, one Lord, one God and Father).

The Spirit-Son-Father ecclesial triadic order empowers and tests *oneness* and *giftedness* within missional *koinonia* (participation) and *diakonia* (service and ministry).

The Evangelistic Triad: Acceptance (S-Sp-F)

Son-Spirit-Father occurs sixteen times in the New Testament and expresses an evangelistic triadic order. Acts 2:38–39 records Peter's Trinitarian framed answer to temple congregants asking, "Is there any way that we can be saved?" To which Peter answers, "Repent and be baptized, each of you, in the name of Jesus Christ for the forgiveness of your sins, and you will receive the gift of the Holy Spirit. For the promise is for you and for your children, and for all who are far off, as many as the Lord our God will call." In this procession, the gospel story of the Son convicts hearers via the Spirit and issues in the regenerative cry, "Abba, Father."

The baptismal narratives in the Gospels deploy this triadic order to climax with the words of the heavenly voice, "My beloved Son. I take delight in Him."[16] Also, Romans 15:30 reads, "Now I appeal to you, brothers, through our Lord Jesus Christ and through the love of the Spirit, to join with me in fervent prayers to God on my behalf."

Acceptance seems to be the intent of this Trinitarian order. Acceptance here is not in the sense of acceptance of Christ's place in the divine economy, but rather our experience as disciples of forgiveness and acceptance by God into His household through Spirit-quickened trust in Jesus as Messiah and Savior.

The Liturgical Triad: Reverence and Sustainability (Sp-F-S)

Spirit-Father-Son occurs nine times and expresses a liturgical triadic order. In the well-known Trinitarian benediction in Jude 20–21, the reader is admonished to "pray in the Holy Spirit, keep yourselves in the love of God, expecting the mercy of our Lord Jesus Christ for eternal life."

The liturgical triad follows a worship order that moves from inspiration by the Spirit, to reverence of the Father, to Christ-like action or intervention. The end of worship is the beginning of service.

This triadic order also occurs in the climactic moment of the martyrdom of Stephen in Acts 7:55: "But Stephen, filled by the Holy Spirit, gazed into heaven. He saw God's glory, with Jesus standing at the right hand of God." Stephen's epiphany of the Triune God prompts his declaration before his soon-to-be executioners that Jesus reigns on high. This liturgical moment sustained his witness unto death.

Reverence might be a useful title for the meaning when Scripture uses the Spirit-Father-Son order. Authentic reverence has a passive aspect that receives revelation at God's initiative, but results in the recipient's faithful and sacrificial response.

---

16. See Mark 1:10–11 and Matthew 3:16–17.

The Formational Triad: Consecration (F-Sp-S)

Father-Spirit-Son appears eleven times in the New Testament and represents the formational triad. While having the third fewest occurrences, this triad is significant in the greeting in 1 Peter 1:2: "according to the foreknowledge of God the Father and set apart by the Spirit for obedience and for sprinkling with the blood of Jesus Christ. May grace and peace be multiplied to you."

Romans 14:17 also follows the Father-Spirit-Son order, "for the kingdom of God is not eating and drinking, but righteousness, peace, and joy in the Holy Spirit." Herein, the Father pours the Spirit out upon the Son to initiate incarnational mission and pours the Spirit out on His church that it might continue that mission. Thus, *consecration* is the value conveyed by this sixth triad.

TABLE 2.3: TRIADIC ORDERS COMPARISON CHART		
Triadic Order	**Core Theme**	**Key Feature, Meaning, Value**
Father-Son-Spirit	Missional	Sentness
Son-Father-Spirit	Christological	Service
Spirit-Son-Father	Ecclesial	Oneness/Giftedness (Unity/Diversity)
Son-Spirit-Father	Regenerative	Acceptance
Spirit-Father-Son	Sanctifying	Reverence
Father-Spirit-Son	Formational	Consecration

REVIEW AND PREVIEW

First, let us consider the big picture of where we have been and where we are going. We explored the backdrop of contemporary questions in theology of the Trinity, and then the Trinity in the New Testament. Here we found a framework, painted in broad stokes by identifying the seventy-five instances of triadic references and by classifying those instances according to the six triadic orders. We went through a cursory examination of the meaning of each order, and gave each triadic order a name based on its contextual theme.

If we view the New Testament as descriptive evidence of the worship and life patterns of the earliest churches, then these distilled meanings should express some prescriptive aspects of the Trinity is to be experienced in the church. The experience of the Triune God in Christ brings values into the life of the church as sentness, service, oneness/giftedness (i.e., unity/diversity), acceptance, reverence and consecration.[17] We will explore these six Trinitarian values separately with their respective triadic orders in the chapters so designated. That will lead us toward the full, emerging model for Trinitarian ecclesiology in the final chapter of this book.

Before we move forward into those specific triadic orders, I believe we need to look back first. How did the first-century Palestinian writers of the New Testament learn to think so creatively and obstinately Trinitarian? The obvious answer is that Jesus taught them. If so, what teaching materials might He have used for their instruction?

While Jesus was not averse to going beyond the Pentateuch, Tanakh, and the Apocrypha, in the Gospels He often interpreted those very materials to clarify the theology of the disciples. The Hebrew way of thinking and writing uniquely creates space and taste for a sense of plurality in the Godhead. The next chapter explores Old Testament and intertestamental materials as possible roots for the way that the apostolic writers developed Trinitarian consciousness.

DISCUSSION QUESTIONS—CHAPTER 2

- What was your initial reaction to the realization that all these triadic instances had been right in front of you in the Scriptures and that you just weren't seeing them? How can things hide in plain sight?

- How convinced are you that there really might be a connection between a specific Trinitarian order, say Son-Spirit-Father, and the context in which that triadic order is embedded?

- Try a mini-Trinitarian prayer experiment. Choose a triadic order that has the most appeal to you right now. Pray using those names in that chosen order. What happened?

---

17. Those familiar with the ecclesiological model presented by the Mennonite theologian at Notre Dame, John Howard Yoder, may see some resemblance to his ideas here. In his *Body Politics: Five Practices of the Church before a Watching World* (Scottdale, PA: Herald Press, 1992) Yoder proposed an ecclesiological model of oneness, sharing, binding and loosing, giftedness, and welcoming.

CHAPTER 3

The Antecedent Question: Triadic Presence in the Hebrew Scriptures

If the thesis of these scholars is correct, far from being a foundling left on the porch of the Church by Greek metaphysics, the doctrine of the Trinity is a legitimate and honorable child of Hebrew religion, whose growth was slow, and, in years of exile, somewhat retarded, but who blossomed into the vigorous manhood during the first five centuries of the Christian era.[1]
—Arthur Wainwright, *The Trinity in the New Testament* (1963)

Some have disparaged any attempt to uncover roots for the doctrine of the Triune God in the First Testament, which is so famously monotheistic. After all if, as some assert, the concept of the Trinity is a post-New Testament dogmatic invention of the third- through fifth-century ecumenical councils, then how likely is it that one could locate ancient Hebraic artifacts anticipating the Trinity? If the conception of the Trinity occurs only after the New Testa-

---

1. Arthur W. Wainwright, *The Trinity in the New Testament* (London: SPCK, 1962; republished Wipf and Stock Publishers, 2001), 19; with particular reference to G. A. F. Knight, "A Biblical Approach to the Trinity," in *Scottish Journal of Theology Occasional Papers* no. 1 (Edinburgh: Oliver and Boyd, 1953), 3, and Aubrey R. Johnson, *The One and the Many in the Israelite Conception of God* (Cardiff: University of Wales, 1961).

ment is formed, how successful could we be in finding evidence of the Triune God prior to the New Testament? Gerald O'Collins chastised just this line of thought in 1999 when he wrote: "The OT contains, in anticipation, categories used to express and elaborate the Trinity. To put this point negatively, a theology of the Trinity that ignores or downplays the OT can only be radically deficient. Something essential will be missing from what we mean by *the Trinity* if we ignore the Jewish roots of Jesus and those of his first followers."[2]

The New Testament writers were Trinitarian thinkers. They learned this from their rabbinical Master, who in turn must have developed their awareness of plurality in the One God by building on clues presented throughout the Old Testament.

MORE THAN *MERE* MONOTHEISM

If the triadic expressions of the One God are so artlessly abundant in the New Testament so as to form a default theological mindset for its authors, then surely there must be apparent, if not abundant, indications in the First Testament of the God who is a unity and not unitary. Based on review of the seventy-five "casual" uses of triadic references to God in the Gospels and Epistles, we have to ask, "How did these first-century Palestinian monotheists learn such Triune thinking?"

The mystery of the superabundant witness of the triadic matrix in the New Testament cannot be explained without close investigation for an anticipatory witness in the First Testament.

Having now done this research and written this chapter, it seems inconceivable to me that anyone would attempt to explore the New Testament expressions of the Triune God without first investigating the foundation of those expressions in the prior Testament. How else could the New Testament authors end up as "functional Trinitarians"?

Functionally Trinitarian. In their respective commentaries, C. K. Barrett and Gordon Fee make intriguing comments about the presence of triadic formulae[3] embedded in the text of 1 Corinthians 12. Fee writes, "In passing one must note the clear Trinitarian implications in this set of sentences, the earliest of such texts in

---

2. Gerald O'Collins, *The Tripersonal God: Understanding and Interpreting the Trinity*, (New York: Paulist Press, 1999), 11.
3. "Triadic formulae" refer to any instance of a threefold reference to God as Father, Son, and Spirit, no matter the order that the three are referenced.

the NT. As Barrett notes, 'The Trinitarian formula is the more impressive because it seems to be artless and unconscious.'[4] (This passage itself will be discussed later in chapter 9.) What is impressive to Barrett and Fee is that a first-century Palestinian Jewish monotheist, like Paul, thinks as a functional Trinitarian. If those who support the post-Apostolic advent of Trinitarian thinking theory were correct, then such triadic expressions should not be occurring for three more centuries. Yet, such Trinity thinking and speaking is nearly the default norm of the New Testament.

The better explanation for what Ben Witherington and Laura Ice call the "functionally Trinitarian thinking" of the New Testament authors is twofold.[5]

1. **First, the New Testament writers learned Trinitarian-think and Trinitarian-speak from Jesus.** His teaching imparts awareness, relationship, and commitment to Himself, to the *Abba* Father, and to the other *paraclete*, the Holy Spirit.

2. **Secondly, Jesus mentored Trinitarian believing, praying, and obeying within the differentiated monotheistic thinking embedded in the First Testament.** This more-than-mere-monotheism constituted a familiar mode of thought for first-century Palestinian Jews.[6]

"Differentiated monotheism" means theologizing beyond a rigid monotheism of undifferentiated unitariness. This latter unitarian perspective hears the Hebrew Shema in Deuteronomy 6:4—"Listen, Israel: The Lord our God, the Lord is One"—solely as a polemic countering polytheism, be it the Greco-Roman Olympian version or, anachronistically, a dysfunctional Christian tritheism. A differentiated monotheism hears the Shema with an awareness that the word "God"—*elohenu* is plural and the word for "one"—*echad* can mean oneness in the sense of unity or unified. It is the same word used in Genesis 2:24, "they shall become one flesh." The Shema must not be heard as if the Hebrew

---

4. Gordon D. Fee, *The First Epistle to the Corinthians* (Grand Rapids: Eerdmans, 1987), 588, as quoted from C. K. Barrett, *Commentary on the First Epistle to the Corinthians* (New York: HNTC , 1968), 284.

5. I came across this concept of "functionally Trinitarian" in Ben Witherington III and Laura M. Ice, *In the Shadow of the Almighty: Father, Son and Spirit in Biblical Perspective* (Grand Rapids: Eerdmans, 2002), 67–70.

6. I have incorporated here the threefold forms of Karl Barth's understanding of the church's response to the Trinitarian *perichoresis* of the interpenetrating three modes of the divine way of being. See Peter Oh, *Karl Barth's Trinitarian Theology* (New York: T & T Clark, 2006),133.

word for one unit—*yachidh*—is used.[7] The words *unit* and *union* do not have the same meaning. *Unit* conveys a sense of sameness, where *union* conveys distinction without division, autonomy within intimacy.

Three Clues

In this chapter, we will explore the "intimations" of plurality within the One God as found throughout the Old Testament.[8] These intimations of plurality within the Godhead are of three main types.

1. **Grammatical oscillations** between the singular and the plural in a given text, whether *between pronouns* (what I'll be calling *Oscillation Type A* for our investigations here), or *between subject and verb* (*Oscillation Type B*). An example of Oscillation Type A is found in the pronouns of Genesis 1:26–27, "Let **us** make man in **our** image . . . male and female created **he** them" (KJV). An example of Oscillation Type B is found in Genesis 1:31, "**God saw** [*Elohim*—plural, singular verb] everything **He had made** [singular pronoun, singular verb]."

2. **Personality extensions** of the Holy One, such as appear in phrases like the Angel of His Presence, His Word, and His Spirit.

3. **Economic formulae** in divine dyads and triads in which, for example, what God does He does through His Word and His Spirit, in distinction yet without division. Remarkably, the latter triadic instances occur in the Messianic materials in Isaiah, out of which Jesus shapes His earthly mission and message.

1. The Wizardry of Grammatical Oscillations

The Old Testament is not easy. It is long and it is complex. It is ancient and Eastern in worldview, and not Western and secularized in its paradigms. It is

---

7. Hebrew use of *yachidh* to replace *echad* occurs only after the second century CE and likely occurs as a way to make an anti-Trinitarian and polemical distinction between Judaism and Christianity.

8. John Feinberg uses *intimations* and *incipient* as qualifying descriptors in his discussion of the doctrine of the Trinity in *No One Like Him* (Wheaton, IL: Crossway Books, 2001), 448. Note that Feinberg does not use "dyadic" or "triadic" in this context.

salted with grammatical anomalies that either snag your attention or beg your ignorance.[9] Grammatical oscillations in the Hebrew texts have been observed for centuries, but were aptly so named in the published research of G. A. F. Knight (1953) and Aubrey Johnson (1961).[10] This kind of oscillation refers to the observation of toggling between agreement and non-agreement among subject and verb in the same passage, or between a third person and then a first person pronoun for the same subject.

For instance, Johnson notes that in certain passages, especially those expressing special revelation, the expected agreement between the singular and plural among subjects and verbs is not always to be seen. In fact, within some texts, swings occur between expected agreement of subject and verb and disarming disagreement, especially when the subject is *Elohim*-God or *Yahweh*-the LORD. A singular subject can have a plural verb and *vice versa*, and then later in the same text, an oscillation can occur back to subject-verb agreement.

Knight overaggressively contends that much of the Hebrew theological mindset of the Old Testament is obscured behind the Greek-Platonic worldview idioms incorporated into the Septuagint. He roundly supports the earlier sentiment of Edwin Hatch (1888) that "the Greeks changed the rushing torrent of the river of God into a broad and feeble stream. Christianity was profoundly changed by the habit of mind of those who received it. Around it thronged the race of eloquent talkers, who persuaded it to change its dress and to assimilate its language to their own."[11] Knight bases his analysis of the Hebrew foundations for the New Testament understanding of the Triune God on research using the Masoretic texts, in combination with reviewing the large depository of Rabbinical exegesis and interpretation handed down from the second century to the medieval ages. It is in this light that Knight quotes C. R. North to the effect that "the theology of the Old Testament has been buried for sixteen hundred years."[12]

Less contentiously, Wainwright recalibrates Knight's full-on assertion that the Septuagint obscured the oscillations intimating a plurality in the Godhead. "The Septuagint shows a definite tendency to eliminate suggestions of polytheism, but it retains much that does not easily harmonize with the most

---

9. I learned this idea of "snag points" in Scripture from my colleague at Golden Gate Seminary, Dr. Faith Kim.
10. Knight, 3; Johnson, "A Biblical Approach to the Trinity," *The One and the Many in the Israelite Conception of God*.
11. Ibid.
12. Ibid., 4; C. R. North, *Scottish Journal of Theology* (July 1949).

rigid form of monotheism . . . the plural forms in Genesis and Isaiah are retained. . . . The oscillations from singular to plural in Genesis 18 and in Deuteronomy 6 have not been eliminated."[13] When studying these oscillations, readers will be challenged to at least tentatively conclude whether these grammatical inconsistencies are: (1) translation or transmission glosses, (2) evidence of not-so-well blended sources.[14] The Old Testament has intimations of plurality within the Godhead. What were the ancient readers and hearers of these texts to think? In the words of Larry Hurtado: "I agree with the general drift of these studies, that Jewish monotheism was much more complex and diverse than has sometimes been recognized."[15]

Oscillation Type A: Among "Divine" Pronouns

The God(s) must be crazy! The biblical Scriptures waste no time in hinting at plurality within the Godhead.[16] Why does the Hebrew text in Genesis 1:26 say, "Let *Us* make man in *Our* image?" and then in the very next verse say, "So God created man in *His* own image; *He* created him in the image of God, He created them male and female." Careful reading creates tension between the plural "Us" and "Our" and an undifferentiated monotheism, which demands that pronouns for God be singular and only singular. This tension increases between the plural "Us" and the singular in "So God created" and in "He created." Is God a plural "Us" or a singular "He?"

This toggling between the singular and the plural relative to the same subject is the equivalent of oscillating between "the gods must be crazy" and "God must be crazy." Such oscillations are not unusual in the Old Testament. They are found not in obscure, seldom-read or seldom-cited portions, but rather in the very passages that are core to any Hebrew catechism. These passages, like this one in Genesis 1 or the Genesis 18:1–15 account of Abraham and the three visitors, are passages which most Bible readers can recall easily, if not altogether accurately.

---

13. Wainwright, *The Trinity in the New Testament*, 23.
14. *Transmission glosses* here means that those copying texts sometimes copied erroneously or sometimes intentionally emended the text to conform to their expectations.
15. Larry W. Hurtado, *One God One Lord: Early Christian Devotion and Ancient Jewish Monotheism* (Philadelphia: Fortress Press, 1988), 134, n.26. Here Hurtado is concurring with what he calls the "general drift" of the research of J. E. Fossum, *The Name of God and the Angel of the Lord: The Origins of the Idea of Intermediation in Gnosticism*, WUNT 1/36 (Tubingen: JCB Mohr, 1985) and A. F. Segal, *Two Powers in Heaven*, SJLA 25 (Leiden: E.J. Brill, 1978).
16. I first encountered this use of "intimations" with reference to plurality in the Godhead in the monumental study of Feinberg, *No One Like Him*, 445.

Older Christian tradition has explained these textual oscillations between the plural and the singular as early revelations that God is triune.[17] Others more recently contend that the Genesis 1:26–27 oscillation is really a reference to the angelic court in the case of the plural "Us-Our" and to the personal creative work of Yahweh when it is singular "He-Him." However, there is no mention of an angelic court in this entire context, so such a presence would have to be read into the text. Furthermore, humanity is never understood to be in any way in the image of angels. Humanity is either "a little lower than" or being placed in judgment over the angels, but never in the image or likeness of angels. And to place the image of God and the image of angels in the same category would be offensive to the Old Testament theology of "no one like Him." Others have suggested that the plural should be understood as a "magisterial" plural, but such usages are more common to Shakespeare than Hebrew.

The context itself nudges the reader toward a God who is a unity of consciousness rather than merely a unit of consciousness.[18] Note that Genesis 1:27–28 also oscillates between the singular and the plural with reference to humanity, "He created **him** in the image of God; He created **them** male and female." The context suggests a correlation between the singular/plural "Us-Our/He-Him" in God and the "he-them" in humanity. Wouldn't it make sense to think that, just as humanity is a unity with reference to "in His image" yet a differentiation with reference to male and female, so then God also may have a differentiation within Himself?

Knight extrapolates the same idea in terms of the ancient Hebrew being self-aware that he or she was "a *unit* of consciousness indeed, but he was more, he was also a unity of consciousness."[19] Knight provides a starkly literal recitation of Psalm 26:2 and 139:24 as examples of his concept of a unity of consciousness: "Examine me, O LORD, try my kidneys as well as my heart" and "See if there be any offensive way in me."[20] Could not this same concept of unit of consciousness versus unity of consciousness be at least somewhat the Hebrew mindset in hearing the Shema, "The LORD our God, the LORD is One?"

I would here reaffirm Feinberg's assertion, "It is dubious that anyone living in OT times and reading the OT would conclude that three persons—Father, Son and Holy Spirit—are divine, and would understand what that means. On the other

---

17. For example, Irenaeus, *Adversus Heresies*, 4:20, 1,7, cf. Letham, *The Holy Trinity,* 93.
18. This distinction between unit and unity of consciousness is from Knight, "A Biblical Approach to the Trinity," 11.
19. Knight, "A Biblical Approach to the Trinity," 11.
20. Ibid.

hand, a careful student of the OT could have suspected that it teaches something more about God than just monotheism."[21] No attempt should be made to make this molehill of evidence into a mountain of Trinitarian claims. However, more evidence is readily available. The ambiguous use of the plural with reference to God occurs two more times in Genesis and once in Isaiah. Let's take a look at those.

Oscillation Type A in Genesis 3:22 and 11:2–8. Genesis 3:22–24 is another instance of counterintuitive oscillation between the plural and the singular with reference to the LORD God. "The LORD God said, 'Since man has become like one of Us [plural], knowing good and evil . . .' so the LORD God sent him away from the garden . . . He [singular] drove him out . . ." The conversation with or within the Divine is in the plural, but the subject of the action is singular. This oscillation from the plural in the consideration to the singular in the action mirrors the Genesis 1:26–27 passage just discussed. The plural "become like one of Us" indicates that this speech is not the expected soliloquy of unitary monotheism.

In Genesis 11:2–8, this type of oscillation occurs again with, "Then the LORD came down to look over the city and the tower. . . . The LORD said, 'Come let Us [plural] go down there and confuse their language. . . .' So the LORD scattered [singular in subject and verb] scattered them." As Feinberg argues, why use a plural of majesty, if you are alone?[22] Who would hear? Again, no angelic court is identified in the context, so the presence of angels would have to be read into the text. Such dogmatically motivated emendations are rarely a convincing approach. Intimacy within the divine One seems to be the intimation. At least, plurality within the Godhead cannot be ruled out as a conclusion from the text.

Oscillation Type A in Isaiah 6:8. In the call experience of Isaiah, we see a rapid oscillation between the singular and the plural. "Then I heard the voice of the LORD say, 'Whom should I [singular] send? Who will go for us [plural]?'" It is as if, with reference to the divine way of being, the singular and the plural are in synonymous Hebrew parallelism. In contrast to the three instances in Genesis, this oscillation of pronouns in Isaiah from "I" to "Us" to "He" [the latter in verse nine] occurs in the midst of a full angelic court press. Seraphim are hovering and serving. So the "Us" might be proposed as Yahweh including that court, except that there is no other instance in the Old Testament where such inclusive language

---

21. Ibid., 448.
22. Ibid., 449.

occurs clearly. Yahweh, who is alone God, includes created beings only in His bidding and not in His counsel. Thus, in this passage, the seraphim hover and obey, but do not participate as partners with the Lord God in His mission to humanity.

Conclusions about Oscillation Type A

Admittedly, these instances of oscillation between singular and plural use of pronouns is not overwhelming evidence of plurality in the Godhead within the Old Testament. However, these instances, coupled with other indicators, make it very difficult, if not impossible to assert that the Old Testament is monolithically unitary in its monotheism. A unitary monotheism would assert that there is absolutely no plurality or differentiation within the Godhead; Oscillation Type A texts do not support this contention. Thus, the emerging view of Old Testament theology is something more than such mere monotheism.

Oscillation Type B: Between "Divine" Subjects and Verbs

Exclusive Monotheism as *Diastatic* Zion[23] **and Not as Olympic Summit.** Mount Zion is the figurative height where the Lord alone reigns as the One God in Hebrew worship. Mount Olympus is the figurative home for the Greek pantheon of deities. Beyond plurality versus unitariness, the Greek and the Hebrew minds also differenced in their theological concerns. Hebrews are relational; they want to know **who** is God. The Greeks are conceptual; they want to know **what** is deity.

Bauckham helpfully distinguishes divine *identity* from divine *nature*, the former being the Hebrew concern and the latter being the Hellenistic concern. The Old Testament "distinguished the one God from all other reality."[24] The Hebrew word for "one," *echad*, means that Yahweh is in a unique category with no others. Used numerically, *one* makes a distinction from *two* or *three*. However, *one* can also refer to a union, so that in Genesis 1, the man and the woman come together and become one *echad* flesh. Hebrew also has *yachidh*, a word that means "solitary" or "unitary," as in one and only child (Genesis 22:2) or as with a friendless wanderer or exile (Psalm 68:7) [25]

23. Ben Witherington III and Laura M. Ice, *In the Shadow of the Almighty: Father, Son and Spirit in Biblical Perspective* (Grand Rapids: Eerdmans, 2002), 67–69; Richard Bauckham, *God Crucified: Monotheism and Christology in the New Testament* (Grand Rapids: Eerdmans, 1998), 13, 15, 22.
24. Bauckham, *God Crucified: Monotheism and Christology in the New Testament*, 41–42; see also Witherington and Ice, *In the Shadow of the Almighty: Father, Son and Spirit in Biblical Perspective*, 70.
25. Knight, "A Biblical Approach to the Trinity," 17.

Apotheosis is the elevation of another to deity. Within Hebrew monotheism, no apotheosis is possible or permissible. Bauckham concludes: "So the participation of other beings in God's unique supremacy over all things is ruled out. In the case of creation, by excluding them from any role at all, and, in sovereignty over the cosmos, by placing them in strict subordination as servants, excluding any possibility of interpreting their role as co-rulers."[26]

This monotheistic exclusivism is well-pictured by the intertestamental 1 Enoch 14:22, as it describes the court of the Lord, "ten thousand times ten thousand (stood) before Him, yet He needed no counselor." Karl Barth described this wholly otherness of God as diastatic separation—none is like Him. Into this exclusively monotheistic viewpoint comes the ambiguity of Hebrew Shema semantics and the Holy One who is a unity of consciousness and being. (We will consider shortly how the Shema intersects with the divine identity.)

The Dysfunctional Grammar of the Plural of *El*. If the biblical Scriptures are so divinely inspired and the instrumentality of human authorship so superintended that the results are in accord with divine intention while still remaining human words, then why doesn't the Hebrew text follow the grammatical rules of the Hebrew road? Subject and verb should agree in number. Grammatically speaking, "The gods is crazy" ought to be corrected to read either "God is crazy" if you are a monotheist, or "The gods must be crazy" if you are a polytheist.

However, the Jewish writers of the New Testament have no trouble with incorporating this "revelatory grammar" into their own work. Note that Matthew 28:19 reads, "baptizing them in the name [singular] of the Father and of the Son and of the Holy Spirit [three names]." Baptism is to be in the one name of the three.

As has been well researched, when the Old Testament uses the Hebrew root for God *el* with reference to the God of Israel, it does so using *el* in the plural form *Elohim* and almost always follows this plural subject with a verb in the singular. So we see in Genesis 1:31, "God [*Elohim*—plural] saw [verb singular] everything He had made [singular pronoun, singular verb]."

Numerous explanations have been presented for these textual phenomena. Some suggest that it is the plural of majesty, whereby an individual in a position of authority speaks politely of himself or herself as "we" instead of an "I." Fein-

---

26. Bauckham, *God Crucified: Monotheism and Christology in the New Testament*, 13, as quoted in Witherington and Ice, *In the Shadow of the Almighty*, 68.

berg offers a very credible overview and assessment of this well-studied issue of the common use of the plural *Elohim*, which makes the Old Testament theology something other than *mere* monotheism. He does so by investigating the infrequent occasions when the text makes use of *Eloah*, the singular of *Elohim,* and asks, "Unless the intent is to make a point about plurality, why not just use the singular *Eloah*?"[27] (We will see more from Feinberg's studies shortly.)

So, the theological function of these grammatical dysfunctions may be to reveal differentiation within the Godhead. They do create a comfortable space for Trinitarian conceptualization within the thought life of first-century monotheists. These grammatical oscillations create flexibility in the Hebrew mode of thinking for an intimate plurality in the Holy One.

Hebrew Shema-**antics and Greek Ears.** The fourth-century Arians exalted a unitary view of the divine monarchy, asserting that only the Father was the One God. The Son was created and became an angelic incarnation as a human. This Arian subordinationism with its denial of the One God as a unity of Father, Son, and Spirit, was condemned as heresy at the Nicene Council in 325 CE. Since that time, the general Christian and resulting public consensus has been to understand some of the distinction between Judaism and Christianity as being that of Hebrew monotheism versus Christian Trinitarianism.

While we will examine this and other patristic-era theological achievements in some detail in the next chapter, I want here simply to assert that the intent of the bishops at Nicaea was to find the most faithful way to assert how Christians are still monotheists while being faithful to the missional processions of the Son and the Spirit—the Son in the incarnation and crucifixion, and the Holy Spirit in the Pentecostal empowerment of the church. Nicaea resolved that God could be both one and three, and that Christians could be monotheists and Trinitarians.

However, Nicaea did *not* resolve that the ancient Hebrews also could have been other than mathematical monotheists, or as Richard Niebuhr put it, "rigid monotheists." Because Greek was the *lingua franca* of the Mediterranean region and because of the availability of the Greek translation of the Old Testament, those at Nicaea heard the Hebrew Shema with "big fat Greek" ears, really the only ears available. No one at Nicaea knew Hebrew. Their access to the Old Tes-

---

27. Feinberg, *No One Like Him,* 445–449. The author offers examples of the use of *Eloah* as follows: Deuteronomy 32:15; Psalm 18:32, 114:7; Habakkuk 3:3; and frequently in Job.

tament revelation was confined to the Greek Septuagint. Such a hearing aid can-not but hear with a Hellenistic mindset that necessarily diminishes the insights in the Hebrew language and mindset.

This is an important point for our consideration, as all languages have dis-tinct advantages and disadvantages. What exactly may have gotten lost in the translation from Hebrew to Greek?

The Hebrew Language and Two for One. G. A. F. Knight, Aubrey R. Johnson, and H. Wheeler Robinson argue that the divine election of the Hebrew people for covenant consequently meant that their language was also elected as the vehicle for transmission of revelation.[28] And Hebrew communicates some insights that cannot be said in Greek.

For instance, as I mentioned earlier, Hebrew has two words for the "one"—*echad* and *yachidh*. Knight explains, "the Hebrews are seeking to express what was to them essentially true of their god, viz., that He is not to be thought of as a mere monad of being, or as a mathematical 'integer' as in 'one' over against another 'one.'"[29] Hebrew has a word for "one and only" or unique, *yahid*, as in the sense of "Take now your only son." However the word used for "one" in Deuteronomy 6:4 and in Zechariah 14:7 is *echad*. This expression of "one" is also applied in Genesis 2:24, "Therefore a man shall leave his mother and the two shall become *one* flesh." So, when used of humanity, *echad* can mean one with an inner differentiation, or diversity within unity. Normally, *echad* means one in number, but it is also used to mean more than one in a unity.

This linguistic reality begs the question, How can mere monotheism be the prevailing interpretation of the Old Testament when *Elohim*, the key word for the God who is God alone, is itself plural? Feinberg concludes that this gram-matical phenomenon occurs so frequently that it is probably stylistic. But that does not rule out the intimation of plurality in the Godhead being within the ancient Hebrew consciousness.[30]

This problematic use of the plural form of God *Elohim* for the God of Israel is magnified by the equally intriguing "problem" of how often the plural *Elohim* serves as the (plural) subject of a singular verb. It is as if the Hebrew is expressing simul-taneously both the plurality and the oneness of the God of Abraham and Moses.

---

28. Knight, "A Biblical Approach to the Trinity," 6.
29. Ibid., 17.
30. Feinberg, *No One Like Him*, 449.

Witherington and Ice offer this perspective of the Shema: "[T]he issue here is to make a statement against polytheism, not to make a statement in favor of unitariness or undifferentiated nature of the divine identity."[31] Just as oneness is not necessarily sameness, divine uniqueness does not equal divine unitariness. Then, the best way to understand the monotheistic mindset of the New Testament writers is in light of the Shema's oneness. Matthew's missional formulation of Jesus' commission has a strange sounding syntax too, unless you hear this Greek text with Hebrew ears. Having made disciples, these are to be baptized into the Name (singular) of the Father, and of the Son and of the Holy Spirit. This baptismal formula contains the very kind of grammatical oscillation learned from the Hebrew texts revealing the Unique God, who is a unity.[32]

Commonly, the text of the Old Testament uses the plural form of *El* with a singular verb. Feinberg cites additional evidence of Old Testament intimations of plurality in the Godhead, wherein the normal style of using *Elohim* [plural] with a singular verb is instead used with a plural verb. He cites instances of such non-stylistically conforming grammar in Genesis 20:13, where *Elohim* is used with the plural "caused to wander,' in Genesis 35:7 where *Elohim* has "revealed" [plural] himself?/themselves? to Jacob, and in 2 Samuel 7:23 where *Elohim* went to redeem [plural] Israel.[33] What makes these instances noteworthy is their not playing to the normal stylistic form of using the plural *Elohim* with a singular verb as in hundreds of other instances. What is the careful reader to think? Can "bad grammar" be the intentional vehicle of good theology?

Johnson sees this use of *Elohim* as another instance of the one and the many in the Hebrew mindset. He writes, "In short, may one not suggest with a degree of probability that any Israelite who thought of his *Elohim* [the author uses the Hebrew letters] to be Many also thought his *Elohim* to be One?"[34]

In deference to the plural *Elohim*, there are also multiple instances where the plural of "Maker" or "Creator" is used in a context where all other references to deity are singular. In the context of Messianic good news for the barren in Isaiah 55, the plural for "Maker" occurs and is followed by singular references to Yahweh, Redeemer *Goel*, and *Eloah*, the singular form of *Elohim*.

---

31. Witherington and Ice, *In the Shadow of the Almighty,* 70.
32. Ibid., 114. Here Witherington and Ice point out the singularity of name in contrast to the pluralities of names.
33. Feinberg, *No One Like Him,* 449.
34. Johnson, *The One and the Many in the Israelite Conception of God,* 110, n.163.

However, the Septuagint eliminates this plural in the Hebrew and uses a singular Greek participle to translate "Maker" as the one who makes. It is this kind of translation which precipitates the accusations of Knight that the Greek Septuagint has intentionally obscured any intimations of a theology not rigidly monotheistic.[35]

The singular form of *El* is again paired with the plural form of "Maker" in Job 35:10. Why would the Hebrew text use the plural form of "Maker" in these contexts, which predominantly identify singular forms for God? While such textual tremors or oscillations ought not be scored too high on "theological Richter scale" of pro-plurality in God, they do continue to add to the evidence of such plurality being consistent with First Testament revelation.

Conclusions About Oscillation Type B

As I mentioned at the beginning of this chapter, there are three kinds of conclusions that students of Scripture have drawn to explain these kinds of grammatical inconsistencies. Were they translation glosses? Or were they leftover evidence of multiple sources that were not blended well? Or were they intimations of plurality within the Godhead? Here are a few thoughts on each of those explanations which have been put forth.

Explanation #1. Translation Glosses—Correction. The argument here is that ancient Hebrew is primitive and so were the grammatical sensibilities of the writers, thus, the solution is to change the text into grammatical conformity. These textual anomalies plagued the monotheistic mindset of the first-century rabbinical translators, who produced the Greek Septuagint so that the non-Hebrew-reading Hebrews of the Jewish diaspora could understand the Torah and prophets. These translators usually emended the translation in favor of syntax which supported monotheism over polytheism.

There are two arguments which sink this view and its attempts to correct the "problem" of oscillations. First, for millennia, careful readers of the First Testament have emerged with admiration for the capacity of Hebrew to convey spiritual truths and for the writers to eloquently express those truths. These writers did not and do not get "Cs" in grammar and syntax. Secondly, while these syntactical oscillations do not occur on every page, they are so "sprinkled" as seasoning in key passages throughout the Old Testament that it makes more sense to make a case for their occurrence being intentional and tactical. While

---

35. Knight, "A Biblical Approach to the Trinity," 2–3.

our big fat Greek ears do not like the sound of Hebrew speaking outside of *our* grammatical box, such oscillations are music to the ear of divine revelation.

Explanation #2. Source Fusions—Coherence. The argument here is that such oscillations are examples of two sources being fused into one account. The solution is emendation to better fuse the two sources.

What, then, would determine the direction of the oscillation? What criteria guide creating such attempted coherence? Is such literary criticism eisegesis and theological squeezing while fusing texts into conformance?

Explanation #3. Intimations of Plurality—Corroboration. Language is the primary expression of cultural worldview. After all, a culture invents words to value and evaluate its own perspectives of life. My explanation for the oscillations is to affirm the integrity and intentionality of the text, along with the innate capacity of Hebrew to convey God's revelation to us, which includes a worldview that challenges our own. Taken at face value, these oscillations lean us toward hints of plurality within the oneness of the Godhead.

Johnson, following the lead of H. Wheeler Robinson, notes the oscillation within biblical texts "between the conception of the social unit as an association of individuals (with a resultant use of plural forms) and as a corporate personality (with the consequent use of the singular) is unmistakable."[36] He warns against "going astray in textual as well as literary criticism through a desire to secure a 'logical' coherence often foreign to Israelite thinking."[37]

2. EXTENSIONS OF THE DIVINE PERSONALITY

Maturity is the ability to navigate an unanticipated environment. Biblical revelation confronts us with unexpected linguistic phenomena, which we can only gradually come to identify as reliable patterns of theophany. With H. Wheeler Robinson and other Old Testament researchers in the twentieth century, the concepts of personality extension and corporate personality have been identified as peculiar expressions of the Hebrew worldview and the biblical revelation.[38] Personality extension refers to the Hebrew way of being actually present in interactions

---

36. Johnson, *The One and the Many*, 12.
37. Ibid., see also H. Wheeler Robinson, *The Cross of the Servant: a Study in Deutero-Isaiah* (UK: SCM Press, 1926), 58.
38. Robinson, *The Cross of the Servant*, 58.

through intermediaries. For instance, Aubrey Johnson cites the enigmatic Hebrew syntax, wherein servants become extensions of their master's personality and as such are then addressed and even self-identify as the master himself.

In the Old Testament, it is not uncommon for personhood to be extended through the person's name, words, and servants or messengers. For this second clue to plurality in the First Testament, we will look at how interaction with God's Person can occur through the intermediaries of these personality extensions:

- His name
- His word
- His messenger/servant
- The Angel of Yahweh
- The Son
- The Spirit

God's Name as God

With reference to Yahweh, the third commandment warns that His name is not to be misused. To call upon the name of the Lord is to call upon the Lord. Since essence is bound up in the name, Knight asserts that when Yahweh chooses to put His name in the temple of Solomon, then God has used His name in an "objective fashion" to place His alter ego, even His essence, there.[39] Knight argues for this objectification of the name by reference to such passages as "The name of the God of Jacob defend you" (Psalm 20:1), and "The name of the LORD is a strong tower" (Proverbs 18:10).[40] The New Testament picks up this concept of the name as divine alter ego with objective meaning in "all who call upon the name," "there is no other name," and "the name that is above every name" (Acts 2:21, 4:12 and Philippians 2:9).

The concept of personality extension and divine alter ego means that personhood can be extended and such extensions bear the essence of the Godhead. To offend that extension is to offend God.

God's Word as God

Persons within the community are conceived in the Hebrew Bible to have a positive or negative influence by means of their words of blessing or cursing.

---

39. Ibid., 13.
40. Ibid., 13, 18.

"In this way the spoken word may be regarded as an effective 'extension' of the personality."[41] Here Johnson cites the familiar Genesis 27:33 account of Isaac's mistaken blessing on Jacob that, once bestowed, takes on a "quasi-material fashion," and cannot be taken back by Isaac. Having put his soul or self into the blessing on Jacob, Isaac can only bestow a semi-curse upon Esau.[42]

Once spoken, a person's words become a living, objective reality which must accomplish the mission intended by the one who spoke them. So, words then are an alter ego of the person who spoke them, a personality extension. In Isaiah 55:10, "so My word that comes from my mouth will not return to me empty, but it will accomplish what I please and will prosper in what I send it to do." The word is sent and the word is a "living extension of the living God" as in Psalm 107:20: "He sent His word and healed them." Another example is Psalm 130:5–7: "I wait for the LORD; I wait, and put my hope in His word . . . Israel, put your hope in the Lord."[43] Putting your hope in Yahweh's word *is* putting your hope in Yahweh.

In the Word of God, the essential identity of Yahweh is extended so that the One God is to be understood as One, but with a distinction but never a division between God and His word.

> *This is Hebraic metaphysical thinking and it is out of this mindset that New Testament monotheists speak of the Father, Son, and Holy Spirit as the Holy One.*[44] *Hebraic thought permits extension of essence, while maintaining distinction in identity.*

God's Messenger/Servant as God

Extension of the divine personality to His messenger happens in the oracle against Shebna in Isaiah 22:15–19. Using the third person singular in verses 16–18, the messenger informs Shebna, the palace steward, that "He," the Lord of Hosts, is about to shake Shebna violently. The Lord of Hosts is understood to be speaking in person by extension through the messenger. Then in verse 19, the messenger's

---

41. Johnson, *The One and the Many in the Israelite Conception of God*, 2–3.
42. Knight, "A Biblical Approach to the Trinity," 15, who is here referencing Pedersen, *Israel, Its Life and Culture,* vol. 1 (1926), 182. See also H. Wheeler Robinson, "Hebrew Psychology" in Arthur S. Peake, ed., *The People and the Book: Essays on the Old Testament* (Oxford: Clarendeon Press, 1925), 353–382, as significant for his understanding of the Hebrew and Semitic concepts of personality extension and corporate personality.
43. Ibid., 17.
44. The phrase *"Hebraic metaphysical thinking"* comes from Knight, 16.

voice changes to first person singular, "I will remove you from your office." This extension appears more objectively real than just a literary device. It is reminiscent of God's Spirit putting Saul on like a coat to prophesy (1 Samuel 10:10, 19:23–24). In Jeremiah 9:1–2, the prophet presents the LORD's declaration in the first person singular, as the LORD in person. Again the sense is that Judah is to respond as to Yahweh in person rather than as to a prophet speaking with dramatic rhetoric.

Malachi 3:1 is a strong example of extension of the divine personality to a messenger. Notice the oscillating identifications in the text between Yahweh the sender and the messenger as the sent one. "See, I am going to send My messenger, and he will clear the way before Me. Then the Lord will suddenly come to His temple, the Messenger of the covenant you desire—see, He is coming, says the Lord of Hosts." Is "My Messenger" different in identity from the "Messenger of the covenant" or are they the same? The enigmatic answer is likely "yes" on both counts. The sent messenger is differentiated from Yahweh the sender, but indivisible from the Messenger of the covenant as an extension of the divine person. Johnson identifies this oscillation as a movement from "an objective 3rd Person to a subjective 1st Person singular in the case of Yahweh."[45]

> *The insight to be gained is that the divine identity is not static and transcendently isolated, but rather His identity is dynamically and authentically present.*

The Angel of Yahweh as God

The angel of Yahweh or the angel of His presence appears to be an identity distinct from the usual suspects of angelic identities like Michael, Gabriel, etc.[46] When Hagar runs from mistreatment at the hands of Sarah, it is the Angel of the LORD who finds her (Genesis 16:7–13). This angel speaks using the first person singular, "I will greatly multiply your offspring." Yahweh speaks in person through this angel.

In Judges 6:11–14, the Angel of the LORD calls Gideon to deliver Israel from the Philistine oppression. The Angel begins this call in the third person singular voice, "The LORD is with you, mighty warrior." Then the voice changes to first person singular: "Am I not sending you?" Notice that even the person of the voice speaking changes from the Angel of Yahweh to the LORD Himself: "Then

---

45. Johnson, *The One and the Many,* 35.
46. Ibid., *The One and the Many,* 29–36.

the LORD turned to him and said. . . ."[47] This oscillation from the Angel of the LORD to the LORD Himself demonstrates textually that Yahweh's identity is in this sense not static but present in two places.[48] Jesus conveys this same reality of revelation in response to Philip's question about seeing the Father, "The one who has seen me has seen the Father" (John 14:9).

Angel/Yahweh Oscillation in Genesis 18. Yahweh appears to Abraham at the Oaks of Mamre in Genesis 18–19 as an important part of the Sodom judgment saga. This account speaks of the appearance of the LORD, three men as the vehicles of the appearance, and of the LORD's presence, in which Abraham remains standing even as the men continue toward Sodom.

Note the monotheistic progression of the account. The opening sentence sets the theme: Yahweh appears to Abraham. The visible form of the appearance is the three men whom Abraham "beholds" in verse two. Abraham requests opportunity to refresh their "hearts" by offering hospitality. And the three agree and soon also, as a trio, inquire about Sarah's presence (Genesis 18:5, 9). So, to this point in the account, plurality in the revelatory vehicle prevails. Then there is an oscillation to the singular, "And He said, 'I certainly will come back to you in a year's time, and your wife will have a son'" (Genesis 18:10). The voice is singular and the identity is that of Yahweh, "But the LORD asked Abraham, 'Why did Sarah laugh . . . ?'" (Genesis 18:13). Now "the men turned from there and went toward Sodom while Abraham remained standing before the LORD" (Genesis 18:22).[49]

Because of the LORD's appearance as three men, this passage has been a favorite Trinitarian proof text down through the Christian ages. Augustine puzzled over the mysterious oscillations in the text and wondered at the movement from a plurality in voice to singularity to duality in Genesis 19 and yet ending again with singularity in divine action.[50] Recently, Robert Le-

---

47. The Septuagint omits this oscillation and reads "Then the Angel of the Lord . . ."
48. Johnson, 29–36.
49. Philo, *On Abraham,* XXIV: 119–131. Philo, the ancient Jewish philosopher and commentator, reads ahead to the two who are identified as angels in Genesis 19:1, and logically concludes that only two of the "men" went away, and one stayed behind. Philo also observes the oscillation among the personality extensions as being figurative. He interprets the personality extension as symbolic of a threefold image produced when a bright noon sun shines on one subject in such a manner that two shadows are discernible behind the brightly illumined subject himself.
50. Augustine, *On the Trinity,* XI, 20, *Nicene and Post-Nicene Fathers, LCC,* 1st series, Philip Schaff, Part 3, (Peabody, MA: Hendrickson Publishers, 1994), 47; cf. XVII, 33, 53, cf. Letham, *The*

tham has analyzed this text and what he describes as "the bewildering and continuing juxtaposition of men, angels and the Lord. It is as if boundaries have disappeared."[51] Using Wainwright's description of this "mysterious oscillation," Letham concludes that such texts indicate *identification with* yet *distinction from* as operating principles in divine self-disclosure in the Old Testament.[52] Certainly, the text indicates that Yahweh manifests and reveals Himself in plurality, unity, and oneness, and oscillation in terms of plurality and singularity of voice evidence the diversity within that divine unity.[53]

Angel as *Elohim* in Genesis 22. The well-known story of the sacrifice of Isaac uses *Elohim* as the name for God, except in verse 14 and 16 where *Yahweh* is used. (Note that earlier in verse eight, the text says that "*Elohim* will provide for himself.") The story begins with the ominous phrase, "After these things God [*Elohe*] tested Abraham." The divine identity as *Elohim* continues to verse 11 where that identity becomes the Angel of Yahweh. It continues in that identity throughout the remainder of the account.

Beyond this oscillation in identity is the interesting grammar used by this angel. In verse 12, the angel speaks in the first person singular voice as *Elohim* in person: "For now I know that you fear God, since you have not withheld your only son from Me." Later, in verse 16, the Angel of the Lord speaks *from heaven* as *Elohim/Yahweh* in person: "By myself I have sworn, says the Lord."

What is the reader to make of these oscillations in voice? Do they mean that in acts of special revelation, God extends and objectifies His personality as this angel? As the event of the sacrifice increases in intensity with Abraham lifting his blade over the bound body of his only son, then the angelic extension of the divine personality becomes clearly God in person.

The texts intend the reader to understand that, if you have seen and heard this angel, you have seen and heard Yahweh.

Holy Trinity, 23. Partially reading Nicene Trinitarian theology into the text, Augustine repeatedly notes, "since three men appeared, and no one of them is said to be greater than the rest either in form, or age or power, why should we here not understand, as visibly intimated by the visible creature, the equality of the Trinity, and one and the same substance in three persons?"

51. Letham, *The Holy Trinity,* 24.

52. Ibid.; see Wainwright, *The Trinity in the New Testament,* 26–29.

53. It is interesting that of the three transfigured "men"—Jesus, Moses, and Elijah—who are seen by the three apostles on the mountain of Transfiguration in the Gospels, only one, Jesus, is addressed by the apostles (Mark 9:5).

The Lord's Son as God

The Son in Psalm 2:2, 6–7. Monotheistic thinking is not logically toler-
ant of divine Sonship. It is theologically problematic for the Holy One to have
a Son. Yet, the well known Psalm 2 presents the LORD and His chosen one. Of
His messiah, the LORD testifies, "You are My Son, today I have become your
Father."[54] The Hebrew reads literally, "today I have begotten you." The Brown-
Driver-Briggs Hebrew lexicon identifies the usage of the "begotten" *yilad* as
figurative of the bestowal of theocratic rights upon the king.[55] The royal son of
Psalm 2 is to have an earthly, temporal role with eschatological, global implications. The use of "begotten" can convey a sense of sameness in identity and
nature—after all, like begets like. "Begotten" is used to convey recognition or
bestowal of parallel authority.

In the Gospels, Jesus applies this text to Himself at least three times. First is
when the voice from heaven confirms His sonship at the baptism (Mark 1:11).
Second, when He commissions His disciples to go to the nations (Matthew
28:18). And third is when He promises the Spirit as the empowerment necessary
to witness to the nations (Acts 1:4–8).[56]

The Son in Proverbs 30:4. In a similar fashion, a series of theological
questions lead up to Proverbs 30:4. "Who has established all the ends of the
earth? What is His name and what is the name of His Son . . . ?" This context
makes no mention of king or messiah, so it is more difficult to explain this
reference as merely figurative of messianic eschatological action. Earlier in the
chapter, the Holy One is mentioned, and then later, warning is given against
profaning the name (Proverbs 30:3, 9). So, taken in its plain sense, this prov-
erb implies that the Holy One has a son.

The Son in Isaiah 9:6. The figure of a son with unexpected entitlements
also is found in Isaiah 9:6. "For a child will be born to us, a son will be given
to us, and the government will be upon his shoulders. He will be named
Wonderful Counselor, Mighty God, Eternal Father, Prince of Peace." Here
a birthed person is awarded names reserved for deity. What was the ancient
reader to make of this prophecy? This "son" is distinct from the "Lord," yet

---

55. See the New Testament use of Psalm 2:7 in Hebrews 1:5; 5:5.
55. Francis Brown, S. R. Driver, and Charles A. Briggs, *Hebrew and English Lexicon of the OT*
(Oxford: Clarendon Press, 1974).
56. See Psalm 2:8; Matthew 3:17; 28:19–20; and Acts 1:8.

he is seemingly attributed titles denoting equality of authority and essence with the LORD.

The Son in Jeremiah 23:6. The prophet Jeremiah seems here to declare that the Davidic messiah, called Branch, is also to have the name, "Yahweh Our Righteousness." Now, the portent of a literal reading might be avoided by interpreting the name to mean the messiah will take as his throne name, "The LORD is our righteousness." However, such an approach to this theological consciousness-expanding passage cannot be explained away in the same way in Isaiah 9:6.

The Son in Micah 5:2. This passage adds to the accumulated evidence for diversity within the Holy One. Micah 5:2 identifies Bethlehem as the birth place of the LORD's chosen ruler of Israel, but then continues to add a surprising category of pre-existence for this messiah, one that precedes an earthly, temporal birth. "His origin is from antiquity, from eternity (*olam*)."

How can a chosen ruler have both a birth place and pre-exist from everlasting? Resolution of such a problematic prophecy opens the Hebrew mode of thought to reconsider a unitary view of monotheism toward a unity of consciousness from eternity.

Unfaithful responses to discomfiting passages occur either by dismissing them as illogical and inscrutable, or by unnecessarily emending the text. After all, is not the LORD unknowable in all His ways? Richard Bauckham asserts that, "The Second Temple understanding of the divine uniqueness . . . does not make distinctions within the divine identity inconceivable."[57]

> *Such passages do make a unitary view of the Holy One difficult to maintain and the concept of a plurality in the Godhead less foreign to the Hebrew mode of thinking in the Old Testament.*

Yahweh and the Son of Man and the Elect One

Bauckham likewise asserts that "Jews understood the practice of monolatry to be justified, indeed required, because the unique identity of YHWH was so understood to place him, not merely at the summit of a hierarchy of

---

57. Richard Bauckham, *God Crucified: Monotheism and Christology in the New Testament*, 22, as cited by Ben Witherington and Laura Ice, *In the Shadow of the Almighty*, 69.

divinity, but in an absolutely unique category, beyond comparison with anything else."[58] However, the exception to this rule in the Old Testament and the Apocrypha happens in regard to the Son of Man. He exercises judgment on God's behalf, is placed on God's throne, and is to be worshipped.

The Son of Man in Daniel 7:13–14. Daniel 7:13–14 reads that the son of man approaches the Ancient of Days and is "escorted before Him. He was given authority to rule, and glory, and a kingdom; so that every people, nation, and language should serve Him. His dominion is an everlasting dominion that will not pass away."

The Son of Man in 1 Enoch. In 1 Enoch 47:3, the "Head of Days" has "seated himself upon the throne of His glory" and the "books of the living are opened before Him." This view fits well the expected procedures for final judgment by the Lord. However, in 1 Enoch 61:8, the Lord of the Spirits places "the Elect One on the throne of glory" in order that "he shall judge the works of the holy," even to "judge their secret ways according to the word of the name of the Lord of Spirits."

Then, in 1 Enoch 62:2, the Elect One is again seated on the throne of "His glory" by the Lord of the Spirits" to slay sinners by the "word of his mouth." In verse five, the title of the Elect One changes to the "Son of Man," and the "Son of Man is viewed seated on the throne of his glory." In verse nine, the kings and others who rule the earth fall down and "worship and set their hope upon that Son of Man." To this Son of Man "the sum of judgment is given" as he sits on "the throne of his glory," upon which he "has seated himself" (1 Enoch 69:27–29).

So in non-canonical collaboration with Daniel 7, 1 Enoch evidences the Hebrew capacity to conceive a differentiated or shared Oneness, since here the Elect One/son of man is seated on the throne of glory, exercises judgments, and receives worship—all activities reserved in the monotheistic mindset for God alone. Theological conclusions from 1 Enoch must challenge any rigid monotheistic view of the Holy One, which excludes the Elect One/Son of Man sharing the throne of glory, sharing judgment of heavenly and earthly creatures, and even seating himself on that throne. All of these works and this authority are exercised in unity with the Lord.

Ancient Hebrew monotheism continues to appear less and less rigid, and more and more differentiated within His Oneness.

---

58. Ibid., 15.

The Spirit as God

Wainwright begins his analysis of the Holy Spirit as an "Extension" of Yahweh's personality by asserting that the Spirit is personal and not an impersonal force. He argues that as the Spirit of the Lord dons Gideon like a garment, then "it may hardly be said to be regarded as an impersonal force."[59] The extension of a personality must be a person.

In Genesis 6:3, the Lord declares: "My Spirit will not remain with mankind forever, because they are corrupt." Clearly, some distinction is made here between the Lord and His Spirit, but also that when the Spirit refuses to remain, then it is also the Lord who is refusing to remain.

In Psalm 139:7, the Spirit is equated with the Lord's presence. "Where can I go to escape from Your Spirit? Where can I flee from Your presence?" So God extends His presence by means of His Spirit. Where His Spirit is there He is. This distinction between the Lord and His Spirit—coupled with identification of the Lord with His Spirit—is reiterated in Psalm 51:11: "Do not banish me from Your presence or take Your Holy Spirit from me." The Psalmist recognizes that to be banished from God's presence *is* to have His Spirit taken from him.

God's presence and God's Spirit are distinct but indivisible. Johnson identifies Spirit, Word, and Name as "objective realities which are extensions of Yahweh's personality."[60] Wainwright takes it a step further in his analysis of Wisdom as an extension of the divine personality. With reference to Wisdom 7:25, Wainwright asserts that "she [wisdom] is more than an effluence of God. She has a conscious life of her own. She is an extension of the divine personality, an extension which suggests that the idea of the Spirit provided a climate in which plurality in the godhead was conceivable."[61] God's Spirit and Wisdom are more than divine emanation or effulgence; they are objective realities, distinct from God yet indivisible from His identity and activity.

> *Wainwright compellingly asserts that the "concepts of word, spirit and wisdom in the post-exilic period show plurality in the Godhead."[62] This theological principle of distinction without indivisibility constitutes the mindset out of which the New Testament Jewish monotheists were inspired to compose the Gospels and Epistles.*

---

59. Wainwright, *The Trinity in the New Testament*, 15–16.
60. Johnson, *The One and the Many in the Israelite Conception of God*, 16–17.
61. Wainwright, *The Trinity in the New Testament*, 33.
62. Ibid., 37.

3. Incipient Dyadic and Triadic Formulae

Incipient Word/Spirit Dyadic Formulae

Dyad in Psalms 33, Genesis 1, and Ezekiel 37. This Psalm is in the genre of ascent and praise. It early identifies the word of the LORD as the divinely employed instrument of creation: "By the word of the LORD the heavens were made." However, the second part of that couplet references the spirit *ruach*, "And all the host of them by the breath [*ruach*] of his mouth."[63] Physiologically, it is impossible to speak a word without releasing breath, but need this be so of God? In other words, either word and spirit are so intertwined as to be distinctive but inseparable, or this passage is a Hebrew parallelism, in which the second verse is a synonymous underscore of the first? Or, the LORD who creates does so by the dual instrumentality of the divine word and spirit. In this sense, the word and the spirit of Yahweh are certainly distinct but indivisible.

Back in the Genesis 1 story of creation, it is the Spirit who is brooding over the primordial darkness until God speaks and the created takes form. Later, God shapes the dust into an anthropomorph and then breathes His breath (*ruach*) into the shaped humus and the anthropomorph becomes a living soul and self.

In Ezekiel 37, again word and spirit are paired in Yahweh's act of redeeming or recreating his people. First, the prophet is ordered to prophesy to the valley of dry bones and these words cause flesh to come on the bones and now we see a valley of dead bodies. Then the prophet is commanded to prophesy to the *ruach*, the wind created by God's breath, and this spirit-breath-wind causes God's chosen ones, a valley of lifeless anthropomorphs, to live again and stand before Him in mission.

> *This differentiated union of word and spirit is the distinct mark of God's people in terms of the presence of prophets and of Israel being a prophetic people.*

How can prophecy happen apart from the spirit of the Lord, and how can an activity be understood as prophecy unless words are spoken? Whenever words are spoken in God's name without the Spirit, that person is condemned as a seer out for profit, not a prophet out for service. For instance, the strange charismatic

---

63. Psalm 33:6. I wonder if this quickening breath took the form of a breathy whispered command, "Live."

dysfunction of King Saul, when he is among the prophets, underscores the indivisibility of God's words and God's Spirit. Saul ever prophesies truths whenever the Spirit comes upon him and Saul never is identified with the prophets otherwise.

The Pentecostal Prequel of Spirit and Word in Numbers 11 and Joel 2. Note the intriguing Pentecostal prequel in Numbers 11:16–30. Here we see the charismatic confirmation of the advice Moses received from his father-in-law, Jethro. Namely, develop a substructure of qualified and corporately-affirmable leadership and delegate to them appropriately nuanced oversight of tribal domains. In these events, Moses, the tribal elders of the Sanhedrin, and the Hebrew community learn that within the mission and people of the LORD, appointment and anointment are to be inseparable. They learn that call, competency, and charisma are distinct but inseparable gifts to enjoy and to obey the living God.

The LORD instructs Moses to assemble the people at the Tent of Meeting. The seventy elders are called forward, the LORD descends in the cloud to speak with Moses, and the LORD took of "the Spirit that was upon him [Moses], and placed the same Spirit upon the seventy elders; and it happened that when the Spirit rested upon them, they prophesied."[64] Words—to be God's words—must be breathed into and out of the person by the Spirit.

If this Numbers 11 passage is the prequel to Pentecost, then Joel 2:28ff is the prophecy and promise of Pentecost. As the apostle Peter is recorded in Acts 2, theologically interpreted, the divine procession of the incarnation to crucifixion and resurrection culminates in the procession of the Spirit to quicken the church as the body of the Son. In Trinitarian-speak, the Son has ascended to the Father and requested that the Father send the Spirit, and so the "another counselor" has come.[65] Joel 2 articulates the eschatological intention of God to create a prophetic people who will—regardless of gender or age—be marked by worded revelation by the empowering of the Holy Spirit.

*In this mindset of the Hebrew Bible, spirit and word are distinct
but inseparable extensions of the Holy One.*

---

64. The verse in the usually translated manuscript finishes, "although they never did so again." Other manuscripts read the opposite, "prophesied and continued to do so." This alternate reading certainly favors the response of Moses to Joshua when the latter protested what he saw as an attempt to usurp the unique role of Moses. Instead of forbidding the elders to prophesy, Moses aspires, "Oh that all of God's people were prophets and that the LORD would put his Spirit upon them." See Numbers 11:28–29.
65. Acts 2:16; John 14:16.

Incipient Triadic Formulae

Genesis 1:1–3—God, Spirit, Word. In *The Holy Trinity* (2004), Robert Letham introduces his study of the Old Testament background to that doctrine with an observation about the earliest possible incipient triadic instance.[66] He remarks that, in the beginning, God *Elohim* creates and the way of that creation is with the Spirit *ruach* hovering until God speaks and it is with His Word that creation comes into being. So, here in the first three verses of biblical Scripture is an occurrence of an incipient divine triad of God, Spirit, and Word.

Working at the beginning of the third century of the common era, Tertullian wrestled with the Old Testament's way of preserving the divine monarchy, while revealing the divine missional economy as well. He finds such diversity in the Holy unity in Isaiah 42:1; 43:1; 45:1; 49:6; 61:1; Psalm 3:1; 71:18; and 110:1.[67] While I will give Tertullian's contribution wider attention in the next chapter, I will note that his identification of First Testament triadic texts seems appropriate here.

Triad in Isaiah 11:1–2—Branch, Spirit, Lord. This prophecy from Isaiah 11 speaks of the reign of the Davidic king in which the wolf will lay down with the lamb (11:6). The passage indicates that this reign will be the work of the Davidic *ruach*, the Spirit, and the LORD. The Spirit empowers the Davidic branch with wisdom, counsel, and delight to execute justice (11:7–8). The hand of the LORD extends His hand over the nations to create a highway for the remnant of His people (11:11, 16). Who then accomplishes this eschatological work of justice and restoration? The text distinguishes the Branch, the Spirit, and the LORD, yet the distinct sense is that all three act as one in the achievement. No ontological claims can be made from the passage, but the triadic association is the point. Such associations for divine mission are the default way of describing divine actions in the New Testament.

Triad in Isaiah 42:1—LORD, Servant/Chosen One, Spirit. Each song in Isaiah's Suffering Servant hymnal (Isaiah 42; 48; 61; 63) begins with an intriguing triadic cluster. In Isaiah 42:1, the LORD, speaking in the first person

---

66. Robert Letham, *The Holy Trinity: In Scripture, History, Theology and Worship* (Phillipsburg, NJ: P&R Publishing, 2004), 18.
67. Tertullian, *Adversus Praxeaus*, 11; cited in Edmund Fortman, *The Triune God: A Historical Study of the Doctrine of the Trinity* (Philadelphia: Westminster, 1972), 112.

and identified as Yahweh in verse five, introduces "My Servant [*ebedhi*]; I strengthen Him, My Chosen One; I delight in Him; I have put My Spirit on Him." So this song of the mission of the Servant is introduced with a confluence of divine personality extensions and then proceeds to a reaffirmation of monotheism in verse eight, "I am Yahweh, that is My name, I will not give glory to another, or my praise to others."

> *So, here monotheism is defined but not confined since the Holy One acts in mission through His Servant and His Spirit.*

Triad in 48:16–18—Servant, Lord God, Spirit. Whereas Isaiah 42:1 presents a triadic instance where the LORD speaks in the first person, in Isaiah 48, the Servant speaks in the first person of the same triadic cluster. This passage is immediately preceded in verses 11 and 12 by "And I will not give My glory to another. Listen to me, Jacob and Israel, the one called by Me: I am He, I am the first, I am also the last." Then in verse 16 comes the enigmatic triadic expression, "'Approach Me, and listen to this. I have not spoken in secret; from the time anything existed, I was there.' And now the Lord God has sent me and His Spirit." Note the three subjects: "me," the Lord God [*Adonai Yahweh*], and His Spirit.[68]

Who is this "me?" The best understanding would be that it is the messianic servant, who will carry out the divine pleasure in Babylon (see verse 14) and who will also usher in a jubilee as anointed by the Spirit in Isaiah 61. The case can be made that verse 16 appears to attribute pre-existence to this "me," who is to be differentiated from but also identified with the Lord God and His Spirit.[69]

> *So, in the context of an affirmation of unshared monotheistic glory, a diversity of that unity is expressed to carry out the messianic mission of restoration and retribution.*

Triad in Isaiah 61:1—Servant, Spirit, Lord GOD. This same triad of "me," the Lord GOD and His Spirit repeats in Isaiah 61. "The Spirit of the Lord GOD is on Me, because the LORD has anointed Me to bring good news to the poor."

---

68. It is interesting that the Holman Christian Standard Bible translation does not capitalize the second "me" in this verse, which, if intentional, appears to be inconsistent with the first "Me" which it does capitalize, indicating divine identity.
69. Feinberg is cautious about the clarity of this passage as triadic, but is convinced that it is at least a dyadic intimation of plurality in the Godhead.

Clearly, the resulting ministry to the blind, the lame, and others is messianic in expectation. Jesus inserts Himself into this very triad when He reads this text in the Nazarene synagogue service and follows up the reading with the benediction: "Today, as you listen, these words have been fulfilled in your hearing." The history of Christian tradition has seen this passage as a Trinitarian reference identified by Jesus himself.

Triad in Isaiah 63:7–10— LORD, Savior, Angel of the LORD's Presence/ Holy Spirit. This passage identifies Yahweh as savior, the Angel of Yahweh's Presence as the savior, the Holy Spirit as the indwelling Presence of the LORD, which Spirit can be grieved, and the LORD as Father, whose name is everlasting redeemer.[70] Israel is redeemed and the differentiated authorship of that act is Yahweh, "their savior" (vv. 7, 8), "the Angel of His Presence" who "saved them," and "His Holy Spirit" whom the redeemed had grieved in the past.

A differentiation within the redeeming One is apparent between Yahweh as savior and the Angel of Yahweh's Presence, who saves God's people. In verses seven and eight, the LORD bestows His loving kindness and "He became their savior." But then, in the very next verse, it is "the Angel of His Presence" who saved them. So Yahweh saves, but the agent of His salvation is the Angel of His Presence. The passage then moves in reference to God's Spirit, who is grieved by His people's choices.[71]

I would agree with Knight here, that these verses are not proof texts for the presence of Trinitarian teaching in the Old Testament *per se.*[72] Rather, these verses indicate that Yahweh, the LORD, who is one is also a unity of economic differentiation as Angel, Spirit, and Father. I would also agree that in this text, the Angel seems much more closely aligned with the Spirit rather than the Word or the Son. In this passage, redemption comes to the chosen people by Yahweh, by the Angel of His Presence, and by the Father.

Reflections on the Isaiah Passages. These texts teach a theological *identity with* and *distinction from* with reference to the Holy One. The triadic movement

---

70. See Ephesians 4:26–32.
71. The close relation of the LORD's Spirit and His Presence is also seen in Psalm 139:7, where the poetry puts both in synonymous parallelism: "Where can I go to escape Your Spirit? Where can I flee from Your presence?" Isn't the reader to understand that the Lord's Spirit *is* His presence?
72. Wainwright, *The Trinity in the New Testament,* 32.

of reference recalls the previous reference to the observation of C. K. Barrett about the application of triadic formulae in 1 Corinthians, that "the Trinitarian formula is the more impressive because it seems to be artless and unconscious." Letham quotes R. N. Whybray's commentary here, "God's holy spirit . . . is here personified more clearly than anywhere else in the Old Testament, and is on its way to its later development as a distinct hypostasis in late Jewish and Christian thought."[73] Certainly, this incipient triadic reference in Isaiah 63 also appears "artless and unconscious."

> *The inadvertent application of triadic clusters identified with the* LORD *here in the Servant Songs of Isaiah will be seen again in the form of the triadic matrix found throughout the New Testament. In conclusion, it also seems important to state that these incipient triadic instances occur in precisely the messianic material out of which Jesus chooses to launch and live his public ministry.*

The so-called Suffering Servant songs are deeply embedded into the theology and missiology of Jesus the Nazarene. He learned these truths in the incarnation, perhaps at the knees of Mary, whose *magnificat* incorporates this material too. Thus, it is significant that in Isaiah 63:16, Yahweh is called as Jesus called Him, "You, O LORD, are our Father." Does the informal Trinity-speak of Jesus reflect that found here in Isaiah? The answer is yes and no. Wainwright has said it well, "The idea of extension of personality is Hebraic. The idea of interaction within the extended personality is neither Hebraic nor Hellenistic, it is Christian."[74]

Triad in Ezekiel 37—LORD, Spirit/Breath, Word. The famous vision of Ezekiel's valley of the dry bones was discussed earlier with reference to the theological pattern of indivisibility with distinction in the work of the Word and Spirit of the LORD. Let's briefly return to Ezekiel 37 to see this triadic instance of LORD, Spirit/breath and Word. "The Sovereign LORD" commands Ezekiel to "Prophesy to the bones. Hear the word of Yahweh," and then also

---

73. Letham, *The Holy Trinity,* 27; R. N. Whybray, Isaiah 40–66, *New Century Bible Commentary* (Grand Rapids: Eerdmans, 1975), 258.
74. Wainwright, *The Trinity in the New Testament,* 40.

to appeal to the Wind to "Come from the four winds, O Breath, and breathe into these slain that they might live." To achieve His purposes of restoration and reunification of His people, the LORD works through His Word and His Spirit. Should the reader not then understand that the hope of restoration with the LORD is indivisibly caught up in the united work of the Lord, His Word, and His Spirit?

Triad in Haggai 2:4–5—LORD, Word, Spirit. A similar "unconscious" triadic instance occurs in Haggai. "'For I am with you'—the declaration of the LORD of Hosts. 'This is the promise I made to you when you came out of Egypt, and My Spirit is present among you; don't be afraid.'" The Hebrew literally means the "word I covenanted with you." So, the sense of the text is that Yahweh is with His people as promise maker and keeper, the Word of Yahweh is still with them as the substance of the promise, and His Spirit abides among them too as the fulfillment and presence of His promise.

> *This apparently inadvertent threefold way of differentiating the presence of the unique God, while not common in the Old Testament, is not altogether rare either. It will become a common way of speaking of God in the New Testament.*

CONCLUSION

I have made a case for intimations of plurality in the Godhead revealed in the Old Testament. We explored textual evidence in terms of grammatical oscillations, divine personality extensions, and incipient dyadic and triadic formulae—all showing God as a unity of consciousness rather than a conscious unit.

If the research I have presented here is acceptable, then I must assert that these witnesses to a plurality in unity, if not a triadic understanding of God, constitute a theological mode of thought for Jesus and the writers of the New Testament. The presence of the triadic matrix out of which these writers thought and functioned cannot be convincingly explained away by scholarly assertions of late gospel authorship reading historical Trinitarian conclusions back into the New Testament. The only reasonable explanation has to be that this differentiated monotheistic mindset was the inherent mindset of first-century Jews with additional adjustments through the revelation of Jesus.

DISCUSSION QUESTIONS—CHAPTER 3

- Having read chapter 3, explain how first-century Palestinian monotheists like Paul, Peter, and Jude were able to think in sophisticated Trinitarian ways almost casually and unconsciously?

- The clues about the plurality within the One God in the Old Testament were presented in terms of grammatical oscillations, personality extensions, and the presence of divine dyads and triads in the text. Which of these kinds of evidence did you find to be the most compelling? Explain why.

- H. Richard Niebuhr suggests that Jesus was critical of the monotheism of His day for exalting the Word of God to the exclusion of His Spirit. Niebuhr asserts that such rigid monotheism causes legalism. Why is it important that obedience to the One God must hold the Word and the Spirit in balanced reverence? How does the vision of the valley of dry bones in Ezekiel 37 illustrate this truth?

SERMON STARTER: LIVELY, MESSIANIC MONOTHEISMM

Deep Monotheism: Loving the Deep God and Being Deep People: Deuteronomy 6:4-5

Why "deep" monotheism? There are two reasons. First, many people spend their lives in the shallow end of the pool. They can touch bottom easily there and retain a semblance of control. They fear getting in over their heads. As shallow thinkers, livers, and lovers, they are either *practical polytheists* who change their god and values as often as they change their location, or they are *dysfunctional monotheists*, who as legalists overemphasize rules or as behaviorists make their own spiritual experiences the benchmarks of acceptability. Both are shallow-end theologians. It is in the deep end that we discover the deep God who is one and three. It is in the deep of life and love that we discover personal integrity in the midst of a diversity of friends and circumstances. In the deep end, we experience autonomy in intimacy which is in the image of the Triune God.

Listen up to live up to the One who is like no other.

Life often challenges us to let go and move on to fulfill its promise. Our rehearsal of core vision and values is a vital exercise at the tipping point of letting go of the familiar in order to engage the unknown. For instance, as the ancient Hebrews prepared to enter into their promised land, Moses led them through a refresher course in *Torah,* the law and instruction of the LORD God. We call this fifth book of Moses Deuteronomy, which from its Latin roots literally means the "second giving of the law." This law would be the law of their new land. These rules would be the rules of their new homes and the God of that law would be their God. So the Hebrews must hear and heed His words.

We find in Deuteronomy, the Torah refresher course, Judaism's most famous call to worship—the Shema. This thrice-daily prayer had the following words: "Listen, Israel: The Lord our God, the Lord is One. Love the Lord your God with all your heart, with all your soul, and with all your strength." This prayer takes its name from its first word, Shema, which means "hear" or "listen up." It is in first person plural imperative—the voice of command and exhortation. "Listen up to live up to the promise of the covenant made between God and Abraham, Isaac, and Jacob. Ancient promises are being fulfilled in your lifetime! Pay attention." Attentive worship is ever the engine of promise fulfillment.

Renew your core before entering new ground.

The Hebrews were about to cross borders to settle into new opportunities. But like the Chinese double-sided character for crisis, the Hebrew people were to be living "dangerous opportunities." Their promised land was well marked and marketed on every high hill with alternate competing idols, values, and practices. Many gods makes for fragmented living and moral disintegration. One God makes for integrated living and loving with integrity.

"One band, one sound" was the mantra of the band leader in the 2002 film *Drumline.* The plot was about the capacity of the band to incorporate a talented but autonomous and aggressive new snare drummer into the band. We discover in the plot development that autonomy and unity are not mutually exclusive when intimacy is an active principle. Similarly for the immigrant Hebrews and for we who follow Christ, "one God, one devotion" is to be the "Shema/mantra." We are made in the image of God, so we always are becoming like our passions. Our passion either empowers our integrity or dismantles it into compartmentalized and fragmented lives, values, and relationships. Deuteronomy 6:4–5 gives the wise exercise of renewing core theology and priorities as preparation to entering and settling new domains:

> "Listen, Israel: The LORD our God, the LORD is One. Love the
> LORD your God with all your heart, with all your soul, and
> with all your strength."

In this passage, we see four words that are critical to understanding the promise and plan of this Shema. They are: naming God, locating God, numbering God, and loving God. Let's look at these four words and think through the practical Shema theology that each supplies.

Theology 101: Naming God

The first principle in biblical theology is that the LORD is the living God who calls into relationships and commissions into adventures. The word *LORD*, all in capitals is the way that Bible translators working in English have decided to translate the personal name of the God, who called Moses to lead the Hebrews out of Egypt. You may recall from the Exodus that Moses asked the voice from the burning bush what name was to be used in telling Pharaoh just who had sent Moses to demand Israel's release. "I will be who I will be" or literally "Yahweh is who I am."

The rabbis considered it disrespectful and dangerous to say God's personal name out loud so they always substituted *Adonai* (pronounced a/done/eye)—the Hebrew word for *Lord*—whenever God's personal name occurred in the biblical text. Christian teachers have followed this same practice. So remember, whenever you see Lord all in capitals, you can know that the personal name of God is being used in the original language.

This name, the Lord, reminds the Hebrews and us that He never changes, and that He has plans for us to be in relationship with Him and in service with Him for the nations. This Lord makes and keeps covenants and promises. This Lord lives, loves, and leads into new places and spaces for His glory and our redemption. This God lives and is the High One, 'high' more in the sense of holiness than in transcendent remoteness. This Lord invades and acts to transform our confused stories into His story.

This name, the Lord, reminds Israel that this God is reliable even as we say the same of the name of Jesus, who is reliable yesterday, today, and forever (Hebrews 13:8). And reliability is necessary in a rapidly changing world of diverse peoples and pressures.

Theology 102: Locating God

The ancient world was as transient as ours. Diverse peoples were always interacting, sometimes violently, but usually for reasons of commerce and trade. Good cross-cultural salesmanship requires the gift of polite gab. Theology was an integral part of that conversation. "What god do you serve?" was as common a question as "What's your sign?" is today. The Hebrews were to answer, "The Lord is our God." The word, *God*, in the original is *Elohim*, and it is the usual word that we translate "deity" or "divinity." However, it is in the plural here and as it is usually throughout the Old Testament whenever used in reference to the Lord God of Israel. So, quite literally, biblical theology declares, "The Lord is our Gods." Polytheism, of course, refers to people whose worldview and theology incorporate more than one god.

Did you know that classic polytheism assigns such gods to specific geographies? For instance, when the ancient Assyrian government applied its defeated nations resettlement policy in northern Israel, a plague of lion attacks disrupted the relocation process. Having a polytheistic worldview, the solution for the Assyrian administrators in Nineveh was simple. Step one: Determine what god dwells in northern Canaan. Step two: Locate and dispatch a priest of that deity to teach the resettled peoples how to placate the angry deity. Step three: Have the resettled immigrants offer worship to that deity. Step four: The lion problem is solved (2 Kings 17:24–34).

These importees adopted worship of the LORD, but also blended that worship with worship of "their own gods according to the customs of the nations where they had been deported from" (2 Kings 17:33). This blending of beliefs is the syncretism Jesus rejected as salt that had lost its taste to God by being polluted with pluralisms of convenience and custom. Using God in this way is the lukewarm response that God spews from His mouth (Revelation 3:16). These resettled, insta-Hebrews are known in New Testament times as the Samaritans. It is to them that Jesus will say, "But an hour is coming, and is here now, when the true worshippers will worship the Father in spirit and in truth" (John 4:23).

Beware practical polytheism.

Polytheism literally means belief and adherence to more than one god. We learn practical polytheism as children watching the duplicity of our elders, and we master it as teens. Christian teenagers drift into the dynamic of two sets of friends—church friends and schools friends. These school friends often are their real friends in the sense of when you choose your community, you choose your conscience. Most adolescents can tolerate having two sets of friends and two sets of values, which means they really have two gods. They are for all practical purposes polytheists. Adults are no different, just more subtle. If you are not subtle with your value duplicities, you are just not trying hard enough. In the words of the famous Oakland Raider theologian, John Madden, "If you're not cheating, you're not trying hard enough."

All of this works well until we hear the Shema, "The Lord our God is One, there is no other." You cannot have one and the same God wherever you go and whatever you do, without also needing to be the same person. That's called having integrity.

Daniel would hear the call to oneness and become a functional monotheist even when he and his three buddies were accepted into the Babylonian Academy and later appointed into the Chaldean government administration. This fear-Him-foursome learned that undivided love for the Holy One led them to do exploits for His glory.

In a sea of polytheism and a regional supermarket of deities, Scripture reveals that all authentic divinity is summed up in the LORD. Clearly, the LORD of Moses and Jesus is offended by habits of plural deities and mixed faiths. It's not so much "my way or the highway" but "Yahweh is the high way." Biblical monotheism is the antidote to polytheism and syncretism as social and spiritual practices. Biblical monotheism is monotheism without borders. This is the One God wherever we go and before whomever we bow.

Theology 103: Numbering God

The third key word in Shema-antics is the word "One"—*echad*. "The LORD is *one*." Hebrew has two words for "one." *Yachidh* is used to identify something or someone that is the sole or unique one-of-a-kind. In Genesis 22:2, this word is used to identify Isaac as the only child of Abraham and Sarah, while not negating the reality that Abraham also had a child with Hagar. This word also refers in Psalm 35:17 to the threat of losing your one and only physical life, and in Psalm 25:16 to being solitary and alone without friend or family.

However, the word used for *one* in Deuteronomy 6:4 is the usual word for the number one. So, a literal translation of the passage could be, "Listen up, Israel, the LORD is our gods, and the LORD is one."

This word also includes the idea of unity. For instance, Adam and Eve serve as the Genesis model for marriage as the "two become *one* flesh." So the LORD is one in number and yet in this oneness, He is more a unity than a unit. In the film *About a Boy*, Hugh Grant's character conceives of his life as an island to which he invites occasional, temporary guests. He sees himself and his time as isolated units. He learns from a lonely, socially inept boy that life as a unit is not good: "You have to have backup." Goodness in life is the capacity to find and nurture unity, not unitariness. Dwelling as a unity is good and fosters integrity.

Biblical monotheism begets unity and is at the core of biblical theology.

Monotheism matters because it is the hardest challenge in the world to maintain personal and corporate integrity. God's oneness is the foundation for our wholeness. His oneness corrects our double-mindedness. How can you be one, if your God isn't? If your god has two faces, why can't you? Biblical monotheism begets unity in the midst of fragmentation, subordination, and compartmentalization. "Listen up, Israel, there is none but the One God." Biblical monotheism refuses to play to the audience of circumstances or peers.

Biblical monotheists play to an audience of One. Relationship with this One is better than any resume. Keeping faith and covenant with this One God is difficult but worth it. In His oneness lies the hope of our one individually and as a believing community. Our integrity depends on His. Personal, professional, and corporate crises all weigh in to hammer at our wholeness.

But the One God, faithfully heard, heals our fragmented souls and calls us to reconciliation and restoration. Fragmentation occurs whenever one part of us is not on speaking terms with another part of us. It is impossible to be the same person if we have multiple deity disorder. Revolving gods means resolving selves, like the mother in the book *The Kitchen God's Wife* who complains that her daughter thinks she does not have to keep her promises if something she thinks is more important comes along.

Psalm 15 clarifies the "tent rules" of the "no God but One." Whoever keeps promises, even to the little people, is welcome under the flap to sit at His fire. Integrity means reliable character, no matter time or place. False or rigid monotheism is practiced whenever we try to fragment or subordinate God.

The New Testament Shema. In Acts 4:20, we find Peter standing before an investigative authority of Temple leaders, a recently and quite publicly healed paralytic with him. Peter is being asked, "By what power or in what name have you done this?" (Acts 4:7). Then Peter is filled with the Holy Spirit and boldly reframes the Deuteronomy 6:4 Shema. He declares in their hearing: "by the name of Jesus Christ of Nazareth. . . . There is salvation in no one else, for there is no other name given under heaven by which we must be saved" (Acts 4:10, 12). Exclusivist claims are not the issue here, since Hebrew ears are trained in the exclusive allegiance of monotheism. Peter's bold reformation of the Shema after Jesus, whose name literally means the LORD's salvation, is made all the more compelling with witness of a lifelong paralytic now walking and leaping and praising God by his side.

Certainly, monotheism embraces mystery where God is concerned. Biblical monotheism commits itself to worship the one LORD as He reveals Himself. For instance, the gospel of Matthew restates Christian monotheism in terms of the discipleship mandate to baptize followers in the one Name and then gives three Persons: Father, Son, and Spirit. And the apostle Paul states the New Testament Shema in 1 Corinthians 8:6: "yet for us there is one God, the Father, from whom are all things, and we are for Him; and one Lord, Jesus Christ, through whom are all things, and we through Him."

The Old Testament Shema is promise; the New Testament Shema is fulfillment. The first Shema contains the promise of biblical monotheism in anticipation of the coming of the Messiah. The second Shema renews the first in light of the fulfillment of those promises and prophecies at the cross and resurrection of the Son and the empowerment of the Spirit at Pentecost fifty days later.

Theology 104: Loving God

Shamans are experts at placating and manipulating spirits to conform to human wills. Shema-ans are apprentices at offering their own wills and ways to God in faithfulness.

T. C. Vriezen described the existential impact of Deuteronomy 6:4 in this way: "Because Yahweh is one (we might also say 'single'), the demand follows that Yahweh must be loved with all one's heart. . . . The oneness of God's being demands the heart."[75] The last half of Deuteronomy 6:4 defines the appropriate application to biblical monotheism as unlimited devotion. "Love the LORD your God with all your heart, with all your soul, and with all your strength." The Lord is to be loved voluntarily, intellectually—no checking and leaving your brains at the church door—passionately, and with our talents and time. The return on such investment is suffering service, spiritual resistance, and downward career mobility. However, the return on such investment is also walking with God in the fulfillment of His promises, getting out of hell and getting the hell out of you, and getting into heaven and getting heaven into you.

---

75. As quoted in Anthony C. Thiselton, *The Hermeneutics of Doctrine* (Grand Rapids: Eerdmans, 2007), 461.

CHAPTER 4

The Historical Question: The Karma of Dogma—The Trinity in Tradition

We called what we were doing a "Trinitarian revival"; future historians might want to ask us why.

—Stephen R. Holmes[1]

What is true is that from the third century onwards the distinctive idea of God began to fit itself into a Trinitarian mould.

—John Baillie[2]

T o be human is to name things. Since the first naming in Genesis 2 by Adam, humanity has been both the victor and the victim of our vocabulary. Dogma has to do with the search for the best vocabulary to speak of God and the things of God.

Jaroslav Pelikan was right about the development of Christian dogma. We do think theologically more than we speak, and speak more than we

---

1. Stephen R. Holmes, *The Holy Trinity: Understanding God's Life* (Crown Hill, UK: Paternoster, 2012), 200. This is the last sentence in this book.

2. John Baillie, *The Place of Jesus Christ in Modern Theology* (1929), 185, as quoted in Claude Welch, *In This Name: The Doctrine of the Trinity in Contemporary Theology* (New York: Charles Scribner's Sons, 1952), 48.

believe as our official credo.[3] While ***dogma*** has to do with the historical victories of the orthodox expression of the faith, ***karma***, *as used here,* has to do with being a victim of orthodox theology and vocabulary. Dogmatic theology enlightens and limits. Thank God for the Reformation recovery of *sola scriptura!* Scripture again is the norm for faith and practice; else dogma is idolized without recourse to scriptural evaluation. The point of this book is to bring scriptural evaluation in the form of the diverse triadic orders into the center of the current Trinitarian conversation. The point of this chapter is to gather the key words developed by the church over time to interpret the Trinity as God's self-disclosure.

THE METHOD OF THIS CHAPTER

We have identified the six orders of the three persons of the Trinity that make up the Trinitarian matrix of consciousness in the New Testament (chapter 2) and examined the antecedent way of thinking of the One God with inner differentiation in the Old Testament (chapter 3). Now we are ready to look at how this witness of the New Testament writers affected church history: *What effect, if any, did the seventy-plus triadic witnesses of the New Testament have on the developing Trinitarian dogma of the church?*

William Placher recently pondered about dogmatic Trinitarianism in these words: "The Trinity, so they declared, involves one substance, two emanations, three personal properties, four relations, and five notions—and is an absolute mystery. If the mystery is so absolute, I wondered, where did we get all those numbers?"[4] Naming and numbering in church history is part of our humanity; it is part of what Pelikan observed of our thinking and speaking.

And to be silent is to be less than faithful. Many third- and fourth-century Latin theologians speak of the Trinity using concepts like *essentia* ("essence"), *substantia* ("substance"), and *persona* ("persons")—which, according to Augustine, were not quite accurate, but they used them "in order to not be silenced."[5] Silenced by whom and why?

---

3. Jaroslav Pelikan, *Credo: Historical and Theological Guide to Creeds and Confessions of Faith in Christian Tradition* (New Haven, CT: Yale University Press, 2003), 359–364.

4. William Placher, *The Triune God: An Essay in Postliberal Theology* (Louisville: John Knox Press, 2007), 119.

5. Augustine, *On the Holy Trinity*, Nicene and Post-Nicene Fathers, First Series, Part 3 (Peabody, MA: Hendrickson Publishers, 1994), 5.2.6,10.

Two Siren Songs of Syncretism

Trinity can be tough and difficult thinking. If you want three, why not just go ahead and have three gods? Polytheism, even a modest tritheism, has had a place in world religion in the past and in the present. Of course, the moment Christianity affirms three gods, it has jettisoned any continuity with its Jewish roots and the Hebrew Shema, "Hear, O Israel, the Lord our God is one" (Deuteronomy 6:4). However, disaffection with the illogical idea that one is three and three is one has prompted repeated tritheism dogmas. These limited polytheisms were often disguised as subordinationism in order to preserve rigid, mathematical monotheism. (In other words, they made the Son and the Spirit somehow less than God the Father.) "One is one, and not three" is that reasoning. This is what Arius did and what the Watchtower Society of the Jehovah's Witnesses does. Here Islam agrees with Judaism: One is one and never three.

If polytheism disguised as subordinationism is the Charybdis that endangers the ship of faith on the one side, what is the Scylla that threatens it on the other side? Modalism or unitarianism makes the siren claim that we can have our Father, Son, and Holy Spirit and still be rigidly monotheistic. All we have to say is (1) that the Father is God, the Son is God, and the Spirit is God—and (2) that the Father is the Son is the Spirit. God is one but has three different hats to wear from time to time.

Frankly, the Trinity is so tough that most orthodox Christians live like practical unitarians anyway. Where's my evidence for this charge of common heresy? Look at our congregational prayers and preaching. If you go to a liturgical, high church service, it is the Father this and the Father that. If it is Baptist-like worship, it's "Jesus, Jesus, Jesus." And of course, to hear about the Spirit, you need go to a Pentecostal church. It is safer for pastors to be modalistic within their tradition than to be subordinationist and/or polytheistic. The only way they know to be publicly Trinitarian is at baptism and in benedictions, because they are hard-pressed to preach (much less teach) the practical significance of being functionally Trinitarian.

If Trinitarianism Is So Conceptually Difficult, Why Does It Survive?

But why has Christian history been so relentlessly Trinitarian? Stephen Holmes comments that, "In the immediate sub-apostolic period, virtually every witness we have to the Christian devotional and confessional practice suggests that a threefold naming of God was so normal as to be reflexively assumed."[6] If the

---

6. Holmes, *The Holy Trinity,* 56.

Trinity is so tough intellectually, why doesn't it just fade away? Why did the pastors and thinkers at the ecumenical councils at Nicaea and Chalcedon in the fourth and fifth centuries declare that Christianity must be Trinitarian or it is not Christian? Why did the Reformation leaders in the sixteenth century discard centuries of sacramental theology but keep the doctrine of the Trinity as critical to Protestant faith? Why have so many authors of late sounded a call to return to boisterous affirmation of the Three in One?

The answer is not simply the deep orthodox rut of the Chalcedonian creed of three persons in one substance and tradition for tradition's sake. Trinity existed before the words for it were coined: the Greek *trias* of Athenagoras (170 CE) or the famous Latin *trinitas* of Tertullian (200 CE). The naming of the Trinity as "Trinity" did not make the Trinity precious to the way Christians worshipped. *Lex orandi, lex credendi* means that the belief depends upon prayer and worship. Christians were praying and singing Trinity even before concepts like "economic Trinity" and "immanent Trinity" were invented. The New Testament phenomenon of repeatedly, creatively, but ever consistently naming the God of the gospel as three working together as the One God was how Christians learned to pray, praise, and preach. The need to be Trinitarian is created by the need to be biblical. If revelation is God disclosing of Himself what otherwise is unknowable, and if God is to be worshipped and served as He reveals Himself, then the Scripture keeps compelling the faithful to worship and live as Trinitarians.

DEVELOPING A HISTORICAL GLOSSARY OF THE TRINITY

The history of the development of the doctrine of the Trinity is two thousand years long, and many scholars have devoted volumes to that history. We have one chapter devoted to it, because that is what fits the purpose of this book. However, the key words and concepts of Trinitarian dogma, carefully winnowed from church history, are an important tool for processing the Trinitarian matrix of the New Testament. That matrix is a part of the biblical norm for evaluating the authority such dogmatic expressions should have in our churches and our lives. So, I have chosen to construct a historical glossary of the doctrine's development using three current works on the Trinity as a template.

Three Paradigms on the Historical Development of Trinitarian Dogma

Without stirring up a lengthy discussion about dogmatic historiography, I suggest that there are three prevailing paradigms relative to the history of the development of the doctrine of the Trinity in Christian history: evolution, invention, and revelation. I have selected three contemporary historical theologians for their insights on the development of Trinitarian dogma.

From the **Evangelical (revelation)** perspective, I will be using the Baptist scholar at St. Andrews University, Stephen Holmes, and his readable and credible *The Holy Trinity: Understanding God's Life* (2012), already cited above. From the **Roman Catholic (revelation)** perspective, I will use the carefully researched *The Living and True God: The Mystery of the Trinity* (2010) by the Spanish Archbishop Luis F. Ladaria. And from the more **liberal (evolutionary and invention)** perspective, I will use Marian Hillar's *From Logos to Trinity: The Evolution of Religious Beliefs from Pythagoras to Tertullian* (2012).[7] Let me introduce these authors in reverse order.

Liberal Marian Hillar. Marian Hillar is an international expert on the famous anti-Trinitarian Michael Servetus, who was burned at the stake under John Calvin's watch in Geneva in the sixteenth century. Hillar has much invested in Trinitarian doctrine and its history. He is a theological advocate of the evolutionary theory, and uses the word *evolution* unapologetically in his subtitle.

His theological approach takes its cues from the optimistic Darwinian proposal of gradual survival of the fittest over time, as applied to concepts of dogma. Darwinian evolution presupposes that evolving life will, over time, develop new species. And Hillar wants to make a case for Tertullian being the inventor of a new species, *trinitas*, Trinity, in Christian thinking.[8] Hillar constructs an evolutionary theory of the development of the Trinity from Greek Middle Platonic writings, from the Hebrew tradition of divine plurality, and from Egyptian metaphysical writings and monuments which abound with dyadic, triadic, and tetradic symbols.[9]

Roman Catholic Luis Ladaria. Ladaria takes the expected optimistic view of historical development of doctrine within Christian tradition, most particularly Roman Catholic Church tradition. He carefully reviews and explains Trinitarian developments and heresy with reference to the orthodox

---

7. Luis F. Ladaria, *The Living and True God: The Mystery of the Trinity* (Miami: Convivium Press, 2010, original published in Spanish in 1998); Marian Hillar, *From Logos to Trinity: The Evolution of Religious Beliefs from Pythagoras to Tertullian* (New York: Cambridge University Press, 2012).

8. Hillar calls this Trinitarian conceptualization by Tertullian at the turn of the third century an "innovation," (Hillar, *From Logos to Trinity*, 243).

9. Note the detailed explanation of these possible sources for "Development of the Christian Trinitarian Concepts" in Appendix I (Hillar, *From Logos to Trinity*, 273–305).

affirmations of the church over time. Since most of the key theologians in the West, from the ecumenical councils beginning in the fourth century to the Reformation, were necessarily Roman Catholic (excluding the Orthodox in the East), Ladaria provides a helpful edge to my proposed template.

Evangelical Stephen Holmes. Finally, like any faithful evangelical historian, Stephen Holmes is rather skeptical toward any Trinitarian developments in church history that do not conform to the New Testament and the time-tested fifth-century Chalcedonian creed on the Godhead. Whereas many are thrilled with the revival of Trinitarian thought in the past seventy years, Holmes is not. He is thoughtfully more cautious and tends to see much of this recent constructive theology, beginning with Barth's renaming of the Trinity as revealer, revelation, and revealedness, as revisionism and as "deviation from the received ecumenical doctrine."[10]

Conclusion: Big Words for Big Concepts

When you enter the Martin Luther King, Jr. Peace Memorial in Atlanta, Georgia, very soon you see an enlarged photograph of young Martin with his mother. The caption shares that Martin, having just lost a debate with his older siblings, then declared to his mother, "Someday I am going to get me some big words."

When it comes to the Trinity, we need some good words—for the good faith. I've written this chapter to show the historical development of those big words and phrases Christians have used to understand, explain, and worship the Triune God revealed by Christ and the Gospels. And these three historical theologians will be our Trinitarian etymologists in that discovery process. We will follow the vocabulary trail as it has unfolded in three periods of church history:

- the post-apostolic period
- the era of church councils
- the medieval to modern period

1. POST-APOSTOLIC PERIOD AND THE NAMING OF GOD

Trinity: *Trias* and *Trinitas* (181–200 CE). Theophilus, patriarch of the church at Antioch, first used the word "trinity" (*trias* in Greek) about 181 CE in

---

10. Holmes, 28; see also his assessment on Barth, 5–9.

his defense of Christianity to Autolycum.[11] His use of *trinity* referred to Three Persons in One substance which will come two centuries later, but put it more simply as God, the Word, and His Wisdom (the Spirit). He writes: "The three days that precede the creation of the heavenly bodies are a symbol of the Trinity [*trias*], of God, of his Word, and of his Wisdom."

A little over a decade later, Tertullian—the North African attorney turned theologian—begins to pair the oneness (Latin, *unitas*) of God and His Threeness (*trinitas*). He speaks of the Mystery of God

> which distributes the Unity into a Trinity, placing in their order the three persons—the Father, the Son, and the Holy Spirit: three, however, not in condition, but in degree; not in substance, but in form; not in power, but in aspect; yet of one substance, and of one condition, and of one power, inasmuch as He is one God, from whom these degrees in forms and aspects are reckoned, under the name of the Father, and of the Son, and of the Holy Spirit.[12]

About this theological achievement, Ladaria writes that "together with the concept of unitas and in contraposition to it, we have the trinitas, a fundamental term destined to have great success in the history of theology, the Latin equivalent of the Greek trias, . . . The divinity of the one God must be understood in this 'economy.'"[13] Hillar here is so bold as to name Tertullian as the "Originator of the Trinity," and then proceeds to argue that Tertullian constructs his doctrine as a "profoundly Stoic philosopher . . . from the analysis of four general Stoic logical categories."[14] Note also that Tertullian introduces the concepts of person (*persona* in Latin) and substance (*substantia*) into his theological defense of the faith against the charges of Praxeas.

Three Persons and One Substance (200). In developing a Trinitarian witness, Tertullian assumes a *semi-subordinationist* perspective of the three persons in the Godhead. By semi-subordinationist, Tertullian means the three working as one within a hierarchy of Father, Son, and Spirit, yet without any dispersion

---

11. Theophilus, *Apologia Ad Autolycum*, 2.15.
12. Tertullian, *Against Praxeas*, 2.4 146; see also Holmes, 69–70.
13. Ladaria, *The Living and True God*, 182, citing *Against Praxeas*, 3.1; 11.4; 12.1; 146; 168; 170.
14. Hillar, *From Logos to Trinity*, 217, 246.

on the divinity of the Son and Spirit in rank. Ladaria quotes Tertullian on this point, "God suffers no dispersion due to the fact that the Son and the Holy Spirit hold the second and the third place, participants in (*consortes* [italics in the original to convey the Latin word]) the substance of the Father."[15]

We should be aware that there is an old and influential movement of scholars who contend that Trinitarian doctrine is a philosophical/dogmatic invention well after the apostles and the New Testament. Hillar is an emerging new scholar in that stream and very much wants to convince us as to how Greek philosophy rather than biblical exegesis is the leading edge for the Trinitarian thoughts of Justin and Tertullian.

Ladaria, on the other hand, notes that at this point for Tertullian, the divine three are "united but not identified in all aspects, are frequently called '*personae*' . . . another term that will play a great role in Trinitarian theology and in Christology."[16] "Persons" here means distinct identity within united substance. And that brings us to the concept of *coinherence*.

Coinherence (200). Tertullian invokes the word *coinherence* to describe how the three can be united in substance, but nevertheless be distinct. (*Against Praxeas* 12.7). Coinherence is the first Trinitarian expression in a cluster of words like *perichoresis, circumincession* (sometimes spelled *circuminsession*), and *interpenetration* that define the unity of the three in their operations. (More on these other three terms later.) This terminology cluster maintains Triune distinction without confusion or division.

Ladaria notes Tertullian's application of natural analogies to explain what he means by coinherence. He uses an analogy of sun as source, ray as second, and the apex of the ray as the third. Tertullian also applies the analogy of trees and fruit. He is at pains to show that "nothing, however, is alien from that original source from whence it services its own properties. In like manner the Trinity, flowing down from the Father through intertwined and connected steps, does not at all disturb the Monarchy, whilst it at the same guards the state of the Economy."[17] Ladaria interprets Tertullian here as using *trinitas* for the unity of the three and words like *species, form, status,* and *grade* to define the distinction between the persons.[18]

---

15. Ibid., see *Against Praxeas*, 3.5.
16. Ibid., see *Against Praxeas*, 7.9;11.4; 27.11; 31.2.
17. Ibid., see *Against Praxeas*, 8:5–7.
18. Ibid., 183–184.

Holmes recognizes that the church also borrows Tertullian's vocabulary about the person and divinity of the Holy Spirit in *Against Praxeas*.[19] In this context, Holmes suggests that there was significant backstory to the recognition of the Three as One since "triadic doxologies, a triadic baptismal formula, and a triadic rule of faith were already in existence."[20] I would suggest that these triadic liturgical elements arose from the abundance of such triads in the New Testament.

Monarchy and Economy (pre-200). *Monarchy* and *economy* were used in reference to the Trinity well before Tertullian. Monarchy expresses the concern in Scripture, prayer, and worship that the Father is uniquely the source of the Son and the Spirit and the source of the sending. The developing language of worship in the patristic period has a distinct preference for the monarchy of the Father coupled with a description of the Godhead household, the economy, that is hierarchically decribed as first, second and third, to the degree that will threaten the unity of Trinity later in church history. Hillar assumes this "household" understanding of economy to be lifted from Stoic philosophy.[21] With reference to the divine economy, the Godhead was the household of God of which the Father was the head. In the twentieth century, economy will be used to describe the external procession of the Father-Son-Spirit in creation and redemption. The economic Trinity will become the way of talking about the external movements of God. The immanent Trinity will connote the inner relations of the Three within the Godhead.

Eternal Generation of the Logos/Son (200). The New Testament canon has twenty-seven books, with the Old Testament there is a total of sixty-three. But none of this was conclusively determined until the famous festal letter of Bishop Athanasius of Alexandria in 367. For two hundred years prior, the early church had been debating the books of the Bible and the God of the Bible. Beginning in July of 144, Marcion of Sinope began a movement in Rome to drive a wedge between the God of the Old Testament and the God of the New, between the authority of the Jewish books of the Old Testament and the Jewish influenced works in the New. Marcion preferred Paul and hyper-emphasized Paul's concept of grace versus the Law. He saw all that related to the old covenant,

---

19. Holmes, *The Holy Trinity*, 73.
20. Ibid.
21. Hillar, *From Logos to Trinity*, 215.

including its angry God, as passé and taught that Christians now embrace the gracious God and Father of Jesus Christ. This movement had growing influence when Irenaeus became bishop of Lyon (Gaul then, France now) at the end of the second century. Out of necessity for gospel and church, Irenaeus became an apologist and polemicist against Marcion.

For Irenaeus, the unity of the Godhead and the continuity of the Testaments was essential. He correlated both with the eternal relationship of the Father and the Logos/Son. Taking its cue from John 1:1, "in the beginning was the Word," this kind of *logos* Christology emerged in the patristic period to express the cooperation of the Father and Son and to show the import of the Logos in the Incarnation, Crucifixion, and Resurrection for human salvation and creation restoration.

Ladaria notes the moderation that Irenaeus uses in discussing the generation of the Logos from the Father. Holmes finds this same moderation in the confidence of Justin Martyr (100–165) "that 'generation' is the right language to describe the Father's relationship to the Logos." Though Justin's philosophical background highlights the word "emanation" and "more strikingly—his biblical sources offer 'creation'. . . he [Justin] appears to avoid both terms intentionally."[22] To use *emanation* would have constructed a syncretistic bridge away from the Christian originality, and to use *creation* in this context would have been Greek syncretism offered up as kosher.[23] In other words, it would have been the Atticizing of Moses or the Judaizing of Plato. [24]

Hillar marshals an interesting case for the influence of the late second-century Neoplatonist Numenius, but if that were true, why would Justin have hesitated to use Numenius' word *emanation*? Ladaria also notes that Irenaeus states that this generation is "from all time," "always" "in the sense to say at least since time began . . . the Son has coexisted with the Father."[25]

For our purposes here, it is sufficient to note that to maintain unity and distinction in the One God, the language of generation is used to move toward affirmation of the source monarchy of the Father. It is the Father who generates

---

22. Holmes, *The Holy Trinity,* 61.
23. Hillar attempts a strong case for coherence between the "Metaphysical Triad" of Justin and the "Trinity" of First God or Mind, Second God or Mind, and the Third God (Creation) of Numenius; and includes a three-page chart comparing the thought of both (*From Logos to Trinity,* 170, 183–186).
24. Hillar, *From Logos to Trinity,* 183.
25. Ladaria, *The Living and True God,* 176, compare with Irenaeus in *Against Heresies,* II 11, 28; IV 20.3.

the Logos/Son, and this generation elevates the Son above creation in time and substance. Along this line, Holmes notes that Irenaeus teaches an economic Trinity whereby "the Father works in the world through his 'two hands,' the Son and the Spirit."[26] The Son of course is generated—begotten—and not created by the Father. At this point, to speak of eternal generation is somewhat anachronistic unless eternal is taken to mean before time and creation.

Incidentally, Ladaria also notes that Irenaeus was an early patristic witness to the diverse Trinitarian orders used in texts of what will become the New Testament canon. He writes, "Many texts [cited by Irenaeus] show the Trinitarian structure of salvation with formulations that frequently start with the Holy Spirit who leads man to the Son, who in turn gives him access to the Father."[27] So the triadic order of Spirit-Son-Father was in the patristic literature by the beginning of the third century.

***Homoousia, Hypostases,* Subordination, Procession, and *Autotheos*—Origen (184–254).** As often acknowledged, Origen of Alexandria was the origin of all thoughts orthodox and heterodox.[28] Thomas Merton's poem, "Origen," speaks of his sin as being the first among the mutes to speak and as a lighthouse "emitting incessant pulses of illumination" as navigation points for the entire West.[29] And upon the subject of the Three in One, Origen had much to say, much of which represents the development of technical theological language related to the Trinity.

In his overall perspective, Origen emphasizes the Father and how the divine life integrates around Him. For instance, he focuses on the eternality of the Father to argue for the eternality of the Son: "God does not change, and so the Father could not become the Father by begetting the Son; the Father must be eternally Father, and so the Son must eternally be."[30] So, to be begotten or generated does not mean there was a time when the Son was not, according to this exegesis from Origen.

G. L. Prestige comments on the theological indiscretions of this third-century Alexandrian leader with reference to Trinitarian thought.[31] Specifically, Prestige

26. Holmes, *The Holy Trinity,* 65.
27. Ibid., 175; compare *Adverse Heresies,* IV 20.5.
28. Prestige calls Origen "the father alike of Arian heresy and of Nicene orthodoxy," George Leonard Prestige, *God in Patristic Thought* (London: SPCK, 1952) 131.
29. Thomas Merton, "Origen," *The Westminster Handbook to Origen,* ed. John Anthony McGuckin (Lousiville: Westminster John Knox Press, 2004), i-x.
30. Holmes, *The Holy Trinity,* 76.
31. Prestige, *God in Patristic Thought,* 136–137.

notes that Origen fails to discriminate between the Son as *geneton* ("created") and *genneton* ("begotten" or "generated"), as if the two were synonymous. The Arians would commit the same theological indiscretion in arguing a century later for the Son as a created God. Their motive was to preserve their sense of the Father's monarchy at the expense of the Son's full deity.

Origen did hold to a consubstantiality (of same substance, *homoousia*) of goodness and will within the Trinity. But he also teaches a subordinate taxonomy of function, with the domain of the Son being less than that of the Father, and the domain of the Spirit less still than that of the Son. (More on that shortly.)

So, Origen ultimately is anti-homoousian, due to the ambiguity of the term in his mind; the Three Persons are not fully of the same essence. He applied the philosophical concept of *hypostasis* to communicate the sense of "actual existence of a concrete being" and held *hypostasis*, according to Christoph Markschies, to be a near synonym with *ousia* or essence. Markschies concludes that just where Origen was indiscriminate—namely *geneto* and *genneto* and *ousia* and *hypostasia*—Nicaea became discriminate and "no doubt this cost Origen a great deal in terms of reputation for orthodoxy."[32]

At this point in the patristic period, the theological issue was how to explain the divine life as Trinity. Origen attempts to do so by affirming the three distinct identities, *hypostases*, in the monarchy (one head, none like Him) as distinctions without divisions and without subordination. Origen does use the concept of a taxonomy or economy of subordinate functions. At first blush, he emphasizes the transcendence of the Father; only the unbegotten Father is transcendent over all. In the beginning, everything is derived from Him, for He is also greater than the Son and the Holy Spirit. They are transcendent with respect to other beings, but they are exceeded by the Father.

Origen also introduces the technical understanding of procession with reference to Trinitarianism, with procession being understood as the economic mission of the Son in the incarnation and atonement and as the mission of the Holy Spirit at Pentecost.[33] And Origen discusses the Trinity with his eye on the prize of understanding and communicating salvation. "[I]t is the salvific concern, more than the concern for the life of the Trinity in itself, which characterizes Origen's approach," asserts Ladaria.[34]

---

32. Christoph Markschies, "Trinitarianism," in *The Westminster Handbook to Origen*, 209.
33. Ibid., 208; see Origen, *The Fifth Theological Oration*, (Oration 31), where Gregory incorporates some of Origen.
34. Ibid.

However, the combination of these concepts creates problems. Ladaria notes that in one "extraordinary passage," Origen compares the distance that separates the Son and the Holy Spirit from the Father with the distance that separates all creatures from the Son and Father. For Origen, the Father "is the God, *autotheos*."[35] Ladaria quotes Origen from the *Principles,* "only if he is God in himself can he deify [think eternal generation and salvation as partaking of the divine nature as in 2 Peter 1:4, *Principles* 12.2–3]."[36] Origen affirms the three hypostases, the Father, the Son, and the Holy Spirit, believing that none of them, except for the Father, is unbegotten. Ladaria discerns in Origen's thinking a "growing subordination," a "descending" line of the Three.[37] Holmes sees Origen as "happily and regularly" speaking of the Three sharing the same essence, *ousia.* Holmes unhappily notes "the spectre of Origen's famous subordinationism." He admits that Origen paints himself and the Son into the ontological space between the perfect being of the Father and all creatures below, but then argues that Origen "fairly regularly takes biblical images of the agents of God's rule and applies them to the Son and the Spirit."[38] Resolving this scholarly dissonance is interesting, but outside our present vocabulary task, thankfully.

Modalistic Monarchianism and Patripassionism. Hippolytus of Rome (170–235) was a disciple of Irenaeus. He became estranged from the popes of his period when they moved to lessen the penitential system to accommodate the flood of new pagan converts. He was later martyred under Emperor Serverus (reigned 222–235).[39] Hippolytus is traditionally identified as the writer of *Against All Heresies* and *Against the Heresies of Noetus.* He charges the latter with teaching modalistic Monarchianism, which view is usually identified with Sabellius (early third century) and Callistus.

Modalistic monarchists insist on the absolute monarchy (sole rule, *autotheos*) as the normative doctrine. Although the Father and Son (few eyes were on the Spirit at this point) share in the divine monarchy, there is no real ontological difference between the two. The distinction is in mode of manifestation or presentation. Holmes categorizes this teaching as "an aggressive reassertion of

---

35. Ladaria, *The Living and True God,* 192; see Origen, *John XIII.25.*
36. Ibid., 197.
37. Ibid., 198; see Origen, *John II.10.*
38. Holmes, *The Holy Trinity,* 78.
39. See Holmes, *The Holy Trinity,* 235.

monotheism in the face of the tendency in the Logos theology to speak of two divine persons."[40]

Tertullian coined the word *Patripassionism* and famously ascribed it to the theology of modalistic Monarchianism with these words: "Having driven out the paraclete, he now crucified the Father."[41] The core of the accusation was that if one held to modalistic Monarchianism wherein the Father, Son, and Spirit have no real distinction between them, who then other than the Father was really crucified?

Dynamic Monarchianism. Paul of Samosata (200–275) was bishop of Antioch from 260–268. He had difficulty reconciling Trinitarian worship with a theological commitment to divine monarchy.[42] He appears to affirm the divine monarchy of the Father by diminishing the status of Son and Spirit, and by proposing Jesus of Nazareth as eventually being adopted and exalted into divine fellowship. So, the sole monarchy is preserved by proposing a dynamic of adoption in time of Jesus into Sonship.

We need to note here that both forms of Monarchianism—modalistic and dynamic—keep manifesting in later centuries like an endemic doctrinal plague, at least from the orthodox perspective. For instance, dynamic modalism reappears in the Reformation period in the teachings of Faustus Sozzini (1539–1604, also known as Socinus). His doctrinal assertion that "if God is one in essence, he must be one in person" is preserved in the Racovian Catechism of the Polish Brethren.[43]

Arianism, "The Son Begins to Exist," Subordination, "One God, Alone Unmade," Apophatic Theology. Arius, who was born about 256 in Libya and died in 356 in Constantinople, was an anti-Trinitarian presbyter in the church at Alexandria. His most famous work was entitled, *Thalia,* which Holmes indicates was virtually unknown except as quoted by Athanasius.[44] Arius defines his doctrine in a letter to Bishop Alexander of Alexandria:

> We confess One God, alone unmade, alone eternal, alone un-originate, alone true, alone processing immortality. . . . We be-

---

40. Ibid., 269.
41. Tertullian, *Against Praxeas*, X.
42. Ibid., 80.
43. Holmes, *The Holy Trinity,* 170.
44. Ibid., 84.

lieve that this God gave birth to the Only-begotten before all worlds, through Whom He made the world and all things. . . . God's perfect creature not as His other creatures . . . the Son, put forth by the Father outside of time . . . did not exist before He was born. . . . He is neither eternal, nor co-eternal, nor un-create with the Father. . . .[45]

With Arius, the subordination of the Son to the Father includes essential (substance) and functional subordination. This subordination is a hierarchy of being and doing asserted to preserve the monarchy of the Father as the One God. I will contend in the final chapter that, if salvation is dependent on this subordination in the being of the Son, then are we not created and redeemed in the image of such subordinationist theology? If subordination in being is who God is, then will we not create social structures of subordination of being and function? Isn't that the foundation of racism and gender-ism? Without meaning to be rhetorically adversarial, the leap from Arianism to Aryanism is not difficult. I am not speaking here about subordination in function, in economic mission, which is the teaching of the New Testament. My concern is with subordination of being in the Godhead, which was exactly the point of Arius.

For Ladaria, Arianism meant the loss of the originality of Christianity in order to find cultural acceptance in its prevailing philosophy of Middle Platonism. This neo-Platonism thrived on hierarchies of Urge, Demiurge, and matter produced by the Demiurge.[46] I would also note here that as an Eastern thinker, Arius values apophatic theology, which ever emphasizes the ineffability and unknowability of the true God. Holmes finds this emphasis as distinctively Arius' concern and not that of his supporters in the debate.[47] Since God is mystery, we should keep a careful watch for over-speaking about what we really can know about Him. Mystery cannot be mastered, but He can be worshipped. Apophatic theology belongs in our doctrinal toolbox.

---

45. Text from Hilary of Poitiers, *Trinity,* IV:12–13; VI:5–6 as quoted in Ladaria, *The Living and True God,* 212. Incidentally, in this section of his book, Ladaria does a fine job of analyzing the texts and hermeneutics that Arius used to develop and argue for his position.
46. Ladaria, *The Living and True God,* 214.
47. Holmes, *The Holy Trinity,* 87.

2. THE ERA OF CHURCH COUNCILS AND CONCILIAR DOCTRINAL ACHIEVEMENTS

Nicene Creed: One Substance (325). At the prompting of Emperor Constantine, 318 bishops (the traditional tally, with only five from Western churches) convened May–June 325 in Nicaea, a popular suburb of imperial Constantinople. The agenda of this first ecumenical council in church history was to issue a creedal statement on the Godhead. Hosius of Cordoba, the theological advisor to the emperor, served as president. Over those two months, hearing from all sides and parties, the council hammered out the Nicene Creed. This statement of Trinitarian orthodoxy ruled that

- the Son of God, the only-begotten of the Father was of one substance with the Father.

- the Son was God of God, Light of Light, very God of very God, begotten not made.

- all who declared that there was a time when the Son of God was not or who declared that before he was begotten he was not, or that he was made of a different substance, these the Apostolic Church anathematizes.[48]

The declaration of consubstantiality between the Father and the Son is the normative and formative contribution of the Creed. But Trinitarian theology was on shaky ground for two reasons. First, because the Greek word for essence, *ousia*, is ambiguous and can be taken to affirm modalism, namely that the Father and the Son are consubstantial because they are the same thing and thus the distinction of the Three is compromised. Or, second, *ousia* can be taken to mean the essence of the distinction, and then the oneness is compromised.

These ideas were no doubt among those things that the Arians who came after Arius whispered into the emperor's ears and thereby saw Arianism reinstated and creedal orthodoxy refuted at the "Blasphemy" of the Third Council of Sirmium (357). Under the Arian-leaning Constantius II, this latter council denied both same and like substance (*homoousia* and *homoiousia*) between the Father and the Son, and declared that the Father was ontologically greater than

---

48. Ladaria, *The Living and True God*, 222.

the Son.[49] Into this fray, Athanasius, Hilary of Poitiers, and the Cappadocians plunged and emerged with a victorious Trinitarian creed at Constantinople.

God is One Only in the Trinity—Athanasius (d. 373). Athanasius was bishop of Alexandria for nearly half a century, but seventeen of those years were absorbed by five exiles ordered by four different emperors. He is well remembered for being the first to use the same twenty-seven books as we use in the canon of the New Testament (367).

Athanasius does make a critical contribution to the doctrine of God when he asserts that the Trinity does not depend on the creation of the world, rather it exists independent from creation.[50] Those who apply the Middle Platonic schema to Christian theology subsequently assert that the Father begat the Son in order to make the world through Him. Athanasius teaches the independent existence of the Trinity, that it was not an instrumental means to creation. He also declares that "the Son is the *ousia* [substance] of the Father."[51] While Athanasius does affirm that the deification of persons is by grace, the perfect divinity of the Son was by nature and truth.[52] Ladaria notes that Athanasius also affirms the Spirit as belonging to the "one, eternal, immutable Trinity. The Trinity is the One God. The operational unity of the Trinity, with differentiation of persons, shows that the three are inseparable."[53]

What Athanasius achieves in the East in Greek, so Hilary does in the West in Latin.

Subsistence. Hilary of Poitiers (300–368) is sometimes called "the Athanasius of the West" and at other times "the Hammer of the Arians" (*Malleus Arianum*). He writes that the Son, word of the Father, has in Himself a real subsistence. "This word is a reality . . . a substance . . . is God and not emptiness."[54] Ladaria stresses that for Hilary, because God is supremely simple, He can give Himself totally and

---

49. Here Ladaria references the contrarian view of T. B. Barnes in disputing the authority of the Third Council, finding it to have been by only a few participants, and thereby affirmed the genuineness of the First Council of Surmium, convened in 347 near Emperor Constantius' residence in Surmium. This council had deposed the anti-Arian bishop of Surmium and deleted the "one substance" line from the creed; see Ladaria, *Athanasius and Constantius: Theology and Politics in the Constantine Empire* (Cambridge, MA: Harvard University Press, 1993), 231.
50. Ibid.
51. Ibid.
52. Ibid., see *Contra Arius,* III.15.
53. Ibid., 235, see *Serapion,* 114.
54. Ibid., 237, see *de Trinitate,* II.15.

gives Himself to the Son in this way. The conception of "divine generation eliminates at its roots for Hilary any possibility of subordination."[55] The Son is equal in
everything with the Father except fatherhood, but the eternal generation has no
degeneration in it "because nothing foreign was in it."[56]

Hilary wants to give an account of the divine life in the space between modalism and subordination. He argues, "A birth means there must be two—the
begetter and the one begotten; but it also means the two must have the same
nature, and so there can be no subordination."[57] Now Hilary is ready to explain
Jesus' statement that the "Father is greater than I" (John 14:28) as meaning that
the Father is greater because He gives while the Son receives, "but the Son in as
much as He receives all is not lesser."[58] So, the mystery of the Trinity requires a
paradox—like "greater but not lesser"—to be its faithful witnesses.

**Properties and *Idiomata*—The Cappadocians and the First Council of
Constantinople (381).** The key Arian after Arius was Eunomius of Cyzicus (d.
393). Two of the Cappadocian church fathers, Basil and his brother Gregory of
Nyssa, wrote against the teachings of Eunomius. Holmes considers Eunomius as
"far more than Arius, the crucial heresiarch of the fourth century."[59] In the latter
we see the old idea that the one who is unmade or unbegotten must be prior in
time to anyone who is begotten, and therefore the Son cannot be God. Thus,
if the Son is in the image of God, it is an image of activity and not substance.
Holmes offers this summary of the Eunomian theology in slogan form, "unlike
in essence, but united in activity."[60] Also, the Spirit is third in this taxonomy
because the Father is first and the Spirit is neither the Father nor the begotten
Son, so the Spirit is third.[61]

Eunomius and colleagues are avidly anti-apophatic theologians. Where the
Nicene theologians emphasize the ineffability of God, Eunomius asserts that the
"ingenerate [unbegotten] God can be known 'exactly and exhaustively.'"[62] We
are Cappadocians like Gregory and Basil; we resist such boxing of the mystery of
the Godhead with our words.

---

55. Ibid., 239, see *de Trinitate*, III.3.
56. Ibid., 240.
57. Holmes, *The Holy Trinity*, 128; see Hilary, *The Trinity*, 7.14–16.
58. Ibid., see *de Trinitate*, IX.54.
59. Holmes, 93.
60. Ibid., 99.
61. Ladaria, *The Living and True God*, 248.
62. Holmes, *The Holy Trinity*, 100–101.

Basil (330–379), bishop of Caesarea and founder of the communal monastery at Annesi, became lasting friends with Gregory of Nazianzus while at school in Caesarea Mazaca (modern-day Kayseri, Turkey). Both later were classmates in Athens with the future emperor, Julian, called "the Apostate" for his unsuccessful attempt to roll the Roman Empire back into pre-Christian paganism.

Through the influence of his bishop in Caesarea, Basil moved from his compromise "like substance" (*homoiousia*) position into ardent defense of the Nicene *Homoousian* ("same substance") position. He declares that: "The Son exists since all eternity . . . as begotten to the non-born Father."[63] Basil shapes Trinitarian orthodoxy with the soon-to-be-normative phrase that there is a unity in substance, but uniqueness in properties that do not separate the shared substance. He writes, "For example, the divinity is common, but paternity and filiation are properties (*idiomata*)."

Basil scores Eunomius for his "impropriety" in exalting one *idiomata*—ingeneracy—and making all other names for God subservient if not obsolete before that attribute.[64] For Basil, the properties of the Trinity show "otherness in the identity of essence (*ousia*)." The three *hypostases* or persons in the unity of the divine essence each have "unyielding peculiarity: fatherhood, sonship, sanctification."[65] So now the curbs and boundaries for the road of orthodox Trinitarianism are being laid out. Unity of substance is on one side, coupled with distinction of properties/persons on the other.

The Spirit's Procession; *Anarchoi*; and Three Persons, One Godhead.
Basil's friend, Gregory of Nazianzus (329–389/390), was his partner in defense and clarification of the Nicene Creed. Against the claims of the neo-Arians who asserted that the Son was unlike (*anomoios*) the Father in substance or essence, Gregory coined a new word in the Greek, "procession," to make distinct the relation of the Father and the Son, who came by filiation, begetting. Gregory speaks of the "procession" of the Holy Spirit from the Father as the origin of the third person of the Trinity (see John 15:26).[66]

Insisting on the eternality of the Three, he declares that they are *anarchoi*, "without beginning." He reasons that the Father had no beginning, since He ever had the Son, and likewise that the Son, though begotten, had no beginning.

---

63. Ibid., 250; see *Contra Eunomius*, II.17
64. Ibid., 102.
65. Ibid., 253; see Basil, *Epistles*, 236.6.
66. Ladaria, *The Living and True God,* 256; see Gregory of Nazianzus, *Orations*, 31.8.

He never began to be the Son. Being begotten is not the same thing as having a beginning. The first is true of the Son, the second is not.[67]

The names of Father and Son witness to the *homophuia*, the shared nature of the two.[68] The summary of Basil's Trinitarian witness is stated in these words, "The Three are One in Godhead, and the One Three in properties . . . Three Persons, One Godhead, undivided in honour and glory and substance and kingdom."[69]

Analogy of Three People, One Humanity. Basil (330–394/5), bishop of Nyssa, was the younger brother of Gregory and grew up among nine siblings, four of whom would be declared as saints by the Church. Basil affirms the emerging language of three eternal persons/properties/relations in one God. He explores this formula using an analogy of Peter, James, and John as individual persons but also as one shared humanity.[70] This analogy is fraught with problems, as are many analogies. This analogy is certainly no defense against tritheism.

Conciliar Trinitarianism. The locus of theological development between the first four ecumenical councils—Nicaea (325), Constantinople I (381), Ephesus (431) and Chalcedon (451)—shifts from Trinitarianism to Christology. Nevertheless, the affirmations of belief in the Trinity continue to be refined even into the second Council at Constantinople (553). The formulas of Athanasius and Basil that speak of the triadic unity of action and at the same time take up the personal distinctions in this unique and joint action are reproduced almost verbatim.[71] The phrase "only one" is repeated three times to affirm that each one of the divine persons is unrepeatable and is God entirely. What is common is shared divinity and what are particular are the properties or persons. Ladaria comments that, for Basil, there is no distinction "in rank between the Father, the Son, and the Spirit, because the Scripture never speaks of a first, second, or third . . . thus avoiding polytheism."[72] Holmes summarizes Cappadocian Trinitarianism in these words: "The Godhead is simple, and exists thrice-over, in *hypostases* distinguished by relations of origin, and not otherwise."[73] So, if the doctrinal

---

67. See *Orations*, 31; and Ladaria, *The Living and True God*, 257.
68. Ibid.
69. As quoted by Ladaria, *The Living and True God*, 258–259, from *Orations*, 31.14, 28.
70. Ladaria, *The Living and True God*, 261.
71. Ibid., 269.
72. Ibid., 248.
73. Holmes, *The Holy Trinity*, 116.

boulevard has been paved with Eastern Cappadocian gravel, what's left for theologians in the West to contribute?

The Mission of the Son and the Spirit, Unrepeatable Manifestations, and Psychological Analogy. Augustine (d. 354), bishop of Hippo, asks this question in his *Trinity*: If God is already omnipresent everywhere in creation, how can He be sent anywhere? The answer comes in Augustine's understanding of the sending of the Son and the sending of the Spirit as "unique and unrepeatable perceptible manifestations."[74] Modern theologians refer to this discussion as *ad extra* as opposed to *ad intra*. The latter refers to the internal, eternal relations of the Three who are One, and the former refers to the external operations of the Three who are undivided yet distinct in those operations.

Augustine here wants to make basic to the faith the assertion that God is inseparable in operations—namely, whatever the Father does, the Son does, the Spirit does.[75] He also claims that inseparability in operations does not contradict "the proper ordering of the persons in inseparable work."[76]

Does this mean that the matrix of triadic orders in the New Testament shows both this inseparability of operations and the significance of specific triadic order relative to the context in which that order occurs? I think so. For Augustine, the Father has sent, but cannot be sent, since He does not proceed from anyone. The Son is sent and He sends, while the Spirit is sent but does not send. The mission as manifestation happens in time and not in eternity. Missional manifestation, as becoming visible, constitutes a new way of being present for the divine persons.[77]

Augustine goes beyond these formulations to famously propose two human analogies of the Trinity: the triad of the mind, love, and knowledge; and the triad of memory, intelligence, and will.[78] Holmes thinks that the real point of these analogies is to illustrate "the ordered inseparability of divine operations: each indivisible operation is initiated by the Father, carried through the intelligibility of the Son and perfected in the goodness of the Spirit."[79] Does this mean that the other five triadic orders abundant through the New Testament are aberrations of the Father-Son-Spirit order? I do not see how they could be.

---

74. Ibid., 279; see Augustine, *Trinity*, IV.20, 29–30.
75. Ibid., 132.
76. Ibid., 134.
77. Augustine, *Trinity*, 20, 28; Ladaria, *The Living and True God,* 279.
78. Ibid., IX.5–8 and X.11–18.
79. Holmes, *The Holy Trinity,* 138.

Bishop Augustine does justify his advocating these analogies by arguing that if humanity is made in the image of God, then of course our humanity reflects that Godhead back.[80] Much later, Karl Barth will assert that God is so infinitely qualitatively different that no analogies of humanity or creation can apply. However, Barth will retool Augustine's renaming of the Trinity as lover, beloved, and love (the latter being the Spirit) into revealer, revelation, and revealedness.[81] He makes God the subject, object, and verb of revelation.

3. Medieval Doctrinal Development and Beyond

Filioque Controversy and the 1054 Great Schism. *Filoque* is Latin for "and the Son." The third paragraph of the Nicene Creed reads, "And [we believe] in the Holy Ghost, the Lord and Giver of Life: who proceeds from the Father; who with the Father and the Son together is worshipped and glorified; who spoke by the prophets."

Two issues ultimately arose when the word/phrase "and the Son" was added in the late sixth century by some Western/Latin churches so the Holy Spirit "proceeds from the Father and the Son." First, was this change doctrinally correct? If *filioque* was a way of diminishing or subordinating the Spirit to the Father and the Son, then inclusion was theologically incorrect.

Second, did the church in the West possess sufficient license to amend the words of the ecumenical creed that had stood the church well for centuries? This issue of liciety—whether making such changes was permissible—is an ecclesiastical issue of long and arcane history.

We do not need to solve either in order to achieve our goal of constructing a historical glossary on the doctrine of the Trinity. Thankfully, Edward Siecienski has recently published an incredibly researched and authoritative monograph on both issues. I commend it to the curious.[82]

Rational Necessity of Plurality in the Godhead. Richard of St. Victor (d. 1173) was an Augustinian monk and mystic who served as prior of his

---

80. Ibid., VII.6,12; Ladaria notes that Hilary first used this same defense for use of analogies (Ladaria, *The Living and True God,* 282).

81. Compare Augustine, *Trinity,* IX.2, with Karl Barth, *Church Dogmatics,* vol. 1, Pt. 1, G. W. Bromiley and Thomas Torrance, eds. (Edinburgh: T & T Clark, 1936–1977, 2009), 295–304.

82. A. Edward Siecienski, *The Filioque: History of a Doctrinal Controversy* (New York: Oxford University Press. 2010).

monastery in Paris from 1162 until his death. Richard revisits the analogy of human love to construct a reasonable explanation for the necessity of plurality in the Godhead. Why does God have to be three? Richard argues that perfect realization in God, who is supreme goodness, requires another to be loved. If love is to be perfected, then both must be perfect in being, equal, and co-eternal.[83] However, for love to be fully perfected, says Richard, there must be three and not merely two, so that "when a third person is loved by two persons harmoniously and in community, and then the affection of the two persons is fused into one affection by the flame of love for a third."[84]

But then, if three is good, why not four, five, or more? Richard argues that three alone and not more is essential because without just three, the relations between the three would be confused and lost.[85] In other words, the uniqueness of the Triune relations, the Father begetting the only-begotten Son and "spirating" one Holy Spirit, is destroyed if there is a fourth. (We will look at "spirating" in the next section, about Thomas Aquinas.) There is no biblical warrant or philosophical necessity for more than three. Richard's twelfth-century theology is moving toward the pinnacle of the medieval scholastic synthesis of faith and reason that will be reached in the thirteenth century by Thomas Aquinas.

The Medieval Fourth Lateran Council (Roman Catholic; 1215) summarized the orthodox position with these words:

> ineffable God, Father, Son and Holy Spirit; three persons indeed but one essence, substance or nature absolutely simple [meaning no mixture with any other nature like humanity or demiurge]; the Father (proceeding) from no one, but the Son from the Father only; and the Holy Spirit equally from both, always without beginning and end. The Father begetting, the Son begotten, and the Holy Spirit proceeding; consubstantial and coequal."[86]

Now the stage is set for Doctor Angelicus to infuse the Medieval synthesis of faith and reason with neo-Aristotelian categories.

---

83. Richard St. Victor, *Trinity*, IV.4–7; Ladaria, 287.
84. Ladaria, *The Living and True God*, 287; quoting Richard St. Victor, *Trinity*, III.19.
85. Ibid., 288 from *Trinity*, V.20
86. As quoted in Ladaria, *The Living and True God*, 270.

**Four *Ad Intra* Relations—Paternity, Filiation, Exhalation, and Proces-
sion—and *Ad Extra* Appropriations.** Thomas Aquinas (d. 1254), "Doctor Angelicus," was the Dominican priest who composed the ever-after authoritative
Summa Theologica (Sum of All Theology). His theological contribution is mas-
sive, but for our purposes here, it is sufficient to restate the four relations within
the Trinity as laid out by Thomas. It is these relations which are quoted and
referred to in works on the Trinity even to the current time.

Of these relations in the Trinity, Boethius (480–524) says, "Substance holds
together unity; while relation brings number to the Trinity."[87] In introducing
his position of relations in the Trinity, Thomas states that essence and relation
in God are the same since God is in simplicity and unity.[88] There is no distinction is essence but there is real distinction according to relation. Generation is
the procession of the Son (filiation) from the Father (paternity). So paternity
and filiation comprise the first two relations. Exhalation is the procession of the
Spirit from the Father. So exhalation (later, *spiration* will be used) and passive
exhalation or procession are the third and fourth relations in the Trinity. These
relations are not external to God, they are how God exists internally eternally.[89]
Holmes notes that Thomas saw these relations as "superabundantly dynamic."[90]
Innascibility—self-existence—is usually seen as the fifth relation, though it is
assigned to the Father and thus it is not a true relation.

Thomas also teaches that appropriation happens when an attribute of the
whole is applied to one person in *ad extra* operations.[91] For instance, Jesus said
that the second Paraclete, the Spirit, would lead the disciples into all truth. Omniscience is an attribute of the Godhead that is here appropriated to the Spirit
(John 16:13). Thomas sees the fullness of these internal relations as the source of
God creating the universe as different from Himself.[92]

Perchoresis, Circumcession, and Mutual Inhabitation. As this glossary of
Trinitarian vocabulary comes to an end, we need to look at one final concept,
that of perichoresis or circumincession. These terms have to do with the "interpenetration" of members of the Trinity.

---

87. Boethius, *Trinity*, IV, as quoted in Ladaria, *The Living and True God*, 294.
88. Ibid,. 296, see *Summa Theologica* (*ST*), I.28,4.
89. Ibid.
90. Holmes, *The Holy Trinity*, 158.
91. Ladaria, *The Living and True God*, 308, see Thomas, *ST* I.39.8
92. Ibid.

Thomas Aquinas was not the first to think through these concepts in relation to the One who lives as Trinity. For instance, there was Athenagoras in the second century and Hilary of Poitiers in the fourth. Yet, even before those first church fathers, the New Testament speaks of the Father, Son, and Spirit not only being in relation to each other but also being *in* each other. So Jesus asks the disciples, "Don't you believe that I am in the Father and the Father is in Me?" (John 14:10). Or, as the apostle Paul states, "That is, in Christ, God was reconciling the world to Himself" (2 Corinthians 5:19).

The Spirit of God is the Spirit of Christ is the Holy Spirit—not because the Father is the Son is the Spirit, which is unitarian modalism—but because the Father, Son, and Spirit mutually inhabit one another. *Perichoresis* is the Greek word and *circumincession* is the Latin word for this interpenetration of the Father, Son, and Spirit in their external operations. This idea that each divine person is mutually in the other is evidence of the divinity of each. Hilary asserts that "thus mutually each is in the other, for all is perfect in the unbegotten Father, so all is perfect in the begotten Son. . . . God is in him, and he, in whom God is, is God. God cannot dwell in a nature strange and alien to his nature."[93] John of Damascus (d. 749) was the first to name this Trinitarian mutual inhabitation *perichoresis*. Ladaria says that the Latin term *circumincession* (and a later spelling, *circuminsession*) comes much later out of translating the work of John.[94]

This concept will become very important in the contemporary Trinitarian work of Jürgen Moltmann, Miroslav Volf, John Zizioulas, and others. Ladaria notes Urs von Balthasar's assertion in *Theo-Logic II: The Truth of God,* that "the inhabitation of each person in the others certainly respects the *taxis,* the order of the processions, but at the same time shows the radical equality between them, the perfect communion in which distinction is more fitting than difference."[95] So, now the church has a way of naming the diversity in inseparable unity that is the God who lives in Trinity. In the words of the Council of Toledo (589), "the One true God is not without number, yet is not compromised by number."

PS Barth and the Three Modes of Being (*Seinsweise*). The state of the doctrine of the Trinity has been reviewed in chapter 1 and we will visit it again in chapter 11. By all rights, Karl Barth, a major—if not the major—twentieth-cen-

---

93. Ladaria, *The Living and True God,* 310, quotes Hilary, *Trinity,* IV.40.
94. Ibid.
95. Ibid., 311.

tury theologian falls then into one of those chapters. He is mentioned there, but he has added Trinitarian vocabulary that is now referenced by nearly all schools of theology. So I want to add those words to our historical glossary here.

Barth did not like to use the word *persons* to describe or define the three distinct beings in the Trinity. He argued that those words carried too much cultural and psychological baggage to not be misunderstood in the context of the Trinity. He also had a well-known aversion to any natural theologies which drew analogies between the Creator and the creation and its creatures. So, he proposed substituting "three modes of being or existence" in the place of three distinct persons in the Godhead.

Since the One God exists in Trinity, Barth is not wrong to express that Trinity as "modes of being." Stephen Holmes critiques Barth's rejection of the creedal formulations and finds his proposal as importing impersonal framing and opening the door to modalism all over again.[96] However, it is not our responsibility to sort that out here. I merely want to add it to our glossary as a postscript and give its history and meaning.

PPS *Perichoresis* and *Kenosis.* If *perichoresis* means the interpenetration of the divine persons in and through each other, *kenosis* means the emptying of each person out for and into the other. I am grateful to Anthony Thiselton for pointing out the significance of pairing these concepts for understanding the immanence of God in His Triune mission and operations.

Thiselton's agenda was to examine the hermeneutics of the doctrine of God as Trinity.[97] As I do in this book, Thiselton looks at what he calls "the New Testament narrative of Trinitarian co-agency."[98] He notes the multiple uses of the triadic sending formula, Father, Son, Spirit. He also affirms that statement of Moltmann on this New Testament phenomenon: "We find a Trinitarian co-working of Father, Son, and Spirit, but with changing patterns."[99] Thiselton interprets this narrative of Trinitarian co-agency using the insight that Rowan Williams (former archbishop of Canterbury) draws from Russian thinker Sergius Bulgakov that "an eternal *kenosis* [italics in the original] in the life of God which itself then makes possible the *kenosis* involved in creation. . . . God the

---

96. Holmes, *The Holy Trinity,* 177, n.303.
97. Anthony C. Thiselton, *The Hermeneutics of Doctrine* (Grand Rapids: Eerdmans, 2007), 451–478.
98. Ibid., 456.
99. Ibid., 459.

Father pours out his divine life without remainders into the Son; his identity is constituted in this act of giving away."[100]

Kenosis, emptying, has the prevailing connection with Son in the incarnation and crucifixion as seen in the epistle to the Philippians 2:7. "Instead He emptied Himself by assuming the form of a slave, taking on the likeness of men." However, the Son ascends to the Father that the Spirit might "be poured out on all flesh" just as the Spirit came upon the Son at the baptism (Joel 2:28, cf. Acts 2:17, Luke 3:22). Thiselton is intrigued by the pairing of *perichoresis* and *kenosis* in the life of God, as am I.

CONCLUSION

We always name what is important to us. It is human nature. Christianity has been busy for two thousand years naming and describing the God who has revealed Himself as One and Three, as Father, Son, and Holy Spirit. We have studied two thousand years of those big words and concepts developed painfully in controversy to defend the faith. With those names, words, and concepts in mind, we are ready to dive back into the New Testament to examine the six diverse triadic orders used to reveal the missional operations of the living God. We are ready to enter the seventy-five instances of the Trinitarian matrix of the New Testament.

DISCUSSION QUESTIONS—CHAPTER 4

- Theologians have labored to find the right vocabulary and concepts to describe the Mystery that lives in Trinity. Which Trinitarian concepts discussed in this chapter are likely to enrich your theology of the Triune God? Explain.

- Church history reveals that Christians have been persistently Trinitarian in worship and word throughout the ages. This book contends that a high value placed on apostolic witness in Scripture, plus the superabundant presence of triadic instances in the Scripture, nurtured this call to and appreciation for Trinitarianism. Evaluate that contention.

---

100. Ibid.

- How uncomfortable should Christians feel that the word *trinity* was not coined until the end of the second century?

- This chapter contends that many congregations are "operational modalists" in terms of their worship, song, and prayer. Evaluate your own worship experience in your church. Are you too exclusively focused on just one of the persons in the Trinity? Do you just make reference to the Father or to Jesus or to the Spirit? How could you be resolved to be more Trinitarian and balanced?

SERMON STARTER: THE HISTORY OF THE GOOD FIGHT FOR THE DOCTRINE OF THE TRINITY

Contending for the Faith: Jude 3-4

"Dear friends, although I was eager to write you about the salvation we share, I found it necessary to write and exhort you to contend for the faith that was delivered to the saints once for all. For some men, who were destined for this judgment long ago, have come in by stealth; they are ungodly, turning the grace of God into promiscuity and denying Jesus Christ, our Master and Lord."

—Jude 3–4

Dedicated to those who knew that some things were worth fighting for.

All runners in a relay race know that they have to pass the baton and then their race is over. No matter if they ran well or poorly, they have to pass the baton to the next runner.

Toward the end of his life, the apostle Paul realized his lap was ending and he needed to pass the baton carefully to the next generation of Christian leaders. So he wrote a second letter to Timothy, who had succeeded him as lead pastor at Ephesus. "I have fought the good fight, I have finished the race, I have kept the faith" (2 Timothy 4:7). Previously, he had written Timothy with the exhortation to "Fight the good fight for the faith; take hold of eternal life that you were called to and have made a good confession about in the presence of many witnesses" (1 Timothy 6:12).

If there is such a thing as a "good fight," then mustn't there also be a "bad fight"? When you find yourself in a fight or confrontation, do you ask yourself, "Is this a good fight or a bad fight?" If it is a bad fight, what do you do then? When the Christian finds himself or herself engaged in a bad fight—like arguing to justify your mistakes or your sins—the Christian is to stop, disengage, and even apologize. (Eating crow never tastes good, but it's much better when it's fresh.)

However, Christians are called to engage continually in the good fight of the faith, to contend for the faith. Paul's fellow writer, Jude, wrote it this way: "Dear friends, although I was eager to write you about the salvation we share, I found it necessary to write and exhort you to contend for the faith that was delivered to the saints once for all. For some men, who were destined for this judgment long ago, have come in by stealth; they are ungodly, turning the grace of God into promiscuity and denying Jesus Christ, our Master and Lord" (Jude 3–4). Without sounding too pugnacious, here is some sound ringside advice for those who want to be contenders for the faith. Let me give you a quick cue card with the key points, and then I will expand on them:

- Don't get in the wrong ring.
- Do get in the right fight.
- Know who you're fighting.
- Be ready to box.

1. Don't get in the wrong ring.

A. Beware when what you're contending for is not the faith, but your own *comfort*. Christians and churches have fought over worship music, colors of the carpet, and even whether or not the dove in the baptistery window should face outward or to the side. These are comfort fights, not faith fights. They are bad fights. Blow the whistle, stop the action, and get out of that ring.

B. Beware when what you're contending for is not the faith, but what's *reasonable*. Christianity is full of mystery. Much of it does not fit easily into logic or our scientific rationality. Miracles like the resurrection of Jesus are extraordinary events for which we have no scientific or medical categories. Resurrection does not fit without constructing some new ways of thinking. How can the One God also be three Persons, Father, Son, and Holy Spirit? Dorothy Sayers, mystery writer and Christian intellectual, once wrote in frustration, "The Father is incomprehensible, the Son is incomprehensible, and the whole thing is incomprehensible. Something put in by theologians to make it more difficult."[101] If you are trying to fit the mystery of God into a box, you are in the wrong ring and fight.

C. The faith is full of *brain-busting, life-altering mysteries*. Don't deny them. Don't water them down. Embrace them. Do what Saint Augustine did: He

---

101. Dorothy Sayers, *Creed and Chaos* (New York: Harcourt and Brace, 1949), 52.

embraced the faith without waiting for all the answers to get worked out and then spent his life walking in the faith by seeking understanding. Faith is always on the search for more understanding of the Lord and His ways.

2. Do get in the right fight. For Christians, there are three great faith issues worth fighting for.

   A. We need to fight for *the truthfulness and reliability of the Scripture*. "Your word is a lamp to my feet and a light to my path" (Psalm 119:105).

   B. We need to fight for *the necessity of the cross and the way of Christ for salvation*. "For even the Son of Man did not come to be served, but to serve and give His life—a ransom for many" (Mark 10:45).

   C. We need to fight for *the truth of the Trinity*. The One God exists as Trinity. What's wrong with worshipping God as He has disclosed Himself? "Peter an apostle of Jesus Christ . . . according to the foreknowledge of God the Father and set apart by the Spirit for obedience and for sprinkling with the blood of Christ" (1 Peter 1:1–2).

3. Know who you are fighting. As contenders for the Trinity, we enter the ring against two opponents:

   A. A *rigid monotheism called modalism*. These opponents declare that the Father is God, the Son is God, and the Spirit is God but also the Father is the Son is the Spirit. The One God who has three functions.

   B. A *cagey tritheism called subordinationism*. These opponents argue that there can only be one highest, unbegotten God, so everyone else is less divine than the Father. The Son is divine, but He is a subordinate spiritual creation of the Father.

4. Be ready to box. "Always be ready to give a gentle defense to any who asks you about the hope that is in you" (1 Peter 3:15).

   A. *Read the Word*. The inimitable Christian thinker, G. K. Chesterton, wrote many travel guides. He is famous for showing us that the traveler sees what he sees, the tourist sees what he came to see. The reason that early, medieval, and reformation Christian leaders kept fighting for the Triune faith is because they found it everywhere in the New Testament. There are more than seventy instances in Scripture where all three persons—the Father Son, and Spirit—are mentioned in one order or another. We all know the baptismal triad: "In the name of the Father, the Son, and the Holy Spirit," because right after we heard those words, the pastor dunked us under water. But at the end of 2 Corinthians 13:13, Paul gives us this benediction with a different ordering: "The grace of the Lord Jesus Christ, and the love of God, and the fellowship of the Holy Spirit be with you all." The apostle John gives us yet another ordering when he says in his gospel, verse 15:26, "When the Counselor comes, the One I will send to you from the Father—He will testify about Me." Those Trinitarian references are in nineteen out of twenty-seven books in the New Testament, in all six possible orders, and are about seventy-five in number. Stop being a tourist, become a traveler! Go get some Trinity sightings of your own. Read the Word.

B. *Read the creeds. Creed* comes from *credo*, which is Latin for "I believe." Credibility and credentials are also in this word family. When the early church leaders battled for the Trinity against the Jehovah's Witnesses and Unitarians of their day, they wrote down the results in a Creed or Definition. The Nicene Creed written in 325 defines the Trinity in these words:

We believe in one God, the Father Almighty, Maker of heaven and earth, and of all things visible and invisible. And in one Lord Jesus Christ, the Son of God, the only-begotten, begotten of the Father before all ages. Light of Light; true God of true God; begotten, not made; of one essence with the Father, by whom all things were made; who for us men and for our salvation came down from heaven, and was incarnate of the Holy Spirit and the Virgin Mary, and became man. And He was crucified for us under Pontius Pilate, and suffered, and was buried. And the third day He rose again, according to the Scriptures; and ascended into heaven, and sits at the right hand of the Father; and He shall come again with glory to judge the living and the dead; whose Kingdom shall have no end.

Remember creeds are what church leaders contended for, and they intended it for use in worship, prayer, discipleship. They fought well, and passed on this baton for our benefit. Read the creeds.

C. Pray, live, and speak the Trinity. Be functionally Trinitarian. Medieval Christianity had a Latin phrase: *Lex orandi, lex credendi, lex vivendi.* That basically meant, "What we pray and preach, is what we really believe and will live." If the New Testament uses the Three Persons in prayer and praise in all six orders and does so repeatedly, isn't that permission for us to pray and bless in any of those orders also? Engage in a prayer exercise. If you are worried, why not just tell God that you are just praying like the Scripture prays. You may be amazed what happens when you expand your prayer life beyond the introductory order of Father, Son, and Spirit. Remember, the One God lives as Trinity, so when you talk to One, you talk with all. Use the words of the creed in sharing your hope with others. When they ask, why not say something like, "Look, it's not really my fault that I believe in Trinity. Once I realized I wanted fully to follow Jesus, I started reading the New Testament and saw that Jesus was all about the Father. He was the Father this and the Father that. I discovered that loving the Son is loving the Father, too. And in that loving, the Spirit of God moved into my life in a big way. Then stuff in the Bible or sermons or even songs started bursting into my mind, like God was whispering to me truths, only He was whispering from the inside. So you see, it's not my fault I am a Trinitarian. I worship God as He shows Himself to me. I won't put God in a box. If He says He's One and Three, that's okay by me as long as He lets me keep following Him." Pray, live, and speak the Trinity.

And finally, Paul offers this Trinitarian benediction for those who are boxing in the ring: "The grace of the Lord Jesus Christ, and the love of God, and the fellowship of the Holy Spirit be with all of you" (2 Corinthians 13:13).

PART 2:

The Contextual Question and
the Trinitarian Matrix

Chapter 5

The Sending Triad: Father-Son-Spirit as the Missional Order

The doctrine of the Trinity is nothing other than the conceptual framework needed to understand the story of Jesus as the story of God.

—Pinchas Lapide and Jürgen Moltmann,
Jewish Monotheism and Christian Tradition (1981)[1]

For two millennia, the church has welcomed new members into the fellowship as pastors recite the words "in the name of the Father, the Son, and the Holy Spirit" during the rite of baptism. This book demonstrates that the divine Three-in-One is expressed repeatedly in diverse orders throughout the New Testament. However, most believers hear these baptismal words as the normal, even normative expression of the Trinitarian procession. Such an impression would naturally occur for two reasons. First, the Father-Son-Spirit order became predominant simply by the sheer force of repetition of that order at the significant moments of public worship, baptism, and communion. Second, the order became so predominant as to eclipse all other triadic orders

---

1. Pinchas Lapide and Jürgen Moltmann, "The Christian Doctrine of Trinity," *Jewish Monotheism and Christian Tradition* (Philadelphia: Fortress Press, 1981), 47.

from popular consciousness because no other processional order was applied to a significant religious ritual of equal ecclesial significance. **So, the Father-Son-Spirit order became the norm in the liturgical life and thought of churches, by both commission and omission.** Has this great omission of the five alternate orders inhibited church capacity to participate fully in the divine Great Commission? Could the Great Commission have enjoyed greater achievement wherever the diverse triadic orders were incarnated intentionally or unintentionally?

We will explore these relevant issues of faith and practice in a later chapter. For now, we will examine the nineteen instances of the Father-Son-Spirit triad in context to determine the levels of intentionality in their use and degree of consistency between the contexts in which Father-Son-Spirit triad occurs. What exactly is God doing or being when the New Testament authors appeal to or apply this triad? Listed in Table 5.1 are the nineteen instances of the Father-Son-Spirit order. The chart offers an identification of the context of the passage, a grading of authorial Trinitarian intentionality ("A" through "C"), and an abbreviated citation of the passage.

TABLE 5.1: THE MISSIONAL ORDER REFERENCES—FATHER, SON, SPIRIT

LOCATIONS AND GRADATIONS FOR THE MISSIONAL TRIADIC ORDER OF FATHER-SON-SPIRIT			
Text	Rating	Context	Summary
Matthew 12:18	C	Messianic call	Behold My [God] servant [Son], . . . I will put my Spirit upon Him
Matthew 28:19–20	A	Apostolic mission	baptizing them in the name of the Father, the Son and the Holy Spirit
John 1:33	B	Identifying the Son	but He [God] who sent me to baptize with water . . . told me, 'The One [Son] you see the Spirit descending and resting on—He . . . baptizes with the Holy Spirit
John 20:21–22	B	Apostolic mission	As the Father sent me [Son], so send . . . receive the Holy Sprit

			LOCATIONS AND GRADATIONS FOR THE MISSIONAL TRIADIC ORDER OF FATHER-SON-SPIRIT
Text	**Rating**	**Context**	**Summary**
Acts 4:29–31	B	Apostolic witness	Lord, consider their threats, and grant that Your slaves may speak Your message . . . stretch out your hand for healing . . . in the name of Your holy Servant Jesus. . . . When they had prayed . . . they were all filled with the Holy Spirit . . .
Acts 5:30–32	A	Apostolic witness	God raised Jesus, so is the Holy Spirit whom God has given
Acts 10:38	A	Economic/ mission	how God anointed Jesus of Nazareth with the Holy Spirit and power, and He went about doing good
Acts 20:21–23	C	Farewell address	about repentance toward God and faith in our Lord Jesus . . . except that in town after town the Holy Spirit testifies to me that . . .
Romans 1:1–4	C	Apostolic mission	singled out for God's good news . . . concerning His Son, Jesus Christ our Lord . . . by the resurrection from the dead according to the Spirit of holiness.
Romans 5:1–5	A	Justification	peace with God through our Lord Jesus Christ, poured through Holy Spirit
Romans 15:15–16	A	Mission to Gentiles	given me by God to be a minister of Christ Jesus to the Gentiles . . . sanctified by the Holy Spirit.
1 Corinthians 2:1–4	A	Witness	testimony of God, nothing but Jesus, demonstration of Spirit
1 Corinthians 3:9–16	C	Apostolic mission	Jesus, the Son is the Foundation to God's sanctuary, the Spirit of God lives in believers
Galatians 4:4–6	A	Mission of adoption	When the time had come to completion . . . God sent His Son . . . to redeem . . . so that we might receive adoption as sons. And because you are sons, God sent the Spirit of His Son into our hearts, crying, Abba Father!

Text	Rating	Context	Summary
Ephesians 1:11–14	A	Salvation/ mission	to the purpose of Him, first hoped in Christ, sealed with Spirit
Colossians 1:6–8	B	Greeting/ prayer	grace of God, minister of Christ . . . your love in the Spirit
1 Thessalonians 1:3–5	A	Mission results	our God & Father your . . . hope in Lord Jesus Christ, in power and Holy Spirit
1 Peter 1:3–12	C	Hope of salvation	Praise the God and Father of our Lord Jesus Christ. . . . These things have now been announced to you through those who preached the gospel to you by the Holy Spirit sent from heaven.
Revelation 1:9–10	B	Introduction	word of God . . . testimony of Jesus . . . was in the Spirit

LOCATIONS AND GRADATIONS FOR THE MISSIONAL TRIADIC ORDER OF FATHER-SON-SPIRIT

FATHER-SON-SPIRIT REFERENCES IN THE GOSPELS

The gospels of Matthew and John have two instances each of the Father-Son-Spirit triad. There is no discernible use of this triad in the gospel of Mark. The gospel of Luke has five triadic references, but none use the Father-Son-Spirit order.

Father-Son-Spirit in the Gospel of Matthew

Matthew 12:18. This verse is a Messianic quotation from Isaiah 42:1–4.[2] While this Isaiah passage may be taken as an individual or as the nation (the latter is the preference in the Septuagint), Matthew here identifies Jesus as the authoritative fulfillment of the well-known prophesy from Isaiah: "Here is My Servant whom I have chosen, My beloved in whom My soul delights; I will put My Spirit

---

2. The quotation is a hybrid of the MT and LXX. See John Nolland's convincing textual discussion, *The Gospel of Matthew: A Commentary on the Greek Text* (Grand Rapids: Eerdmans, 2005), 493; and see Craig Blomberg's discussion of Isaiah 42:1 as a messianic text which can be taken individually or corporately, in *Matthew: An Exegetical and Theological Exposition of Holy Scripture*, vol. 22, The New American Commentary (Nashville: Broadman & Holman Publishers, 1992), 200.

on Him. . . ."[3] This prophetic citation is between the record of the Sabbath healings of a man with a paralyzed hand and another who is demonized, blind, and mute. The context is the lordship of Jesus over the Sabbath. The Isaiah passage is quoted as the self-identification of Jesus as the chosen divine servant, who has authority by divine election and spiritual endowment to proclaim justice and effect healing.

I rated the reference here in Matthew as a "C" in terms of clear Trinitarian intentionality by the author for two reasons. First, the Isaiah passage as here used has God as the subject using first-person pronouns: "*My* servant," "*My* soul delights," and "*I* will put *My* Spirit on Him." This is God taking action to keep His covenant of redemption and restoration. By implication and use of the pronouns, I have identified the reference as Father first. However, since no use is made of any of the names of God, just pronouns, the defensibility of a Trinitarian identification is more muted. The use of the Father-first order is merited since the text clearly shows the initiative is Father God driven. The context of the passage describes the missional authority of the Son to proclaim justice due to God's election and the anointing of God's Spirit. Craig Blomberg notes that the mission of the Messiah here is to both the Jews and the nations: "[Matthew 12:]20b–21 promise that he will ultimately bring justice and victory for Gentile as well as Jewish followers. The 'nations' of vv. 18–21 are the *ethnē*—all 'peoples' of the world."[4] This missional economy of the Father-Son-Spirit is clearly God sending.

The missional invocation of the Father-Son-Spirit order becomes more intentional in Matthew 28:19.

Matthew 28:19–20. This passage is often referred to as the Great Commission. Its title notes the missional framework in which Christian baptism is a part of discipleship. "Go, therefore, and make disciples of all nations, baptizing them in the name of the Father and of the Son and of the Holy Spirit, teaching them to observe everything I have commanded you." Blomberg notes, "The singular 'name' followed by the threefold reference to 'Father, Son, and Holy Spirit' suggests both unity and plurality in the Godhead. Here is the clearest Trinitarian 'formula' anywhere in the Gospels. . . ."[5] This baptismal triad is striking in that all other New Testament references to baptism are in the name of "the Lord" (Acts 2:38; 8:16), "Jesus Christ" (10:48), or "the Lord Jesus" (19:5)—or "into Christ Jesus" (Romans 6:3;

---

3. Isaiah 42:1 was examined previously in chapter 3, "The Antecedent Question—Triadic Presence in the Hebrew Scriptures."
4. Blomberg, *Matthew*, 200.
5. Ibid., 432.

Galatians 3:27). Clearly in the age of the New Testament writers, the words of the baptismal formula were not yet settled into the Trinitarian framework of Matthew.

Nolland notes that some scholars have discounted this intentionally Trinitarian passage as a dross or emendation of the original text because of how "baptism in the name" occurs in Acts and in Paul, and because of the way that the fourth-century church historian Eusebius refers to Matthew 28:19 as "in His Name" rather than in the threefold name.[6] Blomberg and Nolland affirm the Trinitarian framework as original and consistent with the vocabulary of Matthew as a whole. Nolland says, "A large number of scholars have pronounced Matthew's language to be a foreign body in Matthew, but this judgment seems to be derived ultimately from reading the language in relation to a (later) baptismal context and not in relation to the Gospel."[7] He concludes his discussion by noting the missional initiative found in Matthew's use of the threefold name of God, "Matthew's story has been about the action of the Father through the Son and by means of the Holy Spirit. And that is what the baptized are joined to."[8]

In the 2005 *Like Father, Like Son*, Tom Smail declares this passage to be "the most explicitly Trinitarian statement in the whole Bible" and "also Trinitarian in the shape of the mission to which it calls us."[9] Morris points out that the expression has implications for our understanding of the Godhead: "[O]ne could hardly imagine a more forceful proclamation of Christ's divinity—and, incidentally, of the Spirit's distinct personality—than this listing together, on a level of equality, of Father, Son, and Spirit. One does not baptize people in the name of a divine person, a holy creature, and an impersonal divine force."[10]

The use of the Triune Name distinguishes this baptism from the baptism of repentance of John the Baptist. It means welcoming the disciple into the redemptive mission of the Triune God. Tasker, as quoted in Leon Morris, is even more adamant: "It was essentially a *new* sacrament, by which men and women were to come under the influence of the Triune God, to be used in His service. The words *in the name of the Father, and of the Son, and of the Holy Ghost* are

---

6. Nolland, *The Gospel of Matthew*, 1268; cf. Blomberg *Matthew*, especially cites the following on this issue: Jane Schaberg, *The Father, the Son, and the Holy Spirit* (Chico, CA: Scholars, 1982); L. Abramowski, "Die Entstehung der dreigliedrigen Taufformel—ein Versuch," *ZTK* 81 (1984): 417–46.
7. John Nolland. *The Gospel of Matthew: A Commentary on the Greek Text* (Grand Rapids: Eerdmans; 2005).
8. Ibid., 1269.
9. Tom Smail, *Like Father, Like Son* (Grand Rapids: Eerdmans, 2005), 292.
10. Leon Morris, *The Gospel according to Matthew* (Grand Rapids; Eerdmans, 1992), 747.

therefore both emphatic and essential to the text. Without them, the reference to baptism would be indeterminate and conventional."[11]

In a doctoral seminar on the history of Christian missions, Francis DuBose noted that the only verb in this text was "make disciples" and that all other verbs in the English translation were actually participles. He suggested translating the word *go* as "as you are going," meaning that the church and its members were to be caught up in the redemptive movement of mission with God.[12] The point here is that this text is a missional text imperative upon all believers in and received into the church. The Father-Son-Spirit order is a missional processional order. The Father-Son-Spirit triad is *God sending and sent.*

While Christian baptism is a welcoming into the household of faith, it is equally a welcoming into the redemptive mission of God and His people. Baptism is also commissioning. Even as baptism is a pledge to God and His people of a clear conscience, the pledge is inextricably tied up with the gospel witness to give a gentle defense for the hope that now informs our going.[13] Baptism is divinely intended as a commissioning into mission with the Triune God. Part of the goodness of the good news is that the cleansing from sin is not to be separated from the commissioning of the baptized into the ministry of the church.

Father-Son-Spirit in the Gospel of John

The Father-Son-Spirit triad in Matthew's account of the Great Commission is reiterated in the gospel of John with the same triad. Two of the ten triadic instances in the gospel of John display the Father-Son-Spirit order.

John 1:33. This passage reads as follows: "[B]ut He [God] who sent me to baptize with water told me, 'The One [the Son] you see the Spirit descending and resting on—He is the One who baptizes with the Holy Spirit." The Trinitarian notation of this passage could be written Father-Son-Spirit-Son-Spirit. The passage is unconsciously Trinitarian and receives a grade of "B" in terms of Trinitarian intentionality.

This passage is as close as this gospel comes to depicting the baptism of Jesus. Unlike the accounts in Matthew, Mark, and Luke, John's gospel has

---

11. Morris, *The Gospel according to Matthew*, 747; cf. R. V. G. Tasker, *The Gospel according to St. Matthew,* Tyndale New Testament Commentary Series (Grand Rapids; Eerdmans, 1973), 278.

12. See Francis M. DuBose, *The God Who Sends: A Fresh Quest for Biblical Mission* (Nashville: Broadman, 1983).

13. See 1 Peter 3:15–21.

John the Baptist make the public announcement of Jesus' mission. The three Synoptic Gospels are also Trinitarian in their framing of the baptismal scene but follow the Son-Spirit-Father order. This will be discussed in detail in the chapter on that triadic order (Matthew 3:16, Mark 1:10–11, Luke 3:21).

D. A. Carson rightly assumes that these words of the Baptist come after the baptism of Jesus. He says, "Apparently John the Baptist had baptized Jesus some time earlier. Up to that point, John himself *did not know him* (v. 31)—which does not mean that John did not know Jesus at all, but only that he did not know him as the Coming One." [14]

The Messianic prophecy in Isaiah 42:1 declares that this pouring out on God's servant is the action of God Himself. Andreas Kostenberger comments that "the expression 'the one who sent me' in John's Gospel is a shorthand for God the Father (e.g., 4:34; 5:23, 24, 30, 37), who is identified as the sender of the Baptist in the prologue (1:6)."[15] Kostenberger concludes that "Jesus comes as the fulfillment of the divine promise to pour out the Spirit in the restoring and empowering of Messianic community." (Ezekiel 36:25–27; 37:9–10; Joel 2:28–32; 2 Esdras 6:26; T. Judah 24:3).[16] The Baptist's declaration here finds further fulfillment at Pentecost with the outpouring of the Holy Spirit upon the gathered believers as described in Acts 2. Incidentally, there are two Trinitarian triads identified in Acts 2. Acts 2:32–33 uses the Son-Father-Spirit order, and the key interpretive passage in Acts 2:38–39 follows the same Son-Spirit-Father order used in the Synoptic Gospels at the baptism of Jesus. These triadic instances will be examined closely in the chapters addressing those specific orders.

John 20:21–22. The second instance of the Father-Son-Spirit order comes at the end of John's gospel. The categorization of the Father-Son-Spirit as the missional and not merely the baptismal order is further validated in the Johannine version of the Great Commission. John 20:21–22 reads, "'Peace to you! As the Father [Father God] has sent Me [Jesus, the Son], I also send you.' After saying this, He breathed on them and said, "'Receive the Holy Spirit.'"[17] The Trinitarian order of Father-Son-Spirit is operational here. An-

---

14. D. A. Carson, *The Gospel according to John* (Grand Rapids: Eerdmans, 1991), 151.
15. Andreas Köstenberger, *John* (Grand Rapids: Baker Academic, 2004), 70.
16. Ibid.
17. Verse 23 immediately follows with the Johannine version of Matthew 16:19 and 18:18 about the keys of the kingdom: "If you forgive the sins of any, they are forgiven them; if you retain the sins of any, they are retained." These texts inform us of the evangelistic task of the believing body to use the keys of Scripture that persons may gain entrance into the kingdom of

dreas Kostenberger recognizes the binitarian nature of the passage, "The disciples are drawn into the unity and mission of Father and Son. . . . Succession is important both in the OT and in Second Temple literature."[18] However, the breathing of Jesus on the disciples coming with the imperative to receive the Holy Spirit follows immediately in the context.[19] D. A. Carson observes that the initiating phrase in verse 22, "Having said this," means that "the commission is thereby tied to the giving of the Spirit."[20] The Father sends, the Son is sent and sending, and the Spirit sent and received is the anointing of succession into the triune mission. Carson makes a helpful contribution again when he writes, "Jesus was sent by his Father into the world (3:17) by means of the incarnation (1:14) with the end of saving the world (1:29); now that Jesus' disciples no longer belong to the world (15:19), they must also be sent back into the world (20:21) in order to bear witness, along with the Paraclete."[21]

As God breathed the first humanity into existence, so now the risen Son breathes the Spirit on His disciples that they might join Him in the new humanity. Jesus is the last Adam and the first new Man and by the Spirit begets a new redeemed humanity (Romans 5:17). Then in a reiteration of the Petrine commission of the keys of the kingdom (Matthew 16:19) and the disciplinary mission of the disciples (Matthew 18:18), Jesus grants missional authority to the disciples to function as the earthly distribution points of forgiveness and denial: "If you forgive the sins of any, they are forgiven them; if you retain the sins of any, they are retained" (John 20:23). Gerald Borchert offers a convincing understanding of Jesus' charge to His disciples when he writes:

> Thus one could say that Jesus' followers are to make the Gospel
> so clear that it is evident where people stand on the nature of sin.
> When these texts are understood in this perspective, it should

---

God or, having entered, to take up the ethical task of informing believers of how to live in a kingly way. See John Howard Yoder's *Body Politics* and Mark Dever's *Nine Marks of a Healthy Church,* new expanded ed. (Wheaton, IL: Crossway Books, 2004).

18. Köstenberger, *John,* 673–574.
19. The text in the Greek reads literally, "receive Holy Spirit," with no definite article, "the." Gerald Borchert explains that this absence of the article is not unusual. He comments, "In fact, 'the Holy Spirit' is referred to more than fifty times in the New Testament without the article, three of them being in John's Gospel (1:33; 14:26; 20:22)," see Borchert's *John 12–21,* vol. 25B, The New American Commentary (Nashville: Broadman & Holman Publishers, 2002), 310.
20. Carson, *The Gospel according to John,* 649.
21. Ibid., 648.

become clear that Jesus' commission to his followers is not one of privileged judgment but of weighty responsibility to represent the will of God in Christ with extreme faithfulness and to be honest and authentic about their evaluations or judgments.[22]

The Father-Son-Spirit order here in John 20:21–22 is clearly less intentional than it is in Matthew 29:19. Therefore this instance is rated a "B" in terms of Trinitarian intentionality. However, if anything, the context is equally missional. God is sending.

FATHER-SON-SPIRIT REFERENCES IN ACTS

Of the thirteen triadic instances in Acts, four make use of the Father-Son-Spirit pattern.

Acts 4:29–31. This is part of the apostle Peter's prayer for boldness following the Sanhedrin's attempt to silence the witness of the post-Pentecost church in Jerusalem. This liturgical application of the Triune name reads as follows:

> "And now, Lord [Father], consider their threats, and grant that Your slaves may speak Your message with complete boldness, while You stretch out Your hand for healing, signs, and wonders to be performed through the name of Your holy Servant Jesus [Son]." When they had prayed, the place where they were assembled was shaken, and they were all filled with the Holy Spirit [Spirit] and began to speak God's message with boldness.

The context gives the understanding of the name "Lord" as referring to God the Father. Interceding for gathered believers, Peter is recognizing that, during times of duress especially, the Father's granting of the Spirit through the Son is necessary for the church to sustain its participation in the mission of God. This instance of the Father-Son-Spirit is graded as a "B" with reference to Trinitarian intentionality because the Spirit is not mentioned inside the prayer of Peter, but rather is described as coming as the answer to Peter's intercession. The Spirit enables continuity of the mission of Jesus in the life of the church.

---

22. Borchert, *John 12–21*, vol. 25B, 310.

Acts 5:31–32. This records the response of Peter and the apostles under examination by the Sanhedrin in Jerusalem. The event is, of course, after the crucifixion, resurrection, and Pentecost. Peter invokes the missional authority of the Father-Son-Spirit order to explain why the apostles must in this instance keep proclaiming the gospel as obedience to God rather than be silent in obedience to the Sanhedrin. Peter witnesses that: "The God [Father] of our fathers raised up Jesus [Son]. . . . God [Father] exalted this man to His right hand as ruler and Savior [Son]. . . . We are witnesses of these things, and so is the Holy Spirit [Spirit], whom God [Father] has given to those who obey Him." The text presents a prolonged Trinitarian framework of Father-Son-Father-Son-Spirit-Father, but the discernible procession of reference to the Godhead falls into the Father-Son-Spirit pattern.

Peter interprets the apostolic actions of those caught up in a divine processional movement intended to bring repentance, forgiveness, and obedience (Acts 5:31–32). He presents his case by invoking all three names by which Jesus has made God known, and does so in the processional order prescribed in Matthew 28:19–20 and John 20:22–23: Father-Son-Spirit. Peter uses this same Triadic order to declare the message of the gospel in the house of Cornelius (Acts 10:38).

Acts 10:38. Peter uses the Father-Son-Spirit triad in his expression of the procession of the incarnation, "how God anointed Jesus of Nazareth with the Holy Spirit and with power, and how He went about doing good and healing." This succinct use of the Father-Son-Spirit order sits in a larger narrative presentation of the same missional order. Verse 34 starts with "God doesn't show favoritism," moves to "proclaiming the good news of peace through Jesus Christ" in verse 36 and then crescendos to the gentile Pentecost of the Spirit in verse 44 with, "While he was still speaking these words, the Holy Spirit came down on all who heard the message." So this passage could be notated theologically as F-S-[Father-Son-Spirit in v.38]-Sp. In the hands of the writer of Acts, it is God the Spirit who sounds the final note in this processional symphony by anointing the Gentiles in fulfillment of and involvement in the divine redemptive mission as providential peers with the Jews. Acts 10:38 as a triadic instance of the Father-Son-Spirit is graded "A" because of the clear Trinitarian intentionality of the brief passage.

Acts 20:21–23. This is the fourth and final instance of the Father-Son-Spirit order found in Acts. This instance is graded as "C" in terms of Trinitarian intentionality. In fact, it is among the weakest of the seventy-five occurrences of

Trinitarian references in the New Testament. The context is the apostle Paul's farewell address to the leaders of the Ephesian church. He says, "I testified to both Jews and Greeks about repentance toward God [Father] and faith in our Lord Jesus [Son]. And now I am on my way to Jerusalem, bound in my spirit, not knowing what I will encounter there, except that in town after town the Holy Spirit testifies to me that chains and afflictions are waiting for me." The apostle has inadvertently referenced each of the divine Three in the course of two sentences. This is an unconscious reference to the Trinity and is rated a "C" in terms of Trinitarian intentionality. However, what is the New Testament reader to think when these unconscious references—such regular triadic namings of the Father, Son, and Spirit—are salted throughout the narrative?

FATHER-SON-SPIRIT REFERENCES IN THE PAULINE EPISTLES

Of the seventy-five occurrences of Trinitarian processional orders in the New Testament, eighteen utilize the triadic procession Father-Son-Spirit. (See Table 5.1 above.) Many of these Father-Son-Spirit texts appear either in an initial greeting section or in a final benediction of a gospel or epistle. The epistle to the Romans has both.

Father-Son-Spirit in Romans

Romans 1:1–4. In the first verses of Romans, Paul introduces himself in terms of his apostolic mission "singled out for God's [Father] good news . . . concerning His Son, Jesus Christ our Lord . . . who has been declared to be the powerful Son of God by the resurrection from the dead according to the Spirit of holiness" (Romans 1:1–4). This lengthy (actually, the first seven verses), intensely theological introductory sentence is rated a "C" in terms of Trinitarian intentionality. The audacity to identify it as a triadic inference rests on whether or not "according to the Spirit of holiness" applies to the personal holiness of the life lived by Jesus or is a reference to the Holy Spirit. Commentators of the caliber of Mounce take it as personal holiness, while other commentators like Morris and Schreiner probably have the better ground to take it as a reference to the Holy Spirit. Morris asserts, citing F. F. Bruce, "*The Spirit of holiness* is the regular Hebrew way of saying 'the Holy Spirit'; Paul here reproduces the Hebrew idiom in Greek."[23]

---

23. Leon Morris, *The Epistle to the Romans* (Grand Rapids: Eerdmans; Leicester, England: Inter-

This incidence is inadvertent at best, with the Spirit referenced in the midst of a rich binitarian symphony of the Father and Son: "Grace to you and peace from God our Father and the Lord Jesus Christ" (Romans 1:7b). While the context is clearly one of Paul's apostolic mission "to bring about the obedience of faith among all the nations" (v. 5), it is debatable whether this triadic instance starts at verse 1 with "slave of Christ Jesus" and so follows the order Son-Father-Spirit. Is it better understood as starting with "God's good news" and so follows the procession Father-Son-Spirit? The intensely missional context slightly tilts favoring the Father-Son-Spirit order for this weaker instance of a Trinitarian reference.

Romans 5:1–5. If Romans 1:1–4 is a weaker triadic instance, then Romans 5:1–5 has a much clearer Trinitarian intention. The passage reads as follows, "we have peace with God [Father] through our Lord Jesus Christ [Son]. . . . (v. 1) and we rejoice in the hope of the glory of God . . . because God's love has been poured out in our hearts through the Holy Spirit [Spirit] who was been given to us." This instance is graded a "B" in terms of intentionality since sixty words, or two full sentences, in the original language separate the reference to the Father-Son and the Holy Spirit. The apostle presents inner peace as the result of the justifying work of Triune God.

Thomas Schreiner comments here, "This saving work ends with the Spirit's infusion of love into believing hearts. Believers know now in their hearts that they will be spared from God's wrath because they presently experience God's love for them through the ministry of the Holy Spirit."[24] Even as the passage moves from Father to Son to Spirit, it also moves from faith to hope to love.[25]

Romans 15:15–16. Chapter 15 of the epistle to the Romans is a veritable symphony of Trinitarian inferences. The distinct persons in the Godhead, as later styled in the ecumenical councils, are named nine times between verses 7 and 13. The notes in that Trinitarian melody read Son-Father (v. 7)-Son-Father-Father-Father (vv. 8–11)-Son-Father-Spirit (vv. 12–13). This triadic line will be examined in

---

Varsity Press, 1988), 46; cf. Robert H. Mounce, *Romans*, vol. 27, The New American Commentary (Nashville: Broadman & Holman Publishers, 1995), 61.

24. Thomas Schreiner, *Romans*, vol. 6, Baker Exegetical Commentary on the New Testament (Grand Rapids: Baker Books,1998), 257.

25. Note the masterful transition from *faith* (vv. 1, 2) to *hope* (vv. 2, 4, 5), to *love* (v. 5). This is the sequence found also in 1 Corinthians 13:13. (In 1 Thessalonians 1:3, the sequence is faith, love, hope.); see W. Hendriksen and S. J. Kistemaker, *Exposition of Paul's Epistle to the Romans*, vol. 12–13 (Grand Rapids: Baker Book House, 1953–2001), 171.

chapter 7 with the Son-Father-Spirit order. What follows in verses 15–17 is Paul's Trinitarian mission statement, "because of the grace given to me by God [Father], to be a minister of Christ Jesus [Son] to the Gentiles . . . that the offering of the Gentiles may be acceptable, sanctified by the Holy Spirit [Spirit]."[26]

Leon Morris recognizes the intentionally Trinitarian formation of this passage when he states, "We ought to notice here the way the three Persons of the Trinity are introduced. This is not yet the full doctrine of the Trinity, but it was from such expressions as these that the church in due time came to formulate this doctrine."[27]

Paul uses priestly words here. The word "minister" is related to liturgy and worship, as is the concept of "acceptable offering" (Hebrews 11:8).[28] This priestly ministry has come to Paul as the gracious gift of the Father, with the message of the gospel of the Son, and results in Gentile coverts being acceptable by the sanctification of the Holy Spirit. This passage is reminiscent of Peter's experience when the Holy Spirit fell upon Cornelius and company when they heard the good news: "While Peter was still speaking these words, the Holy Spirit came down on all who heard the message. The circumcised believers who had come with Peter were astounded because the gift of the Holy Spirit had been poured out on the Gentiles also" (Acts 10:44–45). This triadic instance occurs in two verses—twenty-six words in the original Greek—and noticeably depicts a missional movement of Father-Son-Spirit. So, in terms of Trinitarian intentionality, Romans 15:16–17 is rated an "A." With this identification of the Father-Son-Spirit triad at the end of Romans with the one at the beginning (Romans 1:1–4), the epistle has Trinitarian bookends.

Father-Son-Spirit Triad in the Corinthian Correspondence

Seven Trinitarian references can be found in the apostle Paul's two letters to the church at Corinth.

1 Corinthians 2:1–4. One of those instances uses the Father-Son-Spirit triad, 1 Corinthians 2:1–4. Here Paul explains his missional resolution as follows:

When I came to you, brothers, announcing the testimony of

---

26. Theologically understood, the ritual offerings of people are acceptable to God because the people making the offerings are acceptable. No offering is acceptable if God does not also accept the maker of the offering.
27. Morris, *Romans*, 512.
28. Ibid., 511.

> God [Father] to you, I did not come with brilliance of speech
> or wisdom. For I determined to know nothing among you ex-
> cept Jesus Christ [Son] and Him crucified. . . . My speech and
> proclamation were not with persuasive words of wisdom, but
> with a powerful demonstration by the Spirit [Spirit]."

Clearly Paul here invokes the order of Father-Son-Spirit as he explains his missional strategy among the Corinthians. Anthony Thiselton references the Trinity
in his commentary on this passage, saying, "The Holy Spirit witnesses to his own
presence and activity precisely by witnessing to Christ, to the effectiveness of the
gospel, and to other effects which are themselves the work of the trinitarian God."[29]

1 Corinthians 3:9–16. In this passage, the apostle less clearly reiterates this
order of Father-Son-Spirit. In that context, Paul is explaining the task of apostles,
pastors, and teachers as construction workers on the congregation as God's living
temple. He identifies the Corinthian believers as God's [Father in verse 9] building whose unique foundation is Jesus Christ [Son in verse 11] and that as God's
sanctuary, the Spirit [Spirit in verse 16] of God lives in them. Paul is exhorting the
believers toward faithfulness in their walk by giving them a look into this Trinitarian blueprint of God's redemptive mission with the Father as the builder, the Son
as the foundation upon which the church rests, and the Spirit as the indwelling
presence of God in his people.

Father-Son-Spirit Triad in Other Pauline Epistles
Galatians 4:4–6. The Father-Son-Spirit order also occurs in the apostle's letter
to the Galatians, about two-thirds of the way through the epistle at the beginning
of chapter 4. It occurs in the context of a discussion of baptism (3:27) and summa-
rization of the missional/redemptive movement of the gospel. Paul writes in Galatians 4:4–6 that "God [Father] sent His Son [Son] . . . so that we might receive
adoption as sons. And because you are sons, God has sent the Spirit [Spirit] of His
Son into our hearts, crying 'Abba, Father.'" The triadic procession is most accurately understood as Father-Son-Father-Spirit-Father, but nevertheless the gospel
missional order of Father-Son-Spirit is readily discernible. The Father sending the
Son and the Spirit establishes the context of this triad as missional. The fact that

---

29. Anthony Thiselton, *The First Epistle to the Corinthians: A Commentary on the Greek Text*
(Grand Rapids: Eerdmans, 2000), 222.

this order occurs in the wider context of "as many of you as have been baptized into Christ" (Gal. 3:27), connects the Father-Son-Spirit order to baptism and to mission/commission as it also does in Matthew 28:19–20.

F. F. Bruce comments on the work of Spirit in this context by asserting, "Two sure signs of the indwelling Spirit, for Paul, are the spontaneous invocation of God as 'Abba' and the spontaneous acknowledgement of Jesus as κύριος, 'Lord'" (1 Corinthians 12:3).[30] The passage rated an "A" because it is intentionally Trinitarian in its description of the birthing and first words of the newly begotten.

Ephesians 1:11–14. Some epistles of Paul follow the pattern of Romans in greeting the recipients with a Trinitarian reference in processional order of Father-Son-Spirit as a blessing. Besides Romans, this Trinitarian order is applied in the beginning of the epistles to the Ephesians (1:11–14) and Colossians (1:6–8), and in the first epistle to the Thessalonians (1:3–5).

In the Ephesians passage, the apostle greets his addressees with a cluster of soteriological concepts: redemption, forgiveness, and predestination (Ephesians 1:7–10). Then in verse 11, we find the Father-Son-Spirit triad in the words "according to the purpose of the One [Father] who . . . put our hope in the Messiah [Son] . . . when you heard the word of truth . . . were sealed by the promised Holy Spirit." (1:11–13) Literally, the sentence starts, "We have received an inheritance in Him [Son], predestined according to the purpose of the One [Father] who works out everything." Paul is here laying out the manifold blessings in Christ, starting each new thought with the phrase "in Him" in the Greek. Verses 11–13 are the second of the three "in Him" phrases. So, literally, the Trinitarian notation should be Son-Father-Son-Spirit. However, the context indicates that this "in Him" phrase points to the missional procession of the Father, who purposes from eternity; the Messiah, who receives the hope and faith of believers; and the promised Holy Spirit, who seals believers for an eternal inheritance. This triadic instance should be graded as a "B," in that the passage is clearly Trinitarian in intention but not as clearly Father-Son-Spirit in its triadic presentation.

Colossians 1:6–8. Not unexpectedly, this sister letter sent to Ephesus inadvertently follows this Pauline pattern of use of the Father-Son-Spirit order in the greeting section of the epistle. The context is the fruitfulness of "the word of

---

30. F. F. Bruce, *The Epistle to the Galatians: A Commentary on the Greek Text* (Grand Rapids: Eerdmans, 1982), 199.

truth, the gospel," in the lives of the Colossians believers (Colossians 1:5b). The apostle Paul describes the movement in the growth of their faith in three parts, "since the day you heard it and recognized God's [Father] grace in the truth. You learned this from Epaphras, our dearly loved fellow slave. He is a faithful servant of the Messiah [Son] on your behalf, and he has told us about your love in the Spirit [Spirit]" (Colossians 1:6b–8). This triadic finding should be rated "C-" at best since the close order of the references to God, Christ, and Spirit look entirely inadvertent and unintentionally Trinitarian. However, if Trinitarian thinking is part of the default consciousness of the writers of the New Testament, they might unconsciously speak in a Trinitarian phrasing simply because that seems the right way for Christians to speak.

1 Thessalonians 1:3–5. The apostle Paul loves threes. The first epistle to the Thessalonians introduces the Father-Son-Spirit order in its third verse in a more intentionally Trinitarian way, but embeds this triad among two more triads: "[W]e recall, in the presence of God the Father [Father], your work of faith, labor of love, and endurance of hope in our Lord Jesus Christ [Son]. . . . For our gospel did not come to you in word only, but also in power, in the Holy Spirit [Spirit], and with much assurance" (1 Thessalonians 1:3–5). The well-known Pauline triad of faith, love, and hope is produced in the believer in union with Christ and where the gospel comes with another triad of power, union with the Spirit, and assurance of salvation. Each of the three persons of the Trinity is introduced by the word "in," and demonstrates the results of union with the Father, Son, and Spirit. This text has a casual way of presenting a Trinitarian framework to declare the full affirmation of the faith of the Thessalonians. Since the triad is here used casually in that the Trinity is not the focus of the passage, this passage is graded a "B" for Trinitarian intentionality.

Conclusion about Paul and the Father-Son-Spirit Triad

Paul applies various Trinitarian processional orders twenty-eight times.[31] Five of those Pauline uses occur at or near the beginning of the respective letter. All of these introductory applications use the Father-Son-Spirit order. In no instance does any Trinitarian order other than Father-Son-Spirit occur in the greeting section of a Pauline letter. I conclude that, as far as the Pauline material is concerned, the Father-Son-Spirit order is Paul's way of framing missional

---

31. See Appendix A, "New Testament Census of Triadic Occurrences."

orthodoxy and orthopraxy as one enters the letter, even as this same order of Father-Son-Spirit is used as one enters public missional faith at baptism (Matthew 28:19–20; Galatians 3:27–4:6).

FATHER-SON-SPIRIT REFERENCES IN HEBREWS THROUGH REVELATION

1 Peter 1:3–12. First Peter begins with a concise greeting using the Father-Spirit-Son order which will be discussed in chapter 9. However, at verse 3, the epistle changes to the Father-Son-Spirit missional triad to discuss the believing life as one of a living hope. The apostle begins with "Praise the God and Father [Father] of our Lord Jesus Christ [Son]" in verse 3, continues to express the imperishable inheritance apprehended at the "revelation of Jesus Christ" in verse 7, and then concludes with two references to the Holy Spirit, one each in verse 11 ("the Spirit of Christ within") and in verse 12 ("the Holy Spirit sent from heaven"). This hope-filled life instituted and constituted by God the Father, Son, and Spirit is one which both prophets and angels wished to investigate.

This triadic occurrence is a rated "C" in terms of Trinitarian intentionality since the text inserts seven full verses between identification of the Father-Son and the Holy Spirit, all the while maintaining the hope of salvation as the point of discussion. It is as if full discussion of salvation as what the prophets prophesied and the angels desire to look into cannot be complete without identification of the Holy Spirit's place with the Father and the Son. Such is the missional mystery of the Triune God.

Revelation 1:9–10. The Revelation of John has an inadvertent Trinitarian triad in chapter 1. The text reads: "I, John, your brother and partner in the tribulation, kingdom, and endurance that are in Jesus, was on the island of Patmos because of God's word and the testimony of Jesus. I was in the Spirit on the Lord's day and I heard a loud voice behind me" (Revelation 1:9–10). The three persons of the Trinity are here responsible for words: the word of God [Father], the testimony of Jesus [Son], and the Spirit [Spirit] who revealed words of the revelation that are to be written "on a scroll" (Revelation 1:11). The proximity of the three names within seven words in the Greek text cannot be easily overlooked although no theological intentionality can be discerned. That proximity commends this triad for a "B" in Trinitarian intentionality and the tight proximity keeps it from being rated as a "C."

PRELIMINARY CONCLUSIONS: FATHER-SON-SPIRIT TRIADIC ORDER

I have three preliminary conclusions about the New Testament use of the Father-Son-Spirit Trinitarian procession. First, each of the eighteen instances of this triad has been graded with reference to the level of Trinitarian intentionality. The grading moves from overt or explicit intentionality to inadvertent or casual implicit use. Nine instances (fifty percent) received a grade of "A," five instances (twenty-eight percent) received a "B," and four instances (twenty-two percent) received a "C." Therefore, I conclude that the authors of the New Testament use the Father-Son-Spirit order with greater confidence and intentionality in their Trinitarian thinking than they do the other orders.

Second, in eleven out of the eighteen instances where this triad is used (sixty-one percent), the context is missional and sometimes the word "sent" is used, for instance John 1:33 and 20:21. Therefore I conclude that the Father-Son-Spirit triad is God sending. It is an "apostolic" movement, from the Greek word *apostelo*. The apostle Paul prefers to use the Father-Son-Spirit order early in his letters as a way of framing the tradition of the gospel received. This order depicts the redemptive mission of the Triune God. The Father-Son-Spirit order is echoed in the traditional Trinitarian values of fatherly initiation, obedient sonship in incarnation and atonement, and spiritual regeneration of the repentant into a new humanity as the body of the Son. This processional order *is* the gospel story of heaven come down to earth.

Third, the Father-Son-Spirit is the name of God used in baptism to indicate surrender to and involvement in this divine redemptive mission. Baptism symbolizes

- repentance from human rebellion against the Lord of reality and regenerative union with that Lord by grace through faith.

- union into the body of Christ.

- spiritually gifted entrance and engagement in the redemptive mission of the Body in the world.

In other words, the baptismal certificate, which commemorates public confession of salvation and membership, also commemorates ordination and commission into the mission of God, the Father, Son, and Holy Spirit. There is no

incidence in Scripture where authentic confession of sin is not met by forgiveness *and restoration to community and service.* It is unscriptural, if not heretical,
to separate forgiveness from restoration to communal trust and service.

For instance, note that Isaiah's confession of his and his people's unclean
lips is followed by divinely initiated cleansing and divinely bestowed prophetic
commission (Isaiah 6:6–9). Also, the iconic account of Peter's post-crucifixion
confession in the gospel of John makes this same point three times when, after
each pairing of Jesus' "Do you love me?" and Peter's "You know I do," Jesus re-
commissions Peter with a "Feed my sheep" or "Tend my lambs." So the Father
sends the Son and the Spirit. The Son is sent and sends the Spirit and believers.
The Spirit is sent and sends believers. The church is sent and sending as it re-
sponds to worship of the Father, Son, and Spirit.

In chapter 9, we will examine the eleven occurrences of Father-Spirit-Son triadic order to see how the Father's sending of the Spirit empowers Son-like living.

DISCUSSION QUESTIONS—CHAPTER 5

- How should we account for the difference between baptism in the name
  of the Lord Jesus in Acts and Paul's epistles and baptism in the name of
  the Father, Son, and Spirit in Matthew 28?

- Is it true that the Father-Son-Spirit triad has become so iconic that we
  can hardly see any other orders in the New Testament? Is this rut so
  deep that we can hardly see over the edges? What effect do you think
  that has on our worship and life together?

- Each of the eighteen instances of the Father-Son-Spirit order in the
  New Testament has been graded as to the apparent level of Trinitarian
  intentionality seen in the text. Matthew 28:19–20 received an "A" as the
  highest level of Trinitarian intentionality, but John 20:21–22 received a
  "B," and Romans 1:1–4 received a "C." How helpful do you find it to
  grade intentionality in these references? And in which instances would
  you raise or lower that grade? Why?

- How strong a case does this chapter make that the New Testament writers use the Father-Son-Spirit order to call their readers to engage with
  God in His mission in the world?

SERMON STARTER:
THE FATHER-SON-SPIRIT MISSIONAL ORDER

Trinitarian Discipleship: Matthew 28:18-20

In 2007, a Methodist professor named Allan Coppedge published *The God Who Is Triune.* Coppedge starts with a careful look at the Great Commission passage in Matthew 28:19–20 and ends with advocating what he calls "Trinitarian discipleship."[32] "Christian discipleship" is the phrase we commonly hear. *Trinitarian discipleship* is uncommon, but biblically more accurate. Listen again to this familiar text:

> All authority has been given to Me in heaven and on earth. Go, therefore and make disciples of all nations, baptizing them in the name of the Father and of the Son and of the Holy Spirit, teaching them to observe everything I have commanded you. And remember, I am with you always, to the end of the earth.

The point of the passage, the only active verb in it, is *make disciples*—not baptism. Discipleship accelerates in living out the life and ways of Jesus by baptizing believers as *functional Trinitarians. Traditional Trinitarians* are those able to sing and pray Trinitarian without being able to articulate the implications of Trinitarian discipleship. *Practical Unitarians* are those who reject, ignore, or are befuddled with the mystery of the Trinity and so collapse the three into a one of either the Father or the Son or the Spirit. These closet Unitarians give rise to the denominational joke that the Episcopalians have the Father, the Baptists have the Son, and the Pentecostals have the Spirit.

But Coppedge says, "No, we are Trinitarian or we are nothing." He creates vision for being and serving as functional Trinitarians. Just what would that mean and what would it look like?

Presence before Performance

Please do note that the three verbal commands in this passage, make, baptize and teach, are bookended by declaration of Jesus' universal authority and

---

32. Allan Coppedge, *The God Who Is Triune: Revisioning the Christian Doctrine of God* (Downers Grove, IL: InterVarsity Press, 2007), 36–52.

assurance of His abiding presence. Trinitarian discipleship depends on God's presence for our performance. Even before we attempt great things for God, we must expect great things of God.[33] Or, as the Book of Daniel asserts, "but the people who know their God shall be strong, and carry out great exploits" (Daniel 11:32, New King James Version).

Commission Follows Confession and Cleansing

Looking again at the Great Commission in Matthew 28:19–20; discipleship in the Triune name is the means and "of all nations" is the scope. So, being functionally Trinitarian is being commissionable and missional. As a Baptist advocate of believer's baptism by immersion upon confession of faith, I would witness that water baptism ought at a minimum to mean a public declaration of repentance, regeneration, and reception of forgiveness into God's household in Christ. I would also witness to two consistent patterns in Scripture. First, God never just forgives the repentant person without also engaging or restoring the person in His service. Biblically, confession and cleansing is always followed by commissioning. After Isaiah's confession that "I am a man of unclean lips and I dwell amongst a people of unclean lips," God takes the initiative to make atonement and cleanse Isaiah. Then God invites and commissions Isaiah to take up a prophetic mission (Isaiah 6:8–9). Cleansing is followed by commission.

The gospel of John tells of the restoration of Peter to ministry by Jesus. Peter has of course denied his involvement with Jesus three times within twenty-four hours during the crucifixion event. After His resurrection, Jesus seeks to restore Peter with the question, "Simon, son of John, do you love Me?" (John 21:17) After each of the three questions and responses, Jesus concludes not with an "I forgive you," but with a commission, "Tend my lambs" and "Feed my sheep" (John 21:15–17). Forgiveness is followed by missional assignment. If this is the way God works, then why should we be surprised that baptism as the public acknowledgement of gracious restoration to the Triune God is coupled with commitment to His mission of redemption for the nations? Baptism is both confession of faith and commission to spread that faith with the church to the nations.

Baptism is also an ordination. In it we are acting the Triune God's invitation to join Him in His redemptive mission. Technically, baptism of the spirit

---

33. William Carey, as quoted in "The Missionary Herald," *The Baptist Magazine*, vol. 25 (January 1843), 41.

in regeneration is the calling to mission and ordination and water baptism is the public recognition and confirmation that the church has another member-minister and member-missionary. On mission, we are co-laborers with Christ, at the bidding of the Father, in the power of the Spirit. And we co-labor with each other. Be advised that mission is messy. No mission means no mess. Little mission means little mess, much mission means much mess. However, if mess comes with mission, then so does miracle.

Triune Mission and Miracle

Mission and miracle are regular travel companions. If you want to find regular occurrences of the New Testament type miracles, look to the mission field. Why? Because miracle follows mission. No mission, no miracle. Little mission means little miracle. Much mission means much miracle. All mission, all miracle.

Why? Because the Triune God is committed to recovering His lost sheep. In His threeness, the Father sends the Son, and the Father and the Son send the Spirit. In John's version of the Great Commission in John 20:22–23, baptism is not even mentioned but sending is. "As the Father sent me, so send I you. Receive the Holy Spirit." The "I am with you always" of Matthew 28:20 is fulfilled as the Spirit of Christ is the empowering presence of Jesus to walk and speak His will and way to the nations.

Luke's version of the Great Commission is equally Trinitarian and equally missional, with no water baptism mentioned. "It is not for you to know the times or periods that the Father has set by His own authority. But you will receive power when the Holy Spirit has come on you, and you will be My witnesses in Jerusalem, Judea, Samaria and to the ends of the earth" (Acts 1:7–8). Note the Trinitarian order here: Father, Holy Spirit, and Son. Under the Father's authority, the Spirit empowers, and the nations receive our witness to the Son.

The Triune God Calls and Sends

It was part of their discipleship with Jesus. He made them into Trinitarian disciples. The Father, Son, and Spirit Trinitarian order is used in eighteen different places in the New Testament. When the Father, Son, and Spirit appear in that order, the context is usually about calling and sending. Father, Son, and Holy Spirit is *not* a *baptismal* formula—it is a *missional* formula. God calls and sends. Did you catch that? He does not just call, He calls *and* sends. If the Triune God is calling us, then He will also send us together on mission.

Prayer of Consecration

Living God, You are One and Three. May we also live in oneness with one another and diversity in gifts and ministry. Father, as you have sent the Son to be our Redeemer and Lord, so send us as witnesses to your life and grace. Lord Jesus, as you have been sent to save us and send us, please accept our thanks and surrender to your mission in our world. Spirit of the Living God, we welcome you as sent from the Father and the Son. Indwell and fill us that the overflow of your presence may be salt and light in the lives of those around us.

CHAPTER 6

The Saving Triad: Son-Spirit-Father as the Regenerative Order

While twenty-four percent of the New Testament occurrences of Trinitarian triads are in the historically predominant Father-Son-Spirit order, fully twenty percent present an alternate order of Son-Spirit-Father.[1] These fifteen instances are identified in Table 6.1 and occur in all four Gospels, Acts, various epistles of Paul, Hebrews, the first epistle of John, and in Revelation. If these identifications are valid, three conclusions and one question arise.

First, most readers of the Christian Scriptures are not readily aware of the abundance of Trinitarian references in the New Testament, much less fifteen such references to the Son-Spirit-Father triad alone. Second, this abundance of incidences of a triad ordering different from the Father-Son-Spirit is unexpected and understudied. Third, the logical conclusion of this abundant evidence is that multiple orders are apparent throughout the New Testament.

The question: Could the superabundance and ubiquity of this particular order of Son-Spirit-Father—the second highest number of occurrences of any of the six orders—call for special review of the contexts in which these triads are found?

This chapter gives an exegetical survey of each of these Son-Spirit-Father triad incidents, with particular interest in the contexts in which those triads surface. Hopefully that analysis will make a strong case for the use of this specific triad order.

---

1. See Appendix A, Chart 1, "New Testament Census of Triadic Occurrences."

TABLE 6.1: NEW TESTAMENT OCCURRENCES
OF THE SON-SPIRIT-FATHER TRIAD

LOCATIONS AND GRADATIONS FOR THE EVANGELICAL TRIADIC ORDER OF SON-SPIRIT-FATHER			
Text	**Rating**	**Context**	**Summary**
Matthew 3:16–17	A	Baptism	Jesus was baptized . . . the Spirit of God descended
Mark 1:10–11	A	Baptism	he came up out of the water . . . the Spirit descending
Luke 3:21–22	A	Baptism	Jesus was baptized . . . the Spirit of God descended
Luke 10:21	A	Ministry/mission	he rejoiced in the Holy Spirit and said, "I thank you, Father"
John 1:33–34	C	Baptism	He on whom you see the Spirit . . . is the Son of God
Acts 2:38–39	A	Redemption	name of Jesus Christ . . . gift of the Holy Spirit . . . whom the Lord our God
Romans 8:1–3	A-	Redeemed life	in Christ Jesus. Law of the Spirit of life in Christ Jesus . . . for God has done
Romans 15:30	A	Access in prayer	through the Lord Jesus Christ and through the love of the Spirit . . . your prayers to God
1 Corinthians 6:11	A	Redemption	justified in the name of Lord Jesus Christ and in the Spirit of our God
2 Corinthians 3:3	A	Ministry/mission	letter from Christ written with the Spirit of the living God
Ephesians 2:17–18	A	Life in Christ	through him [Son] we access in one Spirit to the Father
Hebrews 9:14	A	Christology/mission	the blood of Christ, eternal Spirit, to serve a living God
Hebrews 10:29–31	A-	Antichrist/mission	spurned the Son of God. . . outraged the Spirit . . . of the living God
1 John 5:6–9	A-	Christian faith	water and blood, Jesus, the Spirit is witness, the testimony of God
Revelation 22:17–18	B	Maranatha/warning	I Jesus . . . the Spirit and the Bride say . . . God will add

SON-SPIRIT-FATHER REFERENCES
IN THE GOSPELS AND ACTS

The Trinitarian Framework of Jesus' Baptism

Review of Table 6.1 above indicates that all four Gospels apply the Son-Spirit-Father order. The Gospels use this order in their respective narratives of the baptism of Jesus, except for the gospel of John, which employs the missional Father-Son-Spirit order.

The Synoptic Gospels: Matthew 3:16–17; Mark 1:10–11; and Luke 3:21-22. The baptismal narratives in Mark and Luke are more concise than that of Matthew. However, all three Synoptic Gospels capture the processional movement of Son-Spirit-Father: "After Jesus was baptized . . . the Spirit of God descending like a dove . . . and there came a voice from heaven: 'This is My beloved Son. I take delight in Him!'"

Mark 1:10–11. Mark's gospel has only this one triadic instance, and it is found in its narrative of the baptism of Jesus, unless Mark 1:1–8 can also be considered a triadic order. This gospel opens with a paragraph on the preparation and presentation ministry of John the Baptist. This paragraph starts with, "The beginning of the gospel of Jesus Christ, the Son [Son] of God [Father]." It ends with the witness of John that "he will baptize you with the Holy Spirit [Spirit]." So it seems fair to say that within the first eight verses of the opening of the gospel of Mark, all three persons in the Triune Godhead are mentioned and that the order identified is Son-Father-Spirit. This proposal tallies well with the evangelistic purpose of Mark's gospel.

John 1:33–34. The gospel of John does not reiterate the baptismal account *per se*, but it does give the prophecy whereby John, the cousin of Jesus, was to recognize and point out the Messiah. "The One you see the Spirit descending and resting on—He is the One who baptizes with the Holy Spirit. I have seen and testified that He is the Son of God" (John 1:33). I may be "forcing" this Johannine passage into the mold of the Son-Spirit-Father order since the phrase "Son of God" is not indisputably a reference to the Father. But certainly the Son-Spirit movement is quite clear, and it seems obvious that John the Baptist is to look for this triadic order to identify the One is who is coming as the Father's Son. The author wants this Sonship of God to be understood in the light of the previous declaration that this Son is to be the only Son [*monogenes*] from the Father (John 1:14). It is the public baptism of Jesus with the Son-Spirit-Father triad that serves as the starting gun for Jesus' public ministry of preaching, teaching, and healing. Here the evangelistic—literally "good newsing"—ministry of Jesus is initiated.

The Evangelistic Context in Luke and Acts

Luke makes use of the Son-Spirit-Father triad two more times in his gospel. In the narrative of Jesus preaching at His home synagogue in Nazareth, Luke quotes Jesus reading from the Messianic song in Isaiah 61: "He found the place where it was written: 'The Spirit of the Lord is on Me, because He has anointed Me to preach good news" (Luke 4:17–18, cf. Isaiah 61:1).[2] Here Luke's quotation from Isaiah follows the Septuagint, but the Hebrew in Isaiah reads *ruach adonai Yahweh*, which insists on or at least welcomes a stronger emphasis on "Lord." Therefore, identification of the Son-Spirit-Father order appears warranted: Jesus as the Son stands to identify His anointing by the Spirit of Yahweh to call people into a gracious season of jubilee and restoration to the kingdom. The passage yields a context of evangelizing or bringing the good news of the kingdom to those in most need of that news.[3]

Luke 10:21. Luke uses the Son-Spirit-Father order again in chapter 10. The context is Jesus' response to the reports that He has just received from the seventy disciples sent out as spiritual harvest workers in preparation for His own preaching ministry in those same towns and villages. Upon receiving the report of the disciples, "He [Jesus, Son] rejoiced in the Holy Spirit [Spirit], and said, 'I praise You, Father [Father].'" I simply note here that the context of this procession order, Son-Spirit-Father, is one in response to a verbal evangelistic ministry of preaching, healing, and exorcism.

---

2. This ministerial Christology should be integrated with Luke's earlier incarnational Christology, when the Spirit comes upon Mary to conceive the Son in her womb (Luke 1:35).

3. John Howard Yoder, *The Politics of Jesus* (Grand Rapids: Eerdmans 1972, 1994), 162; see also Galatians 2:10. Yoder focuses on this passage in Luke as Jesus' assuming the messianic task of declaring a jubilee year in which comprehensive human interactions—spiritual, relational, economical, and political—were to be realigned with God's will, ways, and word. I recognize the valuable discussion of the relationship, integration, and antinomies between the so-called social gospel and soul-winning. Ministry to lives without the message of repentance unto new life in Christ is a dead end, even as soul winning without remembering the poor is less than apostolic evangelism.

Acts 2:38–39. Luke uses *all six distinct triadic formulae* in just the book of Acts. This comprehensive pattern is matched only by the apostle John, when combining his gospel, epistles, and Revelation; and by the apostle Paul, in the composite of all his epistles.

With the apostle Luke, some of these orders in Acts are used multiple times so that there are thirteen occurrences overall. He uses the Son-Spirit-Father order only once, but it is at a pivotal point in the first gospel sermon of Peter. In answer to the question of the temple onlookers, "What must we do to be saved?" the apostle Peter replies using the Son-Spirit-Father order, "Repent and be baptized . . . in the name of Jesus Christ [Son] for the forgiveness of sins, and you will receive the Holy Spirit [Spirit]. For the promise is for . . . as many as the Lord our God [Father] will call" (Acts 2:38–39).

In the recent history of Christianity, this potent text has been used as a focal text for the "divine order of salvation" in the Restoration Movement of the Disciples of Christ and the "Jesus-only" branch of Pentecostalism. It is the latter movement which advocates a Son-only modalist approach to God and for baptism in the name of Jesus only. The contrast between this baptismal formula and that of Matthew 28:19–20 only appears to be a contrast between modalist unitarianism, which finds no distinctions within the Godhead, and Trinitarian faith, which declares three distinct entities equal in essence but existing in indivisible unity. Though Acts 2:38 calls for baptism in the name of Jesus, the context itself is explicitly Trinitarian, using the Son-Spirit-Father order. The Son is identified with repentance, baptism, and forgiveness of sins; followed by the gift of the Holy Spirit; and all at the call and initiative of the Lord God [Father]. So, Acts 2:38–39 is in reality no less Trinitarian in framework than the so-called Great Commission in Matthew, just in a different order. This passage and order will be further analyzed later in this chapter under the Reformation formula for evangelism: *notitia, assensus, fiducia*—"data, agreement, and faith commitment."

PAULINE APPLICATION OF THE SON-SPIRIT-FATHER TRIAD

Five occurrences of the Son-Spirit-Father order can be found in the epistles of Paul. Two are in Romans, one in 1 Corinthians, and two in Ephesians.

Romans 8:1–3. Romans 8 begins with the famous soteriological declaration, "Therefore, no condemnation now exists for those in Christ Jesus [Son], because the Spirit's [Spirit] law of life . . . has set you free from the law of sin and death. What the law could not do . . . God [Father] did" (Romans 8:1–3). Processional analysis here yields a pattern of Son-Spirit-Father.[4] However, verses 1–11 are an instructive movement of Trinitarian perichoresis. I use *perichoresis* here in the patristic sense of the distinct but indivisible, interpenetrating relations within and by the One God. I have annotated the significant processional movement below.

> **1–3** for those in Christ Jesus [Son], because the Spirit's [Spirit] law of life in Christ Jesus [Son] has set you free from the law of sin and death. What the law could not do . . . God [Father] did.

> **5–6** those who live according to the Spirit [Spirit], about the things of the Spirit [Spirit] . . . the mindset of the Spirit [Spirit] is life and peace.

> **7–8** the flesh is hostile to God [Father] because it does not submit itself to God's [Father] law . . . those who are in the flesh are unable to please God [Father].

> **9** not in the flesh, but in the Spirit [Spirit], since the Spirit of God [Spirit] lives in you. But if anyone does not have the Spirit of Christ [Spirit], he does not belong to Him.

> **10–11** Now if Christ [Son] is in you, the body is dead because of sin, but the Spirit [Spirit] is life because of righteousness. And if the Spirit of Him [Father, or Spirit?] who raised Jesus [Son] from the dead, then He [Father] who raised Christ [Son] from the dead will also bring your mortal bodies to life through His Spirit [Spirit] who lives in you.

---

4. Those notations could be continued beyond verse 3 to verse 17, in which case, the *perichoretic* movement of the Trinitarian mission in the life of believers would be seen as S-Sp-S-F-S-Sp-F-Sp. See Paul Fiddes, who has utilized *perichoresis* (the Greek version of the Latin *cummunicatio idiomatum*) to make a strong contribution to the contemporary discussion of Trinitarian pastoral theology. He might have used this Trinitarian choreography found in Romans 8:1–3 to illustrate his points.

Note that the Son-Spirit-Father order appears both at the beginning in verses 1–3 and at the end in verses 10–11.[5] These twin recitations are separated by Paul's recitation of Spirit-Spirit-Spirit in verses 5 and 6, followed by Father-Father-Father in verses 7 and 8, and then the triple reference to the Spirit in verse 9. The context of these twin Son-Spirit-Father occurrences is Paul's presentation of the believer's life in Christ made possible by the Holy Spirit. So, through faith in the Son, the Spirit brings you to the Father and imparts the gifts of the Father to you.

Romans 15:30. Paul also uses the Son-Spirit-Father triad in requesting intercession from the Roman believers. He writes later in Romans 15:30: "Now I appeal to you, brothers, through our Lord Jesus Christ [Son] and through the love of the Spirit [Spirit], to join with me in fervent prayers to God [Father]." The focal point of the intercession was to be deliverance of Paul from malicious unbelievers during his pending Judean visit. It is intriguing that the triad which usually conveys the divine movement in coming to faith is here being used in intercession regarding those resistant to such faith.

1 Corinthians 6:11. The Son-Spirit-Father triad also occurs in a context in 1 Corinthians similar to the one in Romans 15:30. Here Paul is contrasting the believer's life before and after faith in Christ. He has just listed multiple patterns of unrighteous living in 1 Corinthians 6:9–10 and then moves to explain the cleansing that faith brings. "But you were washed, you were sanctified, you were justified in the name of the Lord Jesus Christ [Son] and by the Spirit [Spirit] of our God [Father]."

Note that the biblical order of these soteriological metaphors—washed, sanctified, and justified—is not in the anticipated theological *ordu salutis* (order of salvation). This word order, which is counterintuitive—at least from the perspective of dogmatic Reformation soteriology looking for justification to precede sanctification—will be discussed later in this chapter for its connection to the Son-Spirit-Father triad. It is sufficient for the moment to reiterate that this triad usage is presented in a context of discussing the kingdom outcome of the righteous life. The Son-Spirit-Father triad here is the vehicle of divine "good newsing," whether it relates to justification at the beginning of the new life or

---

5. Note also that the Spirit-Father-Son triad also appears twice in this passage if extended to the next paragraph. Compare verse 8 and verse 15. This triad will be investigated in the next chapter.

glorification at its culmination in eternity. Reformation soteriology asserts that we *have been saved* by having been justified at the cross, *are being saved* by the sanctifying work of the Spirit, and *will be saved* in glorification at the end of time.[6] The Son-Spirit-Father order *is* God saving.

2 Corinthians 3:3. Paul returns to the Son-Spirit-Father order again in 2 Corinthians 3:3 when he discusses the readability of the lives of believers by outsiders: "It is clear that you are Christ's [Son] letter, produced by us, not written with ink but with the Spirit [Spirit] of the living God [Father]." Could it be that the Son-Spirit-Father order in some way embodies the Christian life in its most authentic expression and with its most favored outcome?

Ephesians 2:17–18. In this passage, Paul is discussing the metacultural unity that believers experience in Christ. "When the Messiah came, He proclaimed the good news of peace to you who were far away and peace to those who were near. For through Him [Son] we both have access by one Spirit [Spirit] to the Father [Father]." This order of Son-Spirit-Father appears to depict the movement of diverse believers into united citizenship, giving us access to God the Father and which is pleasing to Him. As a systematic theologian, I would identify this passage as sanctification.

SON-SPIRIT-FATHER REFERENCES IN HEBREWS THROUGH REVELATION

The Saving Life of the Son in Hebrews

Since the theme of the letter to the Hebrews is intensively christological, note that all five occurrences of Trinitarian triads identifiable in this letter begin with "Son."[7] The order Son-Spirit-Father is found twice (in 9:14 and 10:29) and the Son-Father-Spirit order is found three times (in 2:3–4; 3:1–7; and 10:12–15).

Hebrews 9:14. This passage comes in the well-known christological discussion of Christ as the high priest, who mediates the new covenant through atone-

---

6. Wayne Grudem, *Systematic Theology* (Grand Rapids: Zondervan, 1994), 747–753.
7. See Appendix A, Chart 1, "New Testament Census of Triadic Occurrences." The Son-Father-Spirit triad will be investigated in chapter 7.

ment in the heavenly sanctuary. "How much more will the blood of the Messiah [Son], who through the eternal Spirit [Spirit] offered Himself without blemish to God [Father], cleanse our consciences from dead works to serve the living God?" This triadic movement of God as Son-Spirit-Father mediates to believers the saving life of Christ, empowered by the Spirit, and delivered to the Father, the living God. The order catalyzes and summarizes the experience of coming into the life that faith in Christ offers. People are saved by becoming aware of the Son's priestly atoning work on the cross, by experiencing the conviction and quickening of the Spirit, and then rising into an authentic relationship of adoption into God's household and hope.

Hebrews 10:29–31. If the Son-Spirit-Father order pictures, as I am proposing, the experience of conversion, then theoretically apostasy as deconversion might be expected to invoke this same triadic order.[8] This is exactly what is found in the second of the two infamous "apostasy" passages in the epistle to the Hebrews (Hebrews 6:1–12; 10:19–38). While I do hold the eternal security approach to these passages, it is not within the scope of this book to give full exegetical and theological defense to that position. For those who wish to study this issue more closely, I do recommend *Four Views in the Warning Passages in Hebrews,* edited by Herbert Bateman.[9]

Using my now familiar triadic notation, Hebrews 10:29–31 reads:

> How much worse punishment do you think one will deserve who has trampled on the Son of God [Son], regarded as profane the blood of the covenant by which he was sanctified, and insulted the Spirit of grace [Spirit]? For we know the One who has said, Vengeance belongs to Me I will repay,' and again, The Lord will judge His people. It is a terrifying thing to fall into the hands of the living God [Father].

---

8. Deconversion refers to loss of faith, about which there is a growing body of literature. See Heinz Streib, et al., *Deconversion: Qualitative and Quantitative Results from Cross-Cultural Research in Germany and the United States of America,* vol. 5 in Research in Contemporary Religion (Göttengen, Germany: Vandenhoeck and Ruprecht, 2011) and Christian Smith and Patricia Snell, *Souls in Transition: The Religious and Spiritual Lives of Emerging Adults* (New York: Oxford University Press, 2009).

9. Herbert W. Bateman IV, ed., *Four Views in the Warning Passages in Hebrews* (Grand Rapids: Kregel, 2007).

The author is warning those considering the path of apostasy that what begins with refutation of the Son inevitably involves insulting the Holy Spirit and concludes with invoking retribution from the Father. If the triadic pattern of conversion is Son-Spirit-Father, then deconversion follows this same pattern with an ominous warning. Some commentators focus on the three verbs in verse 29—trampled, regarded as profane, and insulted—to make the connection with verse 28's recitation of the famous Mosaic dictum about the necessity of two or three witnesses to enact the death penalty for flagrant violation of the Law.[10] The author instead states the charges as made by the Son, then the Spirit, and finally the Father, who is identified in verse 31 as "the One," "the Lord," and "the living God"

In Lenski's commentary on this passage, he sees this apostasy as "sin against the supreme institution of grace, the agents of which are the two divine persons themselves."[11] If Lenski can name the two divine persons, Son and Spirit, in verse 29, why can he not name the third in verses 30 and 31? Is this text what Jesus meant by blasphemy against the Holy Spirit in Matthew 12:31–32? Blasphemy against the agent of grace invokes retribution from the Father. Was Jesus alerting His detractors that their apostolic path had moved beyond trampling the Son to insulting the gracious Spirit, and thus divine retribution was the consequence? Because of the transition from offense against the Son and Spirit in verse 29 to retribution from the Father in verse 30, I grade this triadic instance as a "B."

John's Use of Son-Spirit-Father as a Triadic Testimony

The final New Testament occurrences of the Son-Spirit-Father order come from the apostle John. One is found in 1 John and the other in Revelation.

1 John 5:6–9. The context is the discussion of surety of the witness or testimony concerning the Son and the life He imparts. Verse 6 reads, "Jesus Christ [Son]—He is the One who came by water and blood. . . And the Spirit [Spirit] is the One who testifies." And this discussion continues to a climax in verse 9, "God's [Father] testimony is greater, because it is God's testimony that He has given about His Son." The substance of this testimony presented through the Son-Spirit-Father order is given in verse 11: "And this is the testimony: God has

---

10. Paul Ellingworth, *The Epistle to the Hebrews: A Commentary on the Greek Text* (Grand Rapids: Eerdmans, 1993), 578.
11. R. C. H. Lenski, *The Interpretation of the Epistle to the Hebrews and of the Epistle of James* (Columbus, OH: Lutheran Book Concern, 1938), 359.

given us eternal life, and this life is in His Son." It seems that the Son-Spirit-Father Trinitarian order is consistently linked to entrance into and life lived in union with Christ. This order above all others shows the pattern of persons coming into and living in the saving life of Christ.

Revelation 22:16–18. *Maranatha* is Aramaic for "the Lord is coming" and "come, Lord." The verb *come* is used five times in the last five verses of the New Testament, and it relates to the promised return of Jesus. In triadic notation, verses 16–18 read as follows:

> I, Jesus, [Son] have sent My angel to attest these things to you for the churches. I am the Root and the Offspring of David, the Bright Morning Star. Both the Spirit [Spirit] and the bride say, "Come!" Anyone who hears should say, "Come!" And the one who is thirsty should come. Whoever desires should take the living water as a gift. I testify to everyone who hears the prophetic words of this book: If anyone adds to them, God [Father] will add to him the plagues that are written in this book.

This concluding passage expresses aspiration and warning. Either we should be crying out to the Son to come and to the thirsty say, "Drink of the Son!"—or we will find ourselves cut off by the Father from the Tree of Life and life in the holy city.

In a slightly different variation of the triadic instance in Hebrews 10:29–31 discussed above, the Son-Spirit-Father order is a conversion bridge used by people journeying to their eternal destinies in both directions. These triad instances express warning to those who refuse to cross in the right direction. Grant Osborne also recognizes the similarity of Hebrews and Revelation in the warnings against apostasy, but does not reflect on that warning's triadic underpinnings of Son-Spirit-Father.[12] Those who will not rejoice in the provision of the Son and Spirit will experience retribution from the Father.

While the Trinity is a background organizer for this discussion, the focus is how people are living in response to Jesus and the call of the Spirit. G. K. Beale notes that "I, Jesus, will send my angel" is "modeled" on Malachi 3:1 to affirm the

---

12. Grant Osborne, *Revelation* (Grand Rapids: Baker Academic, 2002), 796.

divinity of Jesus.[13] This divine affirmation leads right into the fifth "I am saying" in the Book of Revelation, "I am the Root and . . . " (Revelation 1:8, 17; 2:23; 21:6; 22:16).[14] Beale further comments, "The titles [Root, and Offspring of David] combine two OT prophecies (Num. 24:17 and Isa. 11:1, 10) concerning the messianic king's triumph over his enemies at the end of time."[15] He also identifies the "Spirit" in verse 17 as the Holy Spirit in contradiction to some who see it as another reference either to Christ or to prophetic speech.[16] So, with reference to intentionality, this triadic reference is Trinitarian, but is a "C" because of the relative inadvertence of its invocation over the span of three verses.

PRELIMINARY CONCLUSIONS:
SON-SPIRIT-FATHER TRIADIC ORDER AS GOD SAVING

If the economic Trinitarian order of Father-Son-Spirit is understood as the *missio Dei*—God sending and sent—then the Trinitarian order of Son-Spirit-Father is to be understood based on the above exegetical studies to be God saving. The Reformation thinkers described the experience of being saved from the human side as *notitia, assensus, fidei*, roughly understood as receiving notice of the gospel, assenting to it intellectually, and committing to it in faith. But from the divine side, the Son makes Himself known as the Spirit brings conviction and convincing until regeneration produces the cry of the newborn child of God, "*Abba*, Father" (Galatians 4:6).

Though Jesus commands disciple making to be marked by baptism in the name of the Father, Son, and Spirit, all four Gospels identify the three persons of the Trinity at Jesus' own baptism in the order of Son-Spirit-Father. When Jesus presents Himself to be baptized by John, the latter witnesses the descent of the Spirit upon Jesus as a dove, concluded by the theophany of the Father's declaration, "This is My beloved Son. I take delight in Him!" (See Table 6.1 above.)

With the first evangelistic invitation at Pentecost, Peter invokes this same order to counsel inquirers toward repentance and baptism in the name of Jesus, forgiveness and empowerment by the Holy Spirit, and the fulfillment of promised

---

13. G. K. Beale, *The Book of Revelation: A Commentary on the Greek Text* (Grand Rapids: Eerdmans, 1999), 1143.
14. S. J. Kistemaker and Warren Hendriksen, *Exposition of the Book of Revelation*, vol. 20 (Grand Rapids: Baker Book House, 1953–2001), 592.
15. Beale, 1146.
16. Ibid., 1148.

salvation by the "Lord our God" (Acts 2:38–39). The wise evangelist understands that Jesus must be so introduced to the recipient that the Spirit's work of illumination yields the experience of forgiveness and adoption into the household of the Father. This is the Trinitarian order of salvation, the *ordo salutis*. The Son-Spirit-Father instances in Hebrews 10:28–29 and Revelation 22:16–18 warn us that if this triadic pattern is the Trinitarian bridge of God saving, then it is also the bridge of God condemning. Bridges always have traffic moving in both directions.

DISCUSSION QUESTIONS—CHAPTER 6

- How hard will it be for you to start using the Son-Spirit-Father order in your thinking and praying? If the New Testament writers use this order in their praying and blessing, why can or can't you use that as permission for you to use it too?

- This chapter identifies the Son-Spirit-Father order as God saving. What makes you want to agree or disagree with that identification? Which of the verses examined as Son-Spirit-Father triads supports your opinion? If you agree with this identification as God saving/regenerating, why is it important that the Father is last in this order?

- According to this chapter, the gospel of Mark has only one triadic instance of any kind. Speculate on why you think there are so few in Mark and why Mark would use the Son-Spirit-Father order instead of the Father-Son-Spirit order? While you are speculating, why do you think the Father-Son-Spirit order—God sending—might have the most instances at eighteen and the Son-Spirit-Father triad the second most frequent at sixteen instances?

- How could you use the Son-Spirit-Father order to explain the new birth process and evangelism?

SERMON STARTER:
THE SON-SPIRIT-FATHER EVANGELISTIC ORDER

Triple Play—The End Game of the Triune God: Romans 8:1-3

To envision or "end-vision" means to begin with the end in view. Progress depends on remembering where you are headed. Without such a vision, people lose heart and momentum, and they may disengage.

One Sunday afternoon some urbanites took a long drive into the countryside. The obvious city dwellers interrupted a seasoned field hand to ask for directions. "Where are you headed?" he responded.

"Oh, nowhere in particular," came their reply.

To which the laconic farmer declared, "Then what difference does it make?"

In the matter of God's mission of human reclamation, where is God headed? Knowing His endgame permits us to realize the significance of the direction He is taking in renewing our lives. What's His point? God wants back what was lost to Him in the beginning because of disobedience. His game then is that through faith in Christ, the Holy Spirit rebirths a person into the household of God so that their first words in the new life are *"Abba, Father"* (Romans 8:15).

This is a divine "triple play." Yes, Jesus saves—but so does the Spirit and the Father. Listen how this Triune triple play unfolds in Romans 8:1–3:

> Therefore, no condemnation now exists for those in Christ Jesus, because the Spirit's law of life in Christ Jesus has set you free from the law of sin and of death. What the law could not do since it was limited by the flesh, God did.

To get out of our losing inning in this sudden death game of life, we need the triple play of the Triune God. Most of us know that the lives we are living are not habitable forever. "Our lives last seventy years, or if we are strong, eighty years" (Psalm 90:10). Then that red slip of property condemnation notice is posted, and it is real and right.

We struggle for authentic significance, knowing perfectly well that our way of living and loving is self-centered or self-loathed and is headed at full speed for a dead end. Then comes the good news, Jesus. His words, His walk, and His authority amaze us and draw us in. Union with Christ means letting go of our good intentions that were becoming threadbare and instead becoming transparent in confession and trust.

Our lives then receive a second wind from the Spirit as we come to understand that when the books are opened, we have an Advocate at the final judgment. The fear of death and the anticipation of eternal condemnation lift as we see that Jesus sends us another counselor, the Spirit, who leads us into the experience of forgiveness and gratitude of service. As we are born again by the Spirit, we cry out like any new child. Only our cry is "*Abba*, Father." Note that this passage explains that the law of moral gravitation—which pulls all down to condemnation because of sin—is only overcome by the law of spiritual aerodynamics. The law condemns, but the Spirit gives life.

Shortly after becoming a new believer in high school, a friend of mine was pulled over for speeding. His fresh joy of salvation sweetened any disappointment as the officer took out his pad and started writing. I think my friend even thanked the policemen for doing his duty. At some point, that officer lost his cool, handed my friend the speeding ticket, and turned away with a whispered, "Go to hell."

To which my friend happily replied, "Sorry, officer, I can't."

There is now no condemnation for those in whom the Triune God has done a saving work. We meet Jesus, the Spirit then brings conviction and regeneration, and the Father bestows adoption and commission. Jesus saves. The Spirit saves. The Father saves. The Trinity saves.

My grandparents lived into their nineties in the same house, with only one phone on a land line. If you talked with one, you then had to talk with the other. They were inseparable. God, too, dwells in unimpaired unity. What Jesus starts in making Himself known, the Spirit wants in on, too: to quicken and reboot us for the life God always intended; and then the Father welcomes us into that unimpaired unity as His child.

This Triune pattern of salvation—Son-Spirit-Father—occurs fifteen times in the New Testament. If we want to cooperate with God saving others, we can count on God moving in this pattern. People need sufficient gospel knowledge of Jesus, birth to resurrection, for the Spirit to kindle a fire within their heads and hearts. In the light of that fire, they will recognize the holy love of the Father has accepted and adopted them eternally and will not let them go. This is God saving. When Nicodemus came at night to speak with Jesus, Jesus drew him into the Trinitarian life by challenging him to be born again by the Spirit. The evidence of such regeneration is the inner cry of adoption into the household of God, "*Abba*, Father."

CHAPTER 7

The Indwelling Triad: Son-Father-Spirit as the Christological Witness Order

Thus the things of the Trinity are undivided: and whereas the communion is of the Spirit, it hath been found of the Son; and whereas the grace is of the Son, it is also of the Father and of the Holy Spirit. . . . And I say these things, not confounding the Persons, (away with the thought!) but knowing both the individuality and distinctness of These, and the Unity of the Substance."
—John Chrysostom, Archbishop of Constantinople
(397–405)[1]

There are fourteen occurrences of the Son-Father-Spirit triad in the New Testament. These incidences represent nineteen percent of all Trinitarian references in the New Testament. The Son-Father-Spirit triad is the third most prevalent. The gospels of Luke and John, the book of Acts, and the epistle to the Hebrews make significant use of the Son-Father-Spirit triadic order. See Table 7.1 below. Reflection on this order indicates that this triad is the

1. John Chrysostom, *Saint Chrysostom: Homilies on the Epistles of Paul to the Corinthians*, vol. 12 in Schaff, ed., J. Ashworth & T. B. Chambers, trans. (New York: Christian Literature Company, 1889), 418–419.

Christological order *par excellence.* The Son-Father-Spirit triad is *God descending.* It outlines the christological movement of descent by the Son from the Father, followed by ascent by the Son to the Father, which precipitates the descent of the Spirit upon the church. Let's look at the Scripture to verify this initial reflection on the Son-Father-Spirit order against the actual New Testament instances of that order.

TABLE 7.1: NEW TESTAMENT OCCURRENCES OF THE SON-FATHER-SPIRIT TRIAD

LOCATIONS AND GRADATIONS FOR THE CHRISTOLOGICAL TRIADIC ORDER OF SON-FATHER-SPIRIT			
Text	**Rating**	**Context**	**Summary**
Luke 11:13	NA	Prayer	how much more will the heavenly Father give the Holy Spirit
Luke 24:49–50	A-	Missional power	I send the promise of my Father upon you
John 3:34	B	Christology/ mission	he whom God has sent . . . he gives Spirit without measure
John 14:16	A	Empower/ promise	I will pray the Father and he will give you another Counselor . . . the Spirit
John 14:25–26	B	Indwelling	while I remain with you, but the Counselor, the Holy Spirit—the Father will send Him in My name . . . and will remind you of everything I have told you.
Acts 1:4–5	B	Empowerment	He [Jesus] commanded them . . . . to wait for the Father's promise. . . . What you heard from me [Jesus] . . . but you will be baptized with the Holy Spirit
Acts 2:32–33	A	Economic	This Jesus God raised up . . . received from the Father the promised Holy Spirit
Romans 7:4–6	C	Free to be fruitful	through the body of the Messiah [Son] . . . belong to Him [Son] who was raised . . . that we may bear fruit for God . . . so that we serve in the new way of the Spirit

LOCATIONS AND GRADATIONS FOR THE CHRISTOLOGICAL TRIADIC ORDER OF SON-FATHER-SPIRIT			
Text	**Rating**	**Context**	**Summary**
Romans 15:12–13	B	Empowerment	The root of Jesse will appear [Son]. . . . Now may the God of hope fill you . . . by the power of the Holy Spirit.
2 Corinthians 13:14[1]	A	Benediction	grace of Lord Jesus Christ and the love of God and the fellowship of the Holy Spirit
Ephesians 2:21–22	A	One in Christ	into a holy sanctuary in the Lord [Son] . . . for God's dwelling in the Spirit.
Hebrews 2:3–4	A-	Salvation/ Witness	first by our Lord, God also bore witness . . . by gifts of the Holy Spirit
Hebrews 3:1–7	C	Christology/ mission	Consider Jesus, in God's house, Christ . . . over God's house . . . Holy Spirit says today
Hebrews 10:12–15	B	Redemption	Christ had offered . . . right hand of God . . . Holy Spirit also bears witness

SON-FATHER-SPIRIT REFERENCES IN THE GOSPELS

Luke 11:13 and Luke 24:49. In Luke's eleventh chapter, Jesus makes a promise as He ends His teaching on prayer: "how much more will the heavenly Father give the Holy Spirit to those who ask Him." At His ascension back to glory, Jesus will be the first to ask the Father to give the Spirit. Technically, Luke 11:13 is a binitarian and not Trinitarian reference, hence though it appears in the list of Trinitarian references, it receives a grade of NA. This binitarian instance "grows up" into a Trinitarian reference at the end of Luke's gospel. In the post-resurrection ascension narrative of Luke 24:49, Jesus declares that the time has come for the promise to be fulfilled, "I [Son] am sending you, what My Father [Father] promised . . . . [S]tay in the city until you are empowered from on high [Spirit]." We know from Acts, as Luke's sequel to his gospel, that "you will receive power when the Holy Spirit comes upon you, and you will be My witnesses" (Acts 1:8).

I. Howard Marshall comments that "it is surprising that there is no actual mention of the Spirit here."[2] The ascent of the Son to the Father precipitates the endowment of the Spirit. Darrell Bock identifies Jesus as the mediator of salvation's benefits, and so He is the distributor of the Spirit. He writes, "When Jesus speaks of the Father's promise, he can only have one thing in mind—the Holy Spirit (see esp. Acts 1:4–5 and the contrast to John's baptism [Luke 3:16])."[3] This christological procession of the Triune God reflects the obedience of the Son, the authority and faithfulness of the Father, and the necessity of the empowerment of the Spirit to adequately witness or represent the kingdom of this God on earth. This reference to the Son-Father-Spirit order dovetails significantly with Luke's two fold invocation of the Triune God in this same order in Acts 1 and 2. But before we examine those triads, let's look at the three uses of the Son-Spirit-Father order in the gospel of John.

John 3:34. In His incarnation, Jesus is the visible image of the invisible God (Hebrews 1:3). He is also the perfect model for the life we are to live. (Galatians 2:20). What Jesus wants for us in Acts 1:8 is His life, described here in John 3:34. In triadic notation it reads, "For God [Father] sent Him [Son], and He [Son] speaks God's [Father] words, since He [Father] gives the Spirit [Spirit] without measure." Technically, the order is Father-Son-Son-Father-Father-Spirit. The Father sends the Son (missional order), so that on earth the Son speaks the Father's message, and the responders receive the Father-sent Spirit, that they may replicate the witnessing mission of the Son (the christological order). The missional triad of Father-Son-Spirit has chronological priority to the christological triad of Son-Father-Spirit, and the sending has the intent of enabling the ascending of the Son and the descending of the Spirit. In this context, Gerald Borchert notes the Johannine intention to underscore the unity of the Three in One with these comments:

> The continual affirmation of the Johannine Gospel is the unity of the Son with the Father, which was expressed first by the equating of the *logos* (Word) with *theos* (God) in the Prologue (1:1). . . . But this idea of Jesus being one with God finally began to make sense after the resurrection with the key confes-

---

2. I. H. Marshall, *The Gospel of Luke: A Commentary on the Greek Text* (Exeter, England: Paternoster Press, 1978), 907.
3. D. L. Bock, *Luke: 9:51–24:53*, vol. 2, Baker Exegetical Commentary on the New Testament (Grand Rapids: Baker Academic, 1996), 1942.

sion of Thomas (20:28). . . . Such a statement does not mean
that the Father has abdicated his role in salvation because such
an idea would be a complete misunderstanding of the Johannine view of the unity of the Father and the Son. Indeed, the
Spirit is also part of that unity, and here it said that there was
no partial giving of the Spirit to Jesus (3:34).[4]

So clearly, John 3:34 is a triadic instance expressing the unity of the Three
of redemptive mission. I have listed this as a Son-Father-Spirit triad because of
the context of Jesus explaining to Nicodemus the necessity of being born of the
Spirit in order to participate in the kingdom. I have graded my identification as
an "A-," since there is some ambiguity because of the initial Father-Son introductory dyad.

John 14:16–17. The gospel of John continues to reveal the meaning of
this S-F-Sp processional order in John 14:16. This passage contains some of
the most significant teaching about the doctrines of the Trinity and the Spirit
in the Christian Scriptures. Here Jesus speaks the famous word about "another
Counselor [*paraclete*]." He asserts to the disciples, "And I [Son] will ask the Father [Father], and He will give another Counselor to be with you forever. He is
the Spirit [Spirit] of truth." He who descended, the Son, will ascend to petition
the Father that the Spirit might descend upon the disciples. The triad is clearly
Trinitarian and clearly Son-Father-Spirit, and so I have graded as an "A" in intentionality. Henrichsen's comments on this passage offer exegetical arguments
for the divinity and the personhood of the Spirit. He writes

The passage clearly indicates that the Holy Spirit is not merely
a power but *a person,* just like the Father and the Son. He is *another* Helper, not a *different* Helper. The word *another* indicates
one like myself, who will take my place, do my work. Hence, if
Jesus is a person, the Holy Spirit must also be a person. Moreover, personal attributes are everywhere ascribed to him (14:26;
15:26; Acts 15:28; Rom. 8:26; 1 Cor. 12:11; 1 Tim. 4:1; Rev.
22:17). His relation to the Father and the Son is described as of

---

4. Gerald Borchert, *John 1–11*, vol. 25A, The New American Commentary (Nashville: Broadman & Holman Publishers, 1996), 194.

such a character that if these are persons, he too must be a person (Matt. 28:19; 1 Cor. 12:4–6; 2 Cor. 13:14; 1 Pet. 1:1, 2).

For the same reason, if Jesus is divine, the Spirit, too, must be divine. This too is taught throughout the New Testament, to say nothing of the Old. Thus, divine names are given to him (Acts 5:4; 28:25; Heb. 10:15, 16); divine attributes are ascribed to him; such as, eternity, omnipresence, omnipotence, omniscience (1 Cor. 2:10; 12:4–6; Heb. 9:14); and divine works are predicated of him (Matt. 12:18; Luke 4:18; John 14:16; 1 Cor. 12:2–11; 2 Thess. 2:13; 1 Pet. 1:12). Passages such as Matt. 28:19 and 2 Cor. 13:14 clearly indicate that the three persons are completely equal. One and the same divine essence pervades all.[5]

The context here of the Son-Father-Spirit order is one of Jesus explaining how His life and mission will be replicated in the lives of the disciples via the Spirit of truth. John explains this further in the same chapter and reiterates the same triadic order.

John 14:25–26. Later in that same discourse, Jesus explains that, "I [Son] have spoken these things to you while I [Son] remain with you. But the Counselor, the Holy Spirit [Spirit] —the Father [Father] will send Him [Spirit] in My name [Son]—will teach you all things and remind you of everything I [Son] have told you." So the triadic order is Son-Son-Spirit-Father-Spirit-Son-Son. The logical reconstruction of the advent of the Counselor is that (1) the Father sent Him, and (2) that sending was upon the request of the Son or in the Son's name. So the initiation is the Son's, the permission or commission is the Father's, and the results are the Spirit's. Jesus intends His disciples to understand the movement of the sending of the Spirit to be Son-Father-Spirit. Since the order is somewhat by implication or deduction, I have graded this instance as a "B."

Andreas Köstenberger notes the sending them of this passage and analyzes it in Trinitarian format, "Hence, the Father is never sent; he is sender of both the Son and the Spirit. The Spirit is never sender; he is sent by both the Father

5. William Hendriksen and S. J. Kistemaker, *Exposition of the Gospel according to John*, vol. 2 (Grand Rapids: Baker Book House, 1953–2001), 275–276.

and the Son. Only Jesus is both sent one and sender; sent by the Father, he sends both the Spirit and the disciples."[6] I would agree that the biblical text never explicitly sees the Spirit as sender of one of the other two persons of the Trinity, but the Spirit does "drive" the incarnate Son into the wilderness after His baptism and certainly the Spirit does send the church into mission in the world (Mark 1:12; Acts 13:2–4).

SON-FATHER-SPIRIT REFERENCES IN ACTS

Acts 1:4–5. The Son-Father-Spirit order appears twice in the book of Acts. Acts 1:4–5 reads, "While He [Son] was together with them, He [Son] commanded them not to leave Jerusalem, but to wait for the Father's [Father] promise. 'This,' He said, 'is what you heard from Me; for John baptized with water, but you will be baptized with the Holy Spirit [Spirit] not many days from now.'" So the triadic order here is Son-Father-Spirit. You could argue that it is a dyadic instance of Father-Spirit since the Son is represented here only in pronouns. However, Jesus emphasizes His initiatory role here. He implies, "Wait here until I go get the Spirit from the Father." I have graded this reference as a "B" so as not to force my interpretation.

Acts 2:32–33. In Acts 2:33, the christological theme of ascent and descent is used to explain the events in the Temple at the first post-resurrection Pentecost. Luke writes, "Therefore since He [Son] has been exalted to the right hand of God [Father] and has received from the Father [Father] the promised Holy Spirit [Spirit], He has poured out what you both see and hear." The christological movement of the Son's incarnational descent unto death is offered up to the Father in the Son's ascent and precipitates the descent of the Spirit upon the believers gathered in the Temple. The christological meaning of the Son-Father-Spirit Trinitarian order has to be that ascent will follow descent, the crown will follow the cross, and suffering will be healed in comfort.

With the exception of the Acts 2:33 passage, the texts I have brought forward so far in support of the S-F-Sp processional order have to me not been all together convincing. If no further texts were forthcoming, then my assertion that there is a genuine and significant Son-Father-Spirit Trinitarian processional

---

6. A. J. Köstenberger, *John* (Grand Rapids: Baker Academic, 2004), 442.

order in the New Testament would be fairly weak. However, the next texts we will review are rather convincing. One of them, the benediction found in 2 Corinthians 13:14, actually was the counterintuitive text which first challenged me to do this study and to write this book.

SON-FATHER-SPIRIT REFERENCES IN THE PAULINE EPISTLES

References in Romans

Romans 7:4–6. In this passage, Paul bridges between the freedom that belongs to all Christians because of the death of Christ and the freedom to remarry that is available to the married because of the death of their spouse.[7] Paul uses a Trinitarian framework to construct his bridge in the following way: "you also were put to death in relation to the law through the crucified body of the Messiah [Son] . . . that we may bear fruit for God [Father] . . . so that we may serve in the new way of the Spirit [Spirit] and not the old letter of the law." This application of the S-F-Sp triad encourages believers to experience new life with God by seeing their lives reflected in the Son's atoning work of the cross, their work and lives being offered fruitfully to the Father, and the resulting newness of life as the work of the Spirit. While there is some heavy theology of sanctification being communicated here, Paul is hanging his soteriology on three nails—the Messiah, the Father, and the Spirit—and instructing the Corinthian believers to process this new life using a christological Trinitarian worldview. In this instance, that worldview requires a descent with the Son in the incarnation and cross, followed by an ascent to the Father, and then an empowering of God the Spirit. While most New Testament commentators are preoccupied with the references to the Law, the world, marriage, the flesh, etc., the apostle moves his argument in a Christ-focused Trinitarian order.[8]

Romans 15:12–13. The apostle Paul uses the Son-Father-Spirit order to close his epistle to the Romans with a benediction. With triadic notation Romans 15:12–13 reads: "And again, Isaiah says: The root of Jesse will appear, the One [Messiah,

---

7. Thomas R. Schreiner, *Romans*, vol. 6, Baker Exegetical Commentary on the New Testament (Grand Rapids: Baker Books, 1998), 349.
8. Leon Morris, *The Epistle to the Romans* (Grand Rapids: Eerdmans, 1988), 272; see also Robert H. Mounce, *Romans*, vol. 27, New American Commentary series (Nashville: Broadman & Holman, 1995), 161.

Son] who rises to rule the Gentiles; the Gentiles will hope in Him [Son]. Now may the God [Father] of hope fill you with all joy and peace as you believe in Him so that you may overflow with hope by the power of the Holy Spirit [Spirit]." The formal benediction, "Now may the God of hope fill . . ." is dyadic, Father-Spirit. However, the benediction is introduced with a famous messianic prophecy in Isaiah 11:10. While his readers are focused on Jesus as the fulfillment of Messianic hope to the Jews and to all ethnicities, Paul blesses them in the name of the Father and the Spirit. Since the Son is not within the confines of this benediction—though introduces it—I have graded this triadic instance as a "B." As Thomas Schreiner asserts, "The catchword between verses 12 and 13 is the word 'hope.'"[9] Could this christological order of Son-Father-Spirit be a worship call to hope?

The Counterintuitive Corinthian Benediction

2 Corinthians 13:14. Now we need to look at a second Pauline benediction that invokes God as Son-Father-Spirit. The last words of the apostle Paul's second letter to the believers at Corinth read: "The grace of the Lord Jesus Christ, and the love of God, and the fellowship of the Holy Spirit be with all of you" (numbered as 2 Corinthians 13:13, not 13:14, in the HCSB). This benediction unquestionably reflects a Son-Father-Spirit Trinitarian processional order. But the questions remain of why this order here, and what does this order mean in this context?

Why would the apostle "disorder" the expected F-S-Sp Trinitarian processional reference here at the end of his Corinthian correspondence? Since I affirm the unfailing inspiration of the Scriptures, I do not find error to be an acceptable answer. Neither do I find the idea that the disorder is insignificant. I do wonder if our expectations of a Father-Son-Spirit order were the expectation of neither the apostle nor the Corinthians. Could Paul and the first generation of believers have flourished within the rich diversity of Trinitarian orders, while we have so relied on and reiterated one Trinitarian order, that Paul's benediction here sounds so strange and unwanted?

Why would the apostle end a long pastoral letter with a Son-Father-Spirit reference? Murray Harris offers three reasons for this benedictory triad:

> But why, in this embryonic trinitarian formulation, do we find the unexpected order, Christ-God-Spirit? Three reasons

---

9.   Ibid., 759.

may be suggested for the "priority" of Christ in this triadic structure. (1) Paul began the benediction with his customary reference to "the grace of (our) Lord Jesus (Christ)" and then expanded it. (2) Christ's grace is the means by which God's love reaches the believer. As Paul expresses it in Rom. 8:39, nothing can separate believers "from the love of God that is revealed in [the grace of] Christ Jesus our Lord." . . . The third element of the triad also is dependent on the first. It was through the grace of Christ exhibited in the cross that God demonstrated his love (Rom. 5:8) *and* that believers came to participate in the Spirit's life and so form the community of the new Age. (3) The verse does not describe relationships within the Trinity but the chronological order (so to speak) of the believer's experience of God: we come to Christ and so encounter God and then receive his Spirit.[10]

Murray seems to align his thinking with the triadic order at the end of this comment and even identifies it as somewhat "chronological." I think the meaning of the Son-Father-Spirit triad invoked here is not that difficult. Paul's pastoral technique blends missional exhortation and congregational comfort. He began this letter presenting his theology of ministry initiation. God is the God of all mercy and comfort, and comforted persons are able to comfort others with the comfort they have received from God (2 Corinthians 1:3–4). In the words of Henri Nouwen, we are "wounded healers."[11] People are attracted to those with similar wounds and hurts, who appear to have received or are receiving healing. Jesus is the quintessential wounded healer. Little wonder that Paul decides to conclude his letter as he began it, namely with a word of comfort.

Kistemacher and Hendriksen affirm this benediction with these words, "Because of its Trinitarian formulation, this is the richest benediction in the New Testament." However, they then inadvertently go on to misquote the prayer in this way, "The prayer is that the Father, Son, and Holy Spirit may endow the

---

10. M. J. Harris, *The Second Epistle to the Corinthians: A Commentary on the Greek Text* (Grand Rapids: Eerdmans; Milton Keynes, UK: Paternoster Press, 2005), 938.

11. Henri Nouwen, *The Wounded Healer: Ministry in Contemporary Society* (New York: Image Books, 1979), although the concept was first published in the work of Carl G. Jung, "The Psychology of Transference," *The Practice of Psychotherapy, Collected Works*, vol. 16 (Princeton: Princeton University Press, 1954/1966), 115–116.

worshipers with the virtues of love, grace, and fellowship to equip them for service." Note that they have switched the order to the baptismal missional order. Why could not Paul be richly blessing the Corinthians in the name of God as Son-Father-Spirit? In fairness to Kistemacher and Hendricksen, they go on to explore the "unusual order" in the ensuing paragraph:

> The order of the trinitarian formula differs from the sequence in which the Father is first, the Son second, and the Spirit last. Here the Son precedes the Father, which indeed is unusual. Earlier in the letter Paul alludes to the Trinity in the usual order (1:21–22; compare also Rom. 1:1–4). Peter in his introduction to his first epistle mentions the Trinity in the sequence of God the Father, the Spirit, and Jesus Christ (1 Peter 1:2). We can only surmise that Paul's emphasis on the Lord Jesus Christ caused him to mention the Second Person of the Trinity first. His emphasis on the phrase *our Lord Jesus Christ* is evident throughout the epistle (1:2, 3; 8:9; 11:31; 13:13).[12]

In contrast to contemporary scholars, John Chrysostom also notes the unusual order in a sermon in the late fourth century, but carefully adheres to it throughout. He writes:

> Thus the things of the Trinity are undivided: and whereas the communion is of the Spirit, it hath been found of the Son; and whereas the grace is of the Son, it is also of the Father and of the Holy Spirit; for [we read], "Grace be to you from God the Father." And in another place, having enumerated many forms of it, he added, "But all these works by one and the same Spirit, dividing to each one severally as He will." (1 Cor. 12:11) And I say these things, not confounding the Persons, (away with the thought!) but knowing both the individuality and distinctness of These, and the Unity of the Substance.[13]

---

12. S. J. Kistemaker and W. Hendriksen, *Exposition of the Second Epistle to the Corinthians*, vol. 19 (Grand Rapids: Baker Book House, 1953–2001), 459–460.

13. John Chrysostom, *Saint Chrysostom: Homilies on the Epistles of Paul to the Corinthians*, Philip Schaff, ed., J. Ashworth & T. B. Chambers, trans., Nicene and Post-Nicene Fathers, First Series, vol. 12 (New York: Christian Literature Company, 1889), 418–419.

Chrysostom uses this benediction to affirm the consubstantiality of the three persons of the Trinity, their shared operations without confusion of distinctiveness.

If the Father-Son-Spirit order evokes missional mobilization and suffering, then the Son-Father-Spirit order evokes the immersion in the christological healing comfort which that missional suffering wrought. After all, it was the experience of the gracious words and ways of the Lord Jesus Christ that first attracted the Corinthians to follow the faith. These believers soon discovered that it was the love of God the Father that was the source of the sending of the Son and that it was the Spirit who then enabled the experience of fellowship as the household of God. I believe that Paul employs the S-F-Sp triad to encourage these believers in the life of Christ *as* the christological order is uniquely and divinely choreographed to do. In the exhortation of Fred Sanders, we are "Christ-centered, not Father-forgetful or Spirit-ignoring."[14]

Son-Father-Spirit in Ephesians

Ephesians 2:21–22. "The whole building, being put together by Him [Son], grows into a holy sanctuary in the Lord [Son]. You also are being built together for God's [Father] dwelling in the Spirit [Spirit]." Hendricksen describes the context as one of assurance and comfort for the gentile believers. Very comforting is this assurance.[15] Lenski identifies this passage as a triadic reference, "Here we do have the Trinity, the Lord—God—the Spirit. In neither phrase does 'Lord' or 'Spirit' need the article, both terms designate persons. 'In the Spirit' explains 'in the Lord,' for union with the former mediates union with the latter and thus makes us a habitation of God."[16]

SON-FATHER-SPIRIT REFERENCES IN HEBREWS THROUGH REVELATION

The Christological Witness in Hebrews

The stronger texts in support of the reality and significance of the Son-Father-Spirit are found in the letter to the Hebrews. If this triad communicates the chris-

---

14. Fred Sanders, *The Deep Things of God: How the Trinity Changes Everything* (Wheaton, IL: Crossway, 2010), 68.
15. Kistemaker and Hendriksen, 143.
16. R. C. H. Lenski, *The Interpretation of St. Paul's Epistles to the Galatians, to the Ephesians and to the Philippians* (Columbus, OH: Lutheran Book Concern, 1937), 460.

tological witness of God, it makes sense that the christological theme of this letter would make application of the S-F-Sp order. It is noteworthy that all five of the Trinitarian processional orders identified in the letter to the Hebrew believers begin with the Son in their respective triads.[17] The two instances using the Son-Spirit-Father order (Hebrews 9:14; 10:29) were discussed earlier in chapter 6. Hebrews contains three expressions of the Son-Father-Spirit order: 2:3–4; 3:1–7; and 10:12–15.

Hebrews 2:3–4. This passage reads, "how will we escape if we neglect such a great salvation? It was first spoken by the Lord [Son] and was confirmed to us by those who heard Him. At the same time, God [Father] also testifies by signs and wonders, various miracles, and distributions of gifts from the Holy Spirit [Spirit] according to His will." This verse comes as a warning against neglecting the salvation that has come from God through Christ. This salvation was first declared by the Lord, attested by the first generation of believers, and witnessed to by God through signs and wonders and by distribution of gifts by the Holy Spirit. This warning comes on the threshold of an extended christological discussion of the humanity of the incarnate Son and His subsequent high priesthood (Hebrews 2:5–3:6). The writer invokes the Trinity in terms of the words of the Son about the "such a great salvation."

The author of Hebrews organizes his argument in a Trinitarian framework of Son-Father-Spirit. Commentators debate whether or not God or the Holy Spirit is the subject of "distributed according to His will." (Hebrews 2:4). But Lange says, "It does not matter whether we interpret the phrase *according to his will* as referring to the Holy Spirit or to God the Father. The parallel verse, 1 Corinthians 12:11, says that the Spirit 'gives them [the gifts] to each man, just as he determines.'"[18] Ellingworth notes that, "If so, vv. 3–4 would refer to a co-operation in witness between the three persons of the Trinity."[19] While Ellingworth decides against this interpretation and instead sees God as the distributor, I do not see how his statement about the Trinity in cooperation is set aside, since the author could easily have omitted the phrase about the gifts of the Holy Spirit. The author heightens understanding of the greatness of the word of salvation by invoking the full three Persons of the Triune God and does so in the Son-Father-

---

17. Compare in Appendix A, Chart 1, "New Testament Census of Triadic Occurrences."
18. Kistemaker and Hendriksen, *Exposition of Hebrews*, vol. 15 (Grand Rapids: Baker Book House, 1953–2001), 60.
19. Ellingworth, *The Epistle to the Hebrews: A Commentary on the Greek Text* (Grand Rapids: Eerdmans; Carlisle, England: Paternoster Press, 1993), 142.

Spirit order. Salvation has been given and known through the earthly mission of the Son, and has been confirmed by the Father and the Spirit. This S-F-Sp order is how the New Testament reveals the Triune God in the incarnational, earthly life and mission of the Son. This order is the christological order among the diverse triadic expressions of the One God.

Hebrews 3:1–7. In chapter 3, the author of Hebrews moves the christological argument forward with discussion of Jesus' role in God's house as "apostle and high priest of our confession" (v.1).

> Therefore, holy brothers and companions in a heavenly calling, consider Jesus [Son], the apostle and high priest of our confession; He was faithful to the One [Father] who appointed Him, just as Moses was in all of God's household. For Jesus [Son] is considered worthy of more glory than Moses, just as the builder has more honor than the house. Now every house is built by someone, but the One who built everything is God [Father]. Moses was faithful as a servant in all God's household, as a testimony to what would be said in the future. But Christ was faithful as a Son [Son] over His [Father[20]] household. And we are that household if we hold on to the courage and the confidence of our hope. Therefore, as the Holy Spirit [Spirit] says . . ."

The Trinitarian processional pattern in these seven verses is S-F-S-F-S-F-Sp. That I identify this passage as presenting a Son-Father-Spirit order deserves an explanation. I have seemingly proof-texted my identification by including the phrase "as the Holy Spirit says," when that phrase is the author's way of introducing a tapestry of quotations starting with Psalms 95:7–11. I have graded this instance of the Father-Son-Spirit triad as a "C" level instance. Consider that the epistle to the Hebrews is rife with Old Testament quotations—ten in the first chapter alone! However, these quotations are only twice introduced by the phrase, "as the Holy Spirit says." It is used here in 3:7, in my interpretation, as the close-out of the Son-Father-Spirit processional order. And it is found a second and final time in another instance of the Son-Father-Spirit order, Hebrews 10:12–15.

---

20. Note the immediately prior use of "household" is clearly identified as of "God's"—i.e., the Father's—household.

Hebrews 10:12–15. This latter passage occurs in the writer's assessment of the perfection of the Son's sacrifice for sins. It reads, "But this man [Son], after offering one sacrifice for sins forever, sat down at the right hand of God [Father]. He [Son] is now waiting until His enemies are made His footstool. For by one offering He [Son] has perfected forever those who are sanctified. The Holy Spirit [Spirit] also testifies to us about this."

Both of our Hebrews passages put the Son in the beginning of the triad. Both then highlight the authority and centrality of the Father. But then, unexpectedly, the Holy Spirit is identified as the author-by-inspiration of a text from the Hebrew Scriptures demonstrating the unique value of the high priestly work of the Son. The writer to the Hebrews appears in these passages to be reluctant to witness to the christological order of Son-Father without concluding that order Son-Father-*Spirit*. In view of all the other ways used by the author to introduce references from the Old Testament, to use "Holy Spirit" in this fashion suggests a distinctive need to express the christological processional order in its Trinitarian fullness. I grade this instance as a "B," since the triad appears without intentional coherence in the context.

Explicitly or Implicitly Trinitarian?

Most students of Scripture have heard the assertion, "There is no explicit reference to the Trinity in the New Testament." That assertion is repeated so often that it seems irrefutably true. However, the statement is accurate only if to be explicit means that the word *trinity* must be found in the New Testament. But why should that be the case if it is abundantly clear from text and context that the New Testament authors are thinking and writing in an intentionally Trinitarian framework and want to impart that framework to their readers? If "explicitly Trinitarian" requires the authors to discuss the intra-relations of the so-called immanent Trinity as framed in the Nicene formula, then of course there is no explicit Trinity in the New Testament.

But if that is the criterion imposed, Christology in the New Testament does not discuss the unity of the two natures in the one person of the incarnate Christ either. And yet, no one dares to declare that there is no explicit Christology in the New Testament.

If the range of Trinitarian teaching in the New Testament is configured from explicit to implicit, then how does authorial intentionality or "inadvertency" fit in that framework? For instance, Hebrews 3:1–7 is a discussion of the superiority of Jesus as the Son of God over Moses as the servant of God. The passage is peppered with references to Jesus as Son and to God and one reference to the Holy Spirit. I have rated this passage as a "C" in my schema because the references occur over seven verses, because the focus is more christological than Trinitarian, and because the reference to the Holy Spirit is inadvertent to that christological discussion. Clearly, the Trinity is implicit at best in this text.

However, earlier in Hebrews 2:3–4, the author clearly intends to reference the roles of the Three in his exhortation about the "such a great salvation" that believers experience, "It was first spoken by the Lord and was confirmed to us by those who heard him. At the same time, God also testifies by signs and wonders, various miracles, and distributions of gifts from the Holy Spirit according to His will." If the naming of the Lord, God, and the Holy Spirit here is not dogmatically explicit in the Nicene sense, then at least it is intentionally Trinitarian and not merely inadvertent in its description. How often does implicit reference to the Trinity have to occur before implicit becomes explicit? Does the author of Hebrews really need to include "from the Holy Spirit" here to make his point unless his point is that the great salvation is so great because it is the work and gift of the Lord, God, and the Holy Spirit?

DISCUSSION QUESTIONS—CHAPTER 7

- Of the fourteen Son-Father-Spirit triads examined in this chapter, six received an "A," five received a "B," two received a "C," and one "NA." Looking over those triads and their grades in the "New Testament Triadic Occurrences" (Appendix A, Chart 1), which of the grades need to be adjusted and why?

- Pastors do use Paul's benediction in 1 Corinthians 13:13 as their own benediction to end the service. That text reads: "The grace of our Lord Jesus Christ, and the love of God the Father, and the communion of the Holy Ghost, be with you all." How would you answer if someone in worship with you heard that benediction and asked, "Hey what gives? How come the pastor's benediction wasn't in the right order, Father Son, and Holy Spirit?"

- When John Chrysostom preached on 1 Corinthians 13:13 in the imperial church in Constantinople in the fifth century, he recognized the Trinitarian order of the text. He used the three names, Son-Father-Spirit, to argue for God being one substance with three persons. He asserted that the Spirit was given equal respect with the Father and the Son, and therefore all three are equally God. What do you think of John Chrysostom's argument here for the Trinity? From your perspective, what about his argument is compelling, and what is weak?

- In chapters 5–7, you have looked closely at forty-eight triadic instances of three different orders: Father-Son-Spirit, Son-Spirit-Father, and now Son-Father-Spirit. Those instances occur over a span of eighteen out the twenty-seven books in the Testament. Based on your study, how would you defend or critique the following assertion? *Trinitarian thinking is a default consciousness of the writers of the New Testament. They think Trinitarian because they learned it from Jesus.*

- You have been asked to design the worship service for Pentecost Sunday, which is the traditional celebration of the descent of the Spirit on the apostles at Pentecost, approximately seven weeks after Easter. The pastor has selected Acts 2:32–33 as the preaching focus, which in this chapter was identified as having the Son-Father-Spirit order. With this information in mind, how would you design the worship to invoke an experience of God as Son-Father-Spirit?

SERMON STARTER: THE SON-FATHER-SPIRIT CHRISTOLOGICAL ORDER

The Attractive Witness of a Wounded Healer: 2 Corinthians 13:14

Western culture works hard to get and stay in the fast lane—so hard, that we often neglect taking the high road. Fast economic lanes are more attractive than high ethical or missional roads. We retain the songs of ascent in our corporate worship, but the notes of holiness may not highlight our fellowship. When fellowship is marred by unresolved alienations and un-admonished dalliances with sin, what's to be done? How are we to reengage the holy road of a humble walk with the Master, devotion to justice, and the practice of intentional acts of kindness?

The high road can always be found in the footsteps of Jesus. The way of the cross still leads home.

When the apostle Paul was concluding his final letter to the powerful but troubled church at the Greek megaport of Corinth, he ended with an unfamiliar but memorable Trinitarian benediction. The expected *missiological* order of Father, Son, and Spirit is reordered here to change the emphasis. That is because the Corinthians needed to get the cross back before the crown. This *christological* order of Son-Father-Spirit is used here and in thirteen other places in the New Testament. This triadic order exhorts and empowers discouraged fellowships to reengage as faithful followers of Jesus. Hear carefully the words of Trinitarian benediction that Paul chose to bless with: "The grace of the Lord Jesus Christ, and the love of God, and the fellowship of the Holy Spirit be with all of you" (2 Corinthians 13:13).

When the Hebrews thought of worship, it was ever with up the hill to the Temple. Their hymns of worship were songs of ascent, as in Psalm 24:3. "Who may ascend the mountain of the LORD?" Most of our daily work involves looking down and in on what we are doing, so it is refreshing and inspiring to look up and out in worship. We need holy mountains in our minds, lest we become lost and disillusioned in the valley of daily travail and adversity. Adversity has often been my daily bread, so I am glad worship has an upward focus.

However, Jesus warns us that ascent is possible only if descent has preceded it, "No one has ascended into heaven except the One who descended from heaven—the Son of Man" (John 3:13). So, descent precedes ascent, humiliation comes before exaltation, and the cross before the crown. This is the high road of Jesus Christ, who ascends Golgotha before He ascends to Glory. "The grace of the Lord Jesus Christ, and the love of God, and the fellowship of the Holy Spirit be with all of you" (2 Corinthians 13:13).

A Three-Rung Rope Ladder to Regain Our High Calling

This benediction is a supernaturally made three-point sermon. The context is one in which Paul has asked the Corinthian believers to examine their faith and to shore up their credentials of believing in Jesus and living for Him. The Corinthians are like the prodigy Joseph, whose dysfunctional family and the pleasures of favoritism caused him to go from riches to rags and to learn his high-road lessons from the bottom of a pit looking up.

Paul casts a three-rung rope ladder down to the Corinthian believers, and urges them to climb it and to reengage the pilgrimage of the high calling. The rungs are the Grace of the Lord, the Love of God, and the Fellowship of the Holy Spirit.

Rung #1: The Grace of the Lord

The grace of the Lord Jesus is the saving grace that is no cheap grace. There is the cost of the cross and the cost of following. Grace means God stoops down to touch us and others. "I am gentle and humble in heart, and you will find rest for yourselves" (Matthew 11:29). So, God stoops and God lifts up—and so must we.

Jesus turned the cross into a saving cross and the table of Eucharist. That saving grace toward us is ever reciprocated as serving grace by us. God descending is God cleansing, and whom He cleanses He also commissions. It is not "Simon, do you love me? I forgive you," but "Simon, do you love me? Tend my sheep" (see John 21:16).

If the saving grace of the Son is also serving grace, then it must also be standing grace. Christ's death on the cross is the blood-stained grace in which we stand in justification before the judgment seat and hear the divine pardon. Jesus stood against the temptations of the Adversary and against the threats and betrayals of the religious leaders and His close followers. And so must we. We do not put on the armor of God to play pool in the church basement but to stand battle against spiritual forces and deception (Ephesians 6:13). We cannot outrun the devil, so we must stand and resist him in the grace of the Lord Jesus (James 4:7). If we fear such a life, the fear of the Lord is the antidote to any and every fear.[21] If we fear such a life, perfect love casts out fear (1 John 4:18). The grace of

---

21. I am adapting this notion from my colleague, Dr. Adam Groza, Golden Gate Baptist Theological Seminary.

the Lord Jesus is ours because the love of God sent His Son to be the expiation for our sins (1 John 4:10).

Rung #2: The Love of God

The grace of the Lord Jesus adopts us as the loving act of the Living God. First John defines love as Christ's atonement and tests our love by our caring for the stranger as a brother (1 John 4:12). Love is both the domestic and foreign policy of believers in Pauline poetry; without love, we are clanging cymbals (1 Corinthians 13:1).

The love of God makes and maintains the lasting relationships that He and we call covenants. He practices reconciliation so that nothing is able to separate us from His love, neither life nor death (Romans 8). Because God is love, He makes and keeps covenant, and expects us to do the same. God always goes steady. God is the one who proposes on the first date. The Son sent down as the letter of saving grace is all marked with the x's and o's of the love of Father for the world. If the Son descends, He then ascends with us to receive the loving adoption of God into His forever household as His children. Historically, the ascension of Christ after His atonement mission was completed was to ask the Father to send the Spirit down to be poured out upon the church. And that gives us the third rung of the benediction.

Rung #3: The Fellowship of the Holy Spirit

On the fortieth day of resurrection appearances, the Son ascended back to the Father and asked that the promise of the Spirit's descent be fulfilled. Jesus had instructed His disciples to wait in Jerusalem until the Spirit had come upon them and then they would be His empowered witnesses to the ends of the earth. That shared experience of Pentecost forged a fellowship and participation. The fellowship of the Spirit binds us in boldness to show and tell the great things He has done for us.

The fellowship of the Spirit is also God descending to distribute gifts to make us one and to make us unique. This common participation wrought by the Spirit flattens the church organization, as all believers realize that their diverse gifts cause the oneness of the Spirit to have depth and dimension, rather than a plain conformity of sameness. The Spirit of adoption, whereby we cry "*Abba*, Father," makes us brothers and sisters and gives us brotherly affection. We are indeed fellows on the same ship under the same Captain Jesus, moved by the same wind of the Spirit.

A Benediction as a Beginning

This Trinitarian benediction moves the troubled Corinthian congregation back into mission. It calls them from the bench of despair and dissension back onto the field of significant service and witness.

Recall the Genesis 28 story of Jacob on the run from the retribution of his brother Esau because of the deception and cheat played by the smart, handsome younger son on the hairy, slower first-born. Exhausted by evening, Jacob pulled a stone under his head for a pillow and fell into a dream of a heavenly ladder between heaven and earth. The angels of God were ascending and descending on it and the Lord himself shouts down the ladder to dreaming Jacob. God identifies himself as the Lord God of Abraham and Isaac. He promises the land upon which Jacob rests to his posterity, predicts both the multiplication of Jacob's family and the blessing they will be to all peoples, and ends with the promise of the abiding divine presence (Genesis 28:15). This dream at Bethel lifted Jacob's paradigm of earthly schemes into participation in God's heavenly missional covenant. When Jacob awoke, he exclaimed, "Surely, the LORD is in this place, and I did not know it" (Genesis 28:16). Soon Jacob will have an even deeper encounter and will emerge blessed as the limping leader, Israel, even as the grace of the Lord Jesus means He has become our wounded healer, to invoke the famous metaphor of Henri Nouwen.

In the last words of his second epistle to the church at Corinth, the apostle Paul pronounced his Trinitarian benediction of decent from and ascent to the Father. Only in this benediction, better than angels, it is God the Son descending with grace and then ascending back to the Father, whose love then sends God the Spirit to bind believers into a band of brothers and sisters on mission to bless the nations with the gospel. The formula is simple: No descent, no ministry. Some descent, some ministry. Full descent, full ministry. The outcome of our receiving this benediction is fresh acknowledgment that God is in this place and prompt willingness to descend again into vital care and communication to be a gospel blessing to our neighbors near and far. The Spirit enables us to witness to the wounded healer, Jesus, and to be together the wounded healers of Christ. "The grace of the Lord Jesus Christ, and the love of God, and the fellowship of the Holy Spirit be with all of you" (2 Corinthians 13:13).

CHAPTER 8

The Standing Triad: Spirit-Father-Son as the Sanctifying Order

Lex orandi, lex credendi, lex vivendi
—"the law of prayer is the law of belief and the law of life."[1]

THE TRINITY IN OUR PRAYERS, PREACHING, AND PRACTICES

What can be prayed and preached is what is believed and lived. This assertion informs those Christian expressions which value tradition at or nearly at the level of Scripture. *Lex orandi, lex credendi* has been a venerated value in Roman Catholic and Anglican thought since it first appeared in the writing of Augustine's disciple and defender, Prosper of Aquitaine (390–455).[2] *Lex orandi, lex credendi* supporters argue that if the early church worshipped some seventy years before there was a creed and 350 years before

---

1. See Migne, *Patrologia Latina* 51:209–210. See also "Lex Orandi, Lex Credendi: Vatican Approves Rite for Blessing Children in the Womb," Catholic Online, http://www.catholic.org/national/national_story.php?id=45454 (accessed August 20, 2012).

2. See W. Taylor Stevenson, "Lex Orandi—Lex Credendi," in *The Study of Anglicanism*, ed. Stephen Sykes and John Booty (London: SPCK, 1988), 174–88; and Paul de Clerck, "'Lex orandi, lex credendi': The Original Sense and Historical Avatars of an Equivocal Adage" in *Studia Liturgica* 24 (1994), 178–200.

there was a universally affirmed canon of the New Testament, then isn't it fair to say that the worship tradition of the early church shaped the theological underpinnings for the creed and canon? The church found its creed by singing, saying, and praying it in worship. Of this tradition, Lutheran theologian Robert Jenson writes:

> It is in liturgy, when we talk not about God but to and for him, that we need and use God's name, and that is where the Trinitarian formulas appear, both initially and to this day. In the immediately post-apostolic literature there is no use of a Trinitarian formula as a piece of theology or in such fashion as to depend on antecedent development in theology, yet the formula is there. Its home is in the liturgy, in baptism and the Eucharist. There its use was regularly seen as the heart of the matter.[3]

From an evangelical perspective, ought not the proof of faithfulness to Scripture be found in the pudding of our praying, preaching, and practice? However, with reference to the doctrine of the Trinity, evangelicals seem to present precious little Trinitarian pudding in our liturgy or living. Only reverent vestiges of that doctrine surface. Trinitarian truth might be used in a few prayers, some benedictions, and always at the baptismal recitation of Matthew 28:19–20, but it is not often preached.

There are problems with preaching the Trinity. In a 2006 *festschrift* for the then eighty-year-old Jürgen Moltmann, Reiner Strunk identified several ways that preachers deal with the "Zum Problem der Trinitatis—Predigt" (On the Problem of the Trinity—Preaching):[4]

1. Avoidance lest we become foolish, which was Luther's caution. And avoidance since Kant and Schleiermacher were so convincing that there is nothing practically helpful in the doctrine. If the ecclesiastical

---

3. Robert Jenson, "The Triune God," in Carl E. Braaten and Robert W. Jenson eds., *Christian Dogmatics*, vol. 1 (Philadelphia: Fortress Press, 1984), 92.
4. Reiner Strunk, "Gepredigte Trinität: Zum Problem der Trinitatis-Predigt," in *Der Lebendige Gott als Trinität*, edited by Michael Welker and Miroslav Volf (Gütersloher Verlagshaus, 2006), 395–398. It is regrettable that this article was omitted in the English version of the book, *God's Life in Trinity* (Minneapolis: Fortress Press, 2006).

schedule requires it, the better recourse is to do an exposition of a clear Trinitarian text like Romans 11:26–33 or Ephesians 1:3–14 or a not so clear text such as Numbers 6:22–27;

2. Use indirect references to the Trinity;

3. Select the Trinitarian section of the Confession as the sermon theme, and go with it.

This recommendation is not an encouraging word about the state of preaching on the Trinity, but it gets worse. In the concluding article in the 1999 *The Trinity*, Fuller Seminary Preaching and Theology Professor Marguerite Shuster analyzed sermons in the thirteen-volume *20 Centuries of Great Preaching* and forty-three volumes of the *Pulpit Digest* journal to identify preaching on the Trinity.[5] In more than fifty volumes, only twenty sermons were explicitly on the Trinity—and Shuster found that even these few were characterized by theological imprecision and weak textual exposition. She indicated that although "a moment's reflection reminds us that the Trinity is, at least implicitly, everywhere in Christian worship," still she could recall only two sermons that she had heard on the Trinity, one of which she herself preached.[6]

If evangelicals can find no effective way to preach, pray, and practice the Trinity, how then will it not be forgotten? *The Forgotten Trinity* was the title given to the seminal 1983 British Council of Churches Study Commission on the Trinitarian Doctrine Today. In that study, University of Aberdeen theologian James Torrance concluded, "All of these considerations should not lead us to overlook the fact that, despite their [and may I insert "our"] orthodox confession of the Trinity, Christians are in their practical life, almost mere 'monotheists.'"[7]

---

5. Marguerite Shuster, "Preaching the Trinity: A Preliminary Investigation," in *The Trinity*, eds. Stephen Davis, Daniel Kendall, Gerald O'Collins, S. J. (Oxford: Oxford University Press, 1999), 356–367.

6. Ibid., 356.

7. James Torrance, "The Doctrine of the Trinity in our Contemporary Situation," in *The Forgotten Trinity: A Selection of Papers Presented to the BCC Study Commission on the Trinitarian Doctrine Today*, ed. Alasdair I. C. Heron (London: BCC/CCBI Inter-Church House, 1983), 10 (not to be confused with the useful 1998 Trinitarian apologetic by James R. White by the same title).

A Sixfold Path

"And how can they believe in the one of whom they have not heard? And how can they hear without someone preaching to them?" (Romans 10:14 NIV). If Protestant evangelicals are to restore the doctrine of the Trinity to their preaching, praying, and living, what is the way forward? *Sola Scriptura* provides a path, provided that we approach it as a traveler rather than as a tourist. Tourists look for the Trinity in North Africa with Tertullian or in Turkey at Nicaea. However, as careful travelers, we can observe as many as seventy-five instances in the New Testament where a Trinitarian triadic formula occurs in close word order or in an order more diffused throughout the argument or narrative in question. These triadic formulae occur occasionally in an intentional liturgical form as in Matthew 28:19–20, but most often they occur rather inadvertently as if the New Testament authors casually wrote from a Trinitarian consciousness.

Our perspective affects not only what we see on the surface, but the observable patterns that may be within. For instance, our tourist's eyes habitually expect one triadic order, Father-Son-Spirit, except when delighted by a demented, backward Pauline benediction, "the grace of the Lord Jesus Christ, and the love of God, and the fellowship of the Holy Spirit" (2 Corinthians 13:14 NIV). However, the Trinitarian traveler identifies all six different triadic orders, each used many times throughout nineteen books of the New Testament canon. C. S. Lewis was right: God is not tame. Now let's examine one of the least tame Trinitarian references in the New Testament.

SANCTIFICATION: THE SPIRIT-FATHER-SON ORDER

There are nine occurrences of the Spirit-Father-Son triadic formula in the New Testament. This represents twelve percent of the total seventy-five triadic occurrences. Their range is noteworthy. This ordering appears in every major division of New Testament books and, for its few numbers of occurrences, is relatively even in its overall distribution pattern.

- **The Gospels.** Only one of these instances occurs in any of the Gospels, Luke 4:18. Perhaps, this triad should be understood as God at and after Pentecost—not in the sense that God changes, but in the sense that the way believers approach Him through Trinitarian worship has been renewed.

- **Acts.** Three of the Spirit-Father-Son instances are found in Acts, which means that one third of the thirteen triadic instances in Acts follow this order. (See Table 8.1.) The acts of the apostles were the acts and results of the sanctifying Spirit.

- **Pauline Epistles.** The letters of Paul use the Spirit-Father-Son order three times.

- **Hebrews through Revelation.** In the general epistles, this ordering represents the sole triadic reference in the brief letter of Jude. There is also one instance of it in Revelation.

Intriguingly, these nine instances of the Spirit-Father-Son order normally occur in contexts marked by personal or corporate devotion or liturgy. Could it be that this order expresses the pattern of Trinitarian movement in reverence and sanctification? Could this processional movement be a reprise of the "Song of Ascent" in Psalms, where Hebrew worshippers walked up to the temple to worship and had the restorative experience of genuine reverence? Sanctification means "to make holy or fit for worship and service." Sanctification is a soteriological task of the Holy Spirit. The Spirit sculpts believers inside and outside, with Christ Jesus as the living iconic model.

TABLE 8.1: NEW TESTAMENT OCCURRENCES OF THE SPIRIT-FATHER-SON TRIAD

LOCATIONS AND GRADATIONS FOR THE SANCTIFYING TRIADIC ORDER OF SON-FATHER-SPIRIT			
Text	**Rating**	**Context**	**Summary**
Luke 4:18	A	Nazarene synagogue	The Spirit of the Lord is upon me
Acts 7:55	A-	Martyrdom of Stephen	full of the Holy Spirit . . . saw the glory of God and Jesus standing
Acts 11:15–17	B	Gentile Pentecost	baptized with the Holy Spirit . . . God gave . . . believed in the Lord Jesus Christ
Acts 20:28	A	Ephesian elders' exhortation	Holy Spirit made you . . . for the church of God . . . by blood of the Son

LOCATIONS AND GRADATIONS FOR THE SANCTIFYING TRIADIC ORDER OF SON-FATHER-SPIRIT				
Text	**Rating**	**Context**	**Summary**
Romans 8:9	A-	Redeemed life	the Spirit of God dwells in . . . does not have the Spirit of Christ
Romans 8:16–17	A-	Redeemed life	Spirit witnesses . . . children of God . . . heirs of Christ
Ephesians 4:30–32	B	Christian life	Do not grieve the Holy Spirit of God, sealed, forgiving as God in Christ
Jude 20	A	Warning / exhortation	pray in the Holy Spirit, in the love of God, for the mercy of Lord Jesus Christ
Revelation 22:1	C	New Jerusalem	river of the water of life . . . flowing from the throne of God and of the Lamb

These nine triadic occurrences must be evaluated individually for three reasons:

1. To determine the authenticity and clarity of the occurrence as Trinitarian.

2. To identify the context in which the instance occurs.

3. To state the meaning of that Trinitarian order in that context.

SPIRIT-FATHER-SON REFERENCES IN THE GOSPELS AND ACTS

The First Sermon in Nazareth

Luke 4:18. Luke 4 records the "bar mitzvah" of Jesus in public ministry. He is handed the Isaiah scroll and He unrolls it to chapter 61, the messianic Jubilee prophecy.[8] Having stood to read the text, Jesus now sits to instruct with the words: "Today as you listen, this Scripture has been fulfilled"[9] (Luke 4:21).

---

8. Darrell Bock has a helpful review of the scholarly debate as to whether the Isaiah 61 passage is messianic or that of the eschatological prophet (*Luke: 1:1–9:50*, vol. 1, Baker Exegetical Commentary on the New Testament [Grand Rapids: Baker Academic, 1994], 406); and Robert Stein reviews the scholarly debate over the insertion of Isaiah 58:6b into the quote in Luke 4:18 (*Luke*, vol. 24, The New American Commentary [Nashville: Broadman & Holman Publishers, 1992], 156).
9. Isaiah 61:1 was discussed in chapter 3, in the section on Incipient Triadic Formulae (p. 109).

In four words in verse 18, in both the Greek and the Hebrew, the text presents a triadic order of Spirit, Father (Lord *kurion* in the Greek and *ruach adonai Yahweh* in the Hebrew), and Son.

The passage as we have it in the Greek New Testament is a slightly shortened quote from the Greek Septuagint translation of Isaiah 61:1–2.[10] In triadic notation, Luke 4:18 reads, "The Spirit [Spirit] of the Lord [Father] is on Me [Son], because He [Father] has anointed Me [Son] to preach good news to the poor. He has sent Me to proclaim freedom to the captives and recovery of sight to the blind, to set free the oppressed, to proclaim the year of the Lord's favor." This order of Spirit-Father-Son is invoked as Jesus lays out His intention to fulfill the mission of the Servant of Yahweh in Isaiah. Lange interprets the Isaiah passage in Luke as "the prophet undoubtedly speaks primarily of his own vocation and dignity, but as the servant of Jehovah he was in his work and destiny the type and image of the Messiah, the perfect servant of the Father."[11] Lange omits noting the mark of the anointing by God's Spirit as the authority to do the messianic service. The passage is triadic though the point is identification of the Servant's work. For this reason, I have graded this instance as a "B." The triadic reference does portend the Spirit's commissioning and anointing the Son to heal the infirm and to preach the good news.

The Spirit-Father-Son Triad and Martyrdom

Acts 7:55. Acts 7 presents the New Testament record of Stephen as the first Christian martyr. Before an enraged group attending a meeting of the Jewish Sanhedrin, and at the conclusion of Stephen's self-defense, the text says: "But Stephen, filled by the Holy Spirit [Spirit], gazed into heaven, and He saw God's glory [Father], with Jesus standing at the right hand of God, and he said 'Look! I see the heavens opened and the Son of Man [Son] standing at the right hand of God [Father]!'" The triadic order of the passage, then, is Spirit-Father-Son.

John Polhill reads this passage in the light of the "Son of Man vision in Daniel 7:13–14, where the Son of Man is depicted as standing before the Ancient of Days. The primary role of the Danielic Son of Man was that of judgment, and the New Testament consistently depicts Christ in this role of eschatological

---

10. I. Howard Marshall, *The Gospel of Luke: A Commentary on the Greek Text* (Exeter, England: Paternoster Press, 1978), 182.

11. J. Lange and J. J. van Oosterzee, *A Commentary on the Holy Scriptures: Luke*, P. Schaff and C. C. Starbuck, trans. (Bellingham, WA: Logos Bible Software), 73.

judge."[12] The text suggests that it is the initiation of the Spirit's fullness that enables Stephen's epiphany of the divine court, the Father's glory, and the authoritative position of the Son. The standing of the Son is to be understood as intercession on behalf of Stephen, or as judgment upon those falsely condemning him. Stephen's Spirit-enabled vision of the Father's glory with the Son and heavenly court is immediately followed by his martyrdom, as he is stoned by the attendants at the earthly court of the Sanhedrin.

Note that this movement of God *as* Spirit-Father-Son occurs in a context of suffering for the sake of the gospel, which is exactly the point of the Romans 8:16–17 passage to be discussed momentarily. In other words, the Spirit-Father-Son pattern, as a movement of the God who is Three, anticipates engagement in missional suffering for the gospel preceded by a Spirit-enabled vision of the Father's glory. The Spirit sanctifies—sets apart—the servant by manifesting the glory of the Father and the authority and intercession of the Son. Spirit-directed reverence sustains missional sufferers for the gospel. Mountaintop experiences are intended to equip for ministry in the valleys. Crowns and crosses are inseparable.

The Authorization of the Spirit

Acts 11:15–17. Acts 10 records the Gentile Pentecost. Here, the movement of the gospel message from Jews to Gentiles is divinely initiated and authenticated through the apostle Peter. Chapter 11 records Peter's explanation of those events to the apostolic leadership in Judea. Christianity is learning how to be Christian without being Jewish.

Verses 15–17 read as follows: "As I began to speak, the Holy Spirit [Spirit] came down on them, just as on us. . . . I remembered the word of the Lord [Son] . . . 'you will be baptized with the Holy Spirit [Spirit]' . . . [I]f God [Father] gave them the same gift that He [Father] also gave to us when we believed on the Lord Jesus Christ [Son], how could I possibly hinder God [Father]?" Using a processional analysis, this passage would yield the following order: Spirit-Son-Spirit-Father-Father-Son-Father.

I have graded this instance as a "B," since it roughly conforms to the Spirit-Father-Son movement. That is because the initiation is that of the Spirit, and the conclusion of Peter and the church leaders is that the Spirit's initiation signifies a divine authorization and culminates in anointing to take the mission of the

12. John Polhill, *Acts*, vol. 26, The New American Commentary (Nashville: Broadman & Holman Publishers, 1992), 208.

Son across cultural barriers with minimal acknowledgment of Jewish kosher and ceremonial laws.[13] The Spirit is God's anointing for earthly service in the Son.

Similarly, the Acts 15 Jerusalem Council letter communicates apostolic authorization of the reception of Gentiles into the church. It acknowledges the initiative of the Holy Spirit in this movement, "It seemed good to the Holy Spirit and to us. . . ." The sense then is that we must follow the Holy Spirit to gain insight into the Father's will for carrying out the mission of the Son. This interpretation requires testing against the final use of the Spirit-Father-Son order in the book of Acts. This triadic movement sets the Gentiles aside as God's chosen servants. These Gentile believers have been "declared kosher" by the Spirit to serve the Son.

Acts 20:28. In Acts 20, the elders of the church at Ephesus have been summoned by Paul to a closure conference. Paul anticipates trouble with his intended trip to Jerusalem. His farewell address takes on some sobering notes in verse 28, which invokes the Spirit-Father-Son triad to equip the Ephesian elders for his anticipated permanent absence. With triadic notations, Acts 20:28 reads: "Be on guard for yourselves and for all the flock that the Holy Spirit [Spirit] has appointed you to as overseers, to shepherd the church of God [Father]; which He purchased with His own blood [Son]."[14]

Scholars love to debate this text for its reference to the "overseers" and what that means for early church governance and polity and for its reference to the unusual phrase "purchased with His own blood" when "His" is best seen as referring back to God. About this latter conundrum, Polhill suggests a Trinitarian interpretation. He writes: "It is quite possible to denote this as 'God's blood' from the perspective of sound Trinitarian doctrine, but such an expression is really quite unlike anything else in the New Testament."[15] From my perspective, Paul clearly must have intended it to be understood as Christ's shed blood on the cross. Because of the hermeneutical ambiguity and the inductive leap to read it as the Son's atoning blood, I have graded this instance as a "C."

---

13. Compare Acts 15:23–29 and Galatians 2:6–10, the latter being Paul's own interpretation of the implications of the ruling by the Jerusalem Council with reference to the Gentile mission.
14. Significant older manuscript evidence translates this last phrase as "the blood of the Lord." Textual critics of the caliber of Kurt Aland, Matthew Black, and Bruce Metzger rate this "his own blood" reading as a "C" in *The Greek New Testament*, 3rd ed. (London: United Bible Societies, 1975), 499. So, either the text is a proof text for the deity of the Son, since His blood at the cross is called God's blood, or with the variant readings, the text is intended to reference the cross without proofing the deity of the Son intentionally.
15. Polhill, *Acts,* 428.

The apostle is here reminding these leaders that it was at the initiation of the Spirit that they were called into the service of church oversight. Their oversight must be mindful that the flock is the Father's flock, and that it became the Father's flock at the high price of the Son's blood. The appointment and anointing of the Spirit has sanctified these leaders to stand doctrinal guard over the Father's sheep. This triadic order rings like a bracing charge to the ordination candidate to stand firm for Christian doctrine, no matter the howl of false teachers.

SPIRIT-FATHER-SON REFERENCES IN THE PAULINE EPISTLES

Adoption and Self-Definition

In the epistle to the Romans, Paul gives the Spirit-Father-Son order an even clearer context for the worship-to-serve pattern. Romans 8 is a thorough symphony of triadic processions with a dual emphasis. The apostle first emphasizes the Christian adoption/acceptance triad of Son-Spirit-Father. He uses it in the beginning, in verses 1–3. That triad conveys God saving. Therefore, the first contextual emphasis is salvation. The second emphasis, sanctification, is what I mean by the worship-to-serve order of Spirit-Father-Son, and it is found in verses 9 and 15.

Romans 8:9. This passage reads: "You, however, are not in the flesh, but in the Spirit [Spirit], since the Spirit of God [Father] lives in you. But if anyone does not have the Spirit of Christ [Son], he does not belong to Him." The consistency and contrast between "Spirit," "Spirit of God" and "Spirit of Christ" is clearly Paul's invoking the Triune God in the order of the referents, Spirit-Father-Son. I would point out that the God worshipped by the followers of Christ must be worshipped in spirit—after all, God is spirit—and that God's inner being and outer economy of mission is experienced as a divinely initiated self-differentiation in the movement of Spirit-Father-Son.[16]

Thomas Schreiner notes the Trinitarian significance of this passage in these words: "We should not conclude from this that the Spirit and Christ are identical, only that they are inseparable in terms of the saving benefits communicated to believers. . . . Texts like these provided the raw materials from

---

16. David Cunningham uses this Barthian concept of divine self-differentiation in his *These Three Are One: The Practice of Trinitarian Theology* (Oxford: Blackwell Publishers, 1998), 65.

which the church later hammered out the doctrine of the Trinity."[17] Schreiner also sees the Trinitarian implication of Romans 8:9. "*The Spirit of Christ* is another way of referring to *the Spirit of God* [italics in the original]. The doctrine of the Trinity had not yet been formulated, but it is this kind of expression that led Christians in due time to speak of God as triune. Paul sees the Spirit as integrally related to Christ as well as to the Father."[18] The apostle is not modalistically claiming that the Spirit is the Father is the Son, but rather that though distinctive as Spirit, God, and Christ, their work is together and indivisible. What the Spirit does, the Father does, the Son does. In this sense, then, the Lord God is also understood to be One as in the Hebrew Shema of Deuteronomy 6:4: "Listen, Israel: The LORD our God, the LORD is One." God is one and has one mission. His inner self-differentiation of Spirit-Father-Son has distinction without division. God is one in the "immanent" sense of intra-Trinitarian relations and one in the economic sense of the redemptive and restorative mission for creatures and creation.

Romans 8:16–17. Verses 15–17 read like a birth certificate. The newly adopted cry out in recognition, "*Abba,* Father," in verse 15. But reading down the "adoption signatures," who then confirms this new paternity? None other than the Trinity! Paul explains this spontaneous outpouring of worship and attribution as "the Spirit [Spirit] Himself testifies together with our spirit that we are God's [Father] children . . . heirs of God and coheirs with Christ [Son]" (vv. 16–17). Blessed assurance comes to believers as Spirit-Father-Son.[19] As always, exaltation in worship is inseparable from suffering service, so we are not surprised to see in verse 17b: "seeing that we suffer with Him so that we may also be glorified with Him." The cross and the crown are united in Christ and in faithful Christian living. Suffering service for Christ's sake is evidence of authentic co-heirship with Christ.

This Spirit-Father-Son procession demonstrates the inner differentiation and indivisibility in operations of the living, Triune God. The worshipful experience of the Spirit's testimony that we are the Father and the Son's heirs enables suffering service. We worship to serve.

---

17. Thomas Schreiner, *Romans*, vol. 6, Baker Exegetical Commentary on the New Testament (Grand Rapids: Baker Books, 1998), 413–414.
18. Leon Morris, *The Epistle to the Romans* (Grand Rapids: Eerdmans; 1988), 308.
19. W. Hendriksen and S. J. Kistemaker, *Exposition of Paul's Epistle to the Romans,* vols. 12–13, (Grand Rapids: Baker Book House, 2001), 258.

We should carefully consider this personal experience of adoption into the divine household orchestrated by the Holy Spirit as an initial *and* a continuing experience. Anecdotally, friends of mine who have adopted children or who have been adopted themselves all confirm the reality of what verse 15 expresses. They describe the critical relational breakthrough when a child, who was adopted post-infancy, first learns and becomes comfortable and natural with calling their adopted parents "Dad" and "Mom." That transition marks a change in the adopted child's relationally informed self-image and sense of acceptance.

Certainly, the experience of spirit adoption whereby one identifies with God as Father enables a spiritual authority to walk with Christ in self-definition, if you will, as a devoted servant of Christ. Effectual reverence in worship is the work of the Spirit to bring worshippers into the experience of *the* Father as *our* Father, so that we as worshippers may live in the Son and His gospel mission in the world no matter the trouble that comes. Such worship issues in service. Herein is the value of designing and practicing worship as the movement from Spirit to Father to Son. Real worship sanctifies us for service.

Mountains and Valleys: Liturgical Ascent and Missional Descent in Romans

If there is a Spirit-enabled liturgical ascent to the Father in the Spirit-Father-Son processional movement, then there is also a descent into the missional suffering of the Son. The apostle Paul ends his discussion of the Spirit-Father-Son movement with the clarification that the experience of co-inheritance with Christ is in contingent solidarity with the earthly mission of suffering, "seeing that we suffer with Him so that we may also be glorified with Him" (Romans 8:17). This same contingent solidarity, expressed in the Greek with the conjunction translated "since" or "if," was also used in Paul's earlier application of the Spirit-Father-Son triad in verse 9, you are in the Spirit, if in fact the Spirit of God dwells in you. Therefore, the Spirit-Father-Son procession must mean that God intends for believers to ascend in worship with the sense of adoption, adoration, and exultation—and to descend into earthly missional suffering with the Son.

Being caught up in the Spirit-Father-Son triadic movement is to be both an initial and a lifestyle experience. Spirit-inspired reverence enables Christ-like service and suffering. Mountaintop renewals precipitate re-engagement of ministry and misery in the valleys. Here the crown precipitates the cross because the Son's cross enables our sharing in His crown.

Ephesians: Worship Is the Engine of Ethics

Ephesians 4:30–32. In this passage, Paul applies the Spirit-Father-Son triad.[20] Ephesians chapter 4 is pure Pauline ecclesiology. The theme is ecclesial unity and maturity. Paul advocates unity developed through gifted leadership equipping the membership for ministry. The members are the ministers and the leaders are the equipping administrators. Leaders are to develop missional consensus through nurturing "speaking the truth in love" with one another (Ephesians 4:15). At the end of this practical ecclesiology in Ephesians 4:30–32, the apostle addresses the necessity and practice of conflict management. Paul writes: "And don't grieve God's Holy Spirit [in the original, the Holy Spirit of God, Spirit]. You were sealed by Him for the day of redemption. . . . And be kind and compassionate to one another, forgiving one another, just as God [Father] also forgave you in Christ [Son]." I grade this instance of the Spirit-Father-Son triad as a "B," since verse 31 lists ways of grieving the Spirit—bitterness, wrath, anger, and the like—and comes between the invocation of the Holy Spirit and the references then to the Father and the Son.

The motive for relational reconciliation is the Spirit's bringing to remembrance the forgiveness of the Father through union with the Son. When believers fail to reconcile, they are grieving the Spirit, and falsely imitating or forgetting the Father's forgiveness in Christ (2 Peter 1:9). Holy hugs come with every greeting and departing between believers. The indwelling Spirit is grieved when we fail to reconcile and is exalted when we remember, as at the Lord's Supper, that God has forgiven us because of Christ's atonement. The Spirit-Father-Son order is a call to worship that energizes the service of reconciliation. We don't lose our ministries when we meet resistance; we find it: the ministry of reconciliation (2 Corinthians 5:18).

SPIRIT-FATHER-SON REFERENCES IN HEBREWS THROUGH REVELATION

The Evangelistic Circle

Jude 20. This principle of sanctification as worship-to-serve is reiterated in a Trinitarian exhortation in the conclusion of the epistle of Jude. Verse 20 reads, "as you build yourselves up in your most holy faith and pray in the Holy Spirit [Spirit], keep yourselves in the love of God [Father], expecting the mercy of our Lord Jesus Christ [Son] for eternal life." This nearly explicit Trinitarian reference is identified as

---

20. While I find Pauline authorship of Ephesians defensible and reliable, I do acknowledge that some scholars question Pauline authorship of Ephesians and its twin epistle to the Colossians.

such by most commentators. Thomas Schreiner comments that "the implicit Trinitarianism of the text should be observed. Jude referred to praying in *the Holy Spirit,*
the love of *God,* presumably the Father, and the mercy of *our Lord, Jesus Christ.*[21]

Peter Davids points out the twin triads in the text, "there is a double tril-
ogy here: faith—love—waiting (a paraphrase of hope) and Holy Spirit—God—
Lord Jesus Christ. Now it is true, as we have seen, that Jude loves sets of three,
but one strongly suspects that these groups were influenced by the traditional
groupings in the tradition of the Jesus movement."[22] If Davids' suspicion here
is correct, then faith building is done as a trifold movement of Spirit-involved
prayer and worship, leading to an experience of kept-ness by or in the Father's
love, and ultimately issues in the merciful Messianic hope of Jesus. This hope-
filled focus of the coming mercy of the returning Christ equips believers, according to verse 21, to render mercy ministry to doubters, disputers, and the defiled.
Worship-filled prayer leads to gutter ministry, "snatching them from the fire . . .
hating even the garment defiled by the flesh" (Jude 23).

S. J. Kistemaker twice comments on the Trinitarian reference of this text,
but each time he probably *unconsciously* changes that reference from the Spirit-
Father-Son order used by Jude back to the expected order of Father-Son-Spirit.
He writes: "In a series of four commands Jude tells them to cultivate the familiar
Christian virtues of faith, prayer, love, and hope. Moreover, in these two verses
Jude refers to the Trinity: God, Jesus Christ, and the Holy Spirit."[23] In this instance, Kistemaker rightly understands the text to be Trinitarian and that the
context calls believers to seek the merciful restoration of repentant libertines in
the name of the Trinity. But he fails to understand that the Spirit-Father-Son order embedded in the text of Jude is the very worship movement that empowers
ministry of mercy in Christ to others.

The Spirit-Father-Son order is thus followed with a call to engage in missions of mercy, "Have mercy on those who doubt; save others by snatching them
from the fire" (Jude 21). The conclusion seems to be compelling that participation with God as Spirit-Father-Son makes Trinitarian worship the engine of ethics

---

21. Thomas Schreiner, *1, 2 Peter, Jude,* The New American Commentary, vol. 37 (Nashville:
    Broadman & Holman Publishers, 2003), 481–482.
22. H. Davids, *The Letters of 2 Peter and Jude,* The Pillar New Testament Commentary (Grand
    Rapids: Eerdmans, 2006), 93.
23. S. J. Kistemaker and W. Hendriksen, *Exposition of the Epistles of Peter and the Epistle of
    Jude,* New Testament Commentary, vol. 16 (Grand Rapids: Baker Book House, 2001),
    404.

and evangelism.[24] The reverse order, Son-Father-Spirit, is the experience of God saving, being evangelized—"good newsed." The biblical news about Jesus of Nazareth leads to an experience of the God and Father of Jesus Christ and results in a spiritual transformation. The reflective echo of the saving Son-Father-Spirit triad is the Spirit-Father-Son formula. And it is according to Jude that the experience of God as Spirit-Father-Son leads to engagement in rescue and charitable ministries. The movement of evangelism by which believers are regenerated echoes back in the Spirit-Father-Son triad of worship to serve. This is the sanctifying work of the Spirit. Authentic Christian worship always ends in commission to serve Christ.

In the End, Trinity

Revelation 22:1. The final chapter in the Bible ends with the river of the water of life flowing from the throne of God and the Lamb (Revelation 22:1). Commentators connect the river image with Ezekiel 47, where the measuring of the river becomes deeper and deeper, the further it flows. Or they focus on John 7:37–39, where the Spirit is the water that flows from Christ (see also John 4:14). If the gospel's own interpretation in John 7:39, "He said this about the Spirit," is applied to Revelation 22:1, then a triadic order of Spirit-Father-Son emerges. In that case, this triad should be judged as weak evidence, a grade of "C," over against all the previous examples of the Spirit-Father-Son triad examined above.

PRELIMINARY CONCLUSIONS: SPIRIT-FATHER-SON TRIADIC ORDER—WORSHIP TO SERVE

What could possibly motivate people willingly to practice reconciliation? Most feel when resistance is encountered, when people are non-responsive or even hostile, ministry has been lost. Yet, ministering reconciliation on the giving or the receiving side is normal Christianity. So where do we find the power to do the difficult, to suffer in service, to give good for evil?

---

24. Revelation 22:1 may contain the final occurrence of the Spirit-Father-Son processional order. If it is, it is certainly the most graphic. The context is the post-apocalypse advent of the New Jerusalem. The writer begins the description of the eschatological city with, "Then he showed me river of living water [Spirit?], sparkling like crystal, flowing from the throne of God and of the Lamb [Son]." The image of the river of living water easily recalls the promise of Jesus to the Samaritan women at Jacob's well in John 4:14, "In fact, the water I shall give him will become a well of water springing up within him for eternal life." However, neither the text in Revelation nor the one in John's gospel state directly that the Spirit is that living water.

The Freudian theory of human personality proposes the assumption that to be human is to pursue pleasure and to flee pain. Cultures of comfort and pursuit of the "good life" are the contemporary and ancient norms. Yet the normative calling to live the Christian way is a call to suffering service. But from where comes the motive to start and sustain countercultural and counter-natural behavior?

The motive and power comes from the Triune God, specifically in the experience of the Triune movement of Spirit, Father, Son. The nine New Testament instances of this triadic movement occur in contexts of worship-to-serve. Spirit-inspired reverence for the Father leads to dedicated walk and service with Christ. Worship can and should be designed in this triadic movement. Expository preaching on the Spirit-Father-Son texts can lead hearers to conceptualize and experience the Triune God in this movement.

About eighty years ago, the British pulpiteer Leslie Weatherhead preached a sermon entitled, "The Four Reasons People Go to Church."[25] He asserted that because people live such difficult lives, they come to church for inspiration. Because they look down all week at the grindstone, they come to look up in worship. And because they fail and are lonely, they come for forgiveness and fellowship. Weatherhead inadvertently preached upon this triadic order of Spirit-inspiration, Father-aimed worship, and Son-supplied forgiveness and fellowship.

Riches for Trinitarian preaching and worshipping abound in the New Testament to those willing to move from Scriptural tourism to travelers on divine adventure, or, as Daniel wrote, "the people that know their God shall do exploits" (Daniel 11:32 KJV).

DISCUSSION QUESTIONS—CHAPTER 8

- Of the nine incidences of the Spirit-Father-Son triad examined in this chapter, which two are the strongest examples of that order? Explain your position based on your own exegesis of those two passages. (Refer to the "New Testament Triadic Census of Occurrences" in Appendix A to find listings.)

---

25. The life and sermons of Leslie Weatherhead are featured in *20 Centuries of Great Preaching*, Clyde E. Fant, Jr. and William M. Pinson, Jr., eds. (Waco, TX: Word Books, 1971), 108–141.

- Assuming the Spirit-Father-Son triad describes God sanctifying His servants, and assuming that Revelation 22:1 is an authentic instance of that triad, why would the order Spirit-Father-Son describe the layout of the heavenly kingdom?

- Jude is a one-page book in the New Testament. Jude is not happy with the moral state of the Christian communities to whom he is writing. Yet, at the end of the letter, he offers an encouraging Trinitarian exhortation like a benediction on their behalf. He uses the Spirit-Father-Son order and says, "pray in the Holy Spirit, keep yourselves in the love of God, expecting the mercy of our Lord Jesus Christ for eternal life." Explain the significance of Jude's choice to use that triad.

- You are preparing a church group to go into the community to carry out a mercy ministry of some kind. You are convinced that whomever God uses, He first cleanses and sanctifies. How could you use the Spirit-Father-Son order in the story of Stephen's witness and martyrdom in Acts 7 to lead your team in a prayer of sanctification, worship, and missional suffering?

SERMON STARTER: THE SPIRIT-FATHER-SON SANCTIFYING ORDER

The Trinitarian Motor of Mercy: Jude 20-22

Jude is the author of a one-page letter in the New Testament. His letter is like a bookmark to show where the book of Revelation begins.

Jude identifies himself as the brother of James. Many of us have quiet brothers who don't speak up much. Some are the middle child. Jude is not like that—he speaks short and sharp when he speaks up in this letter. His message is that God has a history of judging the wicked. So stay sharp and don't doubt retribution.

Jude is a name-caller. Here are some of his best zingers against the fakes and phonies of the faith: rainless clouds, perverts (v. 4); unnatural indulgers (v. 7); dreaming defilers (v. 8); jealous murderers, self-seeking grafters, power mongering rebels (v. 11); love feast zits, church carousers, waterless clouds, fruitless trees, foamy rogue waves and wandering asteroids bound for dark holes (vv. 12–13). Just when you think Jude is done with his diatribe, here come five more fast ones: grumblers, malcontents, passion addicts, loud-mouthed braggers, and flattering tricksters (v. 16).

Jude has an edge to him, his tongue is razor-sharp. But he heeds the apostolic warning that these fakes and phonies are the end-time signs. They draw down the heat of God's executed judgment.

Having made this point about pending retribution in nineteen sentences, Jude casts his vision for the mercy mission of the called in three sentences.

> But you, dear friends, as you build yourselves up in your most holy faith and pray in the Holy Spirit, keep yourselves in the love of God, expecting the mercy of our Lord Jesus Christ for eternal life. Have mercy on those who doubt, save others by snatching them from the fire: have mercy on others but with fear, hating even the garment defiled by the flesh (Jude 20–22).

Theologians love to turn verbs into nouns, so believe becomes belief, trust becomes faith. The New Testament writers turn nouns into verbs, so truth becomes truth-ing in love (Ephesians 4:15), and here mercy becomes mercy-making. In fact, Jude's vision is a mercy sandwich, with snatching the burning from the fire between having mercy on doubters on one side and having mercy on gutter-dwellers on the other. But from where does the motivation come to not only stand against the rolling waves of corruptors, but also do rescue jumps into the roiling troubles of those adrift? Mercy needs a motor or it exhausts the caregiver. Jude describes the engine of mercy as found in the Holy Spirit, the love of the Father, and the expectant mercy of the Son. The passage is intentionally Trinitarian, but his order of the divine persons is unexpected.

The order of Spirit-Father-Son is unexpected until we recall how good it is in an emergency. We see this at work in Acts 7, when Stephen had finished his passionate but unconvincing self-defense to the Jewish Sanhedrin, before the rocks began to fly his way. "But Stephen, filled by the Holy Spirit, gazed into heaven. He saw God's glory, with Jesus standing at the right hand of God" (Acts 7:55). Stephen was equipped to endure his stoning as the Spirit filled him with a vision of the Father's glory and the Son's authority and intercession. God moves Spirit-Father-Son when He wants us encouraged to suffer or to serve for Christ's sake. Jude invokes this same trimotor to encourage his readers to stand faithful against corruption and to move in mercy to the doubting and defiled.

Immediately after World War I, many former military aircraft were pressed into commercial service. This did not sit well when a number of well-publicized crashes brought public confidence in air transport to an all-time low. Then Henry Ford changed everything in 1926 with the introduction of the first all-metal, radial-engine, fourteen-passenger Ford Trimotor commercial airline. This is the plane made famous again in the first ten minutes of the 1984 Harrison Ford film *Raiders of the Lost Ark*. The theologically engineered movement of Spirit-Father-Son has the same effects of power, safety, and range of mission. The Spirit lifts the congregation in worship to experience the glory of God the Father in the midst of His heavenly court, and then the movement of the Son at the right hand of authority beckons us to come into His redemption and to go out in His service, name, and power to rescue others.

The work of the Spirit is to make us worthy to worship and serve the living God. The work of the Spirit is to sanctify believers so that what was imputed to us by faith in the finished work of Jesus on the cross—"It is finished. It is paid." (John 19:30)—is now imparted to our character and actions. The Holy Spirit's job is to make us holy and see us commissioned. Whom God cleanses, He also commissions. The Spirit fills us to enable the experience and sight of the living God in glory, to experience *the* Father as *our* Father, and then take on the yoke of Christ in obedience.

Recently, these assumptions and this thesis about the Trinity in the New Testament were tested at a church retreat in the Santa Cruz Mountains of California. Participants were encouraged to trust the permission given in Scripture to address the Godhead as Father, Son, and Spirit in any order that seemed best for them in their present situation. About five minutes were allotted for the Triune prayer experiment, with a debriefing afterward.

One woman shared what happened as she chose to seek God in the Spirit-Father-Son order. She testified that as she first called upon God the Spirit to fill and show her the Father, she experienced God's presence and was immediately envisioned using her weekday children's ministry to share Christ with the parents of those children. Her experience was that when the Spirit makes us ascend to God the Father in prayer, then motivation comes to serve and share Christ. Her worship led to renewed vision for service. Reverence preceded vision to follow Christ.

Are you in need of steadfastness today? Is your resolve shaken in your stand against temptation and half truth? Is your motivation at a loss to embrace ministry and witness to those who struggle with distrust and debasement? Ask the Holy Spirit to restore the joy of your salvation. Then ask Him to show you anew the undiminished love of the Father. Finally, look to the right of the Father and find the grace of the Son. Stand in that grace and move out in the ministries of mercy that Jesus directs you into.

CHAPTER 9

The Shaping Triad: Father-Spirit-Son as the Spiritual Formation Order

The Holy Spirit indwelling the individual Christian is not only the agent of Christ, but he is also the agent of the Father. . . . I am in a personal relationship with each of the members of the Trinity. God the Father is my Father; I am in union with the Son; I am indwelt by the Holy Spirit. This is not just meant to be doctrine; it is what I have now."

—Francis Schaeffer[1]

The Father-Spirit-Son and the Spirit-Son-Father triads occur among the fewest times of all the New Testament instances of Trinitarian expressions. The Father-Spirit-Son triad occurs in the eleven places listed below in Table 9.1. These eleven occurrences represent about fifteen percent of the seventy-five occurrences of all triadic expressions in the New Testament. Though a limited pool for study, these eleven instances do merit close inspection, especially because two of those instances are rather striking and important benedictions.

---

1. Francis Schaeffer, "True Spirituality," in *A Christian Worldview: The Complete Works of Francis Schaeffer*, vol. 3 (Wheaton, IL: Crossway, 1985), 270–271.

TABLE 9.1: NEW TESTAMENT OCCURRENCES OF THE FATHER-SPIRIT-SON TRIAD

LOCATIONS AND GRADATIONS FOR THE FORMATIONAL TRIADIC ORDER OF FATHER-SPIRIT-SON			
Text	**Rating**	**Context**	**Summary**
John 4:23	C	Witness/ prophecy	worship the Father in Spirit and truth
Acts 1:4–8	B	Power/witness	promise of the Father . . . with the Holy Spirit . . . Father has fixed . . . Holy Spirit upon you . . . be my witnesses
Acts 4:24–26	C	Prayer for boldness	Master [*despota*], You are the One who made the heaven, the earth. . . . You said by the Holy Spirit . . . against the LORD and against His Messiah [*christou*]
Romans 14:17–18	A-	Kingdom life	the kingdom of God, joy in the Holy Spirit, serves Christ
1 Corinthians 2:10–16	A-	Spiritual wisdom	God has revealed through Spirit . . . mind of Christ
Galatians 4:6	A	Redemption	God has sent the Spirit of His Son
2 Thes- salonians 2:13–14	B	Calling	give thanks to God for you, beloved by the Lord. . . because God chose . . . through sanctification by the Spirit . . . obtain the glory of our Lord Jesus Christ
Titus 3:4–6	B	Maintaining good works	from God our Savior . . . renewal by the Holy Spirit. . . richly through Jesus Christ
1 Peter 1:2	A	Greeting	destined by God the Father, sanctified by the Spirit for obedience to Jesus Christ
1 John 4:13	A-	Christian testi- mony	he [God] has given us of his own Spirit, the Father sent his Son
Revelation 1:4–5	C	Greeting	From the One who is and is to come; from the seven spirits before His throne; and from Jesus Christ, the faithful witness

FATHER-SPIRIT-SON REFERENCES IN THE GOSPELS

John 4:23. John chapter 4 narrates the encounter of Jesus with the Samaritan woman at Jacob's well. Near the climax of that conversation in verse 23, Jesus asserts, "the true worshippers will worship the Father [Father] in spirit [Spirit] and truth [Son, as the Word]. Yes, the Father [Father] wants such people to worship Him. God is spirit [Spirit], and those who worship Him [Father] must worship in spirit [Spirit] and truth [Son]."

The attribution of [Son] to the word "truth" in this passage is a bit of a speculative gamble. That is why this reference receives a grade of "C" as to authenticity as a triadic reference. What may make this a calculated attribution is that fact that the phrase "spirit and truth" is repeated and that the order in the phrase puts "spirit" before "truth." It is in this gospel that Jesus self-identifies as "the way, the truth, and the life" (John 14:6), and says that the task of the Spirit of truth is to bring all things into remembrance with reference to the truths of the life and words of Jesus (John 14:17, 15:26, 16:13). If this citation is indeed an authentic instance of the Father-Spirit-Son order, then its context is one of application to worship and spiritual formation. To risk saying more is to venture further into speculation about this text, which is secondary in our investigation of the F-Sp-S processional order.

FATHER-SPIRIT-SON REFERENCES IN ACTS

The Great Commission in Acts and the Father-Spirit-Son Triad

Acts 1:4–8. If the Acts of the Apostles were to have a subtitle, certainly, "How the Promised Spirit Empowered the Gospel and the Church to the World" might be it. The work of the Spirit in the lives of the apostles and the believing church is central to Acts. In Acts 1:4–8, Luke takes a fresh approach to the Great Commission via the practical pneumatology and sanctification inherent in the Father-Spirit-Son triad. Immediately prior to His ascension, Jesus orders the disciples to "wait for the Father's promise . . . you will be baptized with the Holy Spirit" (Acts 1:4–5). What God intends next for the disciples and the gospel will happen as the Father pours out His Spirit upon His church.

In verses 7–8, the full Father-Spirit-Son triad is invoked, "It is not for you to know times or periods that the Father [Father] has set by His own authority. But you will receive power when the Holy Spirit [Spirit] has come upon you and you will be My [Son] witnesses." The presence of the Spirit supplies the power for the work of Christian witness. It may be useful to make a distinction between *being* a witness as declared in this text versus the more common Western evangelical phraseology of *doing* witness. The former has the sense of something flowing out of one's inner existence and experience, while the latter flows out of obligation. The force of the promise is that with this work of the Spirit, believers and disciples will be unable not to bear witness.

Acts is the only New Testament document to use all six triadic orders, but does not explicitly allude to the Son beyond the possessive pronoun "My" in "My witnesses." In addition, the triad is configurable from the clarification of Jesus that the Father sets the time on the eschatological clock, then the Spirit comes upon the disciples, and that descent is at the Father's sending both by implication and by explicit indication in the text. Therefore this passage is rated as a "B" with regard to evidential reference to the Trinity. The result of descent of the Spirit is, of course, the capacity of the disciples to be the witnesses for Christ in an increasing geographical sphere of influence.

Acts 4:24–26. This passage records Peter's intercessory prayer for bold witness in the face of emerging post-Pentecost resistance by the Jewish leadership. The apostle incorporates the familiar Messianic Psalm 2:1–2, identifying Jesus as that anointed One, declared by God as His adopted Son. The text in Acts reads:

> "Master [Father], You are the One who made the heaven, the earth, and the sea, and everything in them. You said through the Holy Spirit [Spirit], by the mouth of our father David Your servant: 'Why did the Gentiles rage and the peoples plot futile things? The kings of the earth took their stand and the rules assembled together against the LORD [Father] and against His Messiah [Son].'"

In the next verse (27), Peter identifies Jesus as the Father's "holy Servant." This incidence of the Father-Spirit-Son triad is rated a "B" because of the rather inadvertent identification of the Holy Spirit. However, as discussed earlier in chapter 5, the missional triad Father-Son-Spirit occurs immediately after this text in Acts 4:29–30. The point there is that the sending of the Holy Spirit enables a bold witness to God's message. Certainly, Peter recognizes that the Psalmist's witness to the chosen One is the result of the Holy Spirit's anointing of King David's lips. If the disciples are to remain faithful and fruitful under pressure and persecution, then the Father must supply the Spirit for bold witness to and life in the Son.

FATHER-SPIRIT-SON REFERENCES
IN THE PAULINE EPISTLES

The Roman Triadic Summation

At the end of Romans, Paul briefly overviews acceptable Christian service and ethical decision making with these memorable words, "for the kingdom of God [Father] is not eating and drinking, but righteousness, peace, and joy in the Holy Spirit [Spirit]. Whoever serves Christ [Son] in this way is acceptable to God and approved by men" (Romans 14:17–18). In this passage, the F-Sp-S triad depicts first the recognizable boundaries of the Father's kingdom, namely, where lives are lived in right relationships and reconciliations. The physical activities of eating and drinking are contrasted with the Spirit-habilitating qualities of righteousness, peace, and joy in the Holy Spirit. Such living serves the Messiah and humanity well. Without these threefold attributes of living in the Spirit, how shall the believer's life be found acceptable to Christ or the community?

This triadic reference is rated "A-" because of the close proximity of the references to God, the Holy Spirit, and Christ—but it recognizes that the notion "Whoever serves Christ in this way" starts a new thought immediately following the attributes of life in the Holy Spirit. The conclusion of the triadic procession from God to Holy Spirit to Christ is the quality and quantity of service that please God and others. So, the intention of the Father-Spirit-Son reference in this instance is God imparting supernatural living and serving.

First Corinthians 2:10-16 and the Mind of Christ

1 Corinthians 2:10–16. Chapter 2 of Paul's first letter to the Corinthians begins with Paul sharing his strategic plan to spread the gospel in Corinth and to see a church flourish there. He expresses the gospel in the framework of the missional order of the trinity: Father-Son-Spirit. This order and this text were reviewed previously in chapter 5.

Now at the end of 1 Corinthians 2, Paul invokes the Father-Spirit-Son triad. The context is a discussion of spiritual maturity and wisdom in terms of being either spiritual or natural (*psuchikos*) persons. Beginning with verse 10, Paul begins a rapid binitarian trill between the Father and the Spirit which culminates at the mind of the Christ.[2] That binitarian trill or perichoresis, the latter being the Greek idea of interpenetration without loss of distinction, has the following movements: "Now God [Father] has revealed these things to us by the Spirit [Spirit], for the Spirit [Spirit] searches everything, even the depths of God [Father]. . . no one knows the thoughts of God [Father] except the Spirit of God [Spirit] . . . the Spirit [Spirit] who comes from God [Father], so that we might understand what has been freely given to us by God [Father]. . . . But the unbeliever does not welcome what comes from God's Spirit [Spirit]. . . . But we have the mind of Christ [Son]."

Using triadic analysis, the order would be Father-Spirit-Spirit-Father-Father-Spirit-Spirit-Father-Father-Spirit-Son. The abbreviated understanding of the passage in terms of triadic analysis is therefore the Father-Spirit-Son order. The context for this processional framework is spiritual formation or maturation of the servants of God. The Father sends the Spirit into the lives of His children that they might take up life in the Son. Sanctification by the Spirit is intended in a Triune way to issue in Christ-minded living.

Anthony Thiselton comments on this passage as the Father-Son-Spirit order by taking the passage as 1 Corinthians 2:6–3:4. He uses the title "A Redefinition of 'Wisdom,' 'Maturity,' and 'Spirituality' in the Light of God, Christ, and the Holy Spirit"[3] Though he is correct in seeing the Father-Son referenced in 2:6–7, "God's hidden wisdom . . . the crucified Lord of glory," the true intent of the passage is to show how the Father imparts His wisdom into the life of believers through the work of His Spirit in the inner person, so that believers have the mind of Christ in their thinking and doing (1 Corinthians 2:16).

This triadic instance is rated as an "A-" because the sixfold binitarian "dance" between the Father and the Spirit that spins forth the mind is Christ in the lives of believers. The minus in the rating shows minor caution, since the reference to the Son is a distinct sentence immediately following the binitarian praise song, "But we have the mind of Christ."

The theme of this chapter is wisdom. It is self-evident that people walk in the wisdom they consider valid and pleasing to those to whom they are held accountable. Worship of the Father to receive the Spirit He sends issues in the capacity to think and walk like Christ Jesus. Christian formation happens in the

---

2. By "binitarian," I mean the One God expressed in terms of only two of the three persons in the Godhead. New Testament binitarian examples of the Father and the Son are the most common, with Son and Spirit, and Father and Spirit being less common.

3. Anthony Thiselton, *The First Epistle to the Corinthians: A Commentary on the Greek Text*, (Grand Rapids: Eerdmans, 2000), 224.

Father-Spirit-Son movement; we grow in walking in Christlike wisdom by the empowering of the Holy Spirit, so we can be pleasing to the Father.

God Forming Believers in Galatians 4:6 and 2 Thessalonians 2:13

Galatians 4:6. The Father-Spirit-Son triad makes its next appearance in Galatians 4:6. Here Paul is again discussing Christian maturity and spiritual formation. He is moving from Christology and soteriology to pneumatology, from the doctrine of Christ and salvation to the doctrine of the Spirit. He is describing the developmental move from childhood to adult Christianity. The verse reads, "And because you are sons, God [Father] has sent the Spirit [Spirit] of His Son [Son] into our hearts, crying, *Abba*, Father [Father]!"

This use of the Aramaic *Abba* is one of three in the New Testament—Mark 14:36 and Romans 8:15 being the others. This verse is very similar to Romans 8:15, which was discussed in chapter 8 under the processional rubric of Spirit-Father-Son. Both texts embed the Aramaic *Abba* Father into the Greek text. Both verses place *Son* at the end of the procession. Paul's application of the Father-Spirit-Son order here in Galatians focuses more on the continuing identity of the Christian self as adopted sons and daughters rather than at the point of adoption.

So, the interpretation that the Father-Spirit-Son order promotes spiritual maturity finds additional support in the remainder of Galatians 4 and on into the next chapter, which aims at calling the Galatian believers not to lapse back into "slavery" and infancy of their earlier identity. This aligns well with the recognition of Timothy George that use of the Aramaic *Abba* is more about adult intimacy than infant adoration:

> The word *Abba* appears in certain legal texts of the Mishna as a designation used by grown children in claiming the inheritance of their deceased father. As a word of address *Abba* is not so much associated with infancy as it is with intimacy. It is a cry of the heart, not a word spoken calmly with personal detachment and reserve, but a word we "call" or "cry out" (*krazō*).[4]

The heart cry of Jesus in the garden of Gethsemane is the call of intimacy, not infancy: "*Abba*, Father! All things are possible for You. Take this cup away

---

4. Timothy George, *Galatians*, vol. 30, The New American Commentary (Nashville: Broadman & Holman, 1994), 307.

from me"[5] (Mark 14:36). The Father sends the Spirit into our lives that we may self-identify as His sons and daughters even as we live our life in union with His Son.

2 Thessalonians 2:13–14. Paul applies this same processional order of Father-Spirit-Son, when he writes to encourage the believers at Thessalonica to stand firm in their faith. In 2 Thessalonians 2:13, Paul exhorts, "God [Father] has chosen you for salvation through sanctification by the Spirit [Spirit] and through belief in the truth. He called you to this through our gospel, so that you might obtain the glory of our Lord Jesus Christ [Son]." This rehearsal of the Thessalonians' own salvation history of Father-Spirit-Son is intended to "encourage" and "strengthen" them for good works and words, and for good hope in the Son's reward and exaltation (2 Thessalonians 2:17).

I find it significant that the Spirit is at the center of this formational triadic formula, with "sanctification by the Spirit" at the center of this particular text. This processional order may express the intention of God as Father to parent or develop His adopted children into maturity in His Son, by the sanctifying work of the Spirit. Note also that this sanctifying or maturational task of the Spirit is accomplished in coordination with "belief in the truth."

The similarity between the Father-Spirit-Son and the Spirit-Father-Son orders may also suggest that Christian development, worship, and devotion—be they personal or corporate—go hand-in-hand. We could speak in many instances of worship as spiritual formation and spiritual formation as worship. Maturity in Christ brings God glory and is what motivates the apostleship of Paul (Colossians 1:28–29). This instance of the Father-Spirit-Son order is rated as a "B" since the final element "Son" arrives at the end of the verse following the one in which the Father and the Son are identified. However, the movement is clearly Trinitarian and intended to shape believers into the glory of the eternal Son.

There is little doubt that "Lord" here refers to the Son, Jesus, since the title "Lord Jesus Christ" is used twice in the following three verses (2 Thessalonians 2:14, 16). Charles Wanamaker entertains the possibility that the reference to spirit here might refer to the human spirit, but then he goes on to conclude it must be the Holy Spirit. He writes: "Although it is possible that πνεῦμα might refer to the human spirit (cf. 1 Thess. 5:23), sanctification in the end comes from God, not from the human spirit (cf. 1 Thess. 4:3–8;

---

5. Ibid.

5:23), and it is elsewhere attributed to the work of the Holy Spirit (Rom. 15:16; cf. 1 Cor. 6:11)."[6]

Michael Martin argues convincingly that "with a singular noun [spirit] and in the absence of a possessive pronoun it seems unlikely that Paul meant 'sanctification of your spirits.'"[7] Gene Green also agrees that spirit here must be the Holy Spirit: "[B]ut the focus of this verse is rather the powerful divine operation in their lives by means of the Holy *Spirit* and *the truth*. These Christians entered into the realm of salvation *through belief in the truth*, that is, through their faith in the gospel that was proclaimed to them"[8]

So, the Thessalonians are chosen by God, loved by the Son, and sanctified by the Spirit in truth. That being so, Paul urges them to "stand firm and hold to the traditions" (2 Thessalonians 2:15).

A Trinitarian Salvation Song in Titus

Titus 3:4–6. The Father-Spirit-Son triad order also appears in Paul's letter to Titus. Here George Knight comments that, "All three persons of the Trinity are mentioned: The Father 'saved us' (v. 5) and 'poured out' the Holy Spirit on us (v. 6) 'through Jesus Christ.'"[9] In the midst of an exhortation to good works, the apostle inserts a portion of what appears to be a Trinitarian-framed hymn of salvation.

> But when the kindness of God [Father] our Savior, and His
> love for mankind appeared
> He saved us—
> not by works of righteousness that we had done,
> but according to His mercy,
> through the washing of regeneration
> and renewal by the Holy Spirit [Spirit].
> He poured out this Spirit on us abundantly
> through Jesus Christ [Son] our Savior (Titus 3:4–6).

---

6. C. A. Wanamaker, *The Epistles to the Thessalonians: A Commentary on the Greek Text* (Grand Rapids: Eerdmans, 1990), 266.
7. Michael Martin, *1, 2 Thessalonians*, vol. 33, The New American Commentary (Nashville: Broadman & Holman, 1995), 253.
8. G. L. Green, *The Letters to the Thessalonians*, (Grand Rapids; Leicester, England: Eerdmans, 2002), 327.
9. G. W. Knight, *The Pastoral Epistles: A Commentary on the Greek Text* (Grand Rapids; Carlisle, England: Eerdmans; Paternoster Press, 1992), 338.

The essential equality between the Father and the Son is certainly conveyed here by the sharing of the title "Savior" in this hymn. The passage presents the Father's initiative in regenerating the elect by His Spirit. "He [God] saved us" is the main verb in this four-verse sentence (Titus 3:5). Paul wants it clear that root comes before fruit: Believers' righteous works are fruit, while the root is the regenerating mercy that washes and renews believers as the Father pours the Holy Spirit upon them (Titus 3:5–6). The Son—both in terms of His earthly person and work and in terms of the faith of the repentant in that person and work—is the channel through which the Father pours out His Spirit.

Though the precise Trinitarian order here is literally Father-Spirit-Son in the text, one could make the case that, logically, the order should be Father-Son-Spirit, since the channel or instrument must be in place before the pouring can be done. Therefore I would rate this passage as definitely Trinitarian in framework but only probably Father-Spirit-Son in its order, thus the rating is a "B." Thomas Lea affirms this recognition, "It is noteworthy that each person of the Trinity is referred to in this passage and particularly in this text: *God* poured out the *Holy Spirit* through *Jesus Christ*."[10] The context of this Father-Spirit-Son instance is exhortation to devote oneself to good works (Titus 3:8). The energy for such devotion is the regenerative and renewing overflow of the Spirit freely poured out by the Father, by whom believers move beyond justification by grace to full heirs of the heavenly hope and inheritance (Titus 3:7).

FATHER-SPIRIT-SON REFERENCES IN HEBREWS THROUGH REVELATION

Peter's First Epistle

1 Peter 1:2. In what reads like instructions to the newly baptized, Peter wastes no time in invoking the names of the divine three Persons, only in an unexpected order of Father, Spirit, and Son. The text reads: " Peter, an apostle of Jesus Christ: To the temporary residents dispersed in Pontus, Galatia, Cappadocia, Asia and Bithynia, chosen according to the foreknowledge of God the Father [Father] and set apart by the Spirit [Spirit] for obedience and for sprinkling with the blood of Jesus Christ."

This instance of the Father-Spirit-Son order is intentionally triadic, and commentators do often recognize it. Thomas Schreiner and others recognize

---

10. Thomas Lea and H. Griffin, *1, 2 Timothy, Titus*, vol. 34, The New American Commentary (Nashville: Broadman & Holman, 1992), 324.

the reality of the triadic order, but also add the disclaimer that by making the disclaimer, "Peter, of course, did not articulate in a full-fledged way the doctrine of the Trinity, but from verses such as this the doctrine was hammered out."[11]

All commentators note that Peter's opening greeting explains that God elects dispersed exiles in a threefold movement, which is communicated textually in three prepositional phrases:

- according to the foreknowledge of God the Father
- by the Holy Spirit set apart (sanctified)
- for obedience and sprinkling of the blood of Jesus Christ.

Seeing that the order is really unarguably triadic in a pre-Trinitarian sense, let's see if we can make the case that the order Father-Spirit-Son is intentional because it is the triadic movement of the Godhead on a mission of Christian formation.

Schreiner is of little help to my case. He notes the triadic framework but "wishes" it were Father-Son-Spirit. He writes, "We should also note in the verse the reference to the Father, Spirit, and the Son. The Father foreknows, the Spirit sanctifies, and the Son cleanses. The idea is close to the traditional theological formulation of the Father as Creator, the Son as Redeemer, and the Spirit as Sanctifier. Similar triadic formulas are found elsewhere in the New Testament (Matt 3:16–17; 28:19; 1 Cor 12:4–6; 2 Cor 13:14; Eph 4:6; 2 Thess 2:13–14; Jude 20–21; Rev 1:4–5)."[12] All the triadic formulas Schreiner identifies are treated in the "New Testament Census of Triadic Occurrences" in Appendix A. It is ironic that Schreiner sees no meaning in the triadic order in relation to the context, though he also sites 2 Thessalonians 2:13 for its triadic formula when it uses the same Father-Spirit-Son order and has a similar context of sanctification and Christian formation, as we discussed earlier in this chapter.

We should applaud Jobes for her attempt to interpret the significance of the triadic order, though I would say that she is slightly off the mark. She comments, "The order—Father, Spirit, Christ—perhaps reflects the logical *ordo salutis* of conversion that finds its ultimate origin in the heart of God, is made operative in human lives by the Holy Spirit, and is evidenced through personal expressions of faith in Jesus Christ."[13]

---

11. Thomas Schreiner, *1, 2 Peter, Jude*, vol. 37, The New American Commentary (Nashville: Broadman & Holman, 2003), 57.
12. Ibid.
13. K. H. Jobes, *1 Peter* (Grand Rapids: Baker Academic, 2005), 68.

Jobes is not alone against my case. For instance, Lange also sees the triadic movement in the context of our salvation, "The three persons of the Holy Trinity cöoperate, according to the Apostle, in the work of our salvation."[14]

Simon Kistemaker votes "yes" on triadic but "no" on order intentionality. He claims that "Peter speaks of God the Father, the Spirit, and Jesus Christ (see also Ephesians 1:3–14). The order he chooses is arbitrary, for he is interested not in sequence but in the function each person of the Trinity performs."[15] No doubt the function of each is significant, but in putting a cake together, it's best to put the icing on last. Order is important. In Kistemaker's defense, he does get half of the point of Peter's declaration when he comments, "In three separate clauses Peter describes three acts of the Triune God. The Father has foreknowledge, the Spirit sanctifies, and Jesus Christ expects obedience from those whom he has cleansed from sin. These three clauses explain the term *elect* (v. 1)."[16] Discussion of God's elect, His chosen, is Peter's point here. In the next verse, he writes, "According to His great mercy, He has given us a new birth into a living hope" (1 Peter 1:3). But Peter's point—no, God's point—is not merely election unto salvation; God and Peter have something more grand in mind than that. I think these interpreters are thinking too small. J. B. Phillips might say to them, "Your God is too small."[17] Now let's see why.

Expanding Our View: Service. First, Peter knows that God never merely forgives and sanctifies. When Jesus restored Peter after his dismal performance at the cross, Jesus did not say, "I forgive you." He said, "Feed My lambs . . . Shepherd My sheep . . . Feed My sheep . . . Follow Me" (John 21:15–19). Peter knows that whomever God cleanses, He also commissions. Whomever He saves, He also calls into His service. So, this Father-Spirit-Son triadic movement reckons on the Father initiating and choosing, the Spirit sanctifying and setting apart, and the Son calling into obedient service. Salvation in 1 Peter 1:2–3 is the stepping stone to commissioning in 1 Peter 2:4–9,

> Coming to Him [Christ the cornerstone], a living stone . . .
> you yourselves, as living stones are being built into a spiritual

---

14. J. Lange, P. Schaff, G. F. C. Fronmüller, J. L. Mombert, *A Commentary on the Holy Scriptures: 1 Peter* (Bellingham, WA: Logos Bible Software, 2008), 12.
15. S. J. Kistemaker and W. Hendriksen, *Exposition of the Epistles of Peter and the Epistle of Jude*, vol. 16, (Grand Rapids: Baker Book House), 36.
16. Ibid., 35.
17. J. B. Phillips, *Your God Is Too Small* (New York: Touchstone, 1997).

> house for a holy priesthood to offer spiritual sacrifices accept-
> able to God through Jesus Christ . . . But you are a chosen race
> [same word as in 1:2!], a royal priesthood, a holy nation . . . so
> that you may proclaim the praises of the One who called you.

So, the Father is the architect, the Spirit cleanses and shapes us into living stones, and the Son calls us to obey and serve Him, to line up in praise with Him as the cornerstone. Kobes notes the work of the Spirit, between the Father and the Son, with this comment, "'[T]he spirit' (*pneuma*) here is almost certainly to be understood as the Holy Spirit, who is the instrument, or agency, by which God makes his electing foreknowledge operative in the lives of those who come to faith in Christ."[18]

Peter knows how the Spirit sanctifies and states: "By obedience to the truth, having purified yourselves for sincere love of the brothers, love one another earnestly from a pure heart" (1 Peter 1:22). He learned this relationship between the Spirit, truth, and cleansing from Jesus Himself and was reminded of it when Jesus insisted on washing his feet: "When the Counselor comes, the One I will send you from the Father—the Spirit of truth . . . Father, . . . [s]anctify them by the truth; Your word is truth" (John 15:26, 17:1, 17 cf. 13:10, 14:26). But Peter also knows that God always assures us of His acceptance and forgiveness and welcomes us as His children by calling and assigning us into His service. We know we are welcome and belong when a place of valued contribution is found for us.

Expanding Our View: Obedience. Now let me bring forward my second exhibit of evidence. I would make a textual case that the triadic order used by Peter here—Father-Spirit-Son—is not only intentionally Trinitarian, it is purposefully in this precise order because it is the order God moves to shape us after Christ.

Commentators love interpreting with the striking third prepositional phrase, "for obedience and for sprinkling with the blood of Jesus Christ" (1 Peter 1:2). Lenski argues that the Father-Spirit-Son order is not arbitrary. He states:

> The order of the three phrases cannot be changed. [For] in
> the third points to intention and to result: "for obedience and
> sprinkling of Jesus Christ's blood." The phrase recalls Exod.

---

18. Jobes, *1 Peter*, 69–70.

24:7, 8: when the people heard what Moses read they said: "All that the Lord hath said we will do and be obedient," and then Moses sprinkled them with the blood. This explains why "obedience" precedes "sprinkling." On the latter compare also Heb. 10:22 and 12:24.[19]

Hebrews 10:22 speaks of standing fast in our faith because our hearts have been sprinkled clean. Hebrews 12:24 invokes us to see ourselves coming to the city of the living God, to the myriads of angels, to the assembly whose names are written in heaven, and to Jesus our Mediator, and to the sprinkled blood.

This business of sprinkling blood has an enlightening backstory in the Old Testament. Let's take a look at four diverse contexts in which sprinkled blood happens there.

1. **Exodus 24:3–8.** Here, the sprinkling of sacrificial blood by Moses on the tabernacle altar and on the people solemnized the event. This sprinkling symbolizes that the people have entered into and accepted the terms of God's covenant and that God accepts their commitment. Jobes insightfully comments about why Peter speaks of obedience and sprinkling in relation to the Son. She says that "This grammatical difficulty can be avoided if the phrase 'obedience and sprinkling' is understood as a hendiadys (expressing a single idea by two words) alluding to the establishment of the Mosaic covenant (Exod. 24:3–8). There the newly formed people of Israel first pledge their obedience (24:3, 7) and then are sprinkled with the blood of the sacrifice (24:8). In this ceremony both sides of the essential nature of the covenant are represented: the people pledge obedience to God, and the blood of the covenant is applied."[20] Lange agrees with Jobes' assessment, "the sprinkling of the people did not take place until they had declared themselves ready to comply with all the demands of the Divine Law without any exception whatsoever."[21] So in Exodus and in 1 Peter, obedience and sprinkling are coupled, with obedience preceding the sprinkling of blood.

---

19. R. C. H. Lenski, *The Interpretation of the Epistles of St. Peter, St. John and St. Jude* (Minneapolis: Augsburg Publishing House, 1966), 26.
20. Jobes, *1 Peter*, 12.
21. Lange, *A Commentary on the Holy Scriptures: 1 Peter*, 12.

2. **Leviticus 1:5; 5:9; 4:6–7, 17–18; 16:14–19.** The holy vessels of the tabernacle are blood sprinkled as a sign of their being set apart for service to the LORD.[22]

3. **Leviticus 4:3–12.** A sevenfold sprinkling of blood in front of the Tent of Meeting is required as a ceremonial cleansing and restoration to ministry of sinning priests. (In the same chapter, **4:13–21**, a similar sevenfold sprinkling and sacrifice is likewise required for when "the whole community of Israel errs" (v. 13) and incurs guilt by violating what the LORD prohibits.

4. **Numbers 19:1–8.** Sevenfold blood sprinkling in front of the Tent of Meeting by the priest for the Israelites. This passage emphasizes the necessary mediation of the high priest that the people might approach the LORD.

We can affirm the interpretation of 1 Peter 1:2 that Peter couples obedience and blood sprinkling of the people bound in the new "holy nation" (1 Peter 2:9) because the Israelites were installed as His people, Israel, as they acknowledged submission to the covenant and then were sprinkled. We need also to see that blood sprinkling occurs repeatedly in the Old Testament in the context of sanctification for service or restoration to service in holiness. Peter wants his readers to know that Christ sprinkles His own sacrifice upon them as a mark of obedience accepted and commission to serve in His name and character.

John's First Epistle

1 John 4:13–14. Some commentators admit that we don't know whether this next passage belongs with the paragraph that comes before it or with what follows after. Perhaps we should see it as both—a sort of a hinge verse. Whatever we decide, we do need to acknowledge the triadic nature of the verses and intent of the author. "This is how we know that we remain in Him [Father] and He in us; He has given assurance to us from His Spirit [Spirit]. And we have seen and we testify that the Father [Father] has sent His Son [Son] as the world's Savior." So the technical triadic order is Father-Spirit-Father-Son, but the intent of the passage must be both assurance of abiding and confession of the life, work, and personal experience of the Son. Daniel Akin states that "their message is rooted

---

22. Ibid.

in historical reality and personal experience."[23] John here recognizes that the saved are supplied with an assurance of salvation.

"We" is the commanding pronoun of the passage. Akin believes that this must refer to the apostles and their witness.[24] But even if that is correct, the intent is that the readers also share in the Spirit's assurance and the apostolic confession that the Father sent the Son. Such assurance comes in the presence of the Holy Spirit as the gift of the Father. The result of that Spirit empowered assurance is the witness that the Father has sent the Son as the world's Savior. "World's Savior" does not, of course, necessarily imply that all people in or of the world will be saved, but that there is a God-supplied and assured Savior available.

This is something like the brass snake that Moses placed on a pole in the midst of the viper-plagued Israelites. All who looked upon the brass snake were healed of the viper's bite, but not all bitten took advantage of that opportunity (Numbers 21:4–8).

Confession of the person and work of the Son follows the assurance of the Spirit that we abide in the Father's love. Colin Kruse comments here that "the Spirit teaches the truth about God's sending Jesus as the Saviour of the world and knowing this provides believers with the basis of assurance."[25] The mutual operations of the Trinity in the functional life of the believer are what the text witnesses to in this passage. First John is written throughout as a test for the state of one's Christian formation. Here the Father-Spirit-Son order is used, somewhat inadvertently, to call the readers into fresh spiritual assurance and witness.

In the End, Trinity

Revelation 1:4–5. The final instance of the Father-Spirit-Son order is found in Revelation 1:4–5. This triadic instance frames the opening greeting of John to the seven churches in the Roman province called Asia. Robert Letham rightly asserts that the opening line, "Grace and peace to you from the One who is, who was, and who is coming," is best understood as a reference to God the Father.[26] The phrase is a sound interpretation of the name Yahweh had revealed to Moses in Exodus 3:14. I also agree with Letham that the second phrase, "from the seven

---

23. Daniel L. Akin, *1, 2, 3 John*, vol. 38, The New American Commentary (Nashville: Broadman & Holman Publishers, 2001), 183.

24. Ibid.

25. C. G. Kruse, *The Letters of John* (Grand Rapids; Leicester, England: Eerdmans, 2000), 163.

26. Robert Letham, *The Holy Trinity: In Scripture, History, Theology and Worship* (Phillipsburg, NJ: P & R Publishing, 2004), 67.

spirits before His throne," should likely be understood as the Spirit, since the pattern of the next two chapters of letters in Revelation to the individual churches has a common refrain, "let him hear what the Spirit says to the churches."[27] The greeting closes with, "and from Jesus Christ, the faithful witness." The insertion of the reference to the spirits in between the references to the eternal One and the Son makes an interpretation of "the seven spirits" as the Holy Spirit an even likelier understanding. The reference to seven spirits is evocative of the phrase "Lord of the Spirits" common in the intertestamental work, 1 Enoch:

> And I heard the voices of those four presences as they uttered praises before the Lord of glory. The first voice blesses the Lord of Spirits forever and ever. And the second voice I heard blessing the Elect One and the elect ones who hang upon the Lord of Spirits (1 Enoch 40:3–5, 69:29).

This introductory doxology in Revelation 1:4–5 displays a triadic framework marked by three *from* phrases: "from the One who is . . . from the seven spirits . . . and from Jesus Christ." This doxology concludes with a formational overview marked by three verbs of which the redeemed are the object: "loves us . . . has set us free . . . made us a kingdom, priests to His God and Father" (Revelation 1:5b–6). So, here the context interprets the meaning of the Father-Spirit-Son order, namely to be lovingly formed, freed from sin, and empowered to minister to God as priests together. The triadic order Father-Spirit-Son is God forming us in the Son for priesting.

But now the question emerges as to why use the Father-Spirit-Son order to introduce the Revelation? The book does begin and end with a vision of the Son, first as the white-robed Alpha and Omega in 1:8–17 and then as fiery-eyed rider—the Word who is King of Kings—in 19:11–16. The intent of Revelation is to call believers to "patient endurance" in anticipation of the coming of Christ on the clouds (Revelation 1:7). Thus, out of reverence for the One God and Father, the churches are to receive the cleansing, correcting, and comforting words sent by the Spirit and thereby to persevere in witness until the Son appears. With this understanding, then, I conclude that the Father-Spirit-Son order is God forming believers for patient witness and suffering for Christ in anticipation of His return. This order shapes believers in an eschatological hope that endures.

---

27. Ibid., 68.

DISCUSSION QUESTIONS—CHAPTER 9

- Look carefully again at Romans 14:17–18. What makes you confident that this passage is an instance of the Father-Spirit-Son order? If you graded this instance in terms of Trinitarian intentionality by Paul, what grade would you give it: "A," "B, " or "C"? Explain your grading.

- This chapter identifies the Father-Spirit-Son order as God shaping believers in the likeness of His Son. Look at Peter's introduction to what might be his post-baptismal letter to new believers (1 Peter 1:1–2). Explain why Peter chooses this order above the other five possible triads to engage his readers.

- Your pastor has been teaching through the book of Romans and now will cover Romans 14. Design a worship service around that chapter, using the Father-Spirit-Son order seen in Romans 14:17–18, the focal passage for the sermon. What songs or choruses will you select to lead your worshippers in exalting God according to that triadic order?

SERMON STARTER: THE FATHER-SPIRIT-SON FORMATIONAL ORDER

Roots and Fruits: 1 Peter 1:2

If the promise keeper is not as great as the promise maker, what difference does it make how great the promise is? No promise can ever be greater than the one who keeps it. The God of Abraham, Isaac, and Jacob—who is the God and Father of Jesus Christ—makes and keeps promises.

God's promises typically fuse holiness and hope. His promise is moral preparation for high placement. His promise imparts character to guarantee career.

Peter was no Paul. Peter has two letters in the New Testament, compared to Paul's thirteen. Paul's letters are pastoral in response to local church needs or personal encouragement to leaders whom he is mentoring. Peter's letters are general epistles aimed at encouragement and enlightenment for any and all who believe. I wonder how much nagging it took to get Simon Peter to put down the fishing pole and take up the pen. How excited the early Christians must have been to read this letter in worship. Finally, something in writing from Peter the Rock, someone close to Jesus from His baptism to His ascension!

Those that design and lead worship often put doxology at the end just before the benediction. But Peter puts doxology, giving thanks, right at the beginning of his letter. Though he thanks the Triune God, he does so in an order that is unexpected, but carefully chosen: the Promise and its Maker, the Power to Keep the Promise, the Product of the Promise.

THE PROMISE AND ITS MAKER

The essence of intelligence is the ability to discern patterns and relationships. The Trinitarian pattern of Father-Spirit-Son for Christian formation occurs in eleven places in the New Testament. Here are five of those places. Listen to see if you can discern the Trinitarian pattern and the intent of God in working this pattern:

> "from the beginning God has chosen you for salvation through sanctification by the Spirit and through belief in the truth. He called you to this through our gospel, so that you might obtain the glory of our Lord Jesus Christ. There-

fore, brothers, stand firm and hold to the traditions you were taught" (2 Thessalonians 2:13–15).

"And because you are sons, God has sent the Spirit of His Son into our hearts, crying *Abba*, Father!' So you are no longer a slave but a son, and if a son, then an heir through God" (Galatians 4:6–7).

"for the kingdom of God is not eating and drinking, but righteousness, peace, and joy in the Holy Spirit. Whoever serves Christ in this way is acceptable to God and approved by men" (Romans 14:17–18).

"But when the kindness of God our Savior and His love for mankind appeared, He saved us—not by works of righteousness that we had done, but according to His mercy, through the washing of regeneration and renewal by the Holy Spirit. He poured out this Spirit on us abundantly through Jesus Christ our Savior, so that having been justified by His grace, we may become heirs with the hope of eternal life" (Titus 3:4–7).

"according to the foreknowledge of God the Father and set apart by the Spirit for obedience and for [the] sprinkling with the blood of Jesus" (1 Peter 1:2).

FOCUSING IN ON 1 PETER 1:2

The Trinitarian pattern of God working Father to Spirit to Son is God's work in sanctifying believers for Christian service in holiness and in hope. We see this when the Spirit provides just-in-time regeneration and renewal so that our backs fit the cross and our heads fit the crown. We see this when the Father pours out the Spirit that we might become sons like His Son. God wants joint heirs. Jesus longs to share His throne. The Father sends the Spirit into our lives to equip us for obedient mission now and for eternal glory later. All of this is in accord with His promise to form us into mature heirs with and in Christ. The Father authorizes the water pressure, the Spirit is the refreshing and cleansing water of life, and Christ is the shower head that shapes the spray.

THE PLAN: FOREKNOWLEDGE OF GOD

Just before returning to the heavenly Father, Jesus told the disciples to wait in Jerusalem while He ascended to ask the Father to keep His promise to pour out the Spirit. When was the promise made? Well, that is difficult to answer, since it was made before dates and calendars had been invented—probably before time had even started.

Paul said that "we speak God's hidden wisdom in a mystery, which God predestined before the ages for our glory" (1 Corinthians 2:7). Peter wrote that God plans everything and what He plans, He promises and what He promises He delivers: "chosen according to the foreknowledge of God the Father and set apart by the Spirit for obedience and for [the] sprinkling with the blood of Jesus" (1 Peter 1:2).

So, the God who is ever Father, Son, and Spirit worked out this plan and promise according to His own choice and foreknowledge. God, being God, plans the past from the future. Foreknowledge means He knows and promises events and responses with reliable confidence because He is sovereign. God is not making this up as He goes along. He has planned it, and us, all along. But He has waited for us to come along to fulfill His promise and plan in Christ for us.

To whom was the promise made? Did you ever make a promise to yourself? Do you keep promises to yourself? God does. God promised His triune self that He would pour out Himself in redemption and transformation of repentant humanity. Why was the promise made? God so loved the world that He made and kept the promise to send the Son and the Spirit. Prophecy is little more than this promise being whispered to prophets and prophetesses, followed by their speaking the promise out loud.

"What eye did not see and ear did not hear, and what never entered the human mind—God prepared this for those who love Him." (1 Corinthians 2:9; Isaiah 52:15, 64:4). God planned to turn rebellious but repentant creatures into obedient heirs and children. This is the gospel according to Pinocchio. Wooden heads and hearts ever acting in foolishness can have the dream come true; they can become real and have a Father instead of merely a carver. God Himself promises that He will so pour the Spirit of Christ on and into them that they will become His children and heirs. He destines them for the throne in glory. He calls them to the cross in service, witness, and mission.

THE POWER: KEEPING A PROMISE TAKES AUTHORITY AND RESOURCE

We are "set apart by the Spirit for obedience," engaged by God the Spirit through sanctifying, washing, adopting, regenerating, renewing, separating, revealing. When the kingdom comes, when heaven's will is done on earth, the Spirit empowers three kingdom virtues, as laid out in Romans 14:17: "for the kingdom of God is not eating and drinking, but righteousness, peace, and joy in the Holy Spirit."

Righteousness. When Paul uses righteousness language, he sometimes means the righteousness declared to us on behalf of the atoning death of Christ on the cross for our sin. But here, the empowering work of the Holy Spirit is not merely to save us from hell and save us for heaven; rather, the saint making work of the Spirit is to get the hell of destructed and demented patterns out of us, and the heaven of right deciding and relating into us.

Peace. The reality of the Spirit's capacity to engraft right ways into us is that we become peaceable and peacemaking. We wage peace because the Spirit is the Spirit of *shalom*. Rather than grieving the Holy Spirit, we give and receive forgiveness since the Son has forgiven us (Ephesians 4:30–32). We are at peace with God and determined to keep the bonds of peace with each other.

Joy. And we are happy. We are not merely enduring our salvation, we are enjoying it. We are happy and we know it! In Eugene Peterson's review of Psalm 129 in *A Long Obedience in the Same Direction*, he quotes G. K. Chesterton to the effect that, "Joy, which was the small publicity of the pagan, is the gigantic secret of the Christian." Peterson goes on to invoke H. H. Farmer's metaphor of "the grain of the universe."[28] Frustration at fighting the grain of God's planned universe is transformed by the Spirit into joy of finding the groove of original intention.

Being Alive. Regenerating means that what was dead to God, us, and others in our lives is made alive with the same power that raised Jesus from the dead. "If the Spirit who raised Jesus from the dead is not in you then . . ." renewing means taking what is worn out and no longer working and re-engineering and rebooting it for service. The pink slip indicating ownership and status of believers is stamped "salvaged." We have been put back into working order. The Spirit is literally the guarantee of that workmanship.

---

28. Eugene H. Peterson, *A Long Obedience in the Same Direction*, 2nd ed. (Downers Grove, IL: InterVarsity Press, 2000), 114.

THE PRODUCT

"And for [the] sprinkling with the blood of Jesus . . ." (1 Peter 1:2). This sprinkling word can mislead you if you are not careful. It does not specifically refer to baptism. These are two separate words in the original, yet really baptism is to be understood in the Old Testament sprinkling sense and context. What is that sense? Sprinkling was done on three occasions.

1. When it had been confirmed that someone was healed of leprosy, they were to be sprinkled to welcome them back into community.

2. When priests were about to engage their duties of leadership in prayer, worship, and confessional ministry, they received the sprinkling of a sacrificial lamb as ordination and commission to carry out that service.

3. In a like manner, the entire congregation of Israel was sprinkled with the blood of a pure lamb as their consecration as God's special people to bless the nations. Peter explains that this is what he means by the "sprinkling" of promise-fulfilled brothers and sisters in the Son who bear the cross and wear the crown.

THE WITNESS OF THE PROMISE MAKER
AND EXPRESSING THE PROMISE

We need to fan the flames of the Spirit in our lives and the lives of others. A reviewer once described the difference between the Rocky Balboa and the John Rambo in the Sylvester Stallone dueling franchises. Rocky always finds victory in the midst of defeat, and Rambo always finds defeat in the midst of victory. In Christ, we are called to be like "Rocky"s, who may experience "set backs, perplexity," but in the midst of trouble and suffering find victory and hope. Soon and very soon, we will surrender crosses for crowns on streets of gold.

Meanwhile, Father, Spirit, and Son have been in the salvage business ever since Eden. God keeps turning wooden-headed Pinocchios into Christ-minded Peters, Pauls, and Priscillas.

CHAPTER 10

The Uniting Triad: Spirit-Son-Father
as the Ecclesial Order

*It is only in the preaching and the sacraments, the prayers and the
hymns of praise, that the Trinitarian confessions come to life.*
—Donald H. Juel, "The Trinity in the New Testament" [1]

O f the seventy-five New Testament triadic instances, ten percent present
the Spirit-Son-Father order.[2] With only these eight instances—the lowest number among all six different triadic orderings—one might be tempted
to overlook this particular identification. However, the biblical injunction
is that "Every fact must be established by the testimony of two or three witnesses" (2 Corinthians 13:1). Since we do have seven witnesses, scattered
across the range of New Testament books, it seems fully warranted that the
meaning of the Spirit-Son-Father order be examined. I have designated this
Spirit-Son-Father pattern as the ecclesial triad and related it to the uniting of
the body of Christ. My rationale for choosing these themes will emerge in my
exegetical work that follows.

---

1. Donald H. Juel, "The Trinity in the New Testament," *Theology Today*, vol. 54, no. 3 (October
   1997), 319.
2. See Appendix A, Chart 1, "New Testament Census of Triadic Occurrences."

TABLE 10.1: NEW TESTAMENT OCCURRENCES OF THE SPIRIT-SON-FATHER TRIAD

LOCATIONS AND GRADATIONS FOR THE ECCLESIAL TRIADIC ORDER OF SPIRIT-SON-FATHER			
Text	**Rating**	**Context**	**Summary**
John 15:26	A-	Empower/promise	Counselor comes, whom I shall send . . . from the Father
John 16:7–9	A-	Empower/promise	the Counselor . . . I will send . . . because . . . to the Father
John 16:13–15	A-	Empower/promise	He will glorify Me . . . all that the Father has is mine . . . He will
Acts 4:8–10	B	Witness	filled with the Holy Spirit . . . "by the name of Jesus Christ . . . whom God . . ."
1 Corinthians 12:4–6	A	Empower/service	gifts, one Spirit, service, one Lord, activities, one God
Ephesians 4:4–6	A-	Church unity	one Spirit, one Lord, one God and Father
Ephesians 5:18–20	B	Christian living	Understand what the Lord's will is . . . but be filled by the Spirit . . . giving thanks always for everything to God the Father
1 John 4:2	A	Christian life	Spirit of God, confesses that Jesus Christ comes in the flesh is of God

SPIRIT-SON-FATHER REFERENCES IN THE GOSPELS

Pneumatology in the Gospel of John

Three instances of the Spirit-Son-Father triad occur in the gospel of John. All three are in the seminal didactic passage John 14–17, especially in the pneumatological sections.

John 15:26. John 15 ends the great "Vine and Branches" discussion by introducing the Spirit in verse 26 as the next *paraclete* ("counselor") after Jesus. The verse reads: "When the Counselor [Spirit] comes, the One I [Son] will send to you from the Father [Father]—the Spirit [Spirit] of truth who proceeds from the Father [Father]—He will testify about Me [Son]."[3] Strung together, the triad emerges as Spirit-Son-Father-Spirit-Father-Son or as a coupling of two triads, Spirit-Son-Father and Spirit-Father-Son. Both of these coupled triads begin with the person of the Spirit. The latter triad reflects a liturgical order, whereby the Spirit empowers believers to cry out to the Father. This cry results in renewed resolve to engage in the life of Christ in the world. We looked at this triad in depth in chapter 8.

I want now to focus on the first order in the coupling. This triad occurs over a mere eight words in the Greek text, which indicates an intentional level of Trinitarian consciousness. Therefore this triad receives an "A-" rating. The Spirit comes because the Son sends Him from the Father. This order is the exact reverse echo of the missional Father-Son-Spirit order. The church powered to witness to the world is the intentional mission of the Triune God. The text conveys that the Spirit descends because the Son will ascend to the Father upon completion of the atoning work on the cross and will ask the Father to fulfill His promise to pour out the Spirit. When the Spirit did come at Pentecost, the church became the temple of the Spirit, the body of Christ, and the people of God (1 Corinthians 6:19–20). The Spirit empowers the capacity to witness, "You also will testify" (John 15:27). This instruction aligns perfectly with the promise of Jesus in Acts 1:8, "But you will receive power when the Holy Spirit has come upon you, and you will be My witnesses in. . . ." The Son represents the earthly investment in kingdom ministry. The Father represents the source from which all the foregoing and continuing proceeds. The Spirit is the energizing presence of God in the witnessing church on Christ's mission in the world.

While John 15:26 is at the center point of the *filioque* [and the Son] controversy between the Western and Eastern branches of Christianity—and certainly this text is sound evidence in favor of the assertion added by the West to the Nicene creed, namely that the Spirit is sent by the Father and the Son—the point of the passage is missional and Trinitarian, and not ontological.[4] Note the comment of D. A. Carson on this text:

---

3. This metaphor of the Spirit *proceeding* from the Father is a major feature in Cunningham's creative reinterpretation of Thomas Aquinas. He entitles his second chapter "Producing," in which he explicates the connection between the real relations of Father, Son, and Spirit, and the subsistent relations in the twofold missional processions of God (incarnation and Pentecost) in terms of this metaphor. See David Cunningham, *These Three Are One* (Oxford: Blackwell, 1998), 55–89.

4. The "and the Son" clause was added to the revered Nicene Creed at the 589 Third Council of Toledo, a Western and non-ecumenical synod from which the Eastern churches felt excluded.

Thus although the clause "who goes out from the Father" refers to the mission of the Spirit, in analogy with the mission of the Son, this is the mission of the Spirit who in certain respects replaces the Son, is sent by the Father and the Son, and belongs (so far as we can meaningfully use such ambiguous terminology) to the Godhead every bit as much as the Son. In short, the elements of a full-blown doctrine of the Trinity crop up repeatedly in the Fourth Gospel; and the early creedal statement, complete with the *filioque* phrase, is eminently defensible, once we allow that this clause in 15:26 does not itself specify a certain ontological status, but joins with the matrix of Johannine Christology and pneumatology to presuppose it.[5]

John 16:7–9 and 16:13–15. The Spirit-Son-Father triad occurs twice more in the succeeding chapter of the gospel of John. John 16:5–15 again focuses on the advent of the ministry of the Spirit as precipitated by the ascension of the Son to the Father. The gospel writer here quotes Jesus as applying the Spirit-Son-Father triad as the vector of the Spirit's tasks: "When He (the Spirit [Spirit] of truth) comes, He will convict the world about sin, righteousness, and judgment. About sin, because they do not believe in Me [Son]; about righteousness, because I am going to the Father [Father] and you will no longer see Me" (John 16:8–10). The order of this instruction would be less significant, were it not for the almost immediate repetition of the order in verses 13–15, "When the Spirit [Spirit] of truth comes, He will guide you into all the truth. . . . He will glorify Me [Son], because He will take from what is Mine and declare it to you. Everything the Father [Father] has is Mine."

The Eastern Church—having a much more developed theology of the Spirit, thanks in part to the Cappadocians: Gregory of Nazianzus, Gregory of Nyssa, and Basil the Great—rejected the *filioque* clause in part because it suggested that the Spirit was of a lesser ontology of being than the Father and the Son. Papal affirmation of this clause was formalized in 1014 over Eastern objections against the clause and against papal primacy, which in turn contributed to the split in 1054 between the Eastern Orthodox and Roman Catholic Church. See A. Edward Siecienski, *The Filioque, History of a Doctrinal Controversy* (New York: Oxford University Press, 2010), and Laurent Cleenewerck, *His Broken Body: Understanding and Healing the Schism between the Roman Catholic and Eastern Orthodox Churches* (Washington, DC: Euclid University Press, 2008).

5. D. A. Carson, *The Gospel according to John* (Leicester: InterVarsity Press; Grand Rapids: Eerdmans, 1991), 529.

Carson sees John 14:26 and 16:12 as complementary texts.[6] In the former, Jesus describes the work of the Spirit to bring to remembrance what He taught the disciples. In the latter, the Spirit moves on to teach them all things pertinent to kingdom living.

About John 16:12, three observations are warranted. First, twice in this brief didactic section, the work of God has been framed in a Trinitarian manner. Second, because the Spirit-Son-Father triad is repeatedly the manner of that framework, it is clear that there is a specific triadic order being applied intentionally. Third, in order for the disciples to be and function as Christ intends, the disciples must receive the new Paraclete sent by the Son to bring glory to Him by declaring to the disciples what the Father has granted to the Son. The Spirit-Son-Father order reflects the inspiring and informing work of the Holy Spirit in the life of the believing community, so that the authoritative ministry of the Son might continue in them.

SPIRIT-SON-FATHER REFERENCES IN ACTS

Peter at Pentecost

Acts 4:8–10. The book of Acts has thirteen instances of Trinitarian processional references. One such reference, Acts 4:8–10, uses the Spirit-Son-Father order. This instance comes at the beginning of the apostle Peter's explanation of the recent Pentecostal events to the Jewish leadership in Jerusalem. Luke's account reads this way: "Then Peter was filled with the Holy Spirit [Spirit] and said to them, 'Rulers of the people and elders: . . . let it be known to all of you . . . that by the name of Jesus Christ [Son] the Nazarene—whom you crucified and whom God [Father] raised from the dead."

When the Spirit comes upon Peter, then his witness is made to the Son and this witness is buttressed by manifested confirmation from the Father. In this instance, the manifestation of the Father's confirmation was the resurrection of the Son from the dead. Peter is here experiencing the fulfillment again of Jesus' promise in Acts 1:8: "But you will receive power when the Holy Spirit has come upon you, and you will be My witnesses in Jerusalem" (see also Joel 2:28–29). This instance of the Spirit-Son-Father is rather inadvertent in that the narration indicates the filling of the Spirit that prompts Peter's speaking the names of the Son and the Father. For that reason this instance should be rated a "B" in

---

6. Ibid., 539.

the taxonomy of Trinitarian instances. However, this inadvertent instance sets a pattern that when believers are Spirit-filled, then witness is made to Son as the Savior and glory is given to the Father for validating that Sonship through the resurrection. I evaluate this thesis further in the next section, with Paul's use of the Spirit-Son-Father triad.

SPIRIT-SON-FATHER REFERENCES
IN THE PAULINE EPISTLES

Pauline Pneumatic Ecclesiology

Two instances of the Spirit-Son-Father triad can be found in the epistles of the apostle Paul: 1 Corinthians 12:4–6 and Ephesians 4:4–6. These locations may be immediately recognizable for their historical and contemporary significance for doctrine of the church. The former passage speaks to the church as one body with many parts, and the latter speaks to the unity of the church that comes through speaking the truth in love. Both locations are discussions of the church and Christian living.

1 Corinthians 12:4–6. In the Corinthian instance, Paul is explaining how the church, as the body of Christ, displays diverse gifts working in unison for the glory of God and the achievement of His mission. As he explains the diversity of member gifting, Paul writes: "Now there are different gifts [*charismaton*], but the same Spirit [Spirit]. There are different ministries [*diakonion*], but the same Lord [Son]. And there are different activities [*energematon*], but the same God [Father] is active in everyone and everything." This complex passage brings together three dimensions of member diversity—gifts, ministries, and activities—with three dimensions of unity via the Triune God expressed in the Spirit-Son-Father triad.

About this triadic occurrence, Gordon Fee writes, "In passing one must note the clear Trinitarian implications in this set of sentences, the earliest of such texts in the NT. Barrett notes, 'The Trinitarian formula is the more impressive because it seems to be artless and unconscious.'"[7] British scholar Anthony Thiselton makes an even bolder Trinitarian interpretation when he writes, "In Barrett's view, 'the Trinitarian formula is the more impressive because it seems to be artless and un-

---

7. Gordon D. Fee, *The First Epistle to the Corinthians* (Grand Rapids: Eerdmans, 1987), 588. Here Fee sites C. K. Barrett, *A Commentary on the First Epistle to the Corinthians* (New York: Hendrickson, 1968), 284.

conscious.' While Richardson's work may serve to question whether it is 'unconscious,' the point remains that it carries no marks of artificial *contrivance*. While the trinitarian stance is implicit in 2 Corinthians 13:13 and Ephesians 4:4–6, here we encounter the earliest 'clear' trinitarian language."[8] My research contends the contrary, that Paul is *intentionally* Trinitarian, even to the degree of choosing the Spirit-Son-Father triad for this context of ecclesiology. He will select this same order to address the unity of the church in Ephesians 4, which we will examine momentarily. Since the passage is so obviously Trinitarian, and the naming of the three comes in such close order, this triad is rated as an "A" in the grading system.

Paul's point here is that the key to the diversity *and* unity of the church is the Triune God, expressed through the diversity of distributed gifts for mutual ministry. The Spirit-Son-Father triad as the Triune God is the primary Trinitarian order for expressing how the church displays its diversity in member gifting within the unity of that body. The Spirit-Son-Father triadic order is God *uniting*.

The passage goes on to expand and underscore both the diversity of the gift manifestations and the unity of the church in the Triune God. The Spirit-Son-Father triad is again invoked, but this time in an expanded form so that the initiation of the Spirit in gift manifestation is explained in 1 Corinthians 12:7–12, with six references to the Spirit—eight if you count verses 12 and 13. The Son is referenced in the context of the church as the body of Christ in verse 12, and then God is referenced three times in verses 18 through 28. Clearly, the apostle is rehearsing the earlier Trinitarian citation in verses 4–6. The inner gift differentiation of the one church is a manifestation of the inner differentiation of the One God.[9] Thiselton's conclusion here, "Thus *in the experience of the believer* the persons of the Trinity are inseparable," should be affirmed with the correction that the experience is corporately *believers* not individual *believer*. Just as the One God has inner differentiation so the Triune God acts on the oneness of the church to affect inner differentiation in community.[10]

---

8. Anthony C. Thiselton, *The First Epistle to the Corinthians: A Commentary on the Greek Text* (Grand Rapids, MI: Eerdmans, 2000). 934.; cf. Neil Richardson, *Paul's Language about God* (Sheffield, UK: Sheffield Academic Press, 1994), 217–218; David Garland calls the Trinitarian notion of the passage "obvious," *1 Corinthians* (Grand Rapids: Baker Academic, 2003), 576.

9. Kenneth Berding has published his argument against the conventional view that the Holy Spirit distributes unique gifting to each member of the body of Christ. Berding emphasizes gifts as ministries that build up the church rather than as abilities which must be discovered. See *What Are Spiritual Gifts? Rethinking Spiritual Gifts* (Grand Rapids: Kregel, 2006).

10. Thiselton, *The First Epistle to the Corinthians,* 935.

Ephesians 4:4–6. This passage leverages this understanding of Pauline Trinitarianism and the church even further. Here Paul emphasizes God *uniting* believers. P. T. O'Brien notes this Trinitarian-achieved oneness with these words: "The sevenfold list [of "ones"] is basically threefold since three of these unities allude to the three persons of the Trinity, while the remaining four refer to believers' relationship to the Spirit, Son, and Father."[11]

This is the second occurrence of the Spirit-Son-Father triad in the writings of Paul. The theme in the fourth chapter of the letter to the Ephesians is one of unity and diversity in the body of Christ, exactly the theme in his prior use of the Spirit-Son-Father triad in 1 Corinthians 12:4–6. This ecclesial unity is not achieved by sameness of gifting, but in a cohesive diversity aimed at being worthy of the high calling shared in Christ. Verses 4–6 read: "There is one body and one Spirit [Spirit]–just as you were called to one hope at your calling–one Lord [Son], one faith, one baptism, one God and Father [Father] of all." Paul is interspersing Christian experiences held in common in relation to the Triune Community, Spirit-Son-Father. O'Brien asserts the reason that Paul begins his Trinitarian acclamations with the Spirit in this way: "The *one Spirit* [italics in the original] brings unity and cohesion to the body by his indwelling and animating activity (v. 3). 'By the one Spirit we were all baptized into one body' (1 Cor. 12:13; cf. Rom. 8:9). Believers are members of the body by virtue of the work of the Holy Spirit. And as there is only one body, so also there is only one Spirit."[12]

Paul thus introduces discussion of the diverse congregational gift matrix to follow in verses 7, 8, and 11 by invoking a Trinitarian reference to unity. Diversity in unity is the oneness that God begets because it instills maturity as believers share the truth in love even as the Godhead does. When One speaks, All speak. When One is spoken to, All are spoken to. Paul intentionally chooses to make his Trinitarian reference using the Spirit-Son-Father triad.

This instance is rated an "A-" in my Trinitarian occurrences taxonomy since the case could be made that the "spirit" here is a reference to the spirit of the church and not the Holy Spirit. However, what follows in the context clearly intersperses references to the persons in the Godhead with attendant Christian experiences. So, one Lord is associated with one faith and one baptism, and one God and Father is praised as transcendent and immanent. And in verse 3, Paul

---

11.   Peter T. O'Brien, *The Letter to the Ephesians* (Grand Rapids: Eerdmans, 1999), 280.
12.   Ibid., 281.

references the Spirit, "diligently keeping the unity of the Spirit with the peace that binds us" (Ephesians 4:3). So, Paul's ground plan is Trinitarian even if the "spirit" in verse 4 is taken in a non-Trinitarian understanding.

So, here again we find Paul uses the Spirit-Son-Father triad to explain the ecclesial oneness and mission of the church as diversity of member gifting. That matrix is choreographed together into a consensus founded upon and uplifted by and to the Triune God. William Hendriksen comments that to "show the unity within the Trinity as ultimate basis for the unity of the church," Paul turns finally to the Father.[13] This Trinitarian narrative of the redeemed church acclaims what the Spirit wrought, what the Son bought, and what God thought.[14] Since the church is birthed and equipped for its earthly mission when the Spirit comes, it makes sense that the Triadic order begins with the person of the Spirit. For Paul in particular, the diversity of member gifting is the initiative of the Holy Spirit so that the body of the Son might be built up by and for the glory of the Father. The rich, differentiated oneness of the church on mission reflects the differentiated oneness of the Triune Godhead.

Ephesians 5:18–20. Note that this instance of what I am calling the ecclesial, or God uniting, order comes in the section just after the Pauline ecclesiology in chapter 4, which of course also uses the Spirit-Son-Father order in Ephesians 4:4–6.

Ephesians 5:18–20 reads: "And don't get drunk with wine, which leads to reckless actions, but be filled with the Spirit [Spirit], speaking to one another in psalms, hymns, and spiritual songs, singing and making music from your heart to the Lord [Son], and giving thanks for everything to God the Father [Father] in the name of our Lord Jesus Christ [Son], submitting to one another in the fear of Christ [Son]." The triadic formula reads Spirit-Son-Father-Son-Son. This order occurs in the context of instruction for sustained living in union with Christ.

Peter O'Brien notes that verses 18–21 are actually one long sentence. That strengthens the case for recognition of the Spirit-Son-Father order, since the sentence starts with being filled with the Spirit, moves to making music to the Lord [Son] and then to thanks to the Father in the Son's name. O'Brien writes,

---

13. W. Hendriksen and S. J. Kistemaker, *Exposition of Ephesians*, vol. 7 (Grand Rapids, MI: Baker Book House, 1953–2001), 187.
14. Ibid.

"Although the point is often missed in the English translations, verses 18–21 form one long sentence, with five participles modifying the imperative 'be filled by the Spirit': 'speaking [to one another]' (v. 19a), 'singing' (v. 19b), 'making music' (v. 19b), 'giving thanks' (v. 20), and 'submitting [to one another]' (v. 21)."[15]

O'Brien goes on to identify this passage twice as Trinitarian. He argues, "Accordingly, Christians filled by the Holy Spirit give thanks to God the Father on the basis of who Jesus is and what he has accomplished for his people by his death and resurrection. The 'unconscious' trinitarian focus of the passage is very powerful indeed."[16] O'Brien goes so far as to describe the fullness achieved in the life of the believer by the Spirit as a triune fullness where "we conclude that the *content* with which believers have been (or are being) filled is the fullness of (the triune) God or of Christ."[17]

If you started the triadic notation with the end of verse 17, you could attempt to make a case for a triadic order of Son-Spirit-Father, but for the reasons just stated, I feel that case is much weaker than the case for the Spirit-Son-Father order in verses 18–20. Clearly, Paul's point in this passage is about how to live in Christian community, in contrast to those who live outside of Christ.

I have graded this triadic instance as a "B" because the order appears so unconscious and because the list in verse 19 puts fifteen words between Spirit and the Lord [Son].

SPIRIT-SON-FATHER REFERENCES IN HEBREWS THROUGH REVELATION

Triadic Discernment and Ecclesial Unity

1 John 4:2. This passage contains the final New Testament occurrence of the Spirit-Son-Father triad. The context is discussion of the practice of spiritual discernment. The concern is that there are deceiving spirits. Not every spirit is from God. The text reads: "This is how you know the Spirit of God [Spirit]: Every spirit who confesses that Jesus Christ [Son] has come in the flesh is from God [Father]."

The seemingly inadvertent use of the Spirit-Son-Father triad occurs in sixteen words in the Greek, in a context of spiritual discernment based on the

---

15. P. T. O'Brien, *The Letter to the Ephesians* (Grand Rapids: Eerdmans, 1999), 385–386.
16. Ibid., 398.
17. Ibid., 391.

individual's capacity to witness to the incarnation of Christ. The theme of the chapter is discernment of authentic theology. The chapter references God (*theos*) twenty-seven times, the Son three times, and the Spirit twice.[18] Authentic theology verbalized is wrought by the Spirit and confirms the historic embodiment of the Son as the redemptive intention of the Father. Commentators on this passage typically focus on the incarnation element of the spiritual test and neglect reference to the Trinitarian framework of the test itself.[19]

This triadic order moves from spiritual infusion to christological content to theological source verification. The progression is similar to that in 1 Corinthians 12:4–6 and Ephesians 4:4–6. In the former, the progression is from inner motivations, hence the use of the Greek *charisma*, to incarnational content in ministries (*diakonia*), and then to external displays of divine action (*energma*). The latter actions verify the Fatherly source of the member's ministry to the body.

First John 4:2 requires believers to live in the promise of Acts 1:8. "You will receive power when the Holy Spirit has come on you, and you will be My witnesses." The Spirit-Son-Father triad is the ecclesial order *par excellence,* God uniting. So the church should consistently evaluate its missional organization in this image of the Triune God. To do so is to live, move, and have our being fully in the One God. Validation of member ministry authenticity is initiated by the Spirit, empowering a witness to the embodied Son, and thereby the member's source is known to be that of the Father. Churches sustain unity by validation in this triadic movement. This movement, Spirit-Son-Father is the parking validation necessary to leave the lot for witness before the world.

Missional and Ecclesial Harmonics

The Father-Son-Spirit triad that we focused on in chapter 5 occurs almost uniformly in the context of discussion of sentness and mission. The reverse of that triad, the Spirit-Son-Father order, usually occurs in a context of the church functioning in diversity and unity. If one visualizes the Father-Son-Spirit order as a *missional descent* into redemptive, earthly ministry, then the Spirit-Son-Father reflects that presence in *ecclesial ascent* back to the One God. The Triune God expresses Himself in the church by distributing gifts that enable united—

---

18. This second reference to the Spirit comes in another triadic reference (Spirit-Father-Son) starting in verse 13, and is discussed in chapter 8.
19. For example, neither Colin G. Kruse, Daniel L. Akin, nor Simon J. Kistemaker make reference to the Trinitarian framework of the passage. See Kruse, *The Letters of John,* 145; Akin, *1, 2, 3 John,* 171–172; and Kistemaker and Hendriksen, *New Testament Commentary,* 325.

but not uniform—ministry as one body. If the Father-Son-Spirit triad is God sending, then the inverse triad, Spirit-Son-Father, is God uniting.

The deep Oneness of Triune Deity has inner distinction without division, interpenetration without mixture and confusion of identity, autonomy in intimacy, if you will. So, the church is the temple of the Holy Spirit, the body of Christ and the people of God. So, the church lives its true oneness in a union of diversely gifted members cooperating and maturing together to represent the kingdom on earth. The Spirit-Son-Father triad is God at work in the church, uniting us as one and gifting us as many.

DISCUSSION QUESTIONS—CHAPTER 10

- The "New Testament Census of Triadic Occurrences" in Appendix A lists three instances of the Spirit-Son-Father order in the gospel of John: 15:16, 16:7–9, and 16:14–15. Which of these passages really does rate an "A" grade for Trinitarian intentionality? If Spirit-Son-Father really is about God creating community, why is this triadic order emphasized in this part of John's gospel?

- This book identifies the Father-Son-Spirit order as God on mission. The reverse reflection of that order is Spirit-Son-Father—God making community. Speculate on how these two orders relate to each other as Trinitarian operations in the world. Why does the Father-Son-Spirit missional order have the most triadic instances in the New Testament with eighteen, and the Spirit-Son-Father ecclesial order have the least with seven instances?

- Reflect on how your church organizes its members for ministry. Study what Paul says in Ephesians 4:4–6 and 1 Corinthians 12:4–6 about how God organizes the church for His glory. Paul's ecclesiology is organized around God as Spirit-Son-Father. How does this insight help you re-think your church's ministry organization? Note in 1 Corinthians 12: 4–6 the order of the charisma gifting of the Spirit, the ministry callings of the Son, and the gifts of God's workings.

SERMON STARTER: SPIRIT-SON-FATHER ECCLESIAL ORDERING

Accidental Ordination—The Trinity in 1 Corinthians 12:4-6

If you climb up 259 steps into the dome of St. Paul's Cathedral in London and whisper on one side of the dome, you will be heard on the other side. The echo is crisp and clear. If you speak the Trinitarian order of Father, Son, and Spirit found in Matthew 28:19, you will hear its echo in 1 Corinthians 12:4 reversed as Spirit, Son, and Father.

> Now there are different gifts, but the same Spirit. There are different ministries, but the same Lord. And there are different activities, but the same God activates each gift in each person (1 Corinthians 12:4–6).

Technically speaking, an echo is the return of one sound while a reverberation is the return of multiple sounds. So, this Trinitarian echo is actually a reverberation because this reversed order of Spirit-Son-Father echoes back from seven different places in the New Testament. Here are several more.

> This is how you know the Spirit of God: Every spirit who confesses that Jesus Christ has come in the flesh is from God (1 John 4:2).

> There is one body and one Spirit —just as you were called to one hope at your calling—one Lord, one faith, one baptism, one God and Father of all, who is above all and through all and in all (Ephesians 4:4–6).

This Ephesian echo of the Holy Three comes in the midst of seven "ones": one body, one Spirit, one hope, one Lord, one faith, one baptism, one God and Father. Just as the Triune God is one, so the church must have unity, community, and oneness as well. Without a deep oneness, the church has no credibility before the watching world.[20] Creating and sustaining that oneness is the work of

---

20. This phrase, "before the watching world," is taken from the title of John Howard Yoder's

God as Spirit-Son-Father in and through us. This Trinitarian order is God uniting us in His image. In our oneness is the world's hope for a true and attractive
community. Sin and self have so broken people's lives, families, and communities that we often resign ourselves merely to polite anonymity.

California, where I live, is notorious for people not knowing their neighbors. But intentional anonymity is a form of hostility, for which the gospel is
the lasting antidote. To have community in a hostile society, we must turn into
the Wind.

That phrase, "into the wind," was made memorable because it was the final
order that World War II aircraft carrier captains gave prior to launching planes.
Launching into the wind gave quick lift to those planes, sending them up and
off to their mission. The biblical word *spirit* has multiple meanings which include spirit, breath, and wind. At Pentecost, the Holy Spirit fell on the praying
believers as a rushing wind (Acts 2:2). Our oneness together in Christ comes
under the lift of the Spirit into trust in Christ and His way to the Father. We
must turn into that Holy Wind and lean forward.

Some of you no doubt have experienced or heard about the winds of the Pali
Lookout in the Nuuanu State Park on the Hawaiian island of Oahu. This viewpoint above a 985-foot cliff is breathtaking for two reasons. First, the view of the
north side of the island from there is panoramic. Second, the two mountains on
either side form a natural wind tunnel. They force the trade winds up the cliff and
over at the Pali Lookout. The warm winds are so strong that you can actually lean
into the wind and it will hold you up. If we resist the wind and lift of the Holy
Spirit, our oneness is at best a bland and oppressive sameness. Such conforming
imitations of spiritual unity do not rely on God's presence to be the church. However, according to the New Testament, there is a way of leaning into the Spirit so
that our unity in diversity is lifted up by the aerodynamic of the Spirit, Son, and
Father. This way of being the church is a Triune God thing.

Charisma Gifts

In 1 Corinthians 12:1, Paul alerts us to the coming discussion of spiritual
gifts—*pneumatikon*. Then he presents spiritual gifts as a threefold reality of the
Trinity in the church. Look carefully again at 1 Corinthians 12:4. "Now there
are different gifts, but the same Spirit. There are different ministries, but the

---

important ecclesiology, *Body Politics: Five Practices of the Christian Community before the
Watching World.* (Scottdale, PA: Herald Press, 2001).

same Lord. And there are different activities but the same God activates each gift in each person." The apostle uses the word *varieties* or *differences* three times successively to refer to the diversity designed into the church membership by each of the persons of the Godhead. If variety is the spice of life, then under supernatural administration, church life is hot curry.

The Holy Spirit breathes diverse charismas into the members. A charisma here can be understood to mean inner motivational grace. In Romans 12:6, Paul used this same vocabulary to introduce a list of grace gifts, charisma. Then in verses 6–8 he lists seven charismas:

1. Prophecy—the motive to forth tell and foretell, and verbally clarify what sin is and is not.

2. Service—the motive to pitch in with your hands to make the mission move forward.

3. Teaching—the motive to clarify and distinguish concepts and relationships in the faith.

4. Exhorting—the motive to encourage people to live faithfully and courageously.

5. Giving—the motive to put personal resources into play in the work of God.

6. Leading—the motive to see God's work and people well organized for effectiveness and to make maximum use of available resources.

7. Mercy—the motive to bring sympathy and relief to those discerned as hurting and troubled.

Christian counselor Gary Chapman has identified five languages of love. He contends that, depending on the individual, we feel most loved when we are being loved in our particular love language. For example, receiving a present, being praised verbally, spending quality time together, having things done for us, or by being touched. Romans 12:6–8 indicates that the Triune God has seven love languages whereby He endows unique motivation to be an expression of our love for Him. These motives are diverse ways of believers together to display love for God through the church body. Just as Adam became a living soul when God breathed into his soil-molded body, so the Spirit breathes motivational grace into our inner beings. We actually gain energy as we follow our unique spiritual charisma into a place of ministry.

Ministry Gifts

The apostle moves beyond these diverse *charisma gifts* of the Spirit to define the second dimension of spiritual gifts as *ministry gifts*: "There are different ministries but the same Lord" (1 Corinthians 12:4). Since his conversion on the Damascus Road, Paul had been calling Jesus "Lord." So, here, too, he must mean Jesus. Also, he is obviously connecting the three dimensions of spiritual gifts—motivations, ministries, and manifestations—respectively with the three persons of the Godhead—Spirit, Son, and Father. [21]

The Greek word for *ministries* has the same root from which the word *deacon* comes. The word means "to stir up the dust to promptly serve one's master." So, a ministry is a place of service. Jesus called His disciples "seeds" and exhorted them to pour out their lives into the ministry hole unto death and from such planting would come much wheat (John 12:24). One seed, one hole. Each believer is called by Christ to discern the place of ministry and service into which to pour out his or her life. No hole, no death, no fruit. One hole, one death, much fruit.

We serve because Christ first served us by pouring out His life on the cross. Now Christ calls us into a place of service. He calls us to be His ministers because His Spirit has regenerated our spirit and supplied us with motivational power. The Spirit ordains and the Son calls into ministry placement. Whom the Spirit cleanses and sanctifies, the Son commissions for His work. There is no instance in Scripture where someone who has been cleansed is not also called to serve. The cleansed are affirmed as forgiven by being commissioned in His service.

When I first met him, Jay was a seventy-one-year-old retired Silicon Valley executive. He volunteered at a local homeless shelter. As he helped and counseled the people who frequent that shelter, one question kept coming up: "Are you a minister?" Jay always answered the same way. "No, I am not a minister; I am just a layman."

---

21. Organizing these dimensions of spiritual gifts into the alliterative terms of motives, ministries, and manifestations comes from a conference at Institute in Youth Conflicts, Oakbook, IL.

The question came up again as one rather emaciated crack addict asked Jay how to help two of his friends who were in a more life-threatening space than he was. Jay affirmed the man for his concern and desire to help his street friends. "The first step to helping them is to help yourself. When it's clear that you have found help, won't your friends be more interested in the help you can give them?"

After a thoughtful pause, the man responded with *the question*: "Are you a minister?"

This time Jay answered differently, "Yes, I am a minister."

What had happened to Jay between the fifth and sixth times that he was asked that? An ordination had occurred in Jay's thinking. Biblical truths had integrated and transformed his perspective. The proverbial light had come on! Jay had worked out the biblical ramifications and concluded that if he belonged to the priesthood of the believers, then he had to be a minister too.

Jay was not the first to reach such a conclusion. Martin Luther, the reluctant entrepreneur of the Protestant Reformation, wrote of what he called this priest-hood of the believers. He dreamed and taught the reality of Ephesians chapter 4 and 1 Corinthians 12, that all Spirit-born believers are called to engage in gifted ministry with their fellow believers.

The phone rang. It was the pastor. After the usual polite banter between friends, the pastor asked, "Would you be willing to teach a class on spiritual gifts?"

"No," came the reply, "but I will help you launch a movement."

Now the pastor was listening, if not completely understanding or believing. "Look, it stands to reason," explained the friend, "if our members really recognized their giftedness for ministry, wouldn't they see God as sort of a venture capitalist willing to invest Himself and His resources into the start-up of new ministers and ministries?"

Ministry Activities/Effects

There are varieties of workings, all done by the same God the Father. The Spirit moves the ship of the church on mission. Christ captains the ship and crew. God the Father flags the ship as His own and makes haven for the ship for His glory. When the right people with the right motives are in the right ministries, we can expect God to do stuff to confirm that this is His heavenly work on earth. His kingdom comes.

God's gift bag of signs and wonders is huge! It includes but is not limited to the divine activities that Paul lists in 1 Corinthians 12:8–10. In this list-ing of God's works are words of wisdom and knowledge, healings, miracles, prophecies, spiritual discernment, and communication gifts. How can we say we love and glorify the Triune God when we risk so little in mission adventures? What are we doing that depends on God the Father's, dare I say it, supernatural and miraculous working, so that all touched are compelled to say, "God is in this place"? God shows up wherever He finds Spirit-motivated service for the Son.

Moving into Ministry Applications

Three applications are urgent if we are to see this culture of ministry participation come to pass. First, we need to re-imagine baptism. It is personal identification of a new believer with Christ and the church. But it is more. Baptism is also ordination into the ministry and mission of the church. It is the watermark that signifies this person belongs to Christ and intends to serve Him until retired to heaven.

Second, if baptism is an ordination, then members become the ministers. So, what then is the pastor's job? Paul explains this in Ephesians 4. Right after affirming the Triune oneness of the congregation in the name of the Spirit, Son, and Father, he says that pastor-teachers are "for the training of the saints in the work of ministry, to build up the body of Christ [the church]" (Ephesians 4:12). So, as the church leans into the wind of the Spirit, the Son and the Father, the pastors become human resource directors and trainers. The Greek word for "pastor"—*episkopos* ("overseer")—takes on new meaning as the pastors look over the mission organization to align gifts with service assignments.

Third, every church needs to recognize entry-level service positions, such as ushering or greeting. New believers and members can do these simple but vital jobs while still new in their growth and discipleship. However, if you will watch closely, you will discern a pattern. If that believer has the charisma of giving, you might see new offering plates or bags appear because that person is motivated by the Spirit to place resources for the kingdom where they are needed. They might give the money themselves or even raise it for that purpose. If the usher has the gift of administration, that person will find it difficult not to organize the schedule of ushers in a more efficient manner, even though he or she is not the chair. If the newbie has the gift of teaching, likely soon you will see them trying to study up on the role of the usher and teaching other ushers how to usher better. You get the pattern. Now these gifted people can either be better aligned in their current position or recruited into a ministry where their gifts can be more fully realized.

Further Application and Conclusion

In most instances where the nature and function of the church is clarified in the New Testament, it is clarified as a movement of the Triune God working from Spirit to Son to Father. Three times in John's gospel, Jesus explains what will happen to the few who remained faithful after His crucifixion. "When the Spirit [Spirit] of truth comes, He will guide you into all the truth. . . . He will glorify Me [Son], because He will take from what is Mine and declare it to you. Everything the Father [Father] has is Mine" (John 16:13–15). The work of the Spirit is to tutor the church about the glorified Son and the possessions of the Son that we have inherited from the Father.

Because of the immoral momentum of the world, the church requires discernment to make sure its practices are authentic. First John 4:2 displays our credentials: "This is how you know the Spirit of God [Spirit]: Every spirit who confesses that Jesus Christ [Son] has come in the flesh is from God [Father]." We are assured that our church is being led by God's Spirit because His Spirit leads us to affirm in word, song, and action that the Son has come in skin and into history, and that this incarnation is the plan of the Father. May we lean into the wind of the Spirit, lay down our lives to serve Christ, and look for the Father to show in wondrous ways that we and our work are His!

PART 3:

Everyday Applications and Further Resources

CHAPTER 11

The Application Question: Becoming a Functional Trinitarian for Everyday Worship, Life, and Ministry

If our creedal affirmations of the mystery of the Trinity are true, then they must be very true, affecting profoundly every dimension of our existence.[1]

—Anne Hunt

This [Trinitarian] faith is at the center of Christian life, for Christ without a Triune God is only 'a noisy gong or a clanging cymbal.'[2]

—Edmund Fortman

The title of this chapter was very nearly the title of this book. After all, the Trinitarian matrix of the New Testament is compelling evidence that Trinitarian thinking was the daily mindset of Jesus and His followers. This triadic consciousness became dogmatically refined and creedalized in the first five centuries to some good and some ill effects. The worst of the latter was the lessened ability of the normal

---

1. Anne Hunt, *What Are They Saying about the Trinity?* (New York: The Paulist Press, 1998), 4.
2. Edmund J. Fortman, *The Triune God: A Historical Study of the Doctrine of the Trinity* (Philadelphia: Westminster, 1972), xxv.

Christian, to borrow from Brother Lawrence, to "practice the Trinitarian presence" of God. At the heart of daily, worship-led Christian living is the God who is One and Three, ever acting in choreographed movements—*perichoresis* in Trinitarian dogmatic discussion—and inviting us into those moves. Faithfulness to Christ is faithfulness to the God in whom Christ disciples us: the Father, the Son, and the Spirit. We must get beyond the mere "What would Jesus do?" ethics of modernity and into a biblically based, postmodern ethic of "What would the Trinity do?" John Feinberg expresses the challenge to be functionally Trinitarian in this way:

> a loud and clear message comes from these contemporary dis-
> cussions (including some evangelicals) that if one wants to wade
> through all the niceties of Greek and Latin terminology that sur-
> round this doctrine and the long history of seemingly esoteric
> controversies that have surrounded it, one had better by the end
> of the discussion show its practical relevance to everyday living.[3]

At the end of each of the preceding chapters on the six Trinitarian orders, I have constructed sermon starters, which tell the "what" and the "so what" of that respective Trinitarian reality. A doctrine preached and prayed is a doctrine believed and practiced. In this chapter, I will briefly rehearse those doctrinal and ethical achievements, to lay the groundwork for a thoroughgoing Trinitarian ecclesiology.

Reimagining the Economic Trinity

Systematic theologians love to divide conversation about the Trinity into two categories: *the immanent Trinity*, which describes the inner life and relations of the Triune God; and *the economic Trinity*, which describes the external action of the Triune God in creation, judgment, and redemption. Theological conversations described in previous chapters spoke of the economic Trinity almost exclusively as the missional procession of Father-Son-Spirit. However, we must not ignore the significant textual evidence studied in this book that either we should be speaking of the "diversity of the economic Trinity" or the "diverse Triune economies."

How are we to preach and practice the Triune God who acts in the church in six distinct but indivisible orders? I do note that all six of the triadic orders studied are economic expressions of the One God sending, saving, indwelling,

---

3. John Feinberg, *No One Like Him: The Doctrine of God,* in the Foundations of Evangelical Theology Series (Wheaton, IL: Crossway Books, 2001), 439.

sanctifying, shaping, or uniting. No matter the processional economy, all three persons participate in unity—but with processional distinction related to one of these six purposes. What happens when we fail to find the everyday differences those various orderings make in our lives? My observation is that an unimaginative and exclusive focus on one economic triad would produce rigidity and even hierarchy in Christian relations, just as an overfocus on one person of the Trinity can skew our theology and worship. (As noted previously, "Episcopalians have the Father, the Baptists have the Son, and the Pentecostals have the Spirit.") If failure to engage evenly with all three persons leaves us as the church impoverished, so does failure to engage evenly in all six biblical triadic orderings. So, how were these processional orderings meant to enrich our practice of ecclesiology?

Identifying the Trinitarian Marks of the Church

The Apostles' Creed identifies four foundational marks of the church: one, holy, catholic, and apostolic. John Calvin teaches that the true church has two marks: right preaching of the gospel and right administration of the sacraments. He may have even added a third, church discipline. Recently, the Mennonite theologian John Howard Yoder identifies five practices of the church "before a watching world": welcoming through believers baptism, sharing through communion and hospitality, recognizing giftedness in members for ministry, living in oneness and intimate known-ness, and applying the Scriptures in mutual admonition as "binding and loosing."[4] In the influential *The Purpose Driven Church,* Rick Warren refreshes the evangelical five tasks of the church: worship, witness, ministry, fellowship, and evangelism.[5] Based on studies of more than one thousand churches in thirty-two countries, *Natural Church Development* by Christian Schwarz concludes that there are eight common characteristics of growing churches: leadership, participatory membership, spirituality, structures, worship service, small groups, evangelism, and relationships.[6] Mark Dever identifies nine marks for "healthy churches": right gospel, right conversion, church membership, leadership, discipleship and growth, expository preaching, biblical evangelism, biblical theology, church discipline.[7]

---

4. John Howard Yoder, *Body Politics: Five Practices of the Christian Community before the Watching World* (Scottdale, PA: Herald Press, 1992).
5. Rick Warren, *The Purpose Driven Church* (Grand Rapids: Zondervan, 1995), 103–107.
6. Christian A. Schwarz, *Natural Church Development: A Practical Guide* (British Church Growth Society, 1996), 15–40.
7. Mark Dever, *Nine Marks of a Healthy Church,* new expanded ed. (Wheaton, IL: Crossway Books, 2004), 245–266. Here Dever also supplies a list of such marks from thirty-five other practical evangelical ecclesiologies.

Our study here has identified six Trinitarian movements in the church, based on seventy-five passages that mention all three persons. These orders are all worship movements. If we live and move and have our being and doing in the Triune God, then these six orders constitute the life into which we as the church are called. I have listed them here in order by descending frequency:

- God sending: Father-Son-Spirit—eighteen occurrences, twenty-four percent of the total (chapter 5).
- God adopting: Son-Spirit-Father—fifteen occurrences, twenty percent of the total (chapter 6).
- God saving and indwelling: Son-Father-Spirit—fourteen occurrences, nineteen percent of the total (chapter 7).
- God sanctifying and shaping: Father-Spirit-Son—eleven occurrences, fifteen percent of the total (chapter 9).
- God sustaining: Spirit-Father-Son—nine occurrences, twelve percent of the total (chapter 8).
- God unifying and gifting: Spirit-Son-Father—eight occurrences, ten percent of the total (chapter 10).

I repeat Chart 2.1 here so you can see what this distribution looks like, clockwise from highest to lowest percentages:

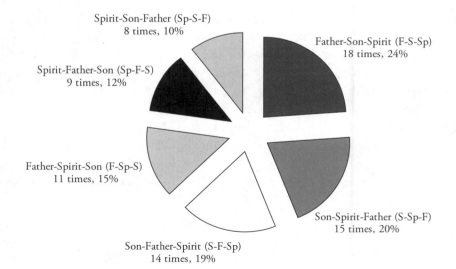

The Trinitarian Church Is the Church in Missional Movement

Much has been written in the last decade about the missional church. Now we can see God moving missionally—Father-Son-Spirit—and we can pray, praise, and preach in that movement. Instead of Trinitarian confusion in the worship service, God sending can be experienced biblically in worship as praise to the Father in song, and word can be the first segment in worship, followed by praise and prayer in honor of the Son, and finally recognition of the Spirit's presence and power in the body of Christ to enable us to show and speak the gospel boldly in the community and world. The eighteen Father-Son-Spirit texts identified in chapter 5 can be adapted for worship and preaching design. This order should be considered in the context of baptism, since that ordinance is a welcoming of a person into communion and commission for the gospel.

As the joy of the Lord is the strength of God's people, that joy of salvation is expressed and experienced in the Son-Spirit-Father triad, which highlights God adopting. When the worship or work of the church is about being gospel mid-wives, we can find parallels for ourselves in all three persons of the Three in One:

- The Father sends the Son and the Spirit, but is never sent, so the Father is sender.

- The Son sends the Spirit and is sent by the Father, so the Son is sender and sent.

- The Spirit is sent by the Father and the Son, but never sends, so the Spirit is sent but not sender.

These realities, plus other aspects of Three-in-Oneness give us guidance for everyday Trinitarian practice of the presence, as we see in the following sections. Christians can render a good defense of the doctrine of the Trinity and can re-imagine our primary relationships in light of this divine intimacy in community.

Realize the Apologetic Impact of the New Testament Witness to the Trinity. Since there are seventy-five Trinitarian references in the New Testament, Christians need no longer make a gentle defense based upon ecumenical tradition. Tertullian names this triadic textual phenomenon "the Trinity." But to say that the concept of the Trinity is a post-apostolic development is evidential nonsense. Muslim anti-Trinitarian apologists still declare that Christians took the Trinity out of the Bible when the 1952 Revised Standard Version corrected the King James Version translations of 1 John 5:7–8. The KJV read: "For there are three that bear record in heaven, the Father, the Word, and the Holy Ghost: and these three are one. And there are three that bear witness in earth, the Spirit, and the water, and the blood: and these three agree in one." The RSV changed it to: "And the Spirit is the witness, because the Spirit is the truth. These are three witnesses; the Spirit, the water, and the blood; and these three agree."

All later translations in English have followed the RSV lead. However, from my study which brings together all of the seventy-five triadic puzzle pieces from the nearly eight thousand verses of the New Testament, we can conclude that Trinitarian thinking and writing is clearly seen to be a default consciousness of the New Testament writers. Triadic orders occur in nineteen of the twenty-seven New Testament books, in every major division (Gospels, Acts, Pauline epistles, other writings), and from every one of its authors other than James.

Christianity did not become Trinitarian *after* the apostles but *with* the apostles. It is not the fault of Christians that they are Trinitarian; they are Trinitarian because God is witnessed to in the life and teaching of Jesus and His apostles. So, to be an "apostolic Christian," you must be Trinitarian—otherwise the New Testament is not taken seriously.

Autonomy in Intimate Community. Western Enlightenment culture emphasizes individuality over community. "I" comes before "us." In the East, community has priority over individuality. "We" comes before "I." Both approaches have distinct advantages, but what would the Trinity do?

The Triune God is neither we nor I. He is like no other. The inner being of the Godhead critiques the false dichotomy of individuality or community, and models a way of oneness and fulfillment by autonomy in intimate community. Technically stated, the three persons in the Godhead have distinction *without* division. If individuality were affirmed in the Trinity—in other words, distinction *with* division— then the result would be three gods as in polytheism, or one high God among two subordinate ones, as in Arianism. If unity were emphasized in the Trinity at the expense of distinction, then modalism or unitarianism would be the result (i.e., neither distinction nor division). Many Christian traditions are operational unitarians in overemphasizing one of the Trinity to the neglect of the others. For instance, "Jesus-only" expressions periodically emerge among churches to this day.

However, the Triune God of Jesus Christ and the apostolic teaching asserts that the One God has an inner being in threeness. God is one but the Father is God, the

Son is God, and the Spirit is God. So God is one and three, but the Father is not the Son is not the Spirit. Moving from information to implications and applications:

- Oneness is not conforming sameness; community demands distinctive identity to be authentic community.

- Autonomy requires community, or else it is hostility.

- Authentic personhood within intimate community means that the gift-edness of individuals in the church enables a deep oneness and effectiveness in that church that reflects the Triune God as the body of Christ.

In the Triune process of Spirit-Son-Father, the Spirit pours out individual charisma while the Son calls persons into ministry in the church or in the community and the Father manifests God's presence in that ministry to show that the power and the glory is His. Such Triune-defined personhood enables believers to live as a non-anxious presence in the community.

Looking at the Core Elements in "Functional Trinitarianism"

The interwoven doctrines of preaching and practicing Trinitarianism are complex because they represent a number of paradoxes—mysteries of the faith. We find ourselves in a singular degree of theological trouble when we split what Scripture presents as both/and paradoxical truths and focus instead on only one of the either/or elements it creates. In the remainder of this final chapter, I will address many of those points of paradox that we should both preach and practice:

1. Monotheism, versus polytheism or henotheism.
2. Radical monotheism, versus rigid monotheism.
3. Responsiveness to God as He reveals Himself.
4. Maturity that reverences mystery.
5. Our hope of oneness lies in God's oneness.
6. Oneness of essence is not sameness of function.
7. Oneness conveys sameness of essence, but not necessarily sameness of function.
8. Submission in time is not subordination in eternity.
9. Differentiation in unity enables mission.
10. Being functionally Trinitarian means being functionally Christian.

Each of these topics represents a sermon starter bite of the feast that is the Trinity. This definitely represents a robust doctrinal meal, that perhaps we will need to partake of in nibbles. So, let's get started.

1. Preach and practice monotheism, versus polytheism or henotheism. Most of us have more than one set of friends. We have church friends, family, neighbors, and work friends. Rarely do we mix those sets. Such mixes work at weddings and funerals but little else.

Christian teenagers feel this distance between their school and church friends, and know intuitively that it tends toward hypocrisy in both worlds. If you have two sets of friends, don't you have two sets of values? And if you have two sets of values, don't you actually then have two gods? That situation parallels the possibilities for polytheism or henotheism, in contrast with monotheism.

Practical polytheism is geographically focused—there is one God and Father at church, but another idol to be served at school or work. Henotheism—serving one God among all possible gods—is similar. But practical monotheism is religion without borders. Wherever I am, there He is. My integrity is affirmed because I am the kind of person who has only one set of values.

The six different orders of the Triune persons we examined in this book show how "portable" our Trinitarian faith is. Trinitarian monotheism works in times and places of joy, sadness, suffering, serving, and saving.

2. Preach radical monotheism, versus rigid monotheism. Richard Niebuhr observed that when religion is practiced as a religion of Word without Spirit, the *rigor mortis* of legalism sets in. He interpreted Jesus' problem with the Pharisees to be this theological disease. Those Palestinian Torah scholars knew every letter of the Torah, loaded those lead letters on their fellow Jews, and did nothing to help them with the crushing load (Matthew 23:4). Paul, himself a recovering legalist, warned that the letter alone kills (2 Corinthians 3:6). To give life, the Word needs the wind of the Spirit. Recall the account of the valley of dry bones in Ezekiel 37. The prophesying of the Word wrought fresh flesh embodiment, but dead bodies stay still until the wind of the Spirit breathes life back in them.

The antipodal disease is Spirit-only religion. Here, the Spirit without the Word produces an "authoritarian experientialism." In other words, you must have my specific experience of the Spirit, or else you are an outsider. Of course, we are enthusiastic about our spiritual experiences and want to share them—and we should. However, we must create safe space for others to have their own experiences and to share them as well. We must conclude that the New Testament authors wrote out of a Trinitarian consciousness that they caught from and were taught by Jesus. Jesus, the Son, quickly introduced His disciples to His Father and enabled in them the indwelling experience of God the Spirit as the abiding teacher. Under the authority of the Father, the Son as the Word and the Spirit are distinct but indivisible. Neither legalism nor experientialism represents Trinitarian faithfulness. The life lived under the authority of the Father depends on the light of the Word and the life of the Spirit.

3. Preach responsiveness to God as He reveals Himself. Who would make up the Trinity? Monotheism or tritheism is much easier to explain.

Some complain that the Trinitarian dogmatic language is technical hairsplitting of Greek and Latin. How could such ancient intellectual constructs be applicable? Don Juel asserts that the mystery of the being of God demands new vocabulary when he writes: "Christians do not believe in three gods but in a God an encounter with whom requires a new language."[8] The seventy-five incidences of the diverse Trinitarian orders put textual pressure on the Christianity community to witness to the God of Jesus revealed in Scripture and experience. If our eyes are open to the text, we experience the Trinitarian way of thinking of the New Testament authors. We must not be that vexing tourist who only sees what he or she came to see. We must be the traveler who sees what is there, unexpected and difficult though it be.

Maturity is the ability to process that kind of unexpected reality. The doctrine of revelation declares that we can only truly know God if and as He chooses to reveal Himself. His self-disclosure is at His initiative. It is also His invitation to redemptive and sustained relationship with Him. Therefore, we must respond to His disclosure as He offers it—and He offers it as Trinitarian. The incredible contributions of the fourth-century conciliar definitions, like three persons in one substance, are not the center of that faithful response to revelation, but they define the orthodox box within which we work creatively and worshipfully. Self-disclosure must be presumed to be without guile or deception, else it will not beget authentic relationship. If we doubt or diminish the disclosure of God's triune being, then we are left in dark and doubt. If we walk fully in the six experiences of the Triune being, then we will enjoy a religion that begets flexibility, recreation, and suffering service.

---

8. Donald H. Juel, "The Trinity in the New Testament," *Theology Today*, vol. 54, no. 3 (April 1997), 323.

4. Preach a maturity that reverences mystery. The Enlightenment project of the eighteenth century begot modernity by exalting human reason. If something could not be explained rationally or proven scientifically, then it was suspect—if not false. For instance, the brief post-World War II philosophical fad called logical positivism insisted that if an assertion could not be verified by reason or experiment, then it was automatically false. So, theological language was marginalized and excluded from the intellectual forum of society. Modernity was in no mood for mystery.

However, the mood is changing. With quantum physics, black holes, dark matter and energy, and neuroscience and neurotheology, exalted rationality is dead or dying in the same way that God was declared dead at the height of modernity and human arrogance. Postmodernity loves mystery and finds more truth in messy, authentic stories than in propositional argumentation. Mystery begets in our humanity maturity that humbly seeks, hears, and receives truth. Some in postmodernity see pre-modern exaltation of divine mystery and mastery as the way forward, a kind of back to the future.

Meanwhile, Scripture has always invited us into the divine mystery of the Holy One and we must not miss out. The mega-mystery of the One True God who is indivisibly Three is the greatest mystery of all. Worship energizes service and joy when that worship finds a bigger God. If your god is too small, surrender to the universe-busting God and Father of Jesus Christ.

5. Preach that our hope of oneness lies in God's oneness. In Jürgen Moltmann's Christian anthropology, he writes, "In God's oneness lies man's hope of oneness."[9] God is indivisibly Three. The Three interpenetrate one another as equal but differentiated community. So, God's Oneness critiques our individualism (not individuality) and our social hierarchies. *Kyriarchy* is a word coined by Elisabeth Schüssler Fiorenza.[10] Kyriarchy comes from her fusion of two Greek words, *kyrios* meaning "Lord," as in *Kyrios Christos* the Lord Jesus, and *archos* meaning "head." For Schüssler Fiorenza, kyriarchy is the propensity of fallen humanity to so lord it over or to so grovel under another in personal, community, or political contexts that the person on the receiving end is inflated or diminished in their own sense of self-worth. Racism and genderism are forms of kyriarchy, lording it over another.

---

9. Jürgen Moltmann, *Man: Christian Anthropology in the Conflicts of the Present* (London: SPCK, 1974), 20.
10. Elisabeth Schüssler Fiorenza, *Jesus—Miriam's Child, Sophia's Prophet: Kritische Anfragen feministischers Christologie* (Gütersloh: Chr. Kaiser, 1997), 46.

Desmond Tutu of South Africa writes poignantly of the power of racism to infect the mind and behavior of all it touches, even inadvertently and unconsciously. He tells the story of a trans-African flight which encountered a distressing level of turbulence. Tutu caught himself hoping that there were white pilots up front and then realized that it was his culture that taught him unconsciously that black Africans were unable to handle such complex challenges.[11]

My point here is that the intimacy shared between the distinct identities in the Trinity as Father, Son, and Spirit witnesses to a "No Hierarchy Zone" with respect to the inner relations of the Divine Three. All are equally the One God, or as in the Nicene formula, three persons in one substance. The New Testament multiplicity of six triadic orders, from Father-Son-Spirit to Spirit-Son-Father to Son-Spirit-Father, etc., demonstrates that God works as One without a hierarchical order, yet with distinctions retained. Whatever God does in the world, He does as Three together.

The diverse orders of the Three communicate oneness, distinction, and missional economy. The oneness is seen in that the Three will not act independently but interdependently. The distinction is seen in the one sending and in the ones sent. The Father sends, but is not sent. Divine transcendence is retained even though descent in immanence, incarnation, and community indwelling is real. The Son is sent and is also the channel and co-sender of the Spirit. The Spirit is sent, but never sends except in sending the Son in the incarnation and earthly ministry into the desert and into service.

So, what does this mean for the church? Our capacity to be credible witnesses to Christ is proportional to our willingness to be inseparably one with one another. If the God we worship is One, then we must be made together as one in His image. This congregational oneness is exactly what Jesus asked of the Father, "I am no longer in the world, but they are in the world, and I am coming to You. Holy Father, protect them by Your name that You have given Me, so that they may be one as We are one" (John 17:11).

In his exhortation to the church at Ephesus, the apostle Paul connects triune oneness with church oneness. As we discussed previously in chapter 10, Paul references eight ones in a row, "accepting one another in love, diligently keeping the unity of the Spirit with the peace that binds us. There is one body and one Spirit—just as you were called to one hope at your calling—one Lord, one faith, one baptism, one God and Father of all, who is above all and through all and in all" (Ephesians 4:2–6).

---

11. Desmond Tutu, *No Future without Forgiveness* (New York: Image Doubleday, 1999), 8, 279.

There are fifty-nine "one another" commands in the Bible. Ephesians 4:32 is an example: "and be kind and compassionate to one another, forgiving one another, just as God also forgave you in Christ."[12] Christians are to hear "the Lord your God is One" by uniting in Christ to live together reconciled and reconciling with one another. Our individuality is expressed and experienced in our belonging together in Christ. This Trinitarian oneness of the church critiques the rationalistic individualism of modernity. "I think, therefore I am" is rejected in favor of the communal affirmation, "I belong, therefore I exist."[13]

6. Preach that oneness of essence is not sameness of function. The One that God is and the oneness that God is after is missional oneness, unity without conformity. Unitarianism begets a totalitarianism of conformity. It substitutes superficial uniformity for mature community. But Trinitarian oneness has no shortcuts to community. It must have inner differentiation in passions and callings.

In Paul's unpacking of the Spirit-Son-Father order in 1 Corinthians 12:3, he makes it clear that the church as the body of Christ is one body by orchestrating the many diverse members into one missional melody. All are gifted, but all are gifted differently, so that in their working together, wholeness and glory are displayed for God's pleasure and ours. This diversity of gifting by the Triune God grants a threefold depth to the resulting unity and reality of the church. Gifts determine functionality, so oneness in Christ means essential value does not consist in sameness of function.

An egalitarianism of sameness fails to reflect the inner differentiation of persons and relations in the Godhead. The social Trinitarians go astray when they attempt to develop this approach to the Trinity and the church.

At the other end of splitting the paradox, the hierarchical or complementarian Trinitarians go astray when they try to base female voluntary submission in the home and the church upon a supposed eternal submission of the Son and Spirit to the Father. Millard Erickson rightly called this attempt "tampering with the Trinity."[14] Over-ordering induces rigidity and hierarchy. Only using the

12. "The 'One Another' Commands in the Bible (N.I.V.), Lutheran Hour Ministries, http://www.lhm.org/roc/2013downloads/robb_oneanother.pdf (accessed December 5, 2014).

13. John Pobee, *Toward an African Theology* (Nashville: Abingdon Press, 1979), 49, as quoted in Velli-Matti Kärkkäinen, *The Trinity: Global Perspectives* (Louisville: Westminster John Knox Press, 2007), 352.

14. Millard Erickson, *Who's Tampering with the Trinity? An Assessment of the Subordination Debate* (Grand Rapids: Kregel, 2009); Kevin Giles, *The Trinity and Subordinationism: The Doctrine of God and the Contemporary Gender Debate* (Downers Grove, IL: IVP Academic,

Father-Son-Spirit misrepresents the scriptural witness to the Triune God and subtly infuses the church with a rigidity that is uninviting. Insisting on sameness of order or gifting is simply unbiblical. Our community must reflect this Lordship in our economy of unity, diversity, mutuality, giftedness, and reciprocity. If there is oneness and equality in that each has unique gifts, why the conversation and controversy about submission of wives to their husbands?

7. Preach that oneness conveys sameness of essence, but not necessarily sameness of function. The three persons in the Godhead are all equally God, so in that sense there is sameness to the oneness. The Nicene Creed affirms that the Three enjoy sameness of divine substance. The sameness of substance is not disturbed or lost by distinction of person or relation. So, the Father is God, the Son is God, and the Spirit is God. But the Father is not the Son is not the Spirit.

- Though the Father sends the Son in incarnation, the Father and the Son are still one in substance and relation.

- The Son is less than the Father in the time of incarnational mission, but not in eternity of being.

- The Father sends the Spirit through the Son, but the Spirit is still the Spirit of the living God and the Spirit of Christ.

No dignity is lost in doing missional service; otherwise, Christ Jesus could never have washed the feet of the disciples. To serve is not to lose or loose one's essence. So then, all service is to God's glory and all leadership is servant leadership. Wives are called to voluntarily submit to their husbands as the Son voluntarily submitted to the mission of the cross. Both do so without loss of dignity of essence. We are not less by serving others, we are more for we bring aid to others and glory and thanksgiving to God. Husbands are also to lay down their lives voluntarily and to live considerately of their wife as she takes a less position at God's call as Christ laid down His life for His bride, the church. He does not lose dignity by laying down His life for His beloved, rather He is exalted (Philippians 2:9–11).

2002); Bruce Ware, *Father, Son and Holy Spirit: Relationships, Roles and Relevance* (Wheaton, IL: Crossway Books, 2005).

I note that in the house rules of Christ in Ephesians 5:21 and in Colossians 3, the undiminished essence of wives, children, and slaves is affirmed in that the ones called to take the weaker position are addressed before the one called to lead and the ones addressed first are also asked to submit voluntarily. Choice indicates autonomy and essence. The oneness of wife and husband, child and parent, and servant and master are seen in the reciprocity in and economic bond of the relationship. Mission requires submission in time, without subordinating essence or value. The wife who submits to her husband in Colossians 3 also prays and prophesies in the Spirit beside that husband in the worship service in 1 Corinthians 11.

8. Preach that submission in time is not subordination in eternity. Some would make the semantic argument that *subordination* and *submission* are synonyms. I would agree that this sometimes is the case but, though the words have the same prefix "sub-," the root words *ordain* and *mission* are not the same.

Ordain comes from the Latin "to put in order, to appoint, to issue orders." It assumes a higher positional authority to issue such orders. It conveys status, rank, and position. *Subordination* has a connotation of ordered levels of essence or being, submission has a connotation of ordered levels of doing. *Mission* has to do with function, task, and purpose. So *subordination* means being ranked in a hierarchy, as with the putting of humanity over creation in Genesis 1:28, and *submission* means to be purposed to function in an economy of doing.

Wherever being is equated with doing, racism and genderism is the result. Jesus asserted that "I and the Father are One," and He asserted that "The Father is greater than I." I would understand the oneness statement to declare the unity of essential being, defined at Nicene as one substance. The "greater than" statement means that the Son had humbled Himself to the Father in the incarnation to carry out the Triune mission of redemption.

The Bible records how God transforms the paradigms of those He calls in order to make them functional. Until Peter became the disciple of Jesus, his paradigm was that submission in service requires subordination of essence. For Peter, function reveals value and essence, doing is being. For this reason Peter objected when Jesus prepared to wash his feet (John 13:8). In Peter's (old) way of thinking, such humble service would have subordinated Jesus to Peter. But Jesus insisted on washing the fisherman's feet to demonstrate that service in no way causes loss or gain in being. Submission in function is not subordination in being. Because God serves, so can we. Because God serves, so must we.

Several theologians have tried to trump the ongoing evangelical male/female roles controversy by reading human relations back into the Trinity and then circling the argument back into that controversy as the solution. Hierarchical complementarians assert that essence drives function, so women are in submission to men because men came first in creation and are somehow higher than women in God's dispensation. Those with this perspective see the submission of the Son in the incarnation as an echo of the eternal submission of the Son to the Father. Bruce Ware's project in his 2005 *Father, Son, and Holy Spirit: Relationships, Roles and Relevance* is an example of this approach.[15] Millard Erickson published a helpful critique of Ware's contention that the eternal submission of the Son to the Father was normative in early church and conciliar conceptions of the relations within the Godhead.[16]

On the contrasting side, evangelical egalitarians read the eternal equality of essence in the three persons in the Godhead down into the essence and function of male and female roles in church and home. Because the Son is of the same substance and essence as the Father, so Kevin Giles reasons, men and women in Christ are also equal in essence and function.[17] However, how can such egalitarian reasoning accommodate the submission of the Son in the incarnation and atonement? Equality of essence in eternity does not equate to equality of function in time.

John Howard Yoder offers a fresh perspective into this issue. In *The Politics of Jesus*, Yoder looks carefully at the house rules passages in Ephesians 5:22–6:9 ("Wives, submit to your husbands") and Colossians 3:18–4:1. Yoder notes that six kinds of persons are addressed here in three pairs: wives and husbands, children and parents, slaves and masters. He comments that Paul in each instance addresses the person in the weaker position before addressing the person in the greater position, wives first then husbands and so forth.[18]

These household rules substitute a kingdom culture for an earthly culture. In the latter, good manners insist that persons in greater authority or prestige be addressed first and those in the lesser roles addressed second, if at all. Yoder strikes the point that the new rules call for each person voluntarily to assume the role and posture indicated in the rule as if each person is a moral agent. Each chooses the calling of Christ in lived-out relations.

---

15. Bruce A. Ware, *Father, Son, and Holy Spirit: Relationships, Roles and Relevance* (Wheaton, IL: Crossway Books, 2005), 131–158.

16. Erickson, *Who's Tampering with the Trinity?*, 247–260.

17. Giles, *The Trinity and Subordinationism*, 194–214.

18. John Howard Yoder, *The Politics of Jesus* (Grand Rapids: Eerdmans, 1994), 162.

Submission and obedience are a calling in Christ. The individual heeds that call between himself or herself and Christ. It is not the job of the husband to get the wife to submit, but rather he must be about his calling to love his wife and lay down his life for her.

The rule also reminds persons in the greater position that they are held accountable to God for how they honor the person in the weaker position. This must be what Peter was speaking to in 1 Peter 3:7, when he cautioned husbands about inconsiderate treatment or attitude toward wives "as the weaker vessel" lest their prayers be hindered. Back in Ephesians 5, Paul says that Christ is glorified and portrayed in the marriage as this oneness of diverse functionality is fulfilled.

So marriage, parenting, and employment all can show the Triune truths of equality of essence and diversity of economic functionality. In temporal mission, the Father sends, but never is sent. The Son both is sent and does send the Spirit. The Spirit is sent, but never sends either the Father or the Son. The six orders of the Trinity identified in the New Testament show that the Godhead is ever united in His work in the world and ever diverse in terms of the six triadic movements. The distinctions of the Three are never blurred, and the unity is never impaired. Whatever God does, He does as three.

9. Preach that differentiation in unity enables mission. Jesuit theologian Karl Rahner famously stated that the "economic" Trinity is the "immanent trinity" and the "immanent" Trinity is the "economic trinity."[19] While some have accused Rahner of modalism (the Father is the Son is the Spirit—one head but three hats), at the least, Rahner wanted to underscore the integrity of the Triune God.[20] The God we meet in the experience of revelation and redemption, the God who is the Son conceived by the Spirit in the womb of Mary by the will of the Father, is the same as the eternal One, whose inner being is one of differentiation—Father, Son, and Spirit. There are not two trinities, one inwardly focused and mutually related in glory, and one externally focused in creation and redemption.

The theological issue here is again to assert that God's oneness is not inner sameness. Part of the point of the New Testament abundant Trinitarian witnesses is that God works in the world as inseparably three, with diversity of order that shows

---

19. Karl Rahner, *The Trinity*, trans. Joseph Donceel (New York: Herder and Herder, 1970), 22–23.
20. Jürgen Moltmann, *The Trinity and the Kingdom: The Doctrine of God*, trans. M. Kohl (London: SCM Press, 1981), 144, where Moltmann uses the phrase "idealistic Modalism"; cf. David Lincicum, "Economy and Immanence: Karl Rahner's Doctrine of the Trinity," *European Journal of Theology*, 2005, vol. 14:2, 111–118.

differentiation, and indivisibility of essence. I want to refer here briefly to what I presented in detail in earlier chapters. The Three is ever united in mission actions. Certainly, the Father-Son-Spirit order is prior to the other five orders. This order is God carrying out His mission of redemption and then including the redeemed in His mission. This order is invoked at baptism as the believer is welcomed into God's mission and into Christ's body. The Father-Son-Spirit order does represent one fourth of the seventy-five triadic occurrences in the New Testament. However, priority is not exclusivity. The five other orders of the Three are revealed repeatedly in the New Testament. The immanent Trinity acts as Trinitarian economies. God is indivisible in being and in action, in immanence and in economy.

There is differentiation in name: Father, Son, and Spirit. There is differentiation in the economy of sending and being sent. There is also differentiation in unity, as the order of the Three does make a difference. Specifically, the usual contexts in which specific orders occur in the text are consistent. The other five orderings show distinct emphases in outcomes:

- The Father-Spirit-Son order appears in contexts of sanctification and shaping believers into the image of Christ. The Father sends the Spirit of Christ to enable life in and for Christ.

- The Son-Father-Spirit order is God saving, causing someone like Nicodemus to be born of the Spirit, born again.

- The Spirit-Son-Father order is usually in a context describing or prescribing the church in unity.

- The Spirit-Father-Son order predominately occurs in contexts of service, even suffering service, for Christ's sake is at stake.

- The Son-Spirit-Father order appears in the Gospel accounts of Jesus' baptism and it appears in contexts describing the experience of regeneration which brings the declaration of the adopted, "*Abba*, Father" (Romans 8:15).

Worship of the Triune God in these six movements empowers missional creativity on the part of the redeemed. To paraphrase Daniel 11:32, "They that so know their God shall do exploits." To the degree that the church fully recognizes and orchestrates the diversity of motives, ministry callings, and divine presence markers in its members, to that degree the church has stepped into the missional wind of God. The unity of the church is deep and rich in that it is composed of an inner differentiation. These many members are gifted uniquely by the Triune God to blend together in effective living and doing in God's mission in the world.

10. Preach that being functionally Trinitarian means neing functionally Christian. Faithfulness and fruitfulness are evidence of authentic worship and life. The church has, of course, been faithful and fruitful for millennia. My hope for this study is to enable Christians and churches to proceed more intentionally and joyfully in the life and ways God has revealed Himself in Christ.

Autonomy in intimacy—being oneself in Christian community—faithfully reflects the differentiation in inner being and outward movement of the Triune God. Resistance to conform is resistance to the false Trinitarian functionality called unitarianism. Christians are called to be distinctive in gifting without division in community or mission. Authentic and creative personhood happens within intimate community. Resistance against being others-directed and valued is resistance against the pseudo-Trinitarianism called subordinationism, which fosters racism and genderism.

Intimate community with unimpaired or repaired dialog is being functionally Trinitarian because this reflects the loving conversation within the One God. Finding and fulfilling your mission in and through the household of the church is being functionally Trinitarian, even as the One God works together in the world in diverse orders, but ever together as one. May we be one in Christ and with each other, even as the Father, Son, and Spirit are One and one with us.

DISCUSSION QUESTIONS—CHAPTER 11

- Having now read this final chapter, what from this chapter of the book do want to share with someone else? When are you going to do it?

- What two ways do you want to be more functionally Trinitarian in your worship and living? How will you implement that resolution?

- If the work of the church is to make disciples, what must be done in your church's discipleship program to make Trinitarian disciples of Christ?

- How convinced are you that real oneness—God's and ours as the church— must be a unity within inner differentiation without division? I would contend that this kind of oneness is an effective antidote to the spiritual abuse of subordinating others to oneself, treating them as less than fully God's children and able ministers. Explain why you agree or disagree.

APPENDIXES

New Testament Census of Triadic Occurrences

APPENDIX CHART 1: NEW TESTAMENT CENSUS OF TRIADIC OCCURRENCES							
NT Book	*Chapter 5* *F-S-Sp*	*Chapter 6* *S-Sp-F*	*Chapter 7* *S-F-Sp*	*Chapter 8* *Sp-F-S*	*Chapter 9* *F-Sp-S*	*Chapter 10* *Sp-S-F*	*Totals*
Core Theme & Feature	*Missional Sending*	*Forma- tional Shaping*	*Evangeli- cal Saving*	*Christologi- cal Indwelling*	*Liturgical Standing*	*Ecclesial Uniting*	
Matthew	C - 12:18		A - 3:16–17				3
	A - 28:19–20						
Mark			A - 1:10–11				1
Luke			A - 3:21	NA - 11:13	A - 4:18		5
			A - 10:21	A- - 24:49–50			
John	B- 1:33	C - 4:23	C - 1:33–34	B - 3:34		A- - 15:26	10

APPENDIX CHART 1: NEW TESTAMENT CENSUS OF TRIADIC OCCURRENCES

NT Book	Chapter 5 F-S-Sp	Chapter 6 S-Sp-F	Chapter 7 S-F-Sp	Chapter 8 Sp-F-S	Chapter 9 F-Sp-S	Chapter 10 Sp-S-F	Totals
Core Theme & Feature	Missional Sending	Formational Shaping	Evangelical Saving	Christological Indwelling	Liturgical Standing	Ecclesial Uniting	
	B - 20:21–22			A - 14:16		A- - 16:7–9	
				B - 14:25–26		A- - 16:14–15	
Gospels 19 (25%)	4 A1–B2–C1	1 A0–B0–C1	5 A4–B0–C1	5 A2–B2–C0–NA1	1 A1–B0–C0	3 A3–B0–C0	19 A11–B4–C3–NA1
Acts	B - 4:29–30	B - 1:4–8	A - 2:38	B - 1:4–5	A- - 7:55	B - 4:8	13
	A - 5:30–32	C - 4:24–25		A - 2:32–33	B - 11:16–17		
	A - 10:38				C - 20:28		
	C - 20:21–23						
Acts 13 (17%)	4 A2–B1–C1	2 A0–B1–C1	1 A1–B0–C0	2 A1–B1–C0	3 A1–B1–C1	1 A0–B1–C0	13 A5–B5–C3
Romans	C - 1:1–4	A- - 14:17	A- - 8:1–3	C - 7:4–6	A- - 8:9		10
	A - 5:1–5		A - 15:30	B - 15:12–13	A- - 8:16–17		
	A - 15:15–16						
1 Cor.	A - 2:1–5	A- - 2:10–15	A - 6:11			A - 12:4–6	4

APPENDIX CHART 1: NEW TESTAMENT CENSUS OF TRIADIC OCCURRENCES

NT Book	Chapter 5 F-S-Sp	Chapter 6 S-Sp-F	Chapter 7 S-F-Sp	Chapter 8 Sp-F-S	Chapter 9 F-Sp-S	Chapter 10 Sp-S-F	Totals
Core Theme & Feature	Missional Sending	Formational Shaping	Evangelical Saving	Christological Indwelling	Liturgical Standing	Ecclesial Uniting	
2 Cor.			A - 3:3	A - 13:14			2
Gal.	A - 4:4–6	A - 4:5–6					2
Eph.	A - 1:11–14		A - 2:17–19	A - 2:22	B - 4:30–32	A- - 4:4–6	6
						B - 5:18–20	
Phil.							0
Col.	B - 1:6–8						1
1 Thess.	A - 1:3–5						1
2 Thess.		B - 2:13					1
1 Tim.							0
2 Tim.							0
Titus		B - 3:4–6					1
Philem.							0
Pauline Epistles 28 (38%)	8 A6–B1–C1	5 A3–B2–C0	5 A5–B0–C0	4 A2–B1–C1	3 A2–B1–C0	3 A2–B1–C0	28 A20–B6–C2
Heb.			A - 9:14	A- - 2:3–4			5
			A- - 10:29	C - 3:1–7			
				B - 10:12–15			

APPENDIX CHART 1: NEW TESTAMENT CENSUS OF TRIADIC OCCURRENCES

NT Book	Chapter 5 F-S-Sp	Chapter 6 S-Sp-F	Chapter 7 S-F-Sp	Chapter 8 Sp-F-S	Chapter 9 F-Sp-S	Chapter 10 Sp-S-F	Totals
Core Theme & Feature	Missional Sending	Formational Shaping	Evangelical Saving	Christological Indwelling	Liturgical Standing	Ecclesial Uniting	
James							0
1 Peter	C - 1:3–11	A - 1:2					2
2 Peter							0
1 John		A- - 4:13	A- - 5:6–9			A - 4:2	3
2 John							0
3 John							0
Jude					A - 20		1
Rev.	B - 1:9–10	C - 1:4–5	B - 22:17–18		C - 22:1		4
Heb. – Rev. 15 (20%)	2 A0–B1–C1	3 A2–B0–C1	4 A3–B1–C0	3 A1–B1–C1	2 A1–B0–C1	1 A1–B0–C0	15 A8–B3–C4
Totals	18 (24%)	11 (15%)	15 (20%)	14 (19%)	9 (12%)	8 (10%)	75
A46–B18–C11	A10–B5–C4	A5–B3–C3	A13–B2–C1	A7–B5–C2	A6–B5–C2–NA1	A6–B2–C1	A6–B1–C0

- Of the twenty-seven books in the New Testament, nineteen (seventy percent) have triadic occurrences. Eight (thirty percent) do not.

- The only author with no Trinitarian references is James.

- There are triadic references in all four gospels, Acts, nine of the thirteen Pauline epistles, and five of the nine books from Hebrews through Revelation.

APPENDIX CHART 1A: NEW TESTAMENT CENSUS OF TRIADIC OCCURRENCES

TRINITARIAN REFERENCES IN THE GOSPELS

NT Book	Chapter 5 F-S-Sp	Chapter 6 S-Sp-F	Chapter 7 S-F-Sp	Chapter 8 Sp-F-S	Chapter 9 F-Sp-S	Chapter 10 Sp-S-F	Totals
Core Theme & Feature	Missional Sending	Evangelical Saving	Christological Indwelling	Liturgical Standing	Formational Shaping	Ecclesial Uniting	
Matthew	C - 12:18	A - 3:16–17					3
	A - 28:19–20						
Mark		A - 1:10–11					1
Luke		A - 3:21	NA - 11:13	A - 4:18			5
		A - 10:21	A- - 24:49–50				
John	B- 1:33	C - 1:33–34	B - 3:34		C - 4:23	A- - 15:26	10
	B - 20:21–22		A - 14:16			A- - 16:7–9	
			B - 14:25–26			A- - 16:14–15	
Gospels 19 (25%)	4 A1–B2–C1	5 A4–B0–C1	5 A2–B2–C0–NA1	1 A1–B0–C0	1 A0–B0–C1	3 A3–B0–C0	19 A11–B4–C3–NA1

APPENDIX CHART 1B: NEW TESTAMENT CENSUS OF TRIADIC OCCURRENCES

TRINITARIAN REFERENCES IN THE BOOK OF ACTS

NT Book	Chapter 5 F-S-Sp	Chapter 6 S-Sp-F	Chapter 7 S-F-Sp	Chapter 8 Sp-F-S	Chapter 9 F-Sp-S	Chapter 10 Sp-S-F	Totals
Core Theme & Feature	Missional Sending	Evangelical Saving	Christological Indwelling	Liturgical Standing	Formational Shaping	Ecclesial Uniting	
Acts	B - 4:29–30	A - 2:38	B - 1:4–5	A- - 7:55	B - 1:4–8	B - 4:8	13
	A - 5:30–32		A - 2:32–33	B - 11:16–17	C - 4:24–25		
	A - 10:38			C - 20:28			
	C - 20:21–23						
Acts 13 (17%)	4 A2–B1–C1	1 A1–B0–C0	2 A1–B1–C0	3 A1–B1–C1	2 A0–B1–C1	1 A0–B1–C0	13 A5–B5–C3

APPENDIX CHART 1C: NEW TESTAMENT CENSUS OF TRIADIC OCCURRENCES

TRINITARIAN REFERENCES IN THE PAULINE EPISTLES

NT Book	Chapter 5 F-S-Sp	Chapter 6 S-Sp-F	Chapter 7 S-F-Sp	Chapter 8 Sp-F-S	Chapter 9 F-Sp-S	Chapter 10 Sp-S-F	Totals
Core Theme & Feature	Missional Sending	Evangelical Saving	Christological Indwelling	Liturgical Standing	Formational Shaping	Ecclesial Uniting	
Romans	C - 1:1–4	A- - 8:1–3	C - 7:4–6	A- - 8:9	A- - 14:17		10
	A - 5:1–5	A - 15:30	B - 15:12–13	A- - 8:16–17			

APPENDIX CHART 1C: NEW TESTAMENT CENSUS OF TRIADIC OCCURRENCES

TRINITARIAN REFERENCES IN THE PAULINE EPISTLES

NT Book	Chapter 5 F-S-Sp	Chapter 6 S-Sp-F	Chapter 7 S-F-Sp	Chapter 8 Sp-F-S	Chapter 9 F-Sp-S	Chapter 10 Sp-S-F	Totals
Core Theme & Feature	Missional Sending	Evangelical Saving	Christological Indwelling	Liturgical Standing	Formational Shaping	Ecclesial Uniting	
	A - 15:15–16						
1 Cor.	A - 2:1–5	A - 6:11			A-- 2:10–15	A - 12:4–6	4
2 Cor.		A - 3:3	A - 13:14				2
Gal.	A - 4:4–6				A - 4:5–6		2
Eph.	A - 1:11–14	A - 2:17–19	A - 2:22	B - 4:30–32		A-- 4:4–6	6
						B - 5:18–20	
Phil.							0
Col.	B - 1:6–8						1
1 Thess.	A - 1:3–5						1
2 Thess.					B - 2:13		1
1 Tim.							0
2 Tim.							0
Titus					B - 3:4–6		1
Philem.							0
Pauline Epistles 28 (38%)	8 A6–B1–C1	5 A5–B0–C0	4 A2–B1–C1	3 A2–B1–C0	5 A3–B2–C0	3 A2–B1–C0	28 A20–B6–C2

APPENDIX CHART 1D: NEW TESTAMENT CENSUS OF TRIADIC OCCURRENCES

TRINITARIAN REFERENCES IN HEBREWS THROUGH REVELATION

NT Book	Chapter 5 F-S-Sp	Chapter 6 S-Sp-F	Chapter 7 S-F-Sp	Chapter 8 Sp-F-S	Chapter 9 F-Sp-S	Chapter 10 Sp-S-F	Totals
Core Theme & Feature	Missional Sending	Evangelical Saving	Christological Indwelling	Liturgical Standing	Formational Shaping	Ecclesial Uniting	
Heb.		A - 9:14	A - - 2:3–4				5
		A - - 10:29	C - 3:1–7				
			B - 10:12–15				
James							0
1 Peter	C - 1:3–11				A - 1:2		2
2 Peter							0
1 John		A - - 5:6–9			A - - 4:13	A - 4:2	3
2 John							0
3 John							0
Jude				A - 20			1
Rev.	B - 1:9–10	B - 22:17–18		C - 22:1	C - 1:4–5		4
Heb. – Rev. 15 (20%)	2 A0–B1–C1	4 A3–B1–C0	3 A1–B1–C1	2 A1–B0–C1	3 A2–B0–C1	1 A1–B0–C0	15 A8–B3–C4

	Appendix Chart 1E: New Testament Census of Triadic Occurrences Summary and Totals for Triadic Locations and Gradations						
NT Book	Chapter 5 F-S-Sp	Chapter 6 S-Sp-F	Chapter 7 S-F-Sp	Chapter 8 Sp-F-S	Chapter 9 F-Sp-S	Chapter 10 Sp-S-F	Totals
Core Theme & Feature	Missional Sending	Evangelical Saving	Christological Indwelling	Liturgical Standing	Formational Shaping	Ecclesial Uniting	
Gospels 19 incidents (25%)	04 A1 B2 C1	05 A4 B0 C1	05 A2 B2 C0 NA1	01 A1 B0 C0	01 A0 B0 C1	03 A3 B0 C0	19 A11 B4 C3 NA1
Acts 13 incidents (17%)	04 A2 B1 C1	01 A1 B0 C0	02 A1 B1 C0	03 A1 B1 C1	02 A0 B1 C1	01 A0 B1 C0	13 A5 B5 C3
Pauline Epistles 28 incidents (38%)	08 A6 B1 C1	05 A5 B0 C0	04 A2 B1 C1	03 A2 B1 C0	05 A3 B2 C0	03 A2 B1 C0	28 A20 B6 C2

APPENDIX CHART 1E: NEW TESTAMENT CENSUS OF TRIADIC OCCURRENCES

SUMMARY AND TOTALS FOR TRIADIC LOCATIONS AND GRADATIONS

NT Book	Chapter 5 F-S-Sp	Chapter 6 S-Sp-F	Chapter 7 S-F-Sp	Chapter 8 Sp-F-S	Chapter 9 F-Sp-S	Chapter 10 Sp-S-F	Totals
Core Theme & Feature	Missional Sending	Evangelical Saving	Christologi-cal Indwelling	Liturgical Standing	Formational Shaping	Ecclesial Uniting	
Heb. – Rev.	02	04	03	02	03	01	15
15 incidents	A0	A3	A1	A1	A2	A1	A8
	B1	B1	B1	B0	B0	B0	B3
	C1	C0	C1	C1	C1	C0	C4
(20%)							
Totals	18 (24%)	15 (20%)	14 (19%)	9 (12%)	11 (15%)	8 (10%)	75 (100%)
A (59%)	A9	A13	A6	A5	A5	A6	A44
B (24%)	B5	B1	B5	B2	B3	B2	B18
C (16%)	C4	C1	C2	C2	C3	C0	C12
NA (1%)			NA1				NA1

Glossary of Trinitarian Terms

Adoptionism	Same as modalistic Monarchianism. It holds that the Son is subordinate to the Father who adopted Jesus into divine Sonship.
Analogy	Describes the Trinity in terms of human psychology or things in nature. Examples: the Trinity is like sun, ray, and illumination—or like mind, memory, and will.
Anamoisis	Greek for "unlike substance"; opposite of *homoousia,* "same substance."
Arnarchoi	Greek for "without beginning." Orthodoxy contends that being begotten is not inconsistent with being eternally in existence.
Arianism	Contends that there was a time when the Son was not, that the Son was created by the Father and was not from eternity.
Autotheos	Less-than-orthodox concept of Origen, used to describe the monarchy of the Father and the subordination of the Son and Spirit. Means "solely God."
Circumincession	Latin-derived translation of the Greek *perichoresis,* which refers to the "mutual interpenetration and inhabitation" of

the three divine Persons, so that what one does, all do; what one says, all say.

Coinherence — Used by Tertullian (c. 200), this word anticipates the Greek *perichoresis* and the Latin *circuminsession*. It means the inseparability, eternal unity, and community of the Father, Son, and Spirit in inner relations and external operations.

Consubstantial — The three persons in the One God are of the same substance, *homoousia*.

Dynamic
Monarchianism — Subordinates the Son and Spirit to the Father, and holds that the Son was adopted by the Father in time as the Son of God.

Economic — Defines and describes the Trinity *ad extra*—the Three acting together toward creation—in contrast to the immanent Trinity, *ad intra,* the Three in inner relation to each other.

Emanation — Concept aligns with a subordination scheme of the Father and the Son along the line of the Son being derived from the Father. It usually connotes that creation also emanated, usually second-hand from the Son and Spirit, and not directly from the Father.

Eternal
Generation — This concept develops in opposition to the Arian contention that there was in eternity a time before the Son was begotten. Eternal generation contends that "begotten" witnesses to the same substance of the Father and Son, and if the Son is of the same substance, then He must be eternally begotten or generated.

Filiation — Having to do with sonship, the Father's eternal begetting of the Son. The Father is in eternal relation to the Son by filiation.

Filioque — Latin word for "and the Son" that was added to the phrase in the Nicene-Constantinople Creed, indicating that the Father sent the Spirit. As emended, it was "the Father and the Son sent the Spirit."

Generation	Notes that the Son was begotten in same substance by the Father. The Son was not made or created.
Homoousia	Greek word that means "same *ousia*" (i.e., "essence" or "substance"). It was incorporated into the Nicene Creed so that God is declared to be three Persons in one substance.
Homoiousia	Greek word that means "like/similar *ousia*" (i.e., "essence" or "substance"). It was offered unsuccessfully for the Nicene Creed as a compromise between the same substance and the unlike substance subordinationism. It was deemed heterodox.
Homophuia	Means the shared nature of the Godhead.
Hypostasis	Greek word that means a "distinct identity or person and relation." It is a Greek synonym for the Latin *persona.*
Idiomata	That which makes the Father, Son, and Spirit distinct from each other, but in eternal relation to each other. Synonymous with *properties.*
Immanent	Defines and describes the Trinity *ad intra,* in inner relations. Namely, the Father begets and sends; the Son is eternally begotten and is sent and sends; the Spirit proceeds from the Father and is sent. Stands in contrast to the economic Trinity, *ad extra*, the Three acting together toward creation.
Kenosis	Greek word for "emptying"; as in, the Son emptied Himself to become the human Jesus; the Father emptied Himself—gave up His Son to the cross; and the Spirit was poured out upon the church.
Logos	Greek word for "Word" as in John 1:1. It is often used to show the unity between the Father and the Logos/Son.
Manifestation	The unrepeatable, perceptible presence of the Son in the incarnation and the Spirit at Pentecost. It is the *ad extra* operation of the Godhead in redemption.

Modalism   The concept that there is one god in substance and person, and that the Father, Son, and Spirit are three functions of that god but not distinct persons. Synonymous with unitarianism.

Modalistic
Monarchianism   Contends that maintaining there is but one God, who alone is from forever, requires seeing the three names as being functional actions and not distinct identities or persons.

Modes of Being   Karl Barth's way of describing the distinct identities within the Godhead without resorting to the concept of *persons*, which in his mind had become radically influenced by modern psychology.

Monarchy   Focuses on the idea of "no one like Him." There can only be one high, first God. This concept tends to cast a subordinationist mindset, but does point to the priority of the Father, not in time but logically in relation with the Son and Spirit.

Monotheism   The concept that there is but one god.

Patripassionism   The seemingly logical consequence of modalism that if there is no real distinction between the Father and the Son, then the Father must have suffered on the cross.

Perichoresis   Greek word synonymous with the Latin *circuminsessio* and refers to the "mutual interpenetration and inhabitation" of the three divine Persons so that what one does, all do.

Person   The concept the Father, Son, and Spirit are distinct identities. Person is to be distinguished from the one substance that the Divine Three share in unity.

Polytheism   The concept that there are more than one god. It is the opposite of monotheism.

Procession	Describes the relational movement from Father to Son to Spirit in inner relations (*ad intra*) in eternity and in external operations (*ad extra*) in creation.
Properties	That which makes the Father, Son, and Spirit distinct, but in eternal relation to each other. Synonymous with *idiomata*.
Spiration	The eternal relation of the Father to the Spirit, who is eternally exhaled or "spirated" by the Father.
Subordin-ationism	The concept that there is one unbegotten God the Father who shares in essence/substance with no one. The Son has divinity, but of a lesser substance than the Father.
Subsistence	The Latin concept that defines the reality of the Son's and Spirit's identity in the One substance of God.
Substance	The stuff of deity, divinity itself, eternal, uncaused but causing all. It is in distinction from Persons in the Trinity. Substance is shared by the Father, Son, and Spirit; identity is not.
Triadic	Something that comes or exists as three.
Trinity	The Latin translation *trinitas* employed by Tertullian (c. 200) from the Greek word *trias* used by Athenagoras (c. 170), to describe the revelatory phenomenon of the One God having an inner plurality of Father, Son, and Spirit, with each one distinct in person but ever united in operations.
Tritheism	The concept that three gods exist who are distinct and not united in substance.
Unitarianism	The concept that there is one god in substance and person, and that the Father, Son, and Spirit are three functions of that god but not distinct persons. Synonymous with modalism.

Appendix C

Spiritual Formation Exercise #1: Trinitarian Prayers

Exercise #1: Praying the Trinity

Most of us are very careful about how we address God when we talk to Him. We call Him by name, "Father," or "Lord," or even just "God." We also practice what we have been taught or seen others do when ending our prayers. We say, "In Jesus' name, amen." We are comfortable with those names and in that order for two good biblical reasons.

First, if we are followers of Christ in a local church, we probably have experienced or soon will experience baptism. That baptism will be carried out in observance of what Jesus said in Matthew 28:18–20. As the administrator of our baptism is about to get us very wet, we will hear words something like, "I baptize you in the name of the Father, and of the Son, and of the Holy Spirit." So, we do use the names of the Father and the Son in our prayers, but usually we omit the name of the Holy Spirit. Why do we leave the Spirit out? I will come back to that momentarily after we look at the second reason that we almost invariably pray to the Father in Jesus' name.

Second, we know the Lord's Prayer. In that prayer, Jesus taught His disciples to pray to God as their Father: "Our Father in heaven" (Matthew 6:9–13). Jesus also taught the disciples to pray in His name. He said, "Whatever you ask in My name, I will do it so that the Father may be glorified in the Son. If you ask Me anything in My name, I will do it" (John 14:13–14). Did you notice that Jesus said to "ask Me"? So, Jesus expects His disciples to speak directly to the Father and to Himself, the Son. Thus, we know we are standing on solid ground when we use the name of the Father and the Son in our prayers. We also know that we can talk to Jesus, the Son, directly in addition to talking to the Father.

However, the writers of the twenty-seven books in the New Testament include prayers, blessings, and benedictions addressing God in all three personal names in the Trinity and in all different orders, too. Often, it is Father, Son, and Spirit—but then sometimes it is the exact opposite, Spirit, Father, Son. Remember your theology: the God and Father of Jesus Christ lives as the One God in three persons. So, when you talk to one—any one—you talk to all. Now you are ready for the experiment!

Look carefully at the chart in Appendix A: New Testament Census of Triadic Occurrences. This chart identifies seventy-five times that the New Testament writers invoked the three persons in the Triune God in one order or another. There are six different possible orders in which you can speak the three different names: Father, Son, and Spirit. If the New Testament writers, inspired by the Holy Spirit to write what God really wanted written, used the three names in every possible order then cannot we also call upon God in those three names in any of those orders?

I think Scripture gives us permission seventy-five times to pray in any of those orders that we feel led to, at any given time. Are you willing to try it?

Look again at the chart. Do you see all six orders? Would you be willing to pray for about five minutes using one of those orders, addressing each person? (Hopefully you won't choose the usual order of Father-Son-Spirit, although it might be very unusual for you to talk directly to the Holy Spirit in the final part of your prayer.)

By now you might feel closest to Jesus as the Son, so start praying to Him, then move to the Father, and then to the Spirit. If you are uncomfortable with such an exercise, you could start your prayer with something like this: "God, I am going to experiment with talking to You from what I understand in Scripture. Please be patient with me. I mean to praise You and not offend You." Praying that disclaimer first might make you more comfortable and even bold in praying through the order you have chosen.

Give your prayer five minutes and then reflect on what happened. I think you'll be surprised at what God will do in your life and what you will learn about Him in this experiment. I would love to hear about your experience. You can contact me through the publisher.

Spiritual Formation Exercise #2: Forty-two Days of Trinitarian Devotion

EXERCISE #2: MEDITATING ON THE TRINITY—ONE ORDER PER WEEK FOR FORTY-TWO DAYS

If you have already tried Exercise #1, you are probably encouraged and even excited about knowing God better through praying in a triadic order that is new to you. You're probably ready to go the next step. I want to challenge you to a twelve-minute-a-day, forty-two-day meditation exercise.

I invite you to spend twelve minutes praying every day at the same time, using one and only one Trinitarian order for seven days straight, then use another order the next week, and so on until six weeks have passed and you have prayed through all six orders. You might want to keep a simple journal to record what happens.

Why the precise discipline of one order only for each week and for a total of six weeks? Habits can work for us or against us. Habits are hard to make and hard to break. Habits and ruts can run deep. The habit of praying in the baptismal order of Father, Son, and Holy Spirit runs very deep indeed. Imagine the spiritual flexibility it will take for you to dig five additional ruts! Most of us can find twelve minutes in our day if we really want to find them. It will take commitment, but it will be worth it.

Some of us have deep experience with Christian, biblical meditation and so are comfortable with the effectiveness of slow repetition of words and prayers in

Scripture. For others, this may be unusual and make you think of the warning Jesus gave against repetitious prayer (Matthew 6:7). Actually, the warning there is not an injunction against meaningful meditation on Scripture. Jesus warns against heaping up prayers and mindless words as if the more we pray that same prayer, the more God is compelled to give us the answer we want.

The longest psalm in the book of Psalms is the slow meditation of King David on the reality of God's word: "I have treasured Your word in my heart so that I may not sin against You" (Psalm 119:11). Meditation is the best way to hide God's words in your heart. For some of us, the best way to spend our twelve minutes in prayer is simply by praising God as each of the three names in the order that we have chosen, and to do it repeatedly until the time is up.

You may find this hard for the first few days, but by the end of the week, you will be glad you stayed with it. You will likely sense that God is doing something new and fresh in your spirit because you are getting to know Him by name in a fresh scriptural way. It may help you to sense what God does in each order by reflecting on something I discussed about these orders in the Introduction. Listed there are all six orders and the context in which you find those orders in the New Testament:

- Chapter 5: The Missional Triad of God *Sending* Us: Father, Son, and Spirit

- Chapter 6: The Evangelistic Triad of God *Saving* Us: Son, Spirit, Father

- Chapter 7: The Christological Triad of God *Indwelling* Us: Son, Father, Spirit

- Chapter 8: The Sanctifying Triad of Our *Standing* in God: Spirit, Father, Son

- Chapter 9: The Formational Triad of God *Shaping* Us: Father, Spirit, Son

- Chapter 10: The Ecclesial Triad of God *Uniting* Us: Spirit, Son, Father

As you give your whole week to praying in one order, note the theological theme of that order as underlined above. For instance, when you pray through the Spirit-Son-Father order, remember how God gives unity in the church: The Spirit gives each of us a specific motivation (*charisma*) to express love for Him and each other, the Son calls us into a specific ministry (*diakonia*) to live out that motivation, and the Father displays workings (*energma*) in that ministry so that people know it is His work that we are doing and they give Him glory. Similarly, the week that you pray through the Son-Spirit-Father order, God saving, remember how you came to faith in Christ and pray for others you know who are still on the way to faith.

If you decide to try this Trinitarian meditation experiment, let me know. Drop me a note through the publisher, and I will pray for you through your forty-two days. I will probably pray for you using the Father-Spirit-Son order, because that is the Triune order when God is shaping us to be more like Christ! See if you can convince two or three others to try the experiment with you, or see if your small group would like to participate. "[B]ut the people that do know their God shall be strong, and do *exploits*" (Daniel 11:32 KJV, italics in the original). Let your Trinitarian drill-deep exploits begin!

Explaining the Trinity to Children and to Adolescents

THE NICENE CREED (325 CE) AS AMENDED BY THE FIRST COUNCIL OF CONSTANTINOPLE (381)

"We believe in one God the Father Almighty, Maker of heaven and earth, and of all things visible and invisible.

"And in one Lord Jesus Christ, the only begotten Son of God, begotten of the Father before all worlds, God of God, Light of Light, Very God of Very God, begotten, not made, being of one substance with the Father by whom all things were made; who for us men, and for our salvation, came down from heaven, and was incarnate by the Holy Spirit of the Virgin Mary, and was made man, and was crucified also for us under Pontius Pilate. He suffered and was buried, and the third day he rose again according to the Scriptures, and ascended into heaven, and sits on the right hand of the Father. And he shall come again with glory to judge both the quick and the dead, whose kingdom shall have no end.

"And we believe in the Holy Spirit, the Lord and Giver of Life, who proceeds from the Father and the Son, who with the Father and the Son together is worshipped and glorified, who spoke by the prophets."

Explaining the Trinity to Children

God is Jesus, the Father, and the Holy Spirit, and They are inseparable.
My grandparents lived into their nineties in the same house with only one phone on a landline. If you talked with one, you then had to talk with the other. They were inseparable. God is like that, too.

Our math classes tell us that $1 + 1 + 1 = 3$, but $1 \times 1 \times 1 = 1$. God is "the three times God." When you talk to Jesus, you are talking to God. When you talk with the Father, you are talking to God. And when you talk with the Holy Spirit, you are talking with God.

Ways to think about three-in-one. There are many different ways that people try to help us understand who this "three times God" is—we call Him the Trinity—and how He can be three persons but just one God. Here are some examples, and maybe you can come up with some more.

- Sometimes people use examples from nature that help us think about the Trinity. For instance, think of an apple. An apple has the skin, the "meat," and the core. Each is the apple, each is unique, but an apple isn't an apple without all three.

- Sometimes they use examples from science where three are one. For instance, a flashlight is the source, it sends out a beam of light, and around where the beam lands there is the glow of illumination.

- Or maybe it would help to think about school—for example, assignments where you have to organize your information and thoughts into a speech. There is you, the speaker, and the speech that you give, and what happens with understanding by the other people who hear you and think about it.

What the Trinity did for us, and what we can do for Him. Jesus called God, "my *Abba*," which means, "my father." When Jesus was baptized, God spoke from heaven and said, "This is My beloved Son. I take delight in Him!" Jesus also said, "I and the Father are one." Later Jesus told His disciples that He was going to return to the glory that He had with His Father before the creation of the world. However, He promised that He would not leave them without another friend, namely, the Holy Spirit. Jesus said He would ask the Father to send the Spirit to the disciples. And that's just what happened.

Fifty days after Jesus died for our sins and was raised from the dead and ascended back to heaven, the Holy Spirit came to the disciples. The Holy Spirit gave them power and they became incredibly bold to share about forgiveness of our sins and living a new life through following Jesus.

The Father sent His Son Jesus to be born, just like us, and to teach us face to face and to die for us so that nothing can separate us from God again. And the Holy Spirit speaking through the Bible is the proof about all of this, plus He is also a "seal"—like a guarantee sticker or a seal of approval—that shows we are forgiven and that we belong to God.

So now, when we are ready to live for God and follow Jesus fully, we should be baptized. This shows our commitment to God the Three-in-One, because Jesus commands us to be baptized in the name of the Father, the Son, and the Holy Spirit.

Explaining the Trinity to Teenagers

More Than a Word. . . . The New Testament has four biographies of Jesus. These we call the Gospels (from a Greek word that means "good news"): Matthew, Mark, Luke, and John. In them we discover that many people loved to hang out with Jesus for His teaching and the way He lived and loved others. Jesus invited some to be His disciples—follower-learner-friends—people like Peter, James, John, Mary, Martha. These disciples learned quickly that Jesus called God Father and that He talked with God in a transforming and intimate way. They asked Him, "Please teach us a prayer." Jesus taught them to call God Father, and as they did, God put His Spirit within them so that Father was more than a word; it was a relationship.

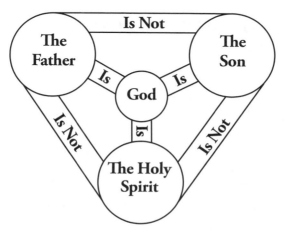

The Reality of the Trinity. The word *trinity* is not found in the New Testament, but the Trinity itself is. In fact, the Trinity appears all over the place there. The three Persons of the One God are named together seventy-five times in the New Testament. At the baptism of Jesus, we see and hear Him as *Christ* (from a Greek word that means a person who is "chosen" or "anointed" for a special task; this was their translation of "Messiah" from a Hebrew word with the same meaning). At the baptism of Jesus Christ, we also hear the Father's voice say, "This is My beloved Son," and we see the Holy Spirit descend like a dove on Jesus. (See Matthew 3:13–17.)

Different Orders, Special Meanings, One Main Message. You can arrange any three items in a total of six different orders. Guess what? All six possible orders of the Father, Son, and Holy Spirit are used in the New Testament. For instance, the order of Father-Son-Spirit is found in the Great Commission of Matthew 28:19–20. The last verses of 2 Corinthians contain a blessing with a different order: Son-Father-Spirit.

There are seventy-five different times that New Testament passages talk about all three Persons in the Trinity, and every one of those six different orderings has at least seven passages that use that specific order. If you search these out, you will find that each order shows up when talking about a particular topic: sending us into a mission, saving us from sin, indwelling us for relationship, setting us apart as family members, shaping us into being more like Jesus Christ, and uniting all disciples into one body as the church. So, there is a diversity of messages in those seventy-five passages and six different orderings. But one thing we can also learn from this is that God is both consistent—we can count on what He says (and He covers a lot of territory about how best to live a life of meaningful worship of Him and service to others)—and He is flexible (He won't be put in a box)!

Autonomy in Intimacy. The best home in which to grow up is the one full of close caring, honest living, and deep trusting. That is an atmosphere of intimacy. Such intimacy implants courage in our hearts to follow our dreams and to stand our ground. Consistent intimacy begets stable autonomy. Autonomy means to be self-directed, free.

When we are children, we know what we are and what we believe—because we believe what our parents believe. But in the adolescent push toward adulthood, we begin to learn to make up our own minds about things. We become more and more autonomous. We get our drivers license, we buy our own things with our own money, and we go away to college or training programs and get jobs.

However, intimacy without autonomy is smothering—too much mothering or fathering. Autonomy without intimacy is isolation, loneliness, and even alienation—too much being our own person. Life works best when we learn to be autonomous within intimacy, just like the perfection that is the Triune God. The Father, Son, and Spirit are distinct conscious Persons, free in decisions and actions, but are a united self-existent community that is decidedly indivisible and committed toward creation and redemption. As Caesarius of Arles declared, "*Fides omnium christianorum in Trinitate consistorum*"—"The faith of all Christians rests on the Trinity."[1]

---

1.   Guilio Maspero and Robert J. Woźniak, eds., *Rethinking Trinitarian Theology: Disputed Questions and Contemporary Issues in Trinitarian Theology*, (New York: T & T Clark International, 2012), viii.

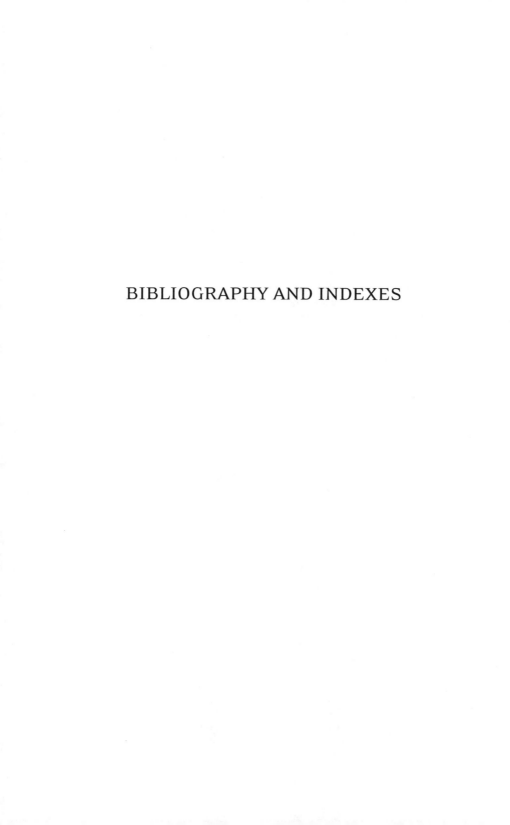

BIBLIOGRAPHY AND INDEXES

Bibliography

JOURNALS

Courth, Franz. "Trintät in der Schrift and Patristik," in *Handbuch der Dog-mengeschichte*, vol. 2, Edited by Michael Schmaus, Alois Grillmeier, Leo Scheffczyk, and Michael Scybold, 11–13. Freiburg: Herder, 1988.

Green, Brad. "Did Augustine's Trinitarian Theology Lead the West Astray?: A Look at a Contemporary Trend in Theology." Paper presented at the 51st National Conference of the Evangelical Theological Society, Danvers, MA, 1999.

Guntin, Colin E. "Augustine, the Trinity and the Crisis of Theology in the West," *Scottish Journal of Theology* 43, no. 1 (January 1, 1990): 33–58.

Husbands, Mark. "The Trinity Is Not Our Social Program: Volf, Gregory of Nyssa and Barth," in *Trinitarian Theology for the Church*. Edited by Daniel J. Treier and David Lauber, 120–141. Downers Grove, IL: InterVarsity Press, 2009.

Johnson, Keith. "Augustine's 'Trinitarian' Redoing of John 5: A Model for Theological Interpretation of Scripture?," *Journal of the Evangelical Theological Society* 52, no. 4 (December 1, 2009): 799–810.

Keener, Craig S. "Is Subordination within the Trinity Really a Heresy? A Study of John 5:18 in Context," *Trinity Journal* 20, no. 1 (March 1, 1999): 39–51.

Luy, David. "The Aesthetic Collision: Urs von Balthasar on the Trinity and the Cross," *International Journal of Systematic Theology* 13, no. 2 (April 2011): 154–169.

North American Orthodox-Catholic Theological Consultation. "The Filioque: A Church Dividing Issue?," http://www.assemblyofbishops.org/ministries/dialogue/orthodox-catholic/2003filioque (accessed January 17, 2015).

Rauser, Randal. "Rahner's Rule: An Emperor without Clothes?," *International Journal of Theology* 7, no. 1 (January 2005): 81–94.

Sanders, Fred. "Entangled in the Trinity: Economic and Immanent Trinity in Recent Theology," *Dialog: A Journal of Theology* 40, no. 3 (September 2001): 175–182.

_____. "The State of the Doctrine of the Trinity in Evangelical Theology," *Southwestern Journal of Theology* 47, no. 2 (March 1, 2005): 153–175.

Sexton, Jason. "The State of the Trinitarian Resurgence," *The Journal of the Evangelical Theological Society* 54, no. 4 (December 1, 2011): 787–807.

Volf, Miroslav. "'The Trinity Is Our Social Program': The Doctrine of the Trinity and the Shape of Social Engagement." *Modern Theology* 14, no. 3 (July 1998): 404–424.

MONOGRAPHS

Anatolios, Khaled, ed. *The Holy Trinity in the Life of the Church.* Holy Cross Studies in the Life of the Church. Grand Rapids: Baker Academic, 2014.

_____. *Retrieving Nicaea: The Development and Meaning of Trinitarian Doctrine.* Grand Rapids: Baker Academic, 2011.

Arendzen, John Peter. *The Holy Trinity: A Theological Treatise for Modern Laymen.* New York: Sheed & Ward, 1937.

Ayres, Lewis. *Nicaea and Its Legacy: An Approach to Fourth-century Trinitarian Theology.* New York: Oxford University Press, 2004.

Bacon, Hannah. *What's Right with the Trinity?: Conversations in Feminist Theology.* Farnham, Surrey: Ashgate, 2013.

Bartlett, Charles Norman. *The Triune God.* New York: American Tract Society, 1937.

Bauckham, Richard. *God Crucified: Monotheism and Christology in the New Testament.* Grand Rapids: Eerdmans, 1999.

Bellinger, Charles K. *The Trinitarian Self: The Key to the Puzzle of Violence.* New York: Oxford University Press, 2001.

Bilezikian, George. *Community 101: Reclaiming the Local Church as a Community of Oneness.* Grand Rapids: Zondervan, 1997.

Bloesch, Donald G. *The Battle for the Trinity: The Debate over Inclusive God-language.* Ann Arbor, MI: Servant, 1985.

Bobrinskoy, Boris. *The Mystery of the Trinity: Trinitarian Experience and Vision in the Biblical and Patristic Tradition.* Translated by Anthony P. Gythiel. Crestwood, NY: St. Vladimir's Seminary Press, 1999.

Boff, Leonard. *Trinity and Society.* 3rd ed. Translated by Paul Burns. Maryknoll, NY: Orbis Books, 1988.

Böhnke, Michael, Assaad Elias Kattan, and Bernd Oberdorfer, eds. *Die Filioque-Kontroverse: Historische, ökumenische und dogmatische Perspektiven 1200 Jahre nach der Aachener Synode.* Freiburg im Breisgau: Herder, 2011.

Boyd, Gregory A. *Satan and the Problem of Evil: Constructing a Trinitarian Warfare Theodicy.* Downers Grove, IL: InterVarsity Press, 2001.

Bracken, Joseph A. *What Are They Saying about the Trinity?* New York: Paulist Press, 1979.

Bray, Gerald Lewis. *The Doctrine of God*. Downers Grove, IL: InterVarsity Press, 1993.

Brown, David. *The Divine Trinity*. La Salle: Open Court Pub. Co., 1985.

Brumback, Carl. *God in Three Persons*. Cleveland: Pathway Press, 1959.

Brümmer, Vincent. *Atonement, Christology and the Trinity: Making Sense of Christian Doctrine*. Burlington, VT: Ashgate, 2005.

Buckley, James J., and David S. Yeago, eds. *Knowing the Triune God: The Work of the Spirit in the Practices of the Church*. Grand Rapids: Eerdmans, 2001.

Butrus, Zachariah. *God is One in the Holy Trinity*. Rikon: The Good Way, 1996.

Buzzard, Anthony F., and Charles F. Hunting. *The Doctrine of the Trinity: Christianity's Self-Inflicted Wound*. Lanham, MD: International Scholars Publications, 1998.

Chalamet, Christophe and Marc Vial, eds. *Recent Developments in Trinitarian Theology: An International Symposium*. Minneapolis: Fortress Press, 2014.

Champion, John Benjamin. *The Holy Trinity*. (s. n.), 1929.

Chester, Tim. *Delighting in the Trinity: Why Father, Son, and Spirit Are Good News*. Oxford: Monarch, 2005.

Clark, Gordon Haddon. *The Trinity*. Jefferson, MD: Trinity Foundation, 1985.

Coffey, David Michael. *Deus Trinitas: The Doctrine of the Triune God*. New York: Oxford University Press, 1999.

Coppedge, Allan. *The God Who Is Triune: Revisioning the Christian Doctrine of God*. Downers Grove, IL: InterVarsity Press, 2007.

Crisp, Oliver D. and Fred Sanders, eds. *Advancing Trinitarian Theology: Explorations in Constructive Dogmatics.* Grand Rapids: Zondervan, 2014.

Cunningham, David. *These Three Are One: The Practice of Trinitarian Theology.* Oxford: Blackwell Publishers, 1998.

Daffara, Marcolino. *De Deo uno et trino.* Cursus manualis theologiae dogmaticae secundum divi Thomae Principia. Taurini: Marietti, 1945.

Dalcour, Edward L. *A Definitive Look at Oneness Theology: Defending the Trinity of God.* New York: University Press of America, 2005.

Davis, Stephen T., Daniel Kendall, and Gerald O'Collins, eds. *The Trinity: An Interdisciplinary Symposium on the Trinity.* New York: Oxford University Press, 2004.

Del Colle, Ralph. *Christ and the Spirit: Spirit-Christology in Trinitarian Perspective.* New York: Oxford University Press, 1994.

Dempsey, Michael T., ed. *Trinity and Election in Contemporary Theology.* Grand Rapids: Eerdmans, 2011.

Dixon, Philip. *Nice and Hot Disputes: The Doctrine of the Trinity in the Seventeenth Century.* London: Continuum, 2003.

Duck, Ruth C. *Gender and the Name of God: The Trinitarian Baptismal Formula.* New York: Pilgrim Press, 1991.

Durrant, Michael. *Theology and Intelligibility: An Examination of the Proposition That God Is the Last End of Rational Creatures and the Doctrine That God Is Three Persons in One Substance (the Doctrine of the Holy Trinity).* Boston: Routledge & K. Paul, 1973.

Edwards, Denis. *The God of Evolution: A Trinitarian Theology.* New York: Paulist Press, 1999.

Edwards, Jonathan. *Observations on the Scriptural Economy of the Trinity and the Covenant of Redemption.* New York: Charles Scribner's Sons, 1880.

Emery, Gilles. *The Trinitarian Theology of Saint Thomas Aquinas.* Translated by Francesca Aran Murphy. New York: Oxford University Press, 2007.

Erickson, Millard. *God in Three Persons: A Contemporary Interpretation of the Trinity.* Grand Rapids: Baker, 1995.

_____. *Who's Tampering with the Trinity? An Assessment of the Subordination Debate.* Grand Rapids: Kregel, 2009.

Faber, Roland. *Freiheit, Theologie und Lehramt: trinitätstheologische Grundlegung und wissenschaftstheoretischer Ausblick.* Innsbruck: Tyrolia, 1992.

Farrelly, John. *The Trinity: Rediscovering the Central Christian Mystery.* Lanham, MD: Rowman & Littlefield, 2005.

Fatula, Mary Ann. *The Triune God of Christian Faith.* Collegeville, MN: Liturgical Press, 1990.

Feenstra, Ronald J. and Cornelius Platinga, eds. *Trinity, Incarnation and Atonement: Philosophical and Theological Essays.* Notre Dame, IN: University of Notre Dame Press, 1989.

Feinberg, John S. *No One Like Him: The Doctrine of God.* Wheaton, IL: Crossway, 2001.

Fiddes, Paul S. *Participating in God: A Pastoral Doctrine of the Trinity.* Louisville: Westminster John Knox Press, 2000.

The Forgotten Trinity: The Report of the B.C.C. Study Committee on Trinitarian Doctrine Today, vol. 2. London: British Council of Churches, 1989.

Forster, Roger. *Trinity: Song and Dance God.* Milton Keynes, UK: Authentic, 2004.

Fortman, Edmund J. *The Triune God: A Historical Study of the Doctrine of the Trinity.* Philadelphia, PA: Westminster, 1972.

Friedman, Russell L. *Medieval Trinitarian Thought from Aquinas to Ockham.* Cambridge: Cambridge University Press, 2010.

Gelpi, Donald L. *The Divine Mother: A Trinitarian Theology of the Holy Spirit.* Lanham, MD: University Press of America, 1984.

Giles, Kevin. *The Trinity and Subordinationism: The Doctrine of God and the Contemporary Gender Debate.* Downers Grove, IL: InterVarsity Press, 2002.

Gill, John. *The Doctrine of the Trinity Stated and Vindicated: Being the Substance of Several Discourses on That Important Subject Reduced into the Form of a Treatise.* London: Printed, and sold by Aaron Ward, at the King's-Arms in Little-Britain; and H. Whitridge, at the Royal-Exchange, 1731.

Girzone, Joseph F. *Trinity.* New York: Doubleday, 2002.

Grant, Robert McQueen. *The Early Christian Doctrine of God.* Charlottesville: University Press of Virginia, 1966.

Grenz, Stanley J. *Rediscovering the Triune God: The Trinity in Contemporary Theology.* Minneapolis: Fortress Press, 2004.

———. *The Social God and the Relational Self: A Trinitarian Theology of the Imago Dei.* Louisville: Westminster John Knox Press, 2001.

———. *The Named God and the Question of Being: A Trinitarian Theo-ontology.* Louisville: Westminster John Knox Press, 2005.

Greshake, Gisbert. *Der dreieine Gott: Eine trinitarische Theologie.* Basel: Herder, 1997.

Grudem, Wayne. A. *Systematic Theology: An Introduction to Biblical Doctrine.* Grand Rapids: Zondervan, 1994.

Gunton, Colin. *Father, Son and Holy Spirit: Essays toward a Fully Trinitarian Theology.* London: T & T Clark, 2003.

_____. *The One, the Three, and the Many: God, Creation, and the Culture of Modernity.* New York: Cambridge University Press, 1993.

_____. *The Promise of Trinitarian Theology.* Edinburgh: T & T Clark, 1991.

_____. *Enlightenment and Alienation: An Essay towards a Trinitarian Theology.* Eugene, OR: Wipf & Stock, 2006.

Hagerty, Cornelius. *The Holy Trinity.* North Quincy, MA: The Christopher Publishing House, 1976.

Hanson, Richard Patrick Crosland. *God: Creator, Saviour, Spirit.* London: SCM Press, 1958.

_____. *The Search for the Christian Doctrine of God: The Arian Controversy, 318–381.* Grand Rapids: Baker Academic, 2005.

Haugh, Richard S. *Photius and the Carolingian: The Trinitarian Controversy.* Belmont, MA: Nordland Publishing Company, 1975.

Hedley, George Percy. *The Holy Trinity: Experience and Interpretation.* Philadelphia: Fortress Press, 1967.

Hilberath, Bernd Jochen. *Der dreieinige Gott und die Gemeinschaft der Menschen: Orientierungen zur christlichen Rede von Gott.* Mainz: Matthias-Grünewald-Verlag, 1990.

_____. *Der Personbegriff der Trinitätstheologie in Rückfrage von Karl Rahner zu Tertullians "Adversus Praxean."* Innsbruck: Tyrolia, 1986.

Hill, Edmund. *The Mystery of the Trinity.* London: Geoffrey Chapman, 1985.

Hillar, Marian. *From Logos to Trinity: The Evolution of Religious Beliefs from Pythagoras to Tertullian.* New York: Cambridge University Press, 2012.

Hodgson, Leonard. *The Doctrine of the Trinity: Croall Lectures, 1942–1943*. New York: Charles Scribner's Sons, 1944.

Holkot, Robert. *Exploring the Boundaries of Reason: Three Questions on the Nature of God*. Edited by Hester Goodenough Gelber. Toronto, ON: Pontifical Institute of Medieval Studies, 1983.

Holmes, Stephen R. *The Holy Trinity: Understanding God's Life*. Christian Doctrines in Historical Perspective Series. Crownhill, UK: Paternoster, 2012.

Horrell, J. Scott. *The Center of Everything*. Grand Rapids: Kregel, 2011.

———. "The Self-giving Triune God, the *Imago Dei* and the Nature of the Local Church: An Ontology of Mission," Evangelical Theological Society papers, 1997.

Hoskins, Richard. *The Doctrine of the Trinity in the Works of John Richardson Illingworth and William Temple, and the Implications for Contemporary Trinitarian Theology*. Lampeter, UK: Edwin Mellen Press, 2000.

Humphreys, Fisher. *The Nature of God*. Nashville: Broadman Press, 1985.

Hunt, Ann. *Trinity: Nexus of the Mysteries of Christian Faith*. Theology in Global Perspectives Series. Maryknoll, NY: Orbis, 2005.

———. *What Are They Saying about the Trinity?* New York: Paulist Press, 1998.

Illingworth, J. R. *The Doctrine of the Trinity: Apologetically Considered*. London: Macmillan and Co., 1907.

Jansen, Reiner. *Studien zu Luthers Trinitätslehre*. Bern: Peter Lang, 1976.

Jenson, Robert W. *The Triune Identity: God according to the Gospel*. Philadelphia: Fortress Press, 1982.

Johnson, Aubrey R. *The One and the Many in the Israelite Conception of God*. Cardiff: University of Wales, 1961.

Johnson, Elizabeth A. *She Who Is: The Mystery of God in Feminist Theological Discourse.* New York: Crossroad, 1992.

Johnson, Keith E. *Rethinking the Trinity and Religious Pluralism: An Augustinian Assessment.* Downers Grove, IL: InterVarsity Press, 2011.

Kärkkäinen, Veli-Matti. *The Trinity: Global Perspectives.* Louisville: Westminster John Knox, 2007.

Kasper, Walter. *The God of Jesus Christ.* Translated by Matthew J. O'Connell. New York: Crossroad, 1989.

Kay, Brian K. *Trinitarian Spirituality: John Owen and the Doctrine of God in Western Devotion.* Waynesboro, GA: Paternoster, 2007.

Kelly, Anthony. *The Trinity of Love: A Theology of the Christian God.* Wilmington, DE: Michael Glazier, 1989.

Kimel, Alvin F., Jr. *Speaking the Christian God: The Holy Trinity and the Challenge of Feminism.* Grand Rapids: Eerdmans, 1992.

Kirby, Reginald. *The Threefold Bond: "Of Communion with God the Father, the Son and the Holy Ghost."* London: Marshall, Morgan & Scott, 1927.

Klein, Félix. *The Doctrine of the Trinity.* Translated by Daniel J. Sullivan. New York: P.J. Kenedy & Sons, 1940.

Koncsik, Imre. *Jesus Christus—Mittler des Glaubens an den dreieinen Gott: Eine ontologische Deutung des Glaubens in Auseinandersetzung mit aktuellen Positionen.* Hamburg: Dr. Kovac, 2001.

Kovach, Stephen D. *The Eternal Subordination of the Son: An Apologetic against Evangelical Feminism* [electronic resource]. Portland, OR: Theological Research Exchange Network, 2005.

Kretschmar, Georg. *Studien zur frühchristlichen Trinitätstheologie.* Tübingen: Mohr, 1956.

LaCugna, Catherine Mowery. *God for Us: The Trinity and Christian Life*. San Francisco: HarperSan Francisco, 1992.

La Due, William J. *The Trinity Guide to the Trinity*. New York: Continuum, 2006.

Lebreton, Jules. *Histoire du dogme de la Trinité: Des origines au concile de Nicée*. Paris: Beauchesne, 1927.

Lee, Jung Young. *The Trinity in Asian Perspective*. Nashville: Abingdon Press, 1996.

Letham, Robert. *The Trinity*. Phillipsburg, NJ: Presbyterian and Reformed, 2004.

Leupp, Roderick T. *The Renewal of Trinitarian Theology: Themes, Patterns and Explorations*. Downers Grove, IL: InterVarsity Press, 2008.

_____. *Knowing the Name of God: A Trinitarian Tapestry of Grace, Faith, and Community*. Downers Grove, IL: InterVarsity Press, 1996.

Levering, Matthew. *Scripture and Metaphysics: Aquinas and the Renewal of Trinitarian Theology*. Malden, MA: Blackwell Publishing, 2004.

Lonergan, Bernard J. F. *The Way to Nicea: The Dialectical Development of Trinitarian Theology*. A Translation by Conn O'Donovan of the first part of De Deo Trino. Philadelphia: Westminster Press, 1976.

Lossky, Vladimir. *Mystical Theology*. London: James Clarke, 1957.

Lowry, Charles W. *The Trinity and Christian Devotion*. London: Eyre and Spottiswoode, 1945.

MacKenzie, Charles Sherrard. *The Trinity and Culture*. New York: Peter Lang, 1987.

Mackey, James Patrick. *The Christian Experience of God as Trinity*. London: SCM Press, 1983.

MacPherson, Camilia Gangasingh. *A Critical Reading of the Development of*

Raimon Panikkar's Thought on the Trinity. Lanham, MD: University Press of America, 1996.

Marsh, Thomas A. *The Triune God: A Biblical, Historical, and Theological Study*. Mystic, CT: Twenty-Third Publications, 1994.

Marshall, Bruce. *Trinity and Truth* [electronic resource]. New York: Cambridge University Press, 2000.

Mascall, Eric Lionel. *The Triune God: An Ecumenical Study*. Allison Park, PA: Pickwick Publications, 1986.

Mattox, Mickey L. and A. G. Roeber. *Changing Churches: An Orthodox, Catholic and Lutheran Conversation*. Grand Rapids: Eerdmans, 2012.

Maurer, Ernstpeter. *Der lebendige Gott: Texte zur Trinitätslehre*. Gütersloh: Kaiser/Gütersloher Verlagshaus, 1999.

McCall, Thomas H. *Which Trinity? Whose Monotheism? Philosophical and Systematic Theologians on the Metaphysics of Trinitarian Theology*. Grand Rapids: Eerdmans, 2011.

McCall, Thomas and Michael C. Rea, eds. *Analytic Theology: New Essays in the Philosophy of Theology as Well as Those in Philosophical and Theological Essays on the Trinity*. Oxford: Oxford University Press, 2009.

McCarty, Shaun. *Partners in the Divine Dance of Our Three Person'd God*. New York: Paulist Press, 1996.

McDowall, Stewart Andrew. *Evolution and the Doctrine of the Trinity*. Cambridge: University Press, 1882.

McGloin, Frank. *The Mystery of the Holy Trinity in Oldest Judaism*. Philadelphia: McVey, 1916.

McGrath, Alister E. *The Christian Vision of God*. Minneapolis: Fortress Press, 2009.

_____. *Understanding the Trinity.* Grand Rapids: Academie Books, 1988.

Merriell, Donald Juvenal. *To the Image of the Trinity: A Study in the Development of Aquinas' Teaching.* Toronto, ON: Pontifical Institute of Mediaeval Studies, 1990.

Metzger, John B. *Discovering the Mystery of the Unity of God: A Theological Study on the Plurality and Tri-unity of God in the Hebrew Scriptures.* San Antonio, TX: Ariel Ministries, 2010.

Metzger, Paul Louis, ed. *Trinitarian Soundings in Systematic Theology.* New York: T & T Clark, 2005.

Miller, David LeRoy. *Three Faces of God: Traces of the Trinity in Literature and Life.* New Orleans: Spring Journal, 2005.

Moingt, Joseph. *Théologie trinitaire de Tertullien.* Paris: Aubier, 1966.

Molnar, Paul D. *Divine Freedom and the Doctrine of the Immanent Trinity: In Dialogue with Karl Barth and Contemporary Theology.* New York: T & T Clark, 2002.

Moltmann, Jürgen. *The Trinity and the Kingdom: The Doctrine of God.* Translated by Margaret Kohl. San Francisco: Harper & Row, 1981.

Morey, Robert A. *The Trinity: Evidences and Issues.* Grand Rapids: World Publishing, 1996.

Murphree, Jon Tal. *The Trinity and Human Personality: God's Model for Relationships.* Nappanee, IN: Evangel Publishing House, 2001.

Murrmann-Kahl, Michael. *"Mysterium trinitatis"?: Fallstudien zur Trinitätslehre in der evangelischen Dogmatik des 20 Jahrhunderts.* New York: W. de Gruyter, 1997.

Ngien, Dennis. *Gifted Response: The Triune God as the Causative Agency of Our Responsive Worship.* Colorado Springs: Paternoster, 2008.

Niebuhr, H. Richard. *Radical Monotheism and Western Culture: With Supplementary Essays.* Louisville: Westminster John Knox Press, 1960.

Nitsche, Bernhard. *Gott und Freiheit: Skizzen zur trinitarischen Gotteslehre.* Regensburg: Friedrich Pustet, 2008.

Oberdorfer, Bernd. *Filioque: Geschichte und Theologie eines ökumenischen Problems.* Göttingen: Vandenhoeck & Ruprecht, 2001.

O'Carroll, Michael. *Trinitas: A Theological Encyclopedia of the Holy Trinity.* Wilmington, DE: Michael Glazier, 1987.

O'Collins, Gerald. *The Tripersonal God: Understanding and Interpreting the Trinity.* New York: Paulist Press, 1999.

O'Donnell, John Joseph. *The Mystery of the Triune God.* New York: Paulist Press, 1989.

_____. *Trinity and Temporality: The Christian Doctrine of God in the Light of Process Theology and the Theology of Hope.* New York: Oxford University Press, 1983.

Oh, Peter S. *Karl Barth's Trinitarian Theology: A Study in Karl Barth's Analogical Use of the Trinitarian Relation.* New York: T & T Clark, 2006.

Ohlig, Karl-Heinz. *Ein Gott in drei Personen?: Vom Vater Jesu zum "Mysterium" der Trinität.* Mainz: Matthias-Grünewald-Verlag; Luzern: Exodus, 1999.

Oischinger, Johann Nep. *Die Einheitslehre der göttlichen Trinität: Nach der kirchlichen Tradition bewiesen und gegen die Irrlehren festgestellt.* München: J.J. Lentner, 1862.

Olson, Roger E. and Christopher A. Hall. *The Trinity.* Grand Rapids: Eerdmans, 2002.

Olson, Roger E. *Trinity and Eschatology: The Historical Being of God in the Theology of Wolfhart Pannenberg.* (s. n.), 1984.

Panikkar, Raimundo. *The Trinity and the Religious Experience of Man: Icon-Person-Mystery.* New York: Orbis, 1973.

Parry, Robin. *Worshipping Trinity: Coming Back to the Heart of Worship.* Milton Keynes, UK: Paternoster, 2005.

Pauw, Amy Plantinga. *The Supreme Harmony of All: The Trinitarian Theology of Jonathan Edwards.* Grand Rapids: Eerdmans, 2002.

Peters, T. F. *God as Trinity: Relationality and Temporality in the Divine Life.* Louisville: Westminster John Knox Press, 1993.

Pfizenmaier, Thomas C. *The Trinitarian Theology of Dr. Samuel Clarke (1675–1729): Context, Sources, and Controversy.* New York: E. J. Brill, 1997.

Piret, Pierre. *Le Christ et la Trinité: Selon Maxime le Confesseur.* Paris: Beauchesne, 1983.

Pittenger, William Norman. *The Divine Triunity.* Philadelphia: United Church Press, 1977.

Placher, William C. *The Domestication of the Transcendence: How Modern Thinking about God Went Wrong.* Louisville: Westminster John Knox Press, 1996.

_____. *The Triune God: An Essay in Postliberal Theology.* Louisville: Westminster John Knox Press, 2007.

Powell, Samuel M. *Participating in God: Creation and Trinity.* Minneapolis: Fortress Press, 2003.

_____. *The Trinity in German Thought.* New York: Cambridge University Press, 2001.

Prestige, George Leonard. *God in Patristic Thought.* London: SPCK, 1952.

Purves, Jim. *The Triune God and the Charismatic Movement: A Critical Appraisal from a Scottish Perspective.* Carlisle, UK: Paternoster, 2004.

Radlbeck, Regina. *Der Personbegriff in der Trinitätstheologie der Gegenwart: untersucht am Beispiel der Entwürfe Jürgen Moltmanns und Walter Kaspers.* Regensburg: F. Pustet, 1989.

Rahner, Karl. *The Trinity.* Translated by Joseph Donceel. New York: Herder and Herder, 1970.

Rawlinson, Alfred Edward John, ed. *Essays on the Trinity and the Incarnation by Members of the Anglican Communion.* New York: Longmans, Green, 1933.

Reymond, Robert L. *A New Systematic Theology of the Christian Faith.* Nashville: Thomas Nelson, 1998.

Richardson, Cyril Charles. *The Doctrine of the Trinity.* New York: Abingdon Press, 1958.

Rusch, William G. *The Trinitarian Controversy.* Philadelphia: Fortress Press, 1980.

Sanders, Fred and Klaus Issler. *Jesus in Trinitarian Perspective: An Introductory Christology.* Nashville: B & H Academic, 2007.

Sanders, Fred. *The Deep Things of God: How the Trinity Changes Everything.* Wheaton, IL: Crossway, 2010.

_____. *The Image of the Immanent Trinity: Rahner's Rule and the Theological Interpretation of Scripture.* New York: Peter Lang, 2004.

Schmidbaur, Hans Christian. *Gottes Handeln in Welt und Geschichte: Eine trinitarische Theologie der Vorsehung.* St. Ottilien: EOS Verlag, 2003.

Schwöbel, Christoph, ed. *Trinitarian Theology Today: Essays on Divine Being and Act.* Edinburgh: T&T Clark, 1995.

Scirghi, Thomas J. *An Examination of the Problems of Inclusive Language in the Trinitarian Formula of Baptism.* Lewiston, NY: Edwin Mellen Press, 2000.

Seamands, Stephen. *Ministry in the Image of God: The Trinitarian Shape of Christian Service.* Downers Grove, IL: InterVarsity Press, 2005.

Servetus, Michael. *The Two Treatises of Servetus on the Trinity: On the Errors of the Trinity and Dialogues on the Trinity (A.D. 1532).* Translated by Earl Morse Wilbur. Harvard Theological Series XVI. London: Cambridge University Press, 1932.

Sexton, Jason S., ed. *Two Views on the Doctrine of the Trinity.* Grand Rapids: Zondervan, 2014.

Sherlock, Charles. *God on the Inside: Trinitarian Spirituality.* Waniassa, Australia: Acorn Press, 1991.

Siecienski, A. Edward. *The Filioque: History of a Doctrinal Controversy.* New York: Oxford University Press. 2010.

Sloyan, Gerard Stephen. *The Three Persons in One God.* Englewood Cliffs, NJ: Prentice Hall, 1964.

Smail, Thomas Allan. *Like Father, Like Son: The Trinity Imaged in Our Humanity.* Grand Rapids: Eerdmans, 2006.

So, Damon W. K. *Jesus' Revelation of His Father: A Narrative-Conceptual Study of the Trinity with Special Reference to Karl Barth.* Waynesboro, GA: Paternoster, 2006.

Soulen, R. Kendall. *The Divine Name(s) and the Holy Trinity: Volume One: Distinguishing the Voices.* Louisville: Westminster John Knox Press, 2011.

Stephens, Bruce M. *God's Last Metaphor: The Doctrine of the Trinity in New England Theology.* Chico, CA: Scholars Press, 1981.

Stewart, Melville Y., ed. *The Trinity: East/West Dialogue.* Translated by Eugene Grushetsky and Xenia Grushetsky. Dordrecht: Kluwer, 2003.

Studer, Basil. *Trinity and Incarnation: The Faith of the Early Church.* Edited by Andrew Louth. Translated by Matthias Westerhoff. Edinburgh: T & T Clark, 1993.

Swain, Scott R. "God According to the Gospel: A Critical Dialogue with Robert W. Jenson on the Hermeneutics of Trinitarian Identification." PhD diss., Trinity Evangelical Divinity School, 2002.

Swinburne, Richard. *The Christian God.* New York: Oxford University Press, 1994.

Swindoll, Charles R. *The Trinity: Discovering the Depth of the Nature of God.* Nashville, TN: Broadman, 1993.

Tavard, George Henry. *The Vision of the Trinity.* Washington, DC: University Press of America, 1981.

Tennent, Timothy. *Invitation to World Missions: A Trinitarian Missiology for the Twenty-First Century.* Grand Rapids: Kregel, 2010.

Thiede, Werner. *Der gekreuzigte Sinn:Eine trinitarische Theodizee.* Gütersloh: Gütersloher Verlagshaus, 2007.

Thompson, John. *Modern Trinitarian Perspectives.* New York: Oxford University Press, 1994.

Toon, Peter and James Spiceland, eds. *One God in Trinity.* Westchester, IL: Cornerstone Books, 1980.

Toon, Peter. *Our Triune God: A Biblical Portrayal of the Trinity.* Wheaton, IL: Victor Books, 1996.

_____. *Yesterday, Today, and Forever: Jesus Christ and the Holy Trinity in the Teaching of the Seven Ecumenical Councils.* Swedesboro, NJ: Preservation Press, 1996.

Torrance, T. F. *The Christian Doctrine of God: One Being, Three Persons.* Edinburgh: T & T Clark, 1996.

_____. *The Trinitarian Faith: The Evangelical Theology of the Ancient Catholic Church*. Edinburgh: T & T Clark, 1988.

_____. *Trinitarian Perspectives: Toward Doctrinal Agreement*. Edinburgh: T & T Clark, 1994.

Torrance, Alan J. *Persons in Communion: An Essay on Trinitarian Description and Human Participation, with Special Reference to Volume One of Karl Barth's Church Dogmatics*. Edinburgh: T & T Clark, 1996.

Treier, Daniel J. and David Lauber, eds. *Trinitarian Theology for the Church: Scripture, Community, Worship*. Downers Grove, IL: InterVarsity Press, 2009.

Turcescu, Lucian. *Gregory of Nyssa and the Concept of Divine Persons*. New York: Oxford University Press, 2005.

Uber, Gottfried. *Vater—Geist—Sohn: Rückführung der Trinitätslehre auf das Neue Testament*. Creglingen Arbeitskreis "Erneuerung der Kirche" 2005.

Vanhoozer, Kevin, J., ed. *The Trinity in a Pluralistic Age: Theological Essays on Culture and Religion*. Grand Rapids: Eerdmans, 1997.

Vickers, Jason E. *Invocation and Ascent: The Making and Remaking of Trinitarian Theology*. Grand Rapids: Eerdmans, 2008.

Volf, Miroslav. *After Our Likeness: The Church as the Image of the Trinity*. Grand Rapids: Eerdmans, 1998.

Volf, Miroslav and Michael Welker, eds. *God's Life in Trinity*. Minneapolis: Fortress Press, 2006.

Wainwright, Arthur W. *The Trinity in the New Testament,* London: SPCK, 1962.

Ware, Bruce A. *Father, Son, and Holy Spirit: Relationships, Roles, and Relevance*. Wheaton, IL: Crossway Books, 2005.

Watts, Isaac. *The Christian Doctrine of the Trinity: Or Father, Son, and Spirit, Three Persons and One God, Asserted and Prov'd, with Their Divine Rights and Honors Vindicated by Plain Evidence of Scripture without the Aid or Incumbrance of Human Schemes: Written Chiefly for the Use of Private Christians.* London: Printed for J. Clark, at the Bible and Crown in the Poultry near Cheapside; E. Mathews at the Bible in Pater-Noster-Row; and R. Ford, at the Angel in the Poultry, 1722.

Weedman, Mark. *The Trinitarian Theology of Hilary of Poitiers. Supplements to Vigiliae Christianae.* Boston: Brill, 2007.

Weinandy, Thomas Gerard. *The Father's Spirit of Sonship: Reconceiving the Trinity.* Edinburgh: T & T Clark, 1995.

Welch, Claude. *In This Name: The Doctrine of the Trinity in Contemporary Theology.* New York: Charles Scribner's Sons, 1952.

Weth, Rudolf, ed. *Der lebendige Gott: auf den Spuren neueren trinitarischen Denkens.* Neukirchen-Vluyn: Neukirchener, 2005.

White, James R. *The Forgotten Trinity: Recovering the Heart of the Christian Faith.* Minneapolis: Bethany House Publishers, 1998.

Wiles, Maurice. *The Making of Christian Doctrine: A Study in the Principles of Early Christian Development.* Cambridge: Cambridge University Press, 1988.

Willis, W. Waite. *Theism, Atheism, and the Doctrine of the Trinity: The Trinitarian Theologies of Karl Barth and Jürgen Moltmann in Response to Protest Atheism.* Atlanta, GA: Scholars Press, 1987.

Winslow, Hubbard. *Discourses on the Nature, Evidence, and Moral Value of the Doctrine of the Trinity.* Boston: (s. n.), 1834.

Wittschier, Sturmius-M. *Kreuz, Trinität, Analogi: Trinitarische Ontologie unter dem Leitbild des Kreuzes, dargestellt als ästhetische Theologie.* Würzburg: Echter, 1987.

Yoder, John Howard. *Body Politics: Five Practices of the Church Before the Watching World*. Scottdale, PA: Herald Press, 2001.

Yu, T'ae-hwa. *The Spirit of Liberation: Jürgen Moltmann's Trinitarian Pneumatology*. Zoetermeer: Uitgeverij Meinema, 2003.

COMMENTARIES

Anderson, Hugh. *The Gospel of Mark*. New Century Bible Commentary. London: Marshall, Morgan and Scott, 1976.

Barrett, C. K. *A Critical and Exegetical Commentary on Acts of the Apostles*. Two volumes. Edinburgh: T & T Clark, 1998.

Beasley-Murray, George R. *John*. Word Biblical Commentary, vol. 36, 2nd ed. Nashville: Thomas Nelson, 1999.

Bock, Darrel L. *Luke 1:1–9:50*. Baker Exegetical Commentary on the New Testament. Grand Rapids: Baker Academic, 1994.

———. *Luke 9:51–24:53*. Baker Exegetical Commentary on the New Testament. Grand Rapids: Baker Academic, 1996.

Bruce, F. F. *The Acts of the Apostles: The Greek Text with Introduction and Commentary*, 3rd revised and enlarged edition. Grand Rapids: Eerdmans, 1990.

Bultmann, Rudolf. *The Gospel of John: A Commentary*. Translated by G. R. Beasley-Murray. Oxford: Basil Blackwell, 1971.

Carson, D. A. *The Gospel according to John*. Grand Rapids: Eerdmans, 1991.

Collins, Adela Yarbro. *Mark: A Commentary*. Minneapolis: Fortress Press, 2007.

Culpepper, R. Alan. *Mark*. Smyth and Helwys Bible Commentary. Macon, GA: Smyth and Helwys, 2007.

Edwards, James R. *The Gospel according to Mark*. Grand Rapids: Eerdmans, 2002.

Evans, C. F. *Saint Luke.* Philadelphia: Trinity Press International, 1990.

France, R. T. *The Gospel of Mark: A Commentary on the Greek Text.* Grand Rapids: Eerdmans, 2002.

_____. *The Gospel of Matthew.* New International Commentary on the New Testament. Grand Rapids: Eerdmans, 2007.

González, Justo L. *Luke: Belief: A Theological Commentary on the Bible.* Louisville: Westminster John Knox Press, 2010.

Gundry, Robert H. *Matthew: A Commentary on His Handbook for a Mixed Church under Persecution,* 2nd ed. Grand Rapids: Eerdman, 1994.

Green, Joel B. *The Gospel of Luke.* Grand Rapids: Eerdmans, 1997.

Gruenler, Royce Gordon. *The Trinity in the Gospel of John: A Thematic Commentary on the Fourth Gospel.* Grand Rapids: Baker Books, 1986.

Hendriksen, William. *Exposition of the Gospel of Luke: New Testament Commentary.* Grand Rapids: Baker Books, 1978.

Hurtado, Larry W. *Mark.* New International Bible Commentary. Peabody, MA: Hendrickson, 1989.

Jeffrey, David Lyle. *Luke.* Brazos Theological Commentary on the Bible. Grand Rapids: Brazos Press, 2012.

Johnson, Luke Timothy. *The Acts of the Apostles,* vol. 5. Sacra Pagina Series. Collegeville, MN: The Liturgical Press, 1992.

Just, Arthur A., Jr., ed. *Luke.* Ancient Christian Commentary on Scripture. New Testament, IIIA, ed. Thomas Oden. Downers Grove, IL: InterVarsity Press, 2003.

Kernaghan, Ronald J. *Mark.* IVP New Testament Commentary Series. Edited by Grant Osborne. Downers Grove, IL: InterVarsity Press, 2007.

Köstenburger, Andreas J. *John*. Baker Exegetical Commentary on the New Testament. Grand Rapids: Baker Academic, 2004.

Luz, Ulrich. *Matthew 1–7: A Commentary.* Translated by James E. Crouch. Minneapolis: Fortress Press, 2007.

_____. *Matthew 21–28: A Commentary.* Translated by James E. Crouch. Minneapolis: Fortress Press, 2005.

Marshall, I. Howard. *The Gospel of Luke: A Commentary on the Greek Text.* Grand Rapids: Eerdmans, 1978.

Michaels, J. Ramsey. *The Gospel of John.* Grand Rapids: Eerdmans, 2010.

Morris, Leon. *The Gospel according to John.* Revised edition. Grand Rapids: Eerdmans, 1995.

Nolland, John. *The Gospel of Matthew: A Commentary on the Greek Text.* Grand Rapids: Eerdmans, 2005.

Patte, Daniel. *The Gospel according to Matthew.* Philadelphia: Fortress Press, 1987.

Placher, William C. *Mark: A Theological Commentary on the Bible.* Louisville: Westminster John Knox Press, 2010.

Pervo, Richard I. *Acts.* Hermenia—A Critical and Historical Commentary on the Bible. Minneapolis: Fortress Press, 2009.

Schnackenburg, Rudolf. *The Gospel according to John, Volume One: Introduction and Commentary on Chapters 1–4.* New York: Crossroad, 1982.

_____. *The Gospel according to John, Volume Three: Commentary on Chapters 13–21.* New York: Crossroad, 1982.

Simonetti, Manlio, ed. *Matthew 1–13.* Ancient Christian Commentary on Scripture. New Testament, IA, ed. Thomas Oden. Downers Grove, IL: InterVarsity Press, 2001.

_____, ed. *Matthew 14–28*. Ancient Christian Commentary on Scripture. New Testament, IB, ed. Thomas Oden. Downers Grove, IL: InterVarsity Press, 2002.

Stein, Robert H. *Mark*. Baker Exegetical Commentary on the New Testament. Grand Rapids: Baker Academic, 2008.

Turner, David L. *Matthew*. Baker Exegetical Commentary on the New Testament. Grand Rapids: Baker Academic, 2008.

Vinson, Rickard B. *Luke*. Smyth and Helwys Bible Commentary. Macon, GA: Smyth and Helwys, 2008.

Whitacre, Rodney A. *John*. The IVP New Testament Commentary Series, ed. Grant Osborne. Downers Grove, IL: InterVarsity Press, 1999.

Witherington, Ben, III. *John's Wisdom: A Commentary of the Fourth Gospel*. Louisville: Westminster John Knox Press, 1995.

_____. *Matthew*. Smyth and Helwys Bible Commentary. Macon, GA: Smyth and Helwys, 2006.

Scripture Index

GENESIS
1:1–3........................ 109
1:26–27.......... 86, 89, 90
1:31...................... 86, 92
2:24...................... 85, 94
6:3........................... 106
11:2–8..................... 90
16:7–13.................. 100
18–19...................... 101
18:5, 9.................... 101
18:10...................... 101
18:22...................... 101
22............... 91, 102, 119
22:2.................... 91, 119
27:33........................ 99
35:7............................ 95

NUMBERS
11:16–30................... 108
11:28–29................... 108

DEUTERONOMY
6:4....... 85, 94, 116, 119,
120, 121, 125, 231

JUDGES
6:11–14..................... 100

1 SAMUEL
10:10........................ 100

2 KINGS
17:24–34.................. 118
17:33........................ 118

PROVERBS
18:10........................... 98
30:3, 9...................... 103
30:4........................... 103

PSALM
2:2............................. 103

3:1............................. 109
15.............................. 120
20:1............................ 98
25:16......................... 119
26:2............................ 89
33.............................. 107
3 3:6.......................... 107
35:17......................... 119
51:11......................... 106
68:7............................ 91
107:20........................ 99
130:5–7...................... 99
139:7................. 106, 111

ISAIAH
6:8...................... 90, 180
9:6.................... 103, 104
42:1............ 59, 109, 110,
162, 163, 166
61:1... 110, 186, 226, 227
63:7–10..................... 111
63:16......................... 112

JEREMIAH
9:1............................. 100
23:6........................... 104

EZEKIEL
37...... 107, 112, 114, 294

DANIEL
7:13–14..................... 105

JOEL
2:28... 108, 149, 166, 269

MICAH
5:2............................. 104

HAGGAI
2:4–5......................... 113

ZECHARIAH
14:7............................. 94

MALACHI
3:1..................... 100, 193

WISDOM
7:25.......................... 106

1 ENOCH
14:22........................... 92
47:3........................... 105
61:8........................... 105
69:27–29.................... 105

MATTHEW
3:16–17....... 80, 184, 185
12:18.......... 79, 160, 162
28:18................ 179, 325
28:19... 15, 18, 49, 52, 58,
60, 64, 66, 73, 74,
92, 160, 163, 164,
169, 174, 176, 178,
179, 180, 187, 222,
224, 277, 334
28:19–20....15, 18, 49, 58,
60, 73, 160, 163,
169, 174, 176, 178,
179, 180, 187, 222,
224, 334

MARK
1:10–11............... 80, 166,
184, 185
1:11........................... 103

LUKE
3:21..................... 60, 166
3:21–22.............. 184, 185
4:18................. 204, 224,
225, 226, 227

10:21.................. 184, 186
11:13............ 75, 200, 201
24:49–50.................... 200

JOHN
1:33............. 79, 160, 165,
                177, 184, 185
1:33–34............. 184, 185
3:34............ 200, 202, 203
4:23............ 118, 242, 243
14:9............................ 101
14:16... 79, 108, 200, 204
14:16–17...................... 203
14:25–26........... 200, 204
15:26................ 141, 253,
                    266, 267
16:7–9............... 266, 268
16:13–15........... 266, 283
20:21–22.......... 160, 166,
                    168, 178

ACTS
1:4–5.......... 200, 202, 205
2 .... 64, 74, 79, 80, 98,
            108, 149, 161, 163,
            166, 169, 184, 187,
            195, 200, 205, 215,
            225, 229, 278
2:16............................ 108
2:21.............................. 98
2:32–33......... 74, 79, 166,
                200, 205, 215
2:38............... 64, 80, 163,
                166, 187, 195
2:38–39...................... 184
4:4–8.......................... 242
4:7.............................. 120
4:8..................... 266, 269
4:10............................ 120
4:20............................ 120
4:24–25...................... 242
4:29–30...................... 244
4:29–31...................... 161
5:30–32...................... 161
7:55..... 80, 225, 227, 239
10:38........... 68, 161, 169
11:16–17.................... 225
20:21–23............ 161, 169

20:28.................. 225, 229

ROMANS
1:1–4.......... 79, 161, 170,
                171, 172, 178
5:1–5.................. 161, 171
7:4–6.................. 200, 206
8:1–3....75, 184, 188, 196
8:1–3........................... 187
8:9............. 226, 230, 231
8:16–17..... 226, 228, 231
14:17............................ 81
14:17–18.......... 242, 245,
                258, 260, 262
15:12–13........... 201, 206
15:15–16........... 161, 171
15:30........... 80, 184, 189

1 CORINTHIANS
2:1–4.......................... 161
2:10–16.............. 242, 245
3:9–16........................ 161
6:11.............. 49, 184, 189
8:6.............................. 120
12:4–6............. 52, 56, 58,
                59, 79, 266, 270,
                272, 275, 276

2 CORINTHIANS
3:3.................. 184, 190
13:14.................... 49, 50,
            57, 58, 59, 60, 79,
        201, 206, 207, 224

GALATIANS
4:4–6........... 56, 161, 173
4:6.............................. 242

EPHESIANS
1:11–14.............. 162, 174
2:17–18...................... 184
2:17–19........................ 16
2:21–22.............. 201, 210
2:22.............................. 79
4:4–6...... 56, 58, 74, 266,
            272, 273, 275, 276
4:26–32...................... 111
4:30–32..... 226, 233, 262
5:18– 20............ 266, 273

PHILIPPIANS
2:9....................... 98, 299

COLOSSIANS
1:6–8................. 162, 174

1 THESSALONIANS
1:3–5................. 162, 175

2 THESSALONIANS
2:13............. 52, 247, 251
2:13–14............. 242, 248
2:13–15...................... 260

TITUS
3:4–6................. 242, 249

HEBREWS
2:3–4... 79, 201, 211, 214
3:1–7......... 201, 212, 213
9:14..... 57, 184, 190, 211
10:12–15... 201, 212, 213
10:29........... 49, 191, 193
10:29–31.................... 184

1 PETER
1:2...... 49, 58, 68, 74, 81,
            209, 242, 250,
            252, 253, 255,
            260, 261, 263
1:3–12....................... 162

1 JOHN
4:2.................... 266, 274,
                275, 277, 283
4:13................... 242, 255
5:6–9................. 184, 192

JUDE
20 80, 226, 233, 238, 251

REVELATION
1:4–5........... 59, 242, 256
1:9–10............... 162, 176
3:16............................ 118
22:1.......... 184, 193, 195,
                226, 235, 237
22:17–18................. 184

Author and Topic Index

A

Ad extra 143, 146, 320, 321, 323
Ad intra 143, 320, 321, 323
Adoptionism 319
Akin, Daniel L. 255, 256, 275
Anamoisis... 319
Anarchoi 141
Anatolios, Khaled 37
Apophatic......................... 136, 137, 140
Arian 20, 64, 93, 133,
                        138, 139, 140, 320
Arianism............. 136, 137, 138, 292, 319
Arius 125, 136, 137, 138, 139, 140
Arnarchoi... 319
Athanasius........... 64, 131, 136, 139, 142
Athenagoras................ 64, 126, 147, 323
Augustine 42, 101, 124,
                        143, 144, 152, 221
Autotheos 133, 135, 319

B

Baillie, Donald 34, 123
Balthasar, Hans Urs von 35, 147
Barnes, T. B................................. 36, 139
Barrett, C. K. 84, 85, 112, 270
Basil 140, 141, 142, 268
Bateman IV, Herbert W..................... 191
Bauer, F. C. 31
Beale, G. K.............................. 193, 194
Berding, Kenneth 271
Blomberg, Craig............... 162, 163, 164
Bobrinskoy, Boris 17, 57
Bock, Darrell............................ 202, 226
Boethius.. 146
Boff, Leonardo 44, 45, 52
Borchert, Gerald........ 167, 168, 202, 203
Bruce, F. F. 170, 174
Brunner, Emil 39
Bulgakov, Sergius............................. 148
Buzzard, Anthony F. 46

C

Caesarius of Arles 32, 335
Calvin, Jean.................. 20, 34, 127, 289
Carson, D. A..... 166, 167, 267, 268, 269
Chalamet, Christopher....................... 37
Chesterton, G. K..... 14, 63, 73, 153, 262
Chrysostom, John 199, 209, 210, 214
Circumincession........ 130, 146, 147, 319
Coinherence............................. 130, 320
Conciliar Trinitarianism 142
Consubstantial 138, 145, 320
Coppedge, Allan........ 17, 18, 38, 66, 179
Crisp, Oliver 37
Cullman, Oscar............................ 64, 65
Cunningham, David 47, 230, 267

D

Demarest, Bruce A. 22, 42
Dever, Mark 167, 289
DuBose, Francis 165
Dynamic Monarchianism.......... 136, 320

E

Economic............. 14, 17, 19, 31, 35, 36,
                    44, 45, 46, 50, 56, 61,
                    86, 111, 126, 131, 133,
                    134, 137, 194, 200, 216,
                    231, 288, 300, 302, 320, 321
Economy...................... 31, 58, 80, 109,
                    129, 130, 131, 134,
                    163, 230, 289,
                    297, 299, 300,
                    302, 303
Ellingworth, P........................... 192, 211
Emanation 106, 132, 320
Erickson, Millard 22, 23, 43,
                    298, 301
Eternal Generation............. 45, 131, 133,
                    135, 140, 320
Eunomius................................. 140, 141

F

Fee, Gordon 84, 85, 270
Feinberg, John 31, 32, 58, 86,
                                          88, 89, 90, 93,
                                          94, 95, 110, 288
Fiddes, Paul 38, 44, 48, 60, 188
Filiation 141, 146, 320
Filioque 40, 144,
                                          267, 268, 320
Fossum, J. E. 88

G

Garland, David 271
Generation 53, 132, 140,
                                          146, 151, 207,
                                          211, 320, 321
George, Timothy 41, 247
Giles, Kevin 43, 45, 298, 301
Gonzalez, Justo 47, 48
Gregory of Nazianzus 141, 268
Gregory of Nyssa 140, 142, 268
Grenz, Stanley 36, 38, 43, 48
Grudem, Wayne 43, 190

H

Harnack, Adolf 31
Hatch, Edwin 87
Heber, Reginald 32, 78
Hendricksen, W. 209, 210
Hilary of Poitiers 20, 139,
                                          140, 144, 147
Hillar, Marian 17, 127, 129,
                                          130, 131, 132
Hippolytus 135
Holmes, Stephen 123, 125, 127, 128,
                                          129, 131, 132, 133,
                                          135, 136, 137, 140,
                                          142, 143, 146, 148
Homoiousia 138, 141, 321
Homoousia ... 133, 134, 138, 319, 320, 321
Homophuia 142, 321
Hunt, Anne 37, 287
Hunting, Charles F. 46
Hurtado, Larry 88
Hypostases, hypostasis ... 34, 112, 133, 134,
                                          135, 141, 142, 321

I

Ice, Laura 85, 91, 92, 95, 104
Idiomata 140, 141, 321, 323
Immanent 17, 19, 30, 31, 33,
                                          35, 36, 39, 43, 44, 45,
                                          46, 47, 126, 131, 213,
                                          231, 272, 288, 302,
                                          303, 320, 321
Irenaeus 89, 132, 133, 135

J

Jenson, Robert 35, 47, 222
Jobes, Karen H. 251, 252, 253, 254
John of Damascus 147
Johnson, Aubrey 83, 87, 94, 95, 97,
                                          98, 99, 100, 101, 106
Juel, Donald H. 265, 295
Justin Martyr 130, 132

K

Kaiser, Christopher 51, 52, 296
Kant, Immanuel 30, 32, 33, 222
Kärkkäinen, Veli-Matti 13, 37, 41,
                                          42, 48, 54, 298
Kelly, J. N. D. 49, 50, 64, 65, 66, 67
Kenosis 148, 149, 321
Kistemaker, S. J. 171, 194, 204, 209,
                                          210, 211, 231, 234,
                                          252, 273, 275
Knight, G. A. F. 83, 87, 89, 91, 94,
                                          96, 98, 99, 111, 249
Köstenberger, Andreas 166, 167, 205
Kruse, C. G. 256, 275
Kyriarchy 296

L

LaCugna, Catherine 43, 44, 45
Ladaria, Louis F. 127, 129, 130,
                                          132, 133, 134, 135,
                                          137, 138, 139, 140,
                                          141, 142, 143, 144,
                                          145, 146, 147
Lapide, Pincha 159
Lee, Jung Young 13, 14, 42,
                                          53, 54, 60
Lenski, R. C. H. 192, 210, 253, 254

Letham, Robert 58, 59, 89, 101, 102, 109, 112, 256
Leupp, Roderick 37
Lewis, C. S. 224
Lewis, Gordon R. 22
lex orandi 18, 126, 155, 221
Logos 17, 127, 131, 132, 133, 136, 227, 252, 321
Lossky, Vladimir 34

M

Manifestation 50, 65, 135, 143, 269, 271, 321
Marcion 131
Markschies, Christoph 134
Marshall, I. Howard 202, 227
Martin, Michael 128, 249, 281
Maspero, Giuliu 29, 37, 335
Metz, Johann Baptist 47
Mishna 247
Modalism 31, 125, 292, 302, 322
Modalistic Monarchianism 135, 322
Modes of being 69, 148
Moltmann, Jürgen 33, 43, 147, 148, 159, 222, 296, 302
Monarchy... 93, 109, 130, 131, 132, 134, 135, 136, 137, 319, 322
Monotheism 20, 22, 33, 39, 46, 47, 64, 84, 85, 88, 90, 91, 92, 93, 94, 96, 104, 105, 110, 114, 115, 119, 120, 121, 125, 136, 153, 159, 293, 294, 295, 322
Morris, Leon 164, 165, 170, 172, 206, 231
Mounce, Robert H. 170, 171, 206

N

Newbigin, Leslie 34
Nicaea 17, 20, 40, 42, 44, 64, 93, 126, 134, 138, 142, 224
Niebuhr, Richard 20, 93, 114, 294
Nolland, John 162, 164
North, C. R. 13, 40, 87, 129, 224
Numenius 132

O

Ordo salutis 195, 251
Origen 20, 133, 134, 135, 319
Osborne, Grant 193

P

Panikar, Raimundo 41, 42
Patripassionism 135, 136, 322
Paul of Samosata 136
Pelikan, Jaroslav 40, 123, 124
Perichoresis 147, 148, 322
Person 14, 41, 60, 72, 87, 98, 99, 100, 102, 103, 106, 107, 108, 109, 110, 115, 118, 120, 129, 131, 136, 141, 145, 146, 147, 148, 163, 164, 180, 196, 203, 209, 213, 246, 250, 252, 256, 267, 273, 282, 289, 291, 294, 296, 299, 301, 302, 321, 322, 323, 326, 335
Persona 124, 129, 321
Peters, Ted 31, 263
Phillips, J. B. 252
Placher, William C. 46, 124
Pobee, John 298
Polhill, John 227, 228, 229
Polytheism 46, 85, 87, 95, 96, 117, 118, 125, 142, 292, 293, 294, 322
Prestige, G. L. 133
Procession 20, 21, 42, 59, 61, 73, 76, 79, 80, 108, 131, 133, 134, 141, 146, 159, 169, 170, 171, 173, 174, 177, 186, 202, 231, 232, 245, 247, 288, 323
Properties 124, 130, 140, 141, 142, 321, 323

R

Rahner, Karl 34, 35, 36, 43, 45, 46, 47, 302
Rauser, Randall 43
Reeves, Michael 29, 31
Relations .. 17, 30, 35, 36, 38, 43, 45, 47, 124, 131, 142, 143, 145, 146, 188, 213, 231, 267, 288, 289, 297, 298, 301, 320, 321, 323

Richard of St. Victor 144
Richardson, Neil 271
Robinson, H. Wheeler 94, 97, 99
Rowe, C. Kavin 46, 48

S

Sabellian 20
Sabellius 135
Sanders, Fred 29, 37, 44, 45, 210
Sayers, Dorothy 13, 152
Schaeffer, Francis 241
Schleiermacher, Friedrich 32, 33, 39,
                                      45, 222
Schreiner, Thomas 170, 171, 206,
                               207, 230, 231,
                               234, 250, 251
Schüssler Fiorenza, Elisabeth 296
Segal, A. E. 88
Sexton, Jason 37
Shuster, Marguerite 223
Siecienski, A. Edward 40, 144, 268
Smail, Tom 164
Sozzini, Faustus 136
Spiceland, James 51, 52
Spiration 146, 323
Stein, Robert 226
Strunk, Reiner 222
Subordination 45, 92, 119, 133,
                               134, 135, 136, 137,
                               140, 293, 298,
                               300, 319, 320
Subordinationism 20, 43, 76, 93,
                               125, 135, 153,
                               298, 301, 304,
                               321, 323
Subsistence 31, 139, 323
Substance 35, 37, 102, 113,
                               124, 126, 129, 130,
                               133, 134, 137, 138,
                               139, 140, 141, 142,
                               145, 146, 192, 199,
                               209, 214, 295, 297,
                               299, 300, 301, 319,
                               320, 321, 322, 323
Substantia 124, 129

T

Tan, Loe-Joo 41
Tertullian 17, 64, 109, 126,
                               127, 129, 130, 131,
                               136, 224, 291, 320, 323
Theophilus 128
Thiselton, Anthony C. 66, 121,
                               148, 149, 173,
                               246, 270, 271
Thomas Aquinas 44, 145,
                               146, 147, 267
Thompson, John 37
Tillich, Paul 22
Toon, Peter 51, 52, 53, 56, 57, 59
Torrance, Thomas 53, 55, 56, 144, 223
Trinity 13, 14, 15, 16, 17, 18, 19, 21,
            22, 23, 24, 25, 29, 30, 31, 32,
            33, 34, 35, 36, 37, 38, 39, 40,
            41, 42, 43, 44, 45, 46, 47, 48,
            50, 51, 52, 53, 54, 55, 56, 57,
            58, 59, 60, 61, 63, 64, 66, 68,
            71, 72, 77, 78, 82, 83, 85, 86,
            101, 109, 112, 123, 124, 125,
            126, 127, 128, 129, 130, 131,
            132, 133, 134, 137, 139, 140,
            141, 142, 143, 144, 145, 146,
            147, 148, 149, 150, 153, 154,
            155, 159, 170, 172, 173, 175,
            179, 193, 194, 197, 199, 203,
            205, 208, 209, 210, 211, 213,
            214, 215, 221, 222, 223, 224,
            231, 234, 235, 240, 241, 244,
            249, 250, 251, 252, 256, 265,
            268, 271, 272, 273, 277, 278,
            287, 288, 289, 291, 292, 294,
            295, 297, 298, 301, 302, 303,
            319, 320, 321, 323, 325, 326,
            327, 331, 332, 333, 334, 335
Tritheism 323
Turner, Harold 34

U

Unitarianism 20, 46, 76, 85,
                               125, 147, 187, 292,
                               298, 304, 322, 323

V

Vanhoozer, Kevin 41
Vial, Marc 37
Vickers, Jason 37
Volf, Miroslav 44, 147, 222
Vriezen, T. C. 121

W

Wainwright, Arthur.......... 17, 35, 51, 52,
59, 66, 83, 87,
88, 102, 106, 112
Wannamaker, C. A. 248
Ware, Bruce............. 43, 44, 45, 299, 301

Welch, Claude.............................. 39, 123
White, James................... 29, 36, 38, 223
Williams, Rowan............................... 148
Witherington, Ben 85, 91, 92, 95, 104
Woźniak, Robert 29, 37, 335

Y

Yoder, John Howard..... 47, 82, 167, 186,
277, 289, 301
Young, William 46

Z

Zizioulas, John 147